Will & Vision

how latecomers grow to dominate markets

Gerard J. Tellis

AND

Peter N. Golder

McGraw-Hill

New York   Chicago   San Francisco
Lisbon   London   Madrid   Mexico City   Milan
New Delhi   San Juan   Seoul   Singapore
Sydney   Toronto

Library of Congress Cataloging-in-Publication Data

Tellis, Gerard J., 1950–
  Will & vision : how latecomers grow to dominate markets / Gerard J. Tellis and Peter N. Golder.
    p.   cm.
  ISBN 0-07-137549-X
    1. Marketing—United States.   2. Brand name products—United States.   I. Golder, Peter N.   II. Title.

HF5415.1 .T45 2001
658.8'00973—dc21   2001044001

McGraw-Hill

A Division of The McGraw·Hill Companies

1 2 3 4 5 6 7 8 9 0   AGM/AGM   0 9 8 7 6 5 4 3 2 1

ISBN 0-07-137549-X

This book was set in Life and Baker Signet by Binghamton Valley Composition.

Printed and bound by Quebecor World/Martinsburg.

McGraw-Hill books are available at special quantity discounts to use as premiums and sales promotions, or for use in corporate training programs. For more information, please write to the Director of Special Sales, Professional Publishing, McGraw-Hill, Two Penn Plaza, New York, NY 10121-2298. Or contact your local bookstore.

 This book is printed on recycled, acid-free paper containing a minimum of 50% recycled, de-inked fiber.

to our families

cheryl, neil, viren, kethan, and sonia
melanie, claire, grace, and julia

who have inspired our efforts, shared our burdens,
and multiplied our joys many times over . . .

contents

foreword

History will prove *Will & Vision* to be an important milestone in our journey to understanding how to manage innovation effectively. Like Utterback's *Mastering the Dynamics of Innovation* of several years ago, the reason for this book's importance is that it delves into the *phenomena* that comprise innovation—the deep historical detail about how this stuff actually happens.

In the context of their respective disciplines, historians of knowledge Kuhn, Popper, Roethlisberger, and Kaplan each have articulated models of how communities of scholars build understanding cumulatively. There is a stunning commonality in their views of how this process works. At the earliest stages, scholars must carefully observe the phenomena of interest and record what they see. Next, they attempt to classify or categorize the phenomena in ways that simplify yet highlight the differences that seem to matter. Third, they generate theories that, if built upon solid classification schemes, can assert what causes what, and why, and under what circumstances.

In the next step, scholars use their theories to predict what they will see when they go back out to observe more phenomena. If their theories accurately predict what they observe, they confirm that their theories are useful. But if they observe what Kuhn called an *anom-*

aly—a phenomenon that the theories-in-use did not cause them to expect or could not explain—then that anomaly forces the researchers to revisit the classification stage. Using puzzles like, "There must be something else going on here," or "These two types of things really aren't meaningfully different," they then refine the classification scheme, which enables them to articulate a better theory of what causes what, and why, and under what circumstances. Earnest scholars continue to work in this cycle, approaching an understanding of the truth asymptomatically. Importantly, this cycle *necessarily* involves both deductive and inductive methods of logic.

In light of this "theory of how theory is built," the vast majority of people who write books and articles about business and management are guilty of academic malpractice in gross and negligent ways. On the inductive side of this cycle, most of them are so anxious to tell managers what to do (what will cause what) that they dive right into theorizing without going through the prerequisite disciplines of observing and classifying the phenomena carefully. Rather, they select a few examples or anecdotes that support what they had already concluded and assert that every manager who is smart ought to do it this way. Year after year their hundreds of books fall into oblivion because their theories are not grounded in careful observation and classification. On the deductive side of the cycle, academics (primarily economists and operations researchers) "test" optimization models on whatever sets of data they can find that can be loaded quickly onto computers. They then leave them there, "tested," without completing the rigors of the rest of the cycle, which entail the search for anomalies and the improvement of classification schemes.

The virture of this book is that it does the first step of this process—the description of the phenomena that comprise innovation—very well. Tellis and Golder also make a strong contribution to the second step, classification, with their assertion that vision, persistence, innovation, commitment, and asset leverage are the five classes of factors that account for the success of the dominant companies in history. This forms the foundation of the theory they then propose—that being *first* isn't nearly so important to ultimate success as doing these other things well. Their corollary is that, quite possibly, being first *reduces* the probability of success.

Subsequent researchers will undoubtedly show that the classification scheme and theory that Tellis and Golder propose in this book are not complete. In fact, as I write this, I can think of an important anomaly or two that their present theory cannot explain, which might be resolved with a somewhat different classification scheme and consequently altered theory. For example, I think that being first-to-market with a technology is different from being first-to-market with a business model. But the neat thing about what the authors have done here is that they have described the phenomena in such a rich way that people like you and I can pick up the baton where they left it off—and carry it for another lap or two around the track that builds understanding. This is what true scholarship is about. I commend Tellis and Golder for what they have done.

Clayton M. Christensen

preface

In the fall of 1990, we began a decade-long investigation into the causes of market dominance, paying special attention to the impact of entry timing on long-term leadership. In particular, we sought a deeper understanding of the importance of pioneering or first-mover advantages. Also, we wanted to understand if it was even possible for late entrants to succeed, and, if so, how exactly they could do it.

What we've discovered over the last 10 years has surprised and amazed us. Some of our initial findings have been published in academic journals and have already begun to be cited in textbooks and some media reports. However, the majority of media reports about pioneers and later entrants make claims that are diametrically opposed to what we have discovered.

We began our study with in-depth research in a limited number of markets. Over the years, we continually increased the number of markets, until now our findings and conclusions are based on in-depth research in 66 different markets and several hundred firms in these markets. We examined each firm's actions over many years and found the impact of these actions on each firm's performance.

Now, for the first time we have compiled in this book all of our research on market dominance and long-term leadership. We include the preliminary results from our earlier academic papers as well as the results of our work on this topic over the past 6 years. Our recent work has focused primarily on expanding our investigation to a broader set of markets, including those in digital and high-technology markets. In the end, we have a high degree of confidence in our findings because our fundamental findings and conclusions have remained the same whether we consider markets like photographic film, which started in the nineteenth century, or those like online stock trading, which began just recently.

We strongly believe that an understanding of these enduring business principles is vital reading for CEOs, entrepreneurs, financial analysts, business school students, and aspiring managers everywhere. In addition, we have been pleased that much broader audiences have enjoyed learning about the long-forgotten details and surprising twists and turns of the business histories we document. After all, these stories of enduring success are used to illustrate important business principles, but they are also the stories of business heroes who overcame great challenges to achieve great success.

The history of our own investigation into the causes of enduring success began with a simple interest in understanding more about the commonly accepted principle that market pioneers tend to dominate their markets. At the time, leading textbooks told us about many dominant firms that were believed to be pioneers—Kodak, Xerox, Apple. Initially, we accepted this conventional wisdom about pioneers, but did not believe that it constituted the whole story. We sought to simply add to the conventional story, not overturn it. When we investigated the market of video recorders, we found surprising insights about the pioneer of that industry and the causes of enduring success. We found that the history of video recorders is much more complex than the widely reported battle between Sony's Beta format and Matsushita's VHS format during the 1970s and 1980s. We detail the exciting history of this market in our book. After investigating only a few markets, we began to see a broader pattern of the strategies that enabled firms to become enduring market leaders, and we still accepted the conventional wisdom about market pioneers.

Our own epiphany came during the investigation of the seemingly well-known history of disposable diapers. As a result of our new understanding of this market, we pursued our research in many more markets. We discovered that important insights about market pioneers and the causes of enduring success tended to hold whether we studied disposable diapers or VCRs, safety razors or Web browsers, photographic film or priority mail, online stock trading or any of a host of other markets.

In the end, each of the 66 markets we investigated represents a fascinating piece of business history. However, our goal is not to simply document these captivating and surprising histories. Rather, we use them to illustrate the principles that enable firms to establish enduring leadership.

Our investigation of these 66 markets was both painstaking and invigorating. It was painstaking in the sense that we had to meticulously compile and analyze so many events, for so many firms, over so many decades. In the course of this effort, we reviewed thousands of articles and hundreds of books to uncover the common principles of enduring leadership as well as to find the best stories to illustrate these principles. Our investigation was invigorating because it led us to think in entirely new ways about the real causes of enduring business success. We'll never forget the excitement of presenting our initial findings and having those in the audience ask if we really believed what we were saying. After much additional work over several years, we think that we have been able to convince most people who have heard about our findings.

In the end, our 10-year effort has been an incredible journey. We have gotten to know many of the key figures in business history by reading about them until we could practically put ourselves in their places as they made important decisions on the future of their enterprises. We learned that conventional wisdom about business success can sometimes be very wrong, and we learned that the success of some business strategies is as enduring as the dominant firms these strategies create. We hope you enjoy your own journey as we try to re-create our discovery of these exciting lessons in business history for you.

acknowledgments

Over the course of 10 years, many relatives and colleagues have contributed to this book. We wish to mention Gary Frazier, who participated in and encouraged us during our very early discussions on market pioneers. Recently, Rajesh Chandy and Joel Huber impacted the shape of the book by reviewing an early draft and suggesting new directions, ideas, and examples. Cheryl Tellis, Stephan Stremersch, and Rajesh Chandy also reviewed each chapter in depth and provided valuable comments and suggestions. Our colleagues at the University of Southern California's Marshall School of Business and New York University's Stern School of Business deserve credit for some specific ideas in the book as well as for encouraging our pursuit of this research by fostering atmospheres of intellectual curiosity. We are very grateful to all of them.

Many individuals helped in the research effort for the book by recommending sources, collecting articles, entering references, or proofing chapters. We wish to recognize the efforts of Stephen Sokoler, Rowena Tse, Katherine (Eng) Van Hemel, Amy Leo, Debanjan Mitra, Elizabeth Floyd, Kimberly Mariash, David Lerner, Jennifer Levy,

Lucy Nguyen, Vy Nguyen, Mithun Vora, and Edward Zelmanovitz (in New York, NY), Philip Birnbaum-Moore, Sangeeta Fernandes, Raechelle Mascarenhas, Cheryl Tellis, Viren Tellis, and Vanessa Patrick (in Los Angeles, CA), and Jan Heide and Jennifer M. Orlowski (in Madison, WI). Some of these individuals helped us very briefly, while others worked for a couple of years.

We appreciate the thoughtfulness of Bernie Jaworski for introducing us to the McGraw-Hill editors and for encouraging us to dialogue with them. We are very grateful to our editor, Michelle Williams, and to the editorial team at McGraw-Hill for believing in this book from the beginning and sharing our vision of what it would become. We deeply appreciate the great enthusiasm of Michelle, who counseled us in our endeavor, repeatedly read and commented on chapters, and supported us strongly throughout. We also thank Judy Duguid for carefully copy-editing the manuscript and Janice Race for efficiently managing the editing process.

We are indebted to Clayton Christensen for generously agreeing to read the book on short notice and for his insightful foreword to the book. Finally, we thank Dave Aaker, George Day, Joel Huber, Phil Kotler, Grant Freeland, and Rajan Varadarajan for their strong endorsement of the book to the public.

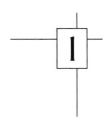

are pioneers really blessed?

the accepted wisdom

Gillette. Coke. Tide. These brands not only dominate their respective categories but have done so for several decades. The thesis of enduring market leadership is not one of isolated examples. Many researchers report that once brands capture leadership they hold that leadership for decades.[1] One article claims that 19 of 25 market leaders held the market leadership for at least 60 years! (See Table 1-1.) The article suggests that enduring market leadership may be a common phenomenon and not a rare occurrence.

This issue of enduring leadership is of paramount importance to managers for several reasons. First, enduring brands are very attractive to consumers. Such brands can charge premium prices while incurring relatively low marketing costs. In contrast, new brands or those with smaller share must resort to costly marketing in order to get known and break into a market. Second, because of economies of scale, a market leader can operate at a more efficient volume and earn higher profits than a rival that commands a narrow market niche. Third, market leaders that dominate in a category can easily extend their franchise into a new related category and dominate that

Table 1-1. Reported Evidence on Stability of Market Share Ranks

Brand	1923 Rank	1983 Rank
Swift's Premium Bacon	1	1
Kellogg's Corn Flakes	1	3
Eastman Kodak Cameras	1	1
Del Monte Canned Fruit	1	1
Hershey's Chocolates	1	2
Crisco Shortening	1	2
Carnation Canned Milk	1	1
Wrigley Chewing Gum	1	1
Nabisco Biscuits	1	1
Eveready Flashlight Batteries	1	1
Gold Medal Flour	1	1
LifeSavers Mint Candies	1	1
Sherwin-Williams Paint	1	1
Hammermill Paper	1	1
Prince Albert Pipe Tobacco	1	1
Gillette Razors	1	1
Singer Sewing Machines	1	1
Manhattan Shirts	1	Top 5
Coca-Cola Soft Drinks	1	1
Campbell's Soup	1	1
Ivory Soap	1	1
Lipton Tea	1	1
Goodyear Tires	1	1
Palmolive Toilet Soap	1	2
Colgate Toothpaste	1	2

Source: "Study: Majority of 25 Leaders in 1923 Still on Top," *Advertising Age*, 1983, p. 32.

one too. On the other hand, other firms introduce thousands of new brands each year. Most vanish entirely from the market.

Why does this occur? Why is it that some brands remain strong and endure as market leaders while others wither away and are quickly forgotten?

The simple answer that many analysts have proposed is the order of market entry. According to this thesis, a firm's probability of surviving and its share of market are in proportion to the order in which it enters a market. In particular, the firm that pioneers or first enters a market is believed to have enormous advantages in terms of success, enduring market share, and long-term market leadership. Thus, market pioneering, or the order of market entry, is assumed to be the principal driver of enduring market leadership. We call this thesis pioneering advantage or first mover advantage.

As a result, analysts are always advising firms to rush to enter, beat the competition, be first to market! Indeed, this admonition is one of the most enduring principles in business theory and practice. Especially in the field of high-technology products, managers assume that being first to market is critical to short- and long-term success. For example, Andrew Grove, CEO of Intel, has this advice for managers, "Opportunity knocks when a technology break or other fundamental change comes your way. Grab it. *The first mover and only the first mover* [italics added], the company that acts while the others dither, has a true opportunity to gain time over its competitors— and time advantage, in this business, is the surest way to gain market share."[2] As a result of this consistent advice, managers are always in a rush to market.

Belief in a pioneering advantage permeates all walks of life. People on Main Street believe it. Analysts on Wall Street believe it. Reporters use it to explain market performance. Researchers develop elaborate studies to validate it. This thesis is strongly supported by academics and practitioners, amateurs and professionals. It is a thesis that has endured through the decades.

Casual observation of markets supports this thesis. Consider six common product categories: razors, copiers, mainframe computers, disposable diapers, laser printers, and online booksellers. Who is the current market leader in each of these categories? Who is the market pioneer? Many people might suggest that the answer to both questions is Gillette in safety razors, Xerox in copiers, IBM in computers, Pampers in disposable diapers, Hewlett-Packard in laser printers, and Amazon.com in online bookstores.

Gillette has had many rivals over the decades. These rivals have fought Gillette on the basis of better products, lower prices, alternate technologies, and alternate forms of shaving. Yet Gillette is still the leader of the safety razor market. Procter & Gamble supposedly created the disposable diaper market with Pampers. Today, Pampers is still one of the best-selling brands. Xerox dominated the copier market for a quarter of a century. At one time Xerox copiers became so pervasive that its name was synonymous with copying. Similarly, IBM's dominance of the mainframe computer market was so complete that reporters could not foresee a computer industry without IBM. While Hewlett-Packard has been involved in a number of businesses, it is perhaps best known for its printers. Today the company dominates the market for printers, including laser printers. Amazon.com has grown so rapidly and consistently that it has become an amazon of Internet retailing, not only of online bookstores.

The assumption that each of these brands is both pioneer and current leader in its respective market underlies the strong belief in a pioneering advantage. Such popular examples feed the belief in people's minds that pioneers have the largest market share and remain long-term market leaders.

Perhaps faith in market pioneering gains its greatest support from the public's simple adherence to the principle of the rights of first movers. The firm that first invents a new design has the right to its patent. The first firm to use a brand name has the right to its long-term use. The first person to develop a new territory has the right to its ownership. Indeed, from childhood, we are taught this principle, with the sayings "The early bird gets the best worm" and "First come, first served." Given the strong support in common observation and common law for the rights of first movers, we have little difficulty in extrapolating to markets. What is true in life and law must be true in markets. The pioneer, or first firm to enter the market, must have the largest share and the most enduring hold on the market.

But does this belief fit in with theory? Is there any good explanation for a pioneering advantage?

accepted theories supporting pioneering advantage

An empirical observation gains scientific validity only when one or more formal theories support it. The abundant evidence in favor of the pioneering advantage from casual observation prompted many authors to try to explain this phenomenon. As a result, researchers in economics, psychology, and marketing have developed formal theories to explain why pioneers should have long-term advantages. Researchers in these fields also refer to pioneers as "first entrants" or "first movers." Some of the theories are quite involved and have been proved through complex mathematical models. Six of these theories are very important and seem quite compelling: ease of recall, brand loyalty, consumer inertia, patent barriers, economies of experience, and resource mobilization. To better appreciate the phenomenon, we present here the basic intuition behind these theories.[3]

EASE OF RECALL

The simplest reason offered in favor of pioneers is the ease of recalling the first brand name in a category. Consumers today are faced with choices from among thousands of brands in hundreds of categories. For example, razors are divided into electric (dry) and manual (wet). The latter fall into disposable and nondisposable razors. Razors are further classified into men's and women's products. Each of these categories has numerous brand names, with newer ones being introduced regularly. Indeed, some analysts estimate that across all categories of products, over 10,000 new brands are introduced each year. Now, the average consumer's vocabulary is a couple of thousand words. How are consumers to keep track of all this information? They may not. They may just remember the first brand encountered in each category—Gillette, or Amazon.com, or Xerox. This is the name that they first encountered. It is also the one that is repeated most often and is most deeply embedded in their memory. Using this argument, some strategists claim that "the leading brand in any category is almost always the first brand into the prospect's mind."[4] To the extent that this is true, pioneers will have a strong advantage over later entrants.

BRAND LOYALTY

Brand loyalty is a preference for a brand that develops from a consumer's prior purchases of the brand. When a market is new, most
consumers are unaware of the product or its important characteristics. They do not know how the new product will satisfy their
needs, or what should be its ideal mix of characteristics. Thus they
approach the new product with an open mind. For example, before
the advent of Coca-Cola, consumers would not have had any idea
of what a cola beverage should look or taste like. In such a context,
the new product can pretty much shape consumers' likes and expectations. For example, once consumers tried and liked Cola-Cola,
they began to think of its mix of sweetness, color, carbonation, and
caramel flavor as typical of a cola and as a sort of ideal for this type
of beverage. The idea, then, is that consumers use the pioneer as a
basis of comparison for new, later entrants. If the new brands are
different, they may not win favor with consumers. If they are similar,
they may be dismissed as me-too followers of the pioneers. Thus the
pioneer has the great advantage of shaping tastes in favor of its
unique formulation. As a result it would develop an enduring preference or loyalty for its specific formulation. Some researchers go
further and claim that "the pioneer can become strongly associated
with the product category as a whole, and as a result, become the
'standard' against which all later entrants are judged."[5] Pioneers then
become so "competitively distinct" that later entrants may not overcome this huge advantage.

CONSUMER INERTIA

Consumer inertia refers to the reluctance of consumers to switch
brands. This reluctance may occur for two reasons. For low-cost or
frequently purchased products, consumers may choose not to switch
brands to minimize the cost of evaluating alternatives and making
fresh decisions on price, quality, and quantity. For example, once a
consumer has decided on a brand of paper for his printer, he may
find it easier just to buy the same brand repeatedly, rather than to
shop for a different brand on each purchase occasion. For high-cost
products, switching brands may incur the cost of learning new

knowledge, forming new habits, or buying new accessories. For example, once a consumer has learned how to use a Xerox copier, she may be reluctant to switch to Canon, even though the latter may offer a little better deal. Similarly, once an office has bought a Xerox machine, it may choose to stick with the Xerox, and not buy machines from other suppliers, to simplify its maintenance and inventory. Since pioneers enter a market first, they are likely to be widely adopted by consumers. As such, consumers may be reluctant to switch to later entrants except for compelling reasons. Thus inertia can provide pioneering brands with an enduring advantage.

PATENT BARRIERS

A patent is legal ownership over a design that prevents a rival from using that design for a set period of time. In the United States, this protection currently lasts for 20 years from the first U.S. filing for most common patents. The goal of patents is to reward firms that carry out the costly research for a new product, giving them a monopoly in that product's market for some time. Pioneering firms can take advantage of this law by protecting not only their initial design, but also a large number of associated designs that are related to the manufacture of the product. Once they own a large set of patents, they may create a formidable barrier that could prevent rivals from entering the market. For example, at one time, Xerox held so many patents in the copier market that it seemed impossible for others to compete. It seemed so formidable that the U.S. government filed an antitrust suit against Xerox to open up competition in this market. Thus, pioneers can use patents to gain and protect market leadership.

ECONOMIES OF EXPERIENCE

The term *economies of experience* refers to the reduction in costs or improvement in quality that accrue to a firm as it gains experience producing and marketing a product. For example, the cost of a long-distance phone call has gone down at a steady rate over the decades since the initiation of phone service. More recently, computer products and peripherals have enjoyed dramatic, regular decreases in costs that have led to a steady increase in the market for these products. Costs decline with experience primarily because workers learn to produce a product more efficiently. Costs also decline with experience because manufacturers learn to produce the product with more efficient technologies, cheaper raw materials, and less waste. Economies of experience can give pioneers a cost advantage over later entrants. So pioneers can either sell the product at a lower price to consumers or keep a higher margin for themselves. In either case, they have a competitive advantage over later entrants. For example, many analysts attribute Intel's dominance of the chip market to the experience it has accumulated with chip production. This experience enables it to produce at a lower cost, introduce new designs earlier, and earn higher margins and profits. It can then reinvest these profits to keep ahead of later entrants into the market.

RESOURCE MOBILIZATION

The mobilization of resources refers to the cornering of essential supplies and outlets. By entering first, pioneers can corner the best resources, such as rich supplies of raw materials, best suppliers, large consumer segments, and best distributors. For example, De-Beers developed dominance in the diamond market by systematically buying up or contracting with diamond mines all over the world. Coke has a formidable network of distributors and franchisees, especially in the fountain business, which Pepsi has had difficulty overcoming. Because pioneers are the first to the market, they are in the best position to quickly corner resources and protect themselves against subsequent rivals.

WHAT THE THEORIES SUGGEST

Each of the above six theories suggests factors that can individually provide a pioneer with a strong advantage over later entrants. The combination of these factors can provide a pioneer with a huge and unassailable advantage over subsequent entrants to a market. This is the rationale that underlies the logic of pioneering advantage. Authors have used one or more of these theories to explain why brands such as Gillette, Tide, and Coke have held their market leadership over so many decades.

evidence supporting the accepted theories

Many skeptical researchers sought more evidence about the thesis of pioneering advantage than these few examples and formal theories. The issue has too many important implications to be left to mere theorizing. Consider that some markets last for centuries. If pioneering is the key to enduring success, then that simple criterion may be the most important factor in assessing future profitability and stock value of firms in that market. On the other hand, technology is in a state of constant flux. It makes some markets obsolete, merges others, and creates entirely new ones. If the timing of market entry is the primary determinant of enduring success, then managers need to focus closely on technology in order to time their market entry at the dawn of a new technology.

So the reader might well ask, how widespread is the phenomenon of the enduring leadership of pioneers? What are the empirical findings supporting this thesis?

Over the last two decades, numerous studies have tried to ascertain whether pioneers have enduring advantages. The studies have sought to determine how widespread or generalizable these advantages really are. A number of these studies use data from a large project called the Profit Impact of Market Strategy, or PIMS for short.

The PIMS project originally started at the General Electric (GE) Company in the 1960s. GE was an early adopter of a scientific system of managing its various businesses for profitability. Today it is a model of a large, dynamic, and profitable multinational corporation. The corporation was highly diversified even in the 1960s. As part of its quest for scientific management, senior managers wanted to know why various business units within the corporation varied in profitability. With this goal in mind, they set up a research project (PIMS), where each of these businesses reported its structure, strategy, and performance on hundreds of variables. The project relocated to Harvard University in the early 1970s and to the independent Strategic Planning Institute in the late 1970s, where it is still available. Over time, the project won support from businesses within other large and small corporations. Thus over the decades, the project accumulated data from thousands of businesses over a vast cross section of consumer and industrial markets. As such, the PIMS data constitute perhaps the largest single repository of information on business structure, strategy, and performance in the world. Various researchers working on these data found some very clear and strong patterns about the advantages of pioneers.

Another important data set on market pioneering comes from a team of professors at the Massachusetts Institute of Technology. The professors originally collected the data to find out why new products succeed or fail. These data are based on a survey of consumers' knowledge, liking, and purchase of products. The professors developed a model, ASSESSOR, for forecasting new-product strategy. Their database is often identified by this name. An important finding from the ASSESSOR data is that market pioneering is one of the most important factors of initial and enduring success.

Findings from the PIMS data are consistent with those from the ASSESSOR data. That two independent databases—collected by different researchers, using different methods, over different time periods, for different purposes, and analyzed at different levels—should yield similar results is impressive. The consistency in findings convinced many managers to believe in a pioneering advantage. In particular, studies using these two databases led to five major conclusions about market pioneers:

1. **Failure rate**. Do pioneers ever fail? Neither database provides any evidence of market pioneers that fail. For that matter, none of these studies reported about pioneers that fail. Thus, the available evidence suggests that *pioneers do not fail*!
2. **Share erosion**. Will not pioneers lose share over time? When pioneers first enter a market, they have a de facto monopoly, which means 100 percent market share. Would not their share erode as competitors and me-too products enter the market? This is a natural question. At least two studies address this question. One study shows that in the short term the market

Figure 1-1. Evolution of Entrants Market Shares by Time of Entry

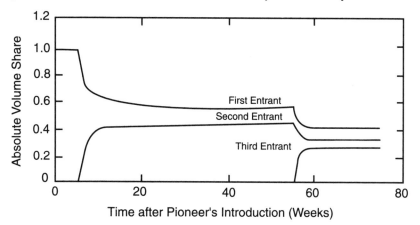

Source: Gurumurthy Kalyanaram and Glen L. Urban, "Dynamic Effects of the Order of Entry on Market Share, Trial, Penetration, and Repeat Purchases for Frequently Purchased Consumer Goods," *Marketing Science*, (1992), 11, 3, p. 237. Courtesy of INFORMS. Reprinted with permission of INFORMS and Glen L. Urban.

share of the pioneer does erode, but only in the first few years (see Figure 1-1). During that time, as each new entrant comes into the market, the pioneer's share falls at a steady rate. However, this decline does not go on indefinitely, but plateaus at a steady-state market share (see Figure 1-1). Another study addresses this issue from a long-term perspective. It shows that in the long term, later entrants are more likely to lose share and leave the market than pioneers. *Thus pioneers' hold on market share appears to be not only strong, but also very enduring.*

3. **Equilibrium market share**. What share of market do pioneers generally hold? At least six different studies address this issue. *They all show that pioneers have a high steady-state market share around 30 percent.* Analyses by several different researchers show that this mean level of share holds over a very large cross section of businesses (see Table 1-2). Based on these studies, average market shares are around 30 percent for pioneers, 20 percent for early followers, and 16 percent for late entrants. Thus pioneers have a 14 percent market share advantage over late entrants. This is a huge number that provides a very strong incentive for market pioneering. Consider

Table 1-2. Market Share Advantage of Pioneers in the PIMS Data

Study	Category	Number of Observations	Pioneer	Early Follower	Late Entrant	Advantage of Pioneer over Late Entrant
Robinson & Fornell (1985)	Consumer goods	371	29	17	12	17
Robinson (1988)	Industrial goods	1209	29	21	15	14
Parry & Bass (1990)	Concentrated consumer goods	437	34	24	17	17
Parry & Bass (1990)	Concentrated industrial goods	994	33	26	20	13
Lambkin (1988)	Start-up firms	129	24	10	10	14
Lambkin (1988)	Adolescent firms	187	33	19	13	20
Average across studies			**30**	**20**	**14**	**16**

Source: Adapted from Peter N. Golder and Gerard J. Tellis (1993, May), "Pioneering Advantage: Marketing Logic or Marketing Legend?" *Journal of Marketing Research*, 30, 158–170.

that, on a day-to-day basis, firms battle for fractions of a point in market share.

4. **Market leadership.** Are pioneers also market leaders? *Past studies claim that market pioneers are generally leaders of their markets.* For example, PIMS data show that over 70 percent of current market leaders are market pioneers.

5. **Stability of market leadership**. How stable are market shares, especially those of market leaders? Studies show that market leadership is very stable. Most market leaders retain their position for very long periods, even as long as half a century. For example, the 1983 article in *Advertising Age*, referred to at the start of this chapter, shows that of 25 market leaders in 1923, 19 were still leaders in 1983, and 24 were still among the top three brands in their respective markets (see Table 1-1).

Thus the available evidence paints a clear picture of the great merits of market pioneering. Market pioneers do not fail. They start off by dominating their respective markets. As new rivals enter the markets, pioneers lose market share slowly, and ultimately reach a stable, high share of market. Even after many decades, they retain that high share of market. Even under intense competition, they are able to endure as market leaders.[6]

the "first immutable law of marketing"?

The confluence of proverb, casual observation, formal theories, and empirical evidence in favor of market pioneers has prompted two authors, Ries and Trout, to call it the "first immutable law of marketing." They state the law quite simply as: "It's better to be first, than it is to be better."[7] These authors themselves give a large number of examples to support the thesis. Some of these examples are the same as the ones that we have cited above and that others have also used: Coke, Gillette, Pampers, Xerox, IBM.

So what begins as a simple proverb, casual observation promotes as a belief, empirical research confirms as a generalization, and economic theory sanctions as dogma. Indeed, faith in the advantages of pioneers has grown so strong that people may have little difficulty believing it really is the first law of marketing.

Analysts in business have yearned for simple answers to the complex problem of formulating strategy and explaining performance. Just as Kepler's three laws of planetary motion greatly simplified our understanding of the universe, such simple laws could explain the complex dynamics of modern markets. In the first law of marketing, analysts have found not only a good explanation for long-term success of many firms, but also a great excuse for the failure of thousands of others.

Moreover, the trade-off between quality and the timing of market entry is one of the most important factors that every manager of a new product must address. If the fruits of this trade-off are clearly and unambiguously known, then it will have a profound impact on strategy for all firms, but especially those in the high-technology area. If it is truly "better to be first than it is to be better," then a firm needs to rush to market with any product it has, even if the product is not quite ready. Quality need not matter. A firm's investments must focus on rapidly gearing up for market entry rather than on lengthy R&D for quality improvement.

The thesis of pioneering advantage is so well accepted that it has also become the single most important basis for designing strategy for Internet and high-tech firms. The prevailing logic hinges on the argument of time. Time moves much faster in the new digital economy than in the old economy. If market pioneering was so advantageous to enduring success in the old economy when change took decades, it must be critical in the new economy when change occurs in days. Strategists repeatedly warn prospects to enter a digital market quickly, if not first, before all doors to future success close. When currently dominant firms seem also to have been the first mover, reporters are quick to emphasize the merits of market pioneering. So in the digital age, the merits of market pioneering are supposed to be as strong as in the old economy, if not overwhelming.

problems with the accepted view

Unfortunately, all the casual observations about pioneers and most of the formal data suffer from three serious problems. These problems are the exclusion of failures, the self-anointing of pioneers, and self-serving definitions of the market. These problems are not difficult to understand. But they are especially pernicious, because they seem quite innocuous. Moreover, these three problems work invariably in the same direction to greatly enhance the perceived rewards to pioneering. We need to carefully evaluate each of these problems in order to assess the validity of pioneering advantage.

EXCLUSION OF FAILURES

A major problem that afflicts the study or observations of pioneers is the human tendency to forget failures. We love success and hate failure. So it is easy to forget about failures. When we exclude from our analysis pioneers that failed and include only pioneers that succeeded, we end up greatly exaggerating the rewards to all pioneers. Economists refer to this problem as *survival bias*.

This problem is quite pervasive. For example, all casual observations of markets completely ignore firms that failed. The press does cover failures *while they occur,* as in its coverage of *current* dotcom disasters. However, the press often forgets about *past* losers, glorifies a current winner, and crowns the latter as a pioneer. The problem of survival bias afflicts not only casual observation. It also afflicts a great deal of formal research. For example, all of the large formal databases on market pioneering are based on surveying current firms or consumers. As such, they exclude firms that failed. Suppose many pioneers actually failed; then these databases would not contain information about those pioneers, grossly undercounting the failure rate of pioneers. Similarly, by computing the average market share of only surviving pioneers, the current databases upwardly bias the rewards to all pioneers.

As a result, the exclusion of failed pioneers runs the risk of wrongly rejecting a reasonable hypothesis that pioneers may be unsuccessful. Indeed, formal research that relies on survey data suffers from the real danger of being circular: stating a hypothesis, excluding conditions that could disprove the hypothesis, then confirming the hypothesis.

For example, many analysts consider the Gillette Company as the pioneer of the safety razor market. They credit King C. Gillette, the cofounder of the company, as the inventor of the safety razor. Others credit him for popularizing the idea of men shaving their own faces. The primary reason for such claims is that the Gillette Company is the oldest *surviving* firm in the razor market. It has a continuous history of dominating this market for close to a hundred years. No other firm in the razor market comes close to it for longevity. Most people either do not know or cannot remember the details of the origin of the safety razor market. As we shall detail later in this book, Gillette did not invent the safety razor. Several brands of safety razors were marketed and advertised before Gillette. Actually, the safety razor was patented and available decades before Gillette. One design was first proposed over a century before Gillette! Once earlier brands failed, they were long forgotten. Omission of such failures biases our observations, distorts our analyses, and leads to erroneous conclusions. In this case, it wrongly enhances the perceived rewards to market pioneering.

Amnesia about failures does not require the passage of a century. Consider the more recent example of the laser printer market. Today, Hewlett-Packard (HP) dominates this market, with its unit market share over 50 percent. Because of its dominance of this category, many people think that HP invented the laser printer or pioneered the market.[8] One author claims that in 1990, when President Bush visited an HP facility in Boise, Idaho, "he congratulated HP engineers for inventing the laser printer" and maintaining the United States' technological leadership.[9] Actually, HP did not invent the laser printer, nor was it the first entrant into this market. IBM was the first firm to commercialize the laser printer. And Xerox was the first firm to develop a working model of the laser printer, 3 years before IBM's market introduction. For reasons we shall discuss later in the book, Xerox stalled on commercializing the product. It finally introduced its laser printer, the Xerox 9700, only after IBM did so.

By the early 1980s, Xerox was marketing a huge laser printer to the professional market costing over $100,000. It also sold an inexpensive model for a little under $30,000. In contrast, with its sights on the mass market, Canon had developed a personal laser printer that could be sold for a few thousand dollars. Canon wanted a U.S. partner to market its product. Its first pick was Xerox. However, Xerox, content with its own technology and failing to see the mass market for the product, turned down the offer. Canon next went to HP. HP was also reluctant to proceed with Canon's machine because, until that time, it did not market products that were not internally produced. However, the company was looking for accessories for its nascent personal computer business, so it accepted Canon's offer and commercialized the laser printer. The product took off. It dwarfed competitors' products that had previously entered the market and became a major product in HP's portfolio. Even today the HP laser printer uses a Canon laser engine. However, its success led to misconceptions about the origin of the market, while the failure of rivals led to amnesia about their early entry. Such errors lead to an exaggeration of the rewards to first movers.

Indeed, our memory for failures is amazingly short. Today Internet Explorer so dominates the market for browsers, that many consumers might not be able to name a rival brand. Yet as recently as 1996, analysts were questioning the prospects of Internet Explorer. Some thought Netscape's hold on the market was insurmountable. Consider this conclusion by one analyst: "When it comes to the Internet, that opportunity is Netscape. Because it was first, because it was originally free and because it has a staggering lead over all its competitors—not just Microsoft."[10] In 1996 many analysts assumed Netscape was the "first" browser or the "Internet market pioneer."[11]

But these assumptions were false. Mosaic clearly predated Netscape. At one time, Mosaic was so popular that it won users at the rate of thousands a month. Indeed, when a small company, Spyglass, bought the rights to Mosaic, one analyst thought that it had "sewn up" the Web browser market! Others considered Spyglass "the pioneering Internet software supplier."[12] Nor was Mosaic the first browser. When it was released, there were many other programs in the market, such as Viola, Erwise, and Midas, some of which probably inspired the authors of Mosaic.[13] Moreover, programs such as Gopher and Lynx were so popular that even the founder of the World Wide Web had doubts whether the Web would take off and succeed. As we shall see in a subsequent chapter, all these brands quickly declined in use and died out. They then quickly faded from the public's consciousness.

As these examples show, a proper understanding of a market requires consideration of successes and failures. Chapter 2 explains a method for such an analysis.

SELF-ANOINTED PIONEERS

Another serious problem with the study of pioneers is the tendency for observers or researchers to survey a few current firms in the market, often interviewing only the leading firms. If these firms have been in the market for a long time, their managers may not know about the early entrants to that market that failed. As such, they tend to refer to their own firm as the pioneer. Sociologists, who do a great deal of research with surveys, find this a common problem with asking respondents to describe themselves. They call such descriptions *self-reports*. What's wrong with self-reports? They are frequently misleading.

Self-reports are a description by a firm's *current* managers of their company's past. Sociologists have long known that in self-reports, respondents claim to possess attributes that the public considers desirable. The title of "pioneer" is especially prestigious and carries no cost to claim it. However, a problem arises if large successful firms call themselves pioneers because the real pioneers have failed. By so doing, they wrongly (and unknowingly) attribute to pioneers rewards that may be due to other causes. As a result, the self-reports will show that pioneering leads to success, even though other factors may be the real causes of success. Sociologists refer to this problem as *social desirability bias*, or just *self-report bias*.[14]

For example, consider the case of the disposable diaper market. In 1991 Procter & Gamble (P&G) celebrated the thirtieth anniversary of its entry in the disposable diaper market. For the millions of parents who benefited from the disposable diaper, that was indeed an occasion for celebration. The disposable diaper has made the job of caring for infants and toddlers much less unpleasant. P&G claimed it "literally created the disposable diaper business in the U.S."[15] Based on such self-reports, many reporters credit P&G with pioneering the disposable diaper market. The subsequent success and dominance of Pampers in the disposable market lends credibility to the claim of pioneering advantage. However, as we shall see in the next chapter, P&G did not create the disposable diaper market. Pampers was not the first disposable diaper. Numerous brands of disposable diapers were sold in the United States prior to the entry of Pampers. All of them failed. In their absence, it was easy for P&G to suggest that Pampers was the pioneer. Really, Pampers success is due not to pioneering but to some important other causes, which this book will reveal. Thus self-reports can greatly distort the collection, analyses, and interpretation of data on market pioneering.

Note that one problem magnifies the effect of the other. Survival bias aggravates self-report bias. By ignoring failed pioneers, survivors have the liberty of appropriating the label of pioneer. Moreover, both biases are similar in that they both wrongly enhance the measured rewards to pioneers. Survival bias and self-report bias are errors that often afflict surveys. Because of the interaction of these two errors, the survey is particularly inappropriate for studying issues relating to market evolution and pioneering. The next chapter describes a method that is much better suited for such strategic analysis.

SELF-SERVING MARKET DEFINITIONS

A third problem with the study of market pioneers is a narrow definition of the relevant market. By defining a market narrowly, a firm's market share automatically looks large. For example, if Motorola defines its market as microprocessors for Apple computers, then its share is 100 percent of this market, because it is the sole supplier of chips to Apple. But if it defines its market as microprocessors for all personal computers, then its share drops to under 10 percent of the chip market.

Since the performance of managers is often evaluated on the market share of the brands or the company that they manage, they have a strong interest in choosing a definition that enhances their market share. One easy way to do so is to define their market narrowly. Indeed, the PIMS study found market share to be such an important predictor of profitability, that at one time, some researchers advised firms to define their business narrowly, so as to increase their market share. Their faulty conclusion was that a mere redefinition of the market would increase profitability!

What is wrong with a narrow definition of the market? The problem with a narrow definition is that it focuses attention on a specific product or technology that a particular firm currently supplies. It blinds a firm to new technologies and products that may capture its share or render its products obsolete.

For example, if one defines the word processor market as the category of *dedicated word processing machines*, then Wang dominated the category in the United States and Europe for the short time it flourished. Wang's dominance in the category was so strong that analysts expected the company to be one of the dominant firms in office automation, rivaling the power of IBM and Xerox. Unfortunately, dedicated word processors were rendered obsolete by word processing software that ran on inexpensive personal computers. Wang's focus on word processing machines blinded it to this change and hindered its timely adaptation to the new environment. It tried to enhance the value of its word processors by including computing capabilities rather than port its software to personal computers that could handle computing and word processing. Once inexpensive personal computers became popular, they obviated the need for costly dedicated word processors. Wang was so closely tied to dedicated word processors that it declined rapidly as word processing shifted to personal computers.

That is the major problem with a narrow market definition. It focuses a firm's attention on the particular technology of a particular category. It blinds the company to the underlying consumer need that is more enduring than the transient technology that currently serves that need. In the above example, consumers have a need to prepare documents or to process words. Thus, defining a market broadly in terms of word processing or document preparation enables managers to be more sensitive to a wide set of competitors, changing technologies, and evolving markets.

Narrowly defined markets will, by definition, easily support the thesis of pioneering advantage. Indeed, firms can always define a market so narrowly that every firm becomes the market leader of the narrow niche it owns. Frequently it would also have pioneered that narrow niche. Thus, we can never refute the thesis of pioneering advantage, and the thesis loses all meaning or managerial relevance. More generally, a narrowly defined market prompts a firm to think of itself as a leader, albeit of a narrow segment of the broad market. It blinds it to competitors of the broader market, who may enter with a superior technology and win all its consumers. That's how Wang lost its position in the word processing market to software programs, such as WordStar, which ran on a general-purpose personal computer. Broad definitions of a market challenge firms to serve underlying consumer needs as technologies change. Narrow definitions of a market lull firms into the false security of pioneering advantage.

Conversely, a problem also arises by defining the term *pioneer* too broadly. For example, firms could define *pioneer* as "one of the early entrants" or "a firm that entered in the early years." All research using the PIMS database adopts this imprecise definition. What's the problem with such definitions?

The most rigorous and useful definition of *pioneer* is the firm to *first* commercialize a product. However, suppose in a market the fourth firm to enter succeeded while the first failed badly. If the term *pioneer* is defined as "one of the first to enter the market," then we would wrongly conclude that pioneers have enduring advantages. As another example, take the safety razor market. By defining a pioneer as a firm that entered the market "sometime in its early history," one can call King C. Gillette the pioneer of the safety razor. Yet the safety razor was first proposed more than 100 years before Gillette. It was commercialized more than 20 years before Gillette and was common in his day!

Thus by selectively redefining the term *pioneer*, one enlarges the number of firms that earn that label and reduces the chances of ever being able to disprove the prevailing thesis of a pioneering advantage. As a result, one may wrongly attribute to market pioneering rewards that may arise from other causes.

Loose definitions of key terms such as the *market* and *pioneer* lead to weak strategic implications. They help managers protect their favorite beliefs at the cost of rendering those beliefs meaningless. Worse still, loose definitions lead to erroneous conclusions.

summary

The issue of enduring leadership is of paramount importance to managers for several reasons. Leading firms enjoy premium prices, incur low marketing costs per unit, have great economies of scale, and can extend their dominance to new categories. The accepted wisdom is that market pioneering, or the order of market entry, is the primary cause of enduring market leadership. Specifically, the following six tenets represent the core of the accepted wisdom:

- Pioneers rarely if ever fail.
- As new firms enter the market, pioneers lose share slowly.
- Pioneers retain a high steady-state market share of about 30 percent.
- Pioneers are generally market leaders.
- Market leadership of pioneers is very stable.
- Because of these many advantages, firms should rush to market. It is better to be first with an inferior product than be late with a superior product.

Several theories explain why pioneers supposedly possess these advantages:

- Brand loyalty. In a new market, pioneers shape consumers' tastes, leading to enduring preferences.
- Inertia. Due to the many costs of switching, consumers prefer to stay with a pioneering brand.
- Patents. Pioneers protect their technological lead with patents.
- Economies of experience. Due to accumulated experience, pioneers have low costs.
- Resource mobilization. Pioneers mobilize the best supplies, suppliers, and distributors and target the best customer segments.

Numerous empirical studies support the accepted wisdom:

- At least five studies based on the PIMS data show that pioneers have large market shares and are leaders of their markets. These studies report no pioneers that failed.
- At least two studies based on the ASSESSOR data report no pioneers that failed. Their market shares decline slowly until they reach a high steady state.

- An article reported in *Advertising Age* shows that most market leaders retain their leadership over more than half a century.

Three problems seriously undermine the validity of the studies that support the accepted wisdom:

- The studies ignored the pioneers that failed, leading to survival bias.
- The studies relied on self-reports of current managers, who tend to describe their own firms as pioneers, leading to social desirability or self-report bias.
- The studies tended to define markets narrowly to enhance their perceived market share, leading to a self-serving bias.

The rest of this book presents the true rewards of pioneering new markets based on research that avoids these three problems.

learning from history

A s the prior chapter shows, asking managers of surviving firms to identify and evaluate pioneers has many problems. To avoid these problems, we need an alternative approach. The historical, or archival, method of getting information about the evolution of markets is a great alternative. This chapter first describes the advantages of the historical method. It then explains the definitions and concepts used in the current research. Next it describes the sample of product categories considered in the research. Finally it provides a glimpse of the total effort involved in this research.

advantages of delving into history

To research the evolution of markets, the historical method is unparalleled in insight and accuracy. The method consists of reconstructing the evolution of markets by evaluating multiple reports about the histories of markets, written as close as possible to the time the events occurred. Among the many advantages of this method, we would especially mention contemporaneity, independence, rich detail, and matched samples. This section briefly explains each of these advantages. Appendix 1 contains a more detailed exposition of the method.

CONTEMPORANEITY

The most important feature of the historical method is that it uses contemporaneous reports, meaning reports written at the time the events occurred. Contemporaneous reports use definitions of the market that differ substantially from those currently in vogue. We need to use those definitions, because that is exactly how the market appeared to entrants at the time. Definitions in use today benefit from hindsight, after one has seen what works and what fails. Contemporaneous reports also reveal an order in which firms entered the market that is different from what respondents now believe. Again, we need to use that order, because the current beliefs suffer from respondents forgetting the firms that failed. When contemporaneous reports are not possible, we use reports as close to the time the events occurred as possible.

The personal computer market provides an example of the importance of contemporaneous records. Micro Instrumentation and Telemetry Systems (MITS) sold the first personal computer, the Altair, in 1975.[1] Yet just 7 years later, the business press referred to Apple Computer as the pioneer of personal computers.[2] Many reporters today credit Apple with pioneering the desktop computer market. Why? The main reason is that among surviving manufacturers of personal computers, Apple Computer is the earliest to have entered the market. Most people and even many industry observers cannot remember any manufacturer that preceded Apple. The Apple computer also became very popular early in the history of the market. So it is easy to label Apple the pioneer.

However, several studies, including one thorough study by two MIT professors and another supported by the National Science Foundation, concluded that MITS is the real pioneer with its entry in 1975.[3] In fact, MITS was so dominant that in 1976 *Business Week* referred to MITS as the "IBM of home computers." Further, it reported that MITS's "early lead has made its design a de facto standard for the industry."[4] MITS's Altair established the notion of a stand-alone personal computer that consumers could own. Most importantly, it launched the public careers of Paul Allen and Bill Gates. They hired full-time programmers after they won a proposal to adapt the computer language BASIC for the Altair. Their initial success convinced them of the future of this market and the potential for a software firm that could serve it. They soon founded Micro-Soft, which, save for a small name change, is the very same company that dominates the software market today.

The early success of MITS certainly did not lead to long-term market leadership. On the contrary, MITS suffered an early death. As the years went by, reporters forgot the pioneer that failed, and crowned the successful brand, Apple, as the pioneer.

INDEPENDENCE

A second important feature of the historical method is that it strives to obtain an *independent* or neutral perspective of the evolution of the market. To do so, we use multiple narratives of more neutral observers of each firm or market than is typically done in survey research. These observers may be reporters or analysts researching the firm or market, in addition to participants within the firm or market. These narratives could be written for various reasons and may adopt a variety of perspectives. Because we use multiple narratives, the overall perspective obtained is not dependent on the information from a single firm or participant. As such, it is independent from the biases that normally afflict such reports, as explained in the first chapter.

Although researchers must sometimes synthesize and interpret the reports, those reports are all publicly available sources of information. Other researchers can easily verify the sources and content of the reports and can question or debate the findings. This approach is particularly well suited for the chronological aspect of research on market pioneering.

To appreciate the insight that can be gained from this approach, let us return to the case of the disposable diaper market. As we stated in the last chapter, P&G suggested that it pioneered the disposable diaper market with the introduction of Pampers. The truth is, disposable diapers were available in the United States long before Pampers. For example, Chux was available before Pampers. Some may argue that Chux was a small, obscure brand. But in 1961 *Consumer Reports* evaluated "nationally available" disposable diapers brands and ranked Chux as clearly the best, ahead of Sears and Montgomery Ward, while Pampers was not even mentioned. A few years later, Pampers and Chux were both ranked as best buys, affirming the arrival of Pampers on the scene and indicating its perception as a competitor to Chux. Again, some readers who know of Pampers might object that Pampers was available in a test market in the early 1960s and was almost a contemporary of Chux. However, the Chux brand was very old. It was introduced as early as 1932. Chux was also not the product of some marginal manufacturer. It was owned by Chicopee Mills, a unit of Johnson & Johnson (J&J). Until J&J withdrew from the branded U.S. market in 1981, it had been in the disposable diaper business for almost 50 years, and for about 30 years before P&G. Thus the passage of time, the success of Pampers, and P&G's self-promotion led to a reinterpretation of the history of this market.

To avoid problems such as these, we use four criteria in selecting various sources and in evaluating and using the information from these sources:

- *Competence*. Is the informant *able* to report correct information?
- *Objectivity*. Is the informant *willing* to report correct information (i.e., no vested interest)?
- *Reliability*. Is the informant a *trusted source* of accurate information?
- *Corroboration*. Is there confirmatory evidence from *other* trusted sources?

In determining competence, we took into account the credentials of the source's authors, the rigor of the methods they used, and the time they devoted to the research. To meet the objectivity criterion, we relied more on disinterested third parties than on participants in the market. To meet the reliability criterion, we used sources that have been respected for a long time. For example, the top periodicals used in this research are *Advertising Age, Business Week, Consumer Reports, Forbes*, and the *Wall Street Journal*. The longevity of and continued respect for these periodicals attest to their reliability. To meet the corroboration criterion, we used multiple sources for each category.

By using these criteria we were able to obtain a more independent, comprehensive, and less biased picture of the evolution of the market than is typically available from a one-shot survey done many years after an event.

RICH DETAIL

A third important feature of the historical method is that it uncovers rich detail that provides a fresh perspective on the evolution of markets. The method may lack the apparent objectivity of random sampling used in surveys. It is also labor intensive, providing only a few numbers after considerable effort. As a result, it may not allow the use of sophisticated statistical methods as can be carried out on survey data. However, the historical method provides fresh insights by uncovering anecdotes and stories that have long been forgotten. It allows for the reconstruction of the temporal evolution of the market that provides important clues about potential causes and effects. Surveys cannot provide the same insights.

In particular, the numerical responses to multiple-choice questions of surveys lack the rich detail of historical analyses, while introducing potentially serious biases. Researchers' use of complex statistical models to analyze survey data may lull managers into a false sense of security in precise estimates of causes that are really spurious. In contrast, time invested in carefully piecing together the evolution of markets can reveal patterns that actors at the time could not see, and unearth facts that the current survivors have long forgotten.

Analysis of the founding of McDonald's Corporation provides an example of the insight obtained from the historical method. In 1991, McDonald's celebrated the thirty-first anniversary of the founding of the chain. The celebration honored "founder Ray Kroc," who had grown the company from its early beginnings to a multinational corporation that dominated the fast-food industry. Reports credited Ray Kroc with pioneering the formula that made McDonald's a success. Indeed, the jacket of Kroc's autobiography, *Grinding It Out*, states that Kroc "founded the McDonald's hamburger chain and built it from a single restaurant in Des Plaines, Illinois, to an international operation with more than $3 billion in annual sales."[5]

Those reports upset Dick McDonald, the surviving brother of two McDonald brothers. "It really burns the hell out of me."[6] It was the brothers who founded the restaurant in San Bernardino, California, in 1948; gave it their name; introduced the golden arches; and most importantly, designed the formula that triggered its success. The formula consisted of fast, clean, inexpensive food, ordered from a simple menu that included hamburgers, fries, and milkshakes. The restaurant was very clean, the brothers used paper and plastic utensils instead of china and glass, and the orders were served in 60 seconds. The brothers got rid of carhops whose deliveries slowed service. These steps led customers to flock to the restaurant. Sales were so strong that the brothers had to order eight milkshake machines, while the typical restaurant ordered one or two. That order attracted the attention of Ray Kroc, a milkshake machine salesman, who decided to see what was happening in San Bernardino.

When Kroc visited the restaurant in 1954, he was struck by the simplicity of the formula and its strong appeal in San Bernardino. He immediately envisioned expanding the formula into a national chain. In his autobiography, Kroc wrote of this experience: "That night in my hotel room I did a lot of heavy thinking of what I had seen during the day. Visions of McDonald's restaurants dotting crossroads all over the country paraded through my brain."[7] The next day he outlined a proposal to the brothers to form a national chain of hamburger restaurants.

The brothers, content with their current profits, were not interested. One of them expressed their feelings about expansion to Kroc in these words: "See that big white house with the wide front porch? That's our home and we love it. We sit out on the porch in the evenings and watch the sunset and look down on our place here. It's peaceful. We don't need any more problems than we have in keeping this place going. More places, more problems. We are in a position to enjoy life now, and that's just what we intend to do."[8] After much persuasion, they finally agreed to let Kroc serve as a franchise salesman for a small commission of 1.4 percent of franchise sales, which was to cover his salary, profit, and expenses. The

McDonald brothers earned a commission of 0.05 percent as franchisers.

Kroc worked relentlessly at selling franchises and expanded sales to $75 million by 1960. However, his net income was only $159,000 because of the small margin he received from the McDonald brothers. Moreover, the brothers were not really interested in his efforts and sometimes undercut him. So he raised $2.7 million to buy them out. That sum was necessary to pay the brothers the amount each wanted from the sale, $1 million after taxes. Kroc then set up the Franchise Realty Corporation that bought prime real estate in promising locations and then leased it to new franchisees. As each franchisee became successful, Kroc could raise the rent on the land, which became the real source of revenues. He started the Hamburger University to train franchisees and employees and instilled in them the principles of quality, service, cleanliness, and value. He started national advertising to popularize the restaurant and its simple formula and establish a clear unique image for the mass market. He also took the formula international, convinced that if it appealed to consumers here, it would also do so in other countries. Most importantly, Kroc never gave up on his vision, persisting tirelessly to expand the chain of franchisees without compromising the original formula. Kroc's clear vision and persistent efforts paid off handsomely and made McDonald's the tremendous success it has become. Ray Kroc had a vision of the mass market that was responsible for McDonald's national and international growth. However, he neither invented the formula nor pioneered the concept.

Historical details of the origins of the fast-food industry not only clarify some facts, but also reveal the unique role of pioneers and visionaries as drivers of success.

MATCHED SAMPLES

A fourth benefit of the historical method is that it allows for the comparison of similar firms at the same stage of market evolution. We call this feature the benefit of matched samples. This characteristic directly mitigates the problem of survival bias caused when failed pioneers are excluded.

We first reconstruct the market as it evolved. We then observe the performance of firms at important moments in the market's evolution. We analyze the factors in each firm's behavior and environment that caused the performance. The important issue is that we try to include all the key firms at the time. We especially include the pioneer, the market leader of the past, the current leader, and the market leader when the current leader entered. While today, the market leader may seem unique and dominant, at the time it entered it may have appeared quite fragile and insignificant relative to the leader at that time. As much as possible, we also include important firms in a market when it was first formed, whether they failed or succeeded.

By following these principles, our research includes not only winners and successful firms, but also failures and unsuccessful firms. It includes small and large firms, incumbents and new entrants. We especially compare firms that *could have made similar decisions*, even though they differed in size, resources, and the order in which they entered the market.

Consider the laser printer market of which HP is the leader today. The question we ask is what were the firms when HP entered? At that time, IBM and Xerox were the dominant suppliers of laser printers. The next question we ask is who was in a better position than HP to succeed with laser printers. At face value, IBM and Xerox not only entered before HP, but were larger firms with extensive resources, strong R&D facilities, and strong experience in office products. So they both had great advantages over HP and strong reasons for succeeding. Yet HP is the current market leader. Why? Subsequent chapters will answer this question. Here we need to emphasize that comparing the behavior and performance of HP versus that of Xerox and IBM not only reveals the real picture of market evolution, but can tell us the true causes of long-term market leadership.

Now consider the browser market. The major organizations in the evolution of this market were CERN (now the European Laboratory for Particle Physics), the National Center for Supercomputing Applications at the University of Illinois, Netscape, and Microsoft. Their entry into the market is in the order listed here. Their control over the technology was also strictly in this order. Yet today, the last of these four to enter, Microsoft, is the market leader. Why? That is the precise question this book attempts to answer. Most importantly, we do so by comparing the behavior and performance of these four major players in the market.

As a third illustration of this point, consider the market of online service providers. Today the market leader is AOL even though it entered quite late. CompuServe and Prodigy were the big players. Moreover, CompuServe had a relatively long history, a strong reputation, and a fine product. Yet these two one-time giants, who had every reason to succeed, are insignificant players today. Ironically, the late entrant AOL purchased the pioneer, CompuServe. Why? This book will answer this question. We do so by carefully comparing the current leader with those firms that had at least as good a chance of succeeding as the current leader. It is such comparison of multiple firms within a market that reveals novel insights and allows for valid conclusions.

To help the reader better understand our findings, we next briefly define the key terms used and the sample of markets covered in our research.

definitions for insight, not comfort

As the discussion above may suggest, the definitions of market and pioneer are crucial for valid analysis. Loose definitions may be comforting, but they can easily lead to empty propositions or self-serving but erroneous conclusions. To avoid these problems we use a precise definition of pioneer and a broad definition of market, while not relying on hindsight.

We define the *pioneer* as the *first* firm to commercialize the product in a new market. This definition is precise and rigorous. It avoids the problem or ambiguity that may occur if one defines pioneer as "one of the first to enter a market." Our definition can clearly differentiate whether being first *by itself* has any enduring advantage. It enables us to distinguish the class of firms that might enter after the pioneer and learn from its errors, yet still enter early enough to shape and dominate the product category.

Using a loose definition of market pioneers, we could consider Internet Explorer as one of the pioneers of the browser market. Then a look at the current position of market shares would imply that market pioneering leads to enduring success. However, by the strict order of entry, Internet Explorer was certainly not the first brand, and thus not the pioneer. Internet Explorer was not even among the first 10 brands to have entered the market. Indeed, in this market, market leadership seems to have gone from Gopher to Mosaic to Netscape to Internet Explorer, in about 6 years, with a host of other rivals that fell by the side.

The prior loose definition of pioneer clouds the facts and confuses the strategic implications. It still leaves unanswered the real questions: Why did the first firm to enter the market fail? Why is Internet Explorer currently on top? How long might its leadership last? These are questions that subsequent chapters directly address.

Second, we define a market as a competitive environment in which firms attempt to satisfy some distinct but enduring consumer need. We use the terms *market* and *product category* interchangeably. We use the term *market* when discussing the consumer and competitive dimensions of the context and the term *product category* when discussing the set of products being marketed.

Examples of a market include browsers, personal computers, and word processors. For personal computers, the definition means any stand-alone computer for consumers' private use. It includes basic products such as the Altair, fully proprietary products such as the Apple, or OEM-assembled products such as the PC. For word processors, it includes either software such as WordStar, dedicated word processors such as the Wang WPS, or memory typewriters such as IBM's electronic typewriters.

In defining markets, we prefer to use broad definitions. The broad definition focuses on enduring consumer needs rather than on transient technologies or products to serve those needs. A narrow definition assures a false sense of security. It leads to smug satisfaction in a firm's current success and reveals no insights about past success or future options. A narrow definition will fallaciously allow any firm with a loyal niche of customers to be designated the pioneer of that small segment that it currently dominates.

The broad definition of personal computers shows that market leadership frequently changed from one brand to another due to a firm's inability to understand and exploit technological changes. For example, market leadership went from MITS to Tandy to Apple to

IBM to Compaq to Dell in just 25 years. In word processors, market leadership went from IBM to Wang to WordStar to WordPerfect to Microsoft Word, also in the last 25 years. In these markets, as in many others covered in this book, market pioneering gave no enduring advantage. The order of market entry was irrelevant. Rather, other key factors played a critical role in success.

Third, we avoid hindsight when identifying pioneers and defining markets or product categories. Every successful, dominant firm has reached that position by doing something right. In a loose sense, that firm has "pioneered" a new technology, business model, or market segment. However, loose definitions of pioneer and market, based on outcomes, are circular: If successful firms are labeled *pioneers* (of a concept or segment), then pioneers must be successful. The key question is how did the firm appear at the time it entered the market, *before we knew the outcomes?* At the time that firms enter, only two observations are certain: (1) the firms' order of entry, whether first, second, etc., and (2) the market of competing firms, each using a particular technology and strategy, any of which could become successful. The case of copiers emphasizes the value of definitions enlightened by historical analysis and not based on hindsight.

Until recently, Xerox was the undisputed leader of the document duplication market. For almost four decades, its leadership was so strong that people did not know of any firm that existed before Xerox. Thus, they considered Xerox to be the pioneer of copiers. But Xerox is actually the name adopted by a small firm, Haloid, which was not originally in the business of making or selling copiers. Indeed, when it entered the market, it was given a poor chance to succeed, as can be ascertained from this quote from *Business Week* (1959): "Office copying is a field where Haloid will find plenty of competition. Most of the 30 or so copying machine manufacturers are already in it with a variety of products and processes—including such strong competition as Minnesota Mining & Mfg. Co. (Thermofax), Eastman Kodak (Verifax), and American Photocopy Equipment Co. (Apeco)."[9]

At the time it entered the category, Haloid was not considered a pioneer, nor was it given much of a chance to succeed. At that time, its technology not only was *not* perceived to be a winner, but was not even considered to be promising. Thus, use of hindsight to define order of entry or market can easily lead to circular or erroneous conclusions.

sample

Because the population of firms and markets is enormous, most in-depth studies of business performance must be based on a sample of markets. This is especially true of historical analyses such as ours that require detailed reconstruction of the evolution of markets, some of which are quite old. We were concerned, as the reader might be, that our results might be biased by the sample we chose. Worse still, we wanted to avoid the chance that our sample would favor a particular position. For this reason, we chose four different samples, each based on different criteria. We also kept track of our results by sample. To assure the reader about the objectivity of our results, we briefly describe each of these samples.

Sample 1 is based on three criteria. First, the sample includes only consumer goods. Second, the sample covers only recent product categories because of the easier availability of information on them. Third, the sample contains both newer product categories (e.g., camcorders) and extensions of existing product categories (e.g., light beer). We found 19 product categories satisfying these criteria. The first sample is not biased toward or against any particular thesis. Our results from this sample ran surprisingly counter to the prevailing thesis of a pioneering advantage. So we selected three more samples on entirely different criteria to validate the findings.

Sample 2 consists of 24 categories from the 25 in the *Advertising Age* article of long-term leaders (see Table 1-1). This research has been extensively cited to support the idea of market share stability. It has also been used to support the notion of a pioneering advantage. Thus researching these categories *biases our results in favor of the prevailing view* that pioneers are successful.

Sample 3 consists of eight product categories, each of which contains a widely believed market pioneer, e.g., Xerox or Polaroid. Thus by definition, sample 3 is strongly favorable to the prevailing belief in a pioneering advantage.

Sample 4 consists of 15 modern markets that represent more high-tech or new-economy products. Examples of such markets are Web browsers, microprocessors, and database software. In such markets, time moves very fast. Many authors assume that because changes in these markets take place very fast, speed in strategy is very important, and order of entry is critical. If this is true, pioneers are more likely to be successful in such markets than in traditional markets. It is definitely worthwhile to test the validity of this belief.

Our total sample consists of 66 separate categories. This number is several times larger than that typically used in longitudinal business studies. The categories were drawn in four batches using substantially different criteria. As the reader can judge, we did not draw these samples selectively to advocate a particular view. On the contrary, three of our four samples are based on criteria that favor the prevailing view of a pioneering advantage.

research effort

The sources of our data are all publicly available documents. We referenced myriad sources for this research. Most of our sources were business periodicals and books, though we also referenced many other journal articles and numerous Web sites. In addition, we reviewed the annual reports of many firms. Based on a rough estimate, we examined about 2000 articles in 30 different periodicals. The periodicals sourced most often were *Consumer Reports, Advertising Age, Business Week, Forbes*, and the *Wall Street Journal*. We also consulted information from over 300 books. Most of these books covered individual product categories or brands. Many of the books were written by professors or scholars based on in-depth research into certain markets. Some of the books contain references to periodicals going back hundreds of years. We had to carry out extensive searches in a number of libraries to access these various sources. Some of these searches led us to different cities and to some very old and long forgotten documents.

We had several reasons for doing this extensive and laborious search. First, we wanted to corroborate our information as much as possible. Second, we wanted to find material written as close to the time each event occurred as was possible. Third, we wanted to evaluate each market from various perspectives to gain greater insight and avoid individual biases.

To illustrate the value of sourcing past articles, consider the following quotes from *Financial World* about a company in the restaurant business[10]:

"World's biggest chain of highway restaurants."
"Pioneer in restaurant franchising."
"Most strongly entrenched factor in the industry."
"Highest quality [investment] vehicle."
"Most fabulous success story in [restaurant chains]."

On reading these quotes, McDonald's probably comes to mind. Indeed, if these quotes were written today, they would probably be describing McDonald's. However, these quotes were written in the 1960s, and they refer not to McDonald's, but to Howard Johnson's restaurants. Since restaurant franchising was developing in the 1960s, information about this market was collected from publications written in the 1960s. This information reveals a fresh perspective on the real role that McDonald's and Howard Johnson's played in this market.

Our total research effort spanned more than a decade, from 1990 to 2001. During this time, we collected and analyzed data, published our initial findings in peer-reviewed, scholarly journals, and presented our conclusions at conferences and seminars.[11] Some colleagues accepted our views, while others conducted rival studies to try to prove us wrong. All along, our understanding of the phenomena kept growing, while our articulation of the thesis grew more precise. Even then, we faced the constant challenge of validating the thesis against the evidence of still evolving markets.

Perhaps the greatest challenge to our ideas came in the last 5 years as the digital age made speed an issue of paramount importance. Analysts kept emphasizing the importance of early if not first entry, to grab at least a foothold in the new markets. So we expanded our sample to research the new and still evolving digital and high-tech economy. What we found is that the patterns of enduring success are as valid today for Bill Gates, Steve Case, and Jeff Bezos as they were over a hundred years ago for George Eastman, King Gillette, Henry Ford, and other entrepreneurs whose names and businesses still endure.

plan of the book

Chapter 3 presents the major findings based on a statistical analysis of the rewards to market pioneering across 66 markets. Chapter 3 also summarizes the true causes of enduring market leadership. Following that, Chapters 4 to 10 each focus on one of the causes of enduring market leadership. To give the reader a sense of how each of these causes leads firms to win, maintain, or lose market leadership, each chapter details the evolution of specific firms in specific markets. In the interests of depth and continuity, we use some of the same firms and markets to illustrate how these causes play out over time. Firms that we repeatedly illustrate in depth are Gillette, Xerox, Microsoft, IBM, Federal Express, Intel, Procter & Gamble, Netscape, Ampex, and Sony. At the same time, to show how widespread our findings are, we also describe examples of other organizations, albeit not as frequently or in as great depth. Examples of the latter class of organizations are Kodak, Amazon.com, Charles Schwab, Eastman Kodak, Johnson & Johnson, McDonald's, Hewlett-Packard, America Online, JVC, Matsushita, Intergalactic Digital Research, the European Laboratory for Particle Physics, Spry, and the National Center for Supercomputing Applications at the University of Illinois. In all cases, we try to contrast the behavior of firms that endured as leaders to those that had as good a chance or even a better chance to do the same. Thus in each market our analysis is always comparative.

In short, the findings of this book are based on a statistical and historical analysis of 66 markets and illustrated by an in-depth description of about 20 firms in these markets.

summary

- If properly conducted, the historical, or archival, method is ideally suited to the research of market evolution and the effects of market pioneering.

- Key features of the historical method, which render it superior to surveys, are contemporaneity, independence, rich detail, and matched samples.
- Contemporaneity means the use of reports written as close as possible to when historical events unfolded. It provides market definitions and order of firms' entry that are not contaminated by hindsight or biased by the omission of failures.
- Independence means the use of multiple reports of neutral observers who do not have a vested interest in the outcomes. As such, the records do not suffer from self-report bias. Since the reports are from publicly available sources, other researchers or readers can evaluate them independently.
- Rich detail refers to the abundant contextual information about markets, actors, and events available in historical reports. Such detail unearths facts that current survivors have long forgotten and reveals patterns that actors at the time could not see.
- When defining the key terms of the research, we use a precise definition of *pioneer* and a broad definition of *market* to avoid biases that plagued past studies. We also rely on historical accounts, not hindsight, to apply these definitions.
- The data for this research come from four sequential samples. The first one is unbiased, while the next three are biased toward supporting the thesis of pioneering advantage. The fourth sample focuses on digital and high-tech markets.
- The ideas in this book are based on research of thousands of articles and hundreds of books over more than a decade. They have been fashioned through publication in peer-reviewed journals and through debate at many conferences and seminars.

3

facts about pioneers and real causes of enduring leadership

This chapter summarizes the main findings of this study, based on the sample of 66 categories that we described in the previous chapter. Our findings emerge from a careful reconstruction and analysis of the evolution of markets. Unlike other chapters of the book, this chapter includes a number of statistics. The statistics describe the performance of pioneers on four key variables: long-term success, market share, market leadership, and duration of leadership. Such statistics give the reader a sense of how common our results are across markets. The remaining chapters illustrate our key results with novel stories of the evolution of these markets. A close scrutiny of these markets reveals the typical characteristics of enduring leaders. We propose that these characteristics are the true causes of enduring market leadership.

We first present a summary of our findings. We then present statistics about market pioneers. Subsequently we highlight the key characteristics of enduring market leaders.

summary findings

Are pioneers really long-term market leaders? What are the true causes of enduring market leadership? Our analysis reveals the following key conclusions:

- Market pioneers rarely endure as leaders. Most of them have low market share or fail completely. Actually, market pioneering is neither necessary nor sufficient for enduring success.
- The real causes of enduring market leadership are *vision* and *will*. Enduring market leaders have a revolutionary and inspiring vision of the mass market, and they exhibit an indomitable will to realize that vision. They persist under adversity, innovate relentlessly, commit financial resources, and leverage assets to realize their vision.

We believe that these are the factors that lead to enduring market leadership. Conversely, pioneers that fail lack one or more of these factors. We next present statistics to support these conclusions and examples to illustrate the causes of enduring leadership.

important statistics about market pioneers

Our statistics focus on four traditional criteria of a pioneer's performance: long-term success, market share, market leadership, and duration of leadership. All our statistics are calculated as of the year 2000.[1]

LONG-TERM SUCCESS

What guarantee does the first entrant to a market have of being ultimately successful?

Since entry in a new category is very difficult and risky, we assume that the pioneer entered to succeed in the long run. This assumption is especially true for the categories that we covered for this book, which all grew to be very large and profitable. The common measure of success is to evaluate the failure rate of pioneers. By failure we mean the end of a brand's sales in a category that it entered. Failure occurs when the brand dies out or exits the market.

Some past studies do not report any pioneers that fail. Others claim that they are unaware of any pioneers that failed, implying an unusually low failure rate of zero![2] In contrast, we found that the failure rate of pioneers was at least 64 percent (see Table 3-1). Examples of pioneers that failed include Daguerreotype (cameras), Star (safety razors), Chux (diapers), Canton (clothes dryer), CP/M (PC operating systems), and Altair (personal computers). Appendix 2 has a complete list of pioneers and current leaders in all 66 categories we studied.

The inclusion of old and new categories raises another question. Is the failure rate of pioneers lower in newer categories? To check this out, we split our sample into three time periods: pre-1940, 1940 to 1974, and post-1974. The failure rate of pioneers that entered before 1940 is quite high at 72 percent. But the failure rate of pioneers in the last 25 years is also quite high at 56 percent. The implication from these statistics is that pioneers tend to fail fairly early in each category's history. Thus the age of the category is not responsible for our results. Even in recent decades, market pioneering does not guarantee success.

Is this high failure rate due to the categories we chose? To evaluate this possibility, we intentionally chose several samples, and compared our results across samples. Table 3-1 shows that in the most representative sample (sample 1) the failure rate of pioneers is very high (68 percent). As we chose samples biased toward the prevailing thesis of pioneer advantage (samples 3 and 4), the failure rate of pioneers seems to go down. Even then in the biased sample 3, which we selected because of well-known pioneers, the failure rate is still quite high (50 percent).

A strong belief among analysts is that because high-tech and digital markets evolve very fast, market pioneering is crucial for success in these markets. For this reason we divided the sample into traditional markets and those that involve high-tech or digital products. We call the latter group modern markets. While the failure rate of pioneers is high in the traditional markets (71 percent), it is also quite high in modern markets (50 percent). Readers need to take into account that many of the latter markets are still quite young, and yet half the pioneers have already failed.

Table 3-1. Failure Rate of Pioneers (as of 2000)

Class	Failure Rate, %	Number of Cases
Total	64	66
Pre-1940	72	36
1940–1974	50	14
Post-1974	56	16
Traditional	71	42
Digital/high-tech	50	24
Sample 1	68	19
Sample 2	75	24
Sample 3	50	8
Sample 4	47	15

MARKET SHARE

The battle for market share is one that firms wage daily. Higher market share bestows numerous benefits such as higher market power, greater economies of scale, greater visibility, and potentially higher profits. In the short term, gains in market share, with positive margins and constant fixed costs, result in higher profits. This outcome is one of the primary reasons that firms battle for market share every day.

How do pioneers fare in terms of market share? Past research suggests that one of the highest rewards of market pioneering is the high market share that pioneers enjoy. According to these studies, on average the pioneers have a market share of 30 percent. Indeed, some researchers think that market share closely tracks the order of market entry: "Not only does the first brand usually become the leader, but also the sales order of follow-up brands often matches the order of their introductions."[3]

In contrast, we found that pioneers had an average market share of only 6 percent (see Table 3-2). This number becomes even smaller (4 percent) for pioneers that entered after 1974. Moreover, the market share of pioneers in sample 1, our most representative sample, is only 3 percent. Even in high-tech and digital markets where pio-

Table 3-2. Market Share of Pioneers (in 2000)

Class	Mean Market Share, %	Number of Cases
Total	6	66
Pre-1940	6	36
1940–1974	10	14
Post-1974	4	16
Traditional	5	42
Digital/high-tech	8	24
Sample 1	3	19
Sample 2	4	24
Sample 3	15	8
Sample 4	9	15

neering is touted to be crucial, pioneers' average market share is only 8 percent. These results indicate that past studies greatly overestimated the market share rewards to pioneering.

MARKET LEADERSHIP

The term *market leader* refers to the brand with the highest market share in a product category. Market leaders enjoy all the tangible benefits that accrue to firms with high market share, such as economies of scale and power over suppliers and prices. In addition, they enjoy some other intangible benefits. For example, to the extent that consumers can recall only one or two brand names per category, they are more likely to recall and choose leading brands. Also, consumers who do not understand product quality may assume that the market leader has the best quality. Stores that can stock only a few brands are more likely to stock brands that lead their categories. Finally, market leadership is a source of great pride for employees of the firm, and of bragging rights for the managers. Perhaps for these reasons, GE, under Jack Welch, adopted a strategy of staying in only those markets in which it could sustain leadership.

How often do market pioneers lead in their product category?

Some past studies suggest that more than half of all market leaders are the pioneers of their respective markets. Others claim that market leadership and being first to market are almost the same. Consider this quote: "The law of leadership applies to any product, any brand, any category. . . . You can always make a good guess by substituting *leading* for *first*."[4] Indeed, in common discourse, most people treat market leaders synonymously with market pioneers.

In contrast, our analysis indicates that market pioneers are *rarely* market leaders! We find that pioneers are current leaders in only 6 of the 66 categories we studied (see Table 3-3). Is this result due to the prevalence of some old categories in which pioneers may have failed. To test this possibility we examined our sample across the three time periods described above. We find that the rate of leadership is lowest in recent decades. For example, after 1974, the market pioneer survives as the leader in just 1 in 16 categories. The rate is even lower in our most representative sample 1—just 1 of 19 categories has a leader that pioneered the category.

Appendix 2 gives the list of pioneers and current leaders in all categories in our sample. Readers can verify for themselves, by perusing this list, that the vast majority of pioneers are no longer leaders in the category they pioneered.

DURATION OF LEADERSHIP

Casual reporters often cite the example of Coca-Cola to suggest that pioneers endure as market leaders. Indeed, from a few such examples (see Table 1-2), many reporters suggest that pioneers endure as leaders for decades. Such questions raise another pertinent question: How long are pioneers able to retain their leadership?

Our results are quite contrary to casual reports. It is true that market pioneers are de facto market leaders upon entry. But we find in most product categories this leadership does not last very long. Overall, pioneers maintained market leadership for a median of 5 years. That is, half of the pioneers in our sample were leaders for more than 5 years, and the other half were leaders for less than 5 years. The reward represented by this short period of leadership is not very great, because it often occurs when sales of the product category are still small.

Table 3-3.   Market Leadership of Pioneers (in 2000)

Class	Pioneers Who Are Current Leaders		Number of Cases
	Number	Percent	
Total	6	9%	66
Pre-1940	3	8%	36
1940–1974	2	14%	14
Post-1974	1	6%	16
Traditional	3	7%	42
Digital/high-tech	3	13%	24
Sample 1	1	5%	19
Sample 2	1	4%	24
Sample 3	2	25%	8
Sample 4	2	13%	15

Not only did few pioneers survive as leaders, but other firms that became leaders often failed to maintain that position. Across our 66 categories, market leadership changed hands many times. To give a sense of this instability of positions, Table 3-4 illustrates some examples with frequent changes in market leadership. Notice how this selection includes very old and very new categories and covers traditional and high-tech markets.

Overall, we find that pioneers are current leaders in only 6 of the 66 product categories studied. Detailed analysis of these six categories shows that attributing current market position to market pioneering may be unambiguously supported in only one case, Crisco shortening. In three other cases the effect of being first in the market is less clear. For instance, Coca-Cola "entered the market as one of thousands of exotic medicinal products belonging to the nationwide patent medicine industry."[5] Coca-Cola contains caffeine, and early in its history contained cocaine, a natural ingredient from coca leaves. These addictive ingredients probably contributed as much to brand loyalty as any other factor posed by economic and psychological theories. In color televisions, while the RCA brand is still in existence, General Electric bought RCA and then sold the entire consumer electronics division to Thomson Electronics of France be-

Table 3-4. Illustrations of Frequent Changes in Market Leadership (as of 2000)

Category	Pioneer	Interim Leaders	Current Leader
Soap		Ivory, Dial	Dove
Liquid dishwashing detergent	Liquid Lux	Joy, Ivory	Dawn
Light beer	Trommer's Red Letter	Rheingold Gablinger's, Meister Brau, Miller Lite	Bud Light
Video games	Magnavox Odyssey	Atari, Nintendo, Sega	Sony
Personal computers	MITS	Tandy, Apple, IBM, Compaq	Dell
PC operating systems	CP/M	Apple II OS, DOS	Windows
Word processors	IBM Memory Writer	Wang, Electric Pencil/Easy Writer, WordStar, WordPerfect	Microsoft Word
Online service providers	CompuServe	Prodigy	America Online
Web browsers	WorldWideWeb	Mosaic, Netscape	Internet Explorer
Online stock trading	K. Aufhauser	Lombard, Ameritrade, E*Trade	Charles Schwab

cause it was not profitable enough. In the telephone product category, Bell was able to dominate this market only after reaching a settlement with Western Union for patent infringement. This settlement called for Bell to pay 20 percent of its revenues to Western Union for 17 years. In two other cases (Sony's leadership of CD players and Intel's of microprocessors), the pioneers face intense competition and still survive today primarily due to relentless innovation. Later chapters detail Sony's and Intel's innovativeness.

In all the other 60 categories, either the pioneers failed, they are not leaders, or current leaders are incorrectly labeled as pioneers (see Appendix 2 for details).

enduring market leaders

These unexpected results raise the following questions: If not the market pioneer, then who? Is there another class of firms that enjoy the advantages attributed to market pioneers? We did find a class of firms that achieve and maintain market leadership over the long haul. We call these firms the enduring market leaders. Some of these firms entered in the early growth stage of the life cycle of a product. Thus, a natural question is how close are these firms to market pioneers? In particular, how soon after the pioneers did current leaders enter the market?

Current leaders tend to enter product categories many years and sometimes decades after the market pioneer. On average across all categories studied, current leaders entered 19 years after market pioneers (see Table 3-5). The time lag is 22, 30, and 24 years for each of our first three samples. It is still 5 years in sample 4. This sample consists of a number of young categories, and new firms might still enter and lead the category in the future, many years after the first or pioneering firm entered in the past.

These time lags are not trivial. In the quest to enter and dominate markets, firms time their entry very carefully, often striving to be first by months or even weeks. Thus current leaders are not firms that we mistakenly failed to classify as pioneers. Nor are they firms that meant to be pioneers but were a few days or months late.

For example, in Web browsers, the current leader Internet Ex-

Table 3-5. Years between Entry of Pioneer and Current Leader (as of 2000)

Class	Number of Years	Number of Cases
Total	19	43
Pre-1940	30	20
1940–1974	17	10
Post-1974	5	13
Traditional	29	24
Digital/high-tech	7	19
Sample 1	22	13
Sample 2	30	11
Sample 3	24	6
Sample 4	5	13

plorer entered 5 years after the pioneer. In personal computers, the current leader Dell entered 9 years after the pioneer. In PC operating systems, the current leader Microsoft Windows entered 10 years after the pioneer. In cameras, the current leader Kodak entered almost 50 years after the pioneer. Yet in all these markets, in the interim years, new entrants kept entering and often rushing to market, as though their success depended primarily on their timing of entry.

At this point, a most pertinent question is why do some firms endure while pioneers fail? What are the common attributes, if any, of enduring market leaders?

While reviewing the evolution of markets, what struck us was how enduring leaders in market after market seemed to share some common characteristics or factors. Many of the markets differed substantially in time, culture, competitive environment, technology, and industry. Yet across all these markets, a few factors seemed to distinguish firms that turned out to be enduring market leaders from those that were minor players in the market or completely failed. Many of these failures were market pioneers or had strong positions at one time.

So what are the characteristics of enduring market leaders? What distinguishes them from firms that fail? More generally, if it is not pioneering, then what are the real causes of enduring market leadership?

We find five factors that drive the superior performance of enduring leaders. These factors are vision, persistence, innovation, commitment, and asset leverage. The latter four factors all have to do with determination or willingness, and so we refer to them collectively as *will*. Alternatively, one may conceive of them as manifestations or components of will.

In subsequent chapters we describe the role of each of these factors. In doing so, we describe the evolution of some notable markets. We present these examples in considerable detail to enable a proper evaluation of our conclusions. Many aspects of these examples will be quite new and surprising. Some readers may be familiar with other examples. However, our goal is not merely to recount histories, but to point out patterns in these histories. Our intention in providing detail is to show the richness and complexity in which these five forces of enduring leadership play out in real markets. We take special care to compare the behavior and performance of pioneers or other early entrants with that of firms that later became enduring market leaders.

As a preview of our thesis, we briefly introduce these five factors here. A short example illustrates the role of each factor.

VISION OF THE MASS MARKET

The word *vision* is an overused and much maligned term in business today. It has often come to mean broad mission statements that are designed for press releases or to induct new employees but are not specific enough to be assessed. Our concept of vision is diametrically opposite these broad meanings. It is very specific and easily assessed. Simply put, the vision of enduring market leaders is a unique perspective of serving the mass market. This notion of vision encompasses two important components.

First, it involves a focus on the mass market with its dynamic and evolving needs. In mature markets today, pursuit of the mass market is considered a flawed strategy. It is synonymous with poor quality, low prices, and low margins. The mass market bears an entirely different perspective for a visionary's new product. At the time a vision is first formulated, competitors may be focusing on the wrong market or on a market niche. For example, in the mid-1970s, Bill Gates and Paul Allen believed that falling prices and improving technology would make computers accessible to most consumers. Thus they envisioned a huge market for desktop computers. This vision of a computer "on every desk and in every home"[6] fired their zeal to develop software for the personal computer market. Others, who preceded them in the market, did not share the same vision and lost their early leadership to Microsoft, the company that Gates and Allen cofounded.

Second, vision involves a unique perspective of serving the mass market. Today, in hindsight, this perspective seems natural and intuitive. Yet at the time it was first expressed, contemporaries criticized or ridiculed such a perspective as too costly or unattainable. For example, when Steve Case took over the helm of what was later to become America Online, he faced numerous competitors, including established firms such as CompuServe and Prodigy. These firms catered to a niche market of sophisticated users or extended the market culture of their founders. In particular, CompuServe provided very valuable financial information for investors, but in a hard-to-use format. In contrast, from the very beginning, Case envisioned America Online to be a service for the mass market. While competitors emphasized information content, AOL emphasized community. While competitors emphasized speed, AOL emphasized a simple intuitive interface. While competitors emphasized sophisticated features, AOL emphasized easy installation. While competitors cultivated niche markets, AOL indulged in costly mailings to sign up a mass market of users. Critics ridiculed AOL as the "Kmart network"[7] of the Internet. They said the firm "dumbed down" information. They claimed its aggressive mass marketing would drive the company broke. Yet today AOL is the market leader. It did well enough to buy out CompuServe, and render Prodigy to an insignificant status in the market. Case's unique approach to serving the mass market paid off handsomely. It grew the company to a position where it could buy the venerable old-media giant, Time Warner.

PERSISTENCE

Many analysts dismiss enduring market leaders as blessed with luck—being in the right place at the right time. However, we find that enduring leaders were not simply blessed with luck. On the contrary, they faced huge obstacles. Indeed, market leadership rarely comes from luck. Rather it comes from a will to persist through many long years to overcome huge obstacles while competing against better-equipped competitors.

For example, it is well known that Sony is a technologically innovative electronics company. However, when Sony first started, it was so small and insignificant that it was not given much of a chance to succeed. Cofounder Masaru Ibuka recounts the reaction he received when he visited Western Electric in the 1950s to seek a license for transistors.

"What do you intend to use transistors for?" managers at Western Electric asked.

"I am considering using them only for radios," he answered.

"Don't waste your time and money"[8] was the response he received, because 12 licensees in the United States had tried and not yet succeeded.

Neither did success come easily to Sony. But in the end, it did succeed. Also, as we shall see in the video recorder market, Sony labored for close to 20 years to develop the Beta videocassette recorder, which was the first product to receive broad market acceptance. Such efforts came from the indomitable will of its founders to realize their vision to serve the mass market. In the same market, the firm that pioneered the technology lacked such vision and persistence.

RELENTLESS INNOVATION

Markets and technology change constantly, rendering once successful products obsolete. The positions of even the most entrenched firms are quite susceptible to the forces of technological and market change. Thus a firm must have the will to innovate relentlessly in order to retain market leadership.

For example, Gillette seems to have dominated the safety razor market for almost a century. A cursory look at its market share shows a relatively stable level of around 70 percent. However, that stability hides enormous turmoil at the model level. As a subsequent chapter details, every decade or so Gillette introduces a new razor and blades, which cannibalize its older products. The few times Gillette failed to innovate, it quickly lost share to rivals.

Similarly, Intel's dominance of the microprocessor market is marked by relentless innovation to introduce a new generation of chip every few years. Each new generation cannibalizes sales of the prior generation of chips. Such innovation is fired by paranoia that competitors will surpass it with a superior technology or product. To firms like Gillette and Intel that face rapid and constant technological change, current market dominance and past market pioneering are practically irrelevant.

FINANCIAL COMMITMENT

Building markets and maintaining leadership through turbulent times require large financial resources. Devoting one's own resources is tough, especially because failure leaves the manager without a job and resources. Obtaining resources from outsiders is tough, because venture capitalists are difficult to persuade and often ask a steep price. Enduring market leaders are firms that had the will to commit their own resources or raise resources from the outside to realize their vision.

For example, Chester Carlson needed the resources of a large firm to develop and market his idea for copying machines based on xerography. He contacted numerous large firms. None of them saw the merit in investing in the primitive technology that he had developed. The only exception was Haloid. As we shall see in a subsequent chapter, Haloid took a huge risk on Carlson's technology. The firm's visionary leader gambled his own and his company's limited resources over a 14-year period to bring to market a good copier based on this technology. The fruit of that investment was the Xerox 914, one of the most successful products in history. As a result of its success, Haloid changed its name to Xerox.

ASSET LEVERAGE

When a category emerges as an offshoot of a parent category (e.g., diet colas from colas, personal computers from computers), firms that dominate the parent category have great potential in the new category. They can leverage their assets to also dominate the new category. For this purpose, the most useful assets are brand name, talent, products, and distribution network. But the decision to leverage assets is not easy. The new category may appear as a threat to the old. Firms that dominate the old may be averse to cannibalizing their established positions or giving the new category credibility. Enduring market leaders are often those firms that are willing to risk their current assets to build positions in the new category.

For example, Apple led the personal computer market in the late 1970s. IBM entered later but quickly surpassed Apple's early lead. The main reason was the IBM brand name, which at that time represented quality products supported by outstanding service. An IBM personal computer inspired confidence in retailers and consumers that the giant corporation would stand behind its product, and that the personal computer market had come of age. However, as the personal computer grew in popularity, IBM felt that it threatened its mainframe computer business. So the firm was not as willing as other firms to promote the growth of personal computers. Other firms proceeded to introduce new personal computers and wrested leadership of this market from IBM.

WILL AND VISION

We find that at the root of enduring market leaders is a unique vision of the mass market. Coupled with this vision is an indomitable will to realize the vision. *Will* manifests itself in four important components: persistence, relentless innovation, financial commitment, and asset leverage. Vision is the starting point. It motivates and directs the other four factors. But all of them are essential for enduring market leadership. Far beyond the naïve hypotheses of pioneering or luck, these factors are probably the real *causes of enduring market leadership*. Figure 3-1 presents a model of how these factors drive enduring market leadership.

Figure 3-1. A Model of Enduring Market Leadership

Firms endured as market leaders because they had most or all of these attributes. On the other hand, many market pioneers failed because they lacked one or more of these factors. The next seven chapters explain each one of these factors and detail supporting evidence. The evidence consists of fascinating histories of the overlooked evolution of well-known product categories.

summary

The historical method reveals the following main findings about market pioneers.

- On average most (64 percent) market pioneers fail. The failure rate is quite high (56 percent) even for recent (post-1974) categories and is also high (50 percent) for high-tech and digital product categories.
- On average, pioneers have only a 6 percent share of the market. For recent categories, this average share falls to 4 percent, while for recent digital and high-tech products it is still only 8 percent.
- Market pioneers are current leaders in only 9 percent of the categories studied. The rate is even lower (6 percent) for recent

categories but a little higher (13 percent) for high-tech and digital product categories.

- Enduring market leaders are rarely pioneers. Rather, they exhibit five important traits: vision, persistence, innovation, commitment, and asset leverage. These are the essential characteristics of long-term market leadership. Market pioneering is neither necessary nor sufficient for such leadership.

envisioning the mass market

An essential component of vision is its focus on the mass market. For example, Ray Kroc had a vision of a national and international mass market for inexpensive fast food. Bill Gates envisioned a mass market of inexpensive personal computers in every home and on every desk.

Yet the mass market is something that marketers tend to shun, especially for mature products. Strategists stress the importance of segmentation and differentiation. Segmentation is the division of a market into groups of consumers who are more similar to each other. The groups are called segments. Differentiation is a strategy in which a marketer tries to change its product design so as to more exactly match the needs of a segment. The primary purpose of segmentation and differentiation is to satisfy consumers within a segment better than competitors do. The underlying assumption is that firms that do so can maintain higher prices than those that market a single undifferentiated product to the mass market. Thus segmentation and differentiation are assumed to be more profitable than mass marketing. As a result, markets, especially for mature products, are flooded with a multiplicity of brands. Most of these brands are me-too products, and yet each claims unique benefits for ever-smaller groups of consumers. Managers avoid the mass market, especially for mature products. It is synonymous with cutthroat competition, low margins, and low profits.

The mass market bears an entirely different perspective for a new product introduced by a visionary. At the time a vision is first formulated, competitors either may not see any market or may focus on a niche. For example, when HP introduced its laser printers, Xerox and IBM were producing big, fast laser printers that cost hundreds of thousands of dollars. These machines were bought by large organizations that alone could afford them. Often, as in this case, the niche arises merely because prices for current products are high. The vision, in this case, involves manufacturing the product at a sufficiently low price to tap the mass market. In this case, HP's printers cost a few thousand dollars and targeted the developing mass market of owners of personal computers. Why focus on the mass market? Such an orientation has three important benefits for a market entrant.

First, reaching out to the mass market requires one to target a price that would appeal to this market. The target can help managers channel the entire research and production effort to achieving that price point. Such goal-oriented planning is especially relevant when a new idea or technology initially results in high-priced products for a market niche. At such times, it requires a visionary to identify the mass market, define the price that would appeal to this market, and direct a firm's efforts to achieve this goal. This chapter describes several examples that illustrate this point.

Second, tapping the mass market allows for economies of scale that lead to low unit costs. The low costs enable the firm to earn a positive margin on each unit even with a low unit price. This margin, when multiplied over the large scale of the mass market, yields far greater profits than a high margin multiplied over the small scale of a market niche. Managers who focus on niche markets may find this difficult to accept and may ignore this point. However, detailed examples in this chapter will show how a mass-market strategy has been more profitable than a niche strategy. It has often propelled a late entrant to market leadership above the market pioneer that focused on a niche.

Third, the large scale of operation that comes with serving the mass market can easily support a big research effort. Such research can lead to rapid reductions in price or improvements in quality. This in turn can attract more consumers, further expanding the mass market. The expansion generates more profits and allows greater investments in research. Thus the cycle of more research, lower prices, market expansion, and higher profits feeds on itself, providing ever-higher benefits to consumers and the firm. The key to triggering this positive cycle is targeting the mass market.

The scale and profits from tapping the mass market allow even a late entrant to surpass the technological lead and experience of a pioneer that focuses on a small segment of the market. At some point such a late entrant may better serve even the market niche on which the pioneer had focused. The pioneer may then be completely forced out of the market. The history of the evolutionary dynamics of four markets shows how these principles play out.

unleashing the potential of the mass market

The *lowly* disposable diaper is a good example of the importance of envisioning the mass market. It powerfully illustrates the enormous potential of targeting the mass market and the futility of defending a market niche.

In the mid-1950s, Procter & Gamble, a market leader in soaps and detergents, sought to diversify into related consumer products, such as paper towels and tissue. In 1957, it bought Charmin Mills, a regional producer of paper products. That purchase further motivated P&G to consider the disposable diaper business. Its research in this market indicated that consumers were dissatisfied with cloth diapers. They found cloth diapers leaky, messy to change, and inconvenient to clean at home or store until pickup by a diaper service. Disposable diapers were available, but not popular. P&G's research indicated that by 1956 disposable diapers had penetrated 80 percent of U.S. homes, but accounted for only 1 percent of diaper changes. The main reason was their high cost, then about 8.6 cents per unit. In comparison, laundry service cost about 3.5 cents per change and home washing about 1.5 cents a change. As such, consumers used disposable diapers sparingly, primarily when traveling with babies.

Indeed, traveling was the precise occasion recommended by *Consumer Reports*.

However, P&G's experience in grocery marketing and its early research with Pampers prompted it to pursue the far greater potential of the mass market. If disposable diapers at the time were used only by travelers and accounted for only 1 percent of diaper changes, then the mass market was potentially 100 times larger than the current market. The big barrier to tapping this market was the high price of disposable diapers. P&G decided to enter this market by producing a superior disposable diaper at a low price of about 6 cents a diaper. However, mass-producing such a diaper was no easy task and took an enormous effort, commitment, and determination to reach the goal.

The importance of the target price in directing P&G's effort is best described by one of the product development managers: "To meet a retail price target of 6.2 cents per diaper, we had to get manufacturing cost down to 3 cents. Clearly we needed substantial reductions in raw material cost and a more efficient manufacturing process. For if we couldn't deliver for 3 cents we would be out of business. And so, with a vision based more on youthful optimism than engineering experience, we committed to the Company that we could achieve the target manufacturing cost of 3 cents per diaper."[1]

It took P&G 5 years to design a product good enough to test-market. It took another 5 years to improve quality and reduce price sufficiently for a national rollout. All along, the firm kept its sights firmly on the mass market, periodically evaluating its progress in a series of test markets. Finally 10 years after starting research, P&G achieved a manufacturing system that could produce diapers at a cost of 3 cents a unit. The firm then began a national launch on a large scale at a profitable price of 5.5 cents a unit. At that price, Pampers' national rollout in 1966 was a huge success, expanding the market from $10 million to $370 million by 1973. That was a market increase of 37 times in just 7 years! P&G had unlocked the mass market for disposable diapers. Demand for the product was so high that the firm could not keep up with it. As a result, sales of Chux also went up. Managers of Chux admitted that their product was inferior in quality and higher in price. They realized that sales grew only because of the popularity but short supply of Pampers.

At the time that P&G entered the market, the best product was probably Chux, produced by Chicopee Mills, a unit of Johnson & Johnson. Why did J&J not pursue the mass market? There were at least four related reasons. First, it was a primary producer of cloth diapers. Growth of disposable diapers may have been a threat to sales and profits of its business in cloth diapers. Second, it saw only a limited market for disposable diapers—parents using the product when traveling. Perhaps what the firm did not realize is that the limited market itself was caused by the high price of Chux. Third, it probably was content with the high price, because it allowed the firm to maintain high margins. Indeed, a low-priced, mass-market diaper may have seemed a threat to the high margins. Fourth, a low-priced diaper may not have seemed feasible. Indeed, it took P&G 10 years to master the manufacturing technology to get the unit price low enough to stimulate the mass market. Thus, J&J probably saw no need to incur the expense or run the risk of cannibalizing its current sales and profits for a questionable future. As an internal company memo sadly reported in 1969, "Up until 1964 the climate at J&J and Chicopee was such that everybody gave lip service to the fact that disposable diapers some day would be a fine business. But that was all to be years in the future."[2] P&G had the vision. J&J did not.

After Pampers' success, J&J tried for over a decade to produce a diaper of equivalent price and quality. However, the scale and intensity of P&G's efforts enabled P&G to lower prices and improve quality faster than J&J could. J&J had to play catch-up, but it did not make an adequate effort to do so. P&G's 10-year research effort and huge investment gave it a technological edge that J&J could not overcome with the resources it devoted to the task. As a result, Chux remained inferior to Pampers. Indeed, there was no need even for consumers who were traveling to prefer Chux to Pampers. Thus J&J could not hold on to the niche it originally served. In the face of mounting losses, J&J withdrew Chux from the market. Through the 1970s, the firm continued to supply retailers with a diaper to market as a store brand (private label). It also introduced a new diaper under the Johnson name. Because the Johnson brand was not profitable, J&J totally withdrew from the branded market in 1981. The firm thus yielded the market it had earlier dominated for 35 years.[3]

More recently, by relying on relentless product innovation, Huggies surpassed Pampers in market share. A subsequent chapter expands on the critical role of relentless innovation for maintaining market leadership.

futility of focusing on a niche

Like the previous example, the early history of photography shows the advantages of focusing on the mass market rather than on a professional niche. In addition, this example shows how a product that is initially targeted to the mass market need not be superior in quality to one that serves a professional niche. It just has to be of adequate quality to meet the current needs of the mass market. However, the price and convenience must be such as to appeal to the mass market. As we alluded to in the disposable diaper example, the economies that come from tapping the mass market are so great that they can support steady improvements in quality and reductions in price. As such, over time, an initially inferior technology that is targeted to the mass market has the potential to surpass the benefits provided by a superior technology that is targeted to a narrow niche of professionals.

Photography initially started in France with the advent of daguerreotype technology in 1839. This technology produced images on silver-coated copper plates that were sensitive to light. When introduced to the United States, the technology caught on quickly, but on a very small scale. In the mid-1840s, the only ones producing daguerreotypes were professional photographers, who took pictures of important sites or the social elite, who could afford the high cost of the technology.

By the mid-1850s, glass-plate technology replaced copper plates. The glass plates were coated with a layer of a transparent sticky substance called collodion. Just before taking an image, the photographer had to coat the collodion with a solution of silver nitrate. When exposed to light, the light-sensitive coating would capture the image. This image could then be developed in a darkroom and printed on photosensitive paper by exposure to sunlight. This technology was called wet collodion plate technology. The black-and-white images obtained by this method were of high quality. As a result, photography flourished. However, the technology was slow and cumbersome and required knowledge of photochemistry. The whole process was also very inconvenient. Indeed, practitioners of the art had to carry a large camera, maintain a large number of plates, have a darkroom, and keep a large stock of chemicals. This was a formidable task. Because these photographers often had to travel to their customers, the technology imposed a huge burden on them. As a result, professionals were nearly the only practitioners of photography.

In the late 1870s a new technology, dry-plate photography, greatly improved the photographic process. In this technology, the glass plates were coated with a dry gelatin emulsion. As a result, ready-to-use glass plates could be manufactured on a large scale, reducing the cost and increasing the convenience of taking images. While the market expanded a little, photography was still restricted to a small set of professionals and full-time amateurs. The reasons were that the processes required many, heavy glass plates, a darkroom for developing pictures, and a stock of chemicals to do so. However, the technology diffused among professional photographers and the business standardized to a commodity status.

George Eastman entered the business at this stage. From the very beginning, he was committed to improving the process of photography with numerous process improvements. He focused on improving two key features of photography: obtaining a more convenient substitute for glass plates and developing a simpler camera to use with the new medium. Eastman took an interest in celluloid, which was just gaining popularity at that time. Like glass, celluloid was transparent and inert to the chemicals used in photography. However, in contrast to glass, it was light in weight, nonbreakable, and flexible. By the spring of 1885, Eastman developed a celluloid film for taking pictures and a camera to use it. However, the quality of the pictures did not match that of the prevailing dry-plate technology and professionals did not adopt the product.

With that failure, Eastman targeted the mass market. He developed a very simple camera that required only three simple steps: users had to advance the film, cock the shutter, and press a button to take a picture (see Figure 4-1). For $25, the Kodak camera (a

Figure 4-1. Early Ad for the Kodak

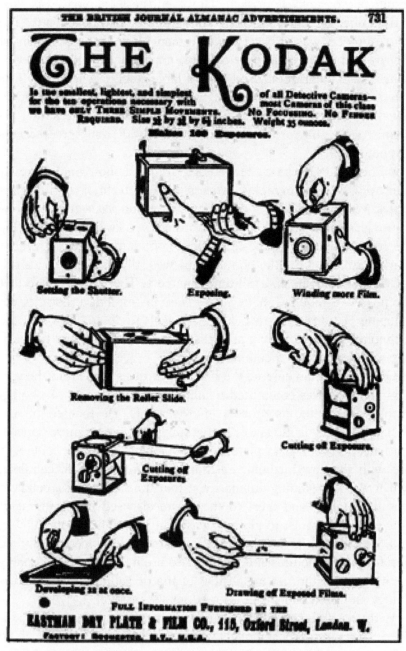

Courtesy of Eastman Kodak Company. Reprinted with permission.

brand name he coined) came loaded with film for 100 pictures. When done, consumers mailed the camera to Eastman's company for developing. For $10, the company developed the pictures, reloaded the camera, and mailed both back to customers. The company's advertising slogan, "You press the button, we do the rest," told amateur photographers all they needed to know. The camera was an immediate success, and sales exploded. With this simple, relatively inexpensive gadget, Eastman unlocked the mass market for photography. The product's success prompted the Eastman Company to change its name to Eastman Kodak in 1892.

Ironically, the incumbent firms that served the professional market did not try to compete with the company. For the next 10 to 16 years, they strove to improve the glass-plate technology. While they were moderately successful, they just could not match the price and convenience of the Kodak camera and film. As such, they were unable to exploit the growth that came primarily from the mass market. In the meantime, Eastman Kodak continued to innovate. The firm improved the camera, the film, and the developing process to provide consumers with better-quality pictures at lower costs. Ultimately, progress in the celluloid technology rendered the dry-plate technology obsolete.

Eastman was neither a pioneer nor a dominant player in glass-plate technology. However, he was a restless innovator, who was wholeheartedly committed to improving the products and process of photography. Moreover, with his sights focused on the mass market, he developed a new technology. It was not superior in quality to existing technology, but it was far simpler and cheaper, and of sufficient quality to appeal strongly to amateurs. This low-margin, high-volume market provided sufficient profits to support research to improve quality and lower costs. Over a few decades of continuous innovation, he was able to make obsolete the older, dominant technology that targeted a niche market of professionals.[4]

envisioning the mass market price

The early history of the video recorder market depicts the sharp contrast between the perspective of a pioneer and the vision of enduring leaders. Like the previous example, it shows the danger of focusing on a small segment instead of the mass market. In addition, it emphasizes a special characteristic of vision—targeting an incredibly low price decades ahead of the ability of technology to deliver that price.

Ampex introduced the first commercial video recorder in 1956. It sold the first three custom-manufactured units for $75,000 each. In doing so, it beat RCA to market. At that time, Ampex was a small company that specialized in magnetic recording technology, while RCA was a giant that dominated the related TV market. Ampex's video recorder used four recording heads scanned transversely across a 2-inch tape. The technology produced high-quality recordings, but it was complex to mass-produce. Mass-manufactured units initially sold for about $50,000. Even at that price the product was an instant hit with the professional market. Video recorder sales grew rapidly, and by 1960 the firm's total revenue grew to seven times its 1956 level. The firm's growth came from video recorders and other businesses, such as sound and data recorders. Yet even in those early years, based on its growth rate and distinctive competence, the most promising of these businesses was video recorders.

Unfortunately, right from the mid-1950s, Ampex focused on neither its video recorders nor its other core businesses, but diversified into related businesses. In some of these businesses, such as audiotapes for home users, Ampex went into competition with several other firms with superior market positions. Partly due to these diversifications and partly due to a recession, Ampex suffered a loss in 1961. The new manager who took over did not seem to understand Ampex's rich potential. In 1962, he articulated a vision of "dynamic growth" in "all" of Ampex's businesses, including video, audio, instrumentation, magnetic tape, and computer memory. In doing so, the firm had to compete for a variety of consumers in a variety of markets, without any clear priorities. In the video recorder market, Ampex had almost a monopoly in sales and R&D. RCA and Toshiba, the only competitors, were well behind. But at the high price at which Ampex sold video recorders, its managers saw only a limited market of professional buyers for the product. They did little to lower costs or expand the market. Indeed, their diversification efforts were partly designed to reduce Ampex's dependence on video recorder sales.

In contrast, three other companies, Sony, JVC, and Matsushita, inspired by their consumer orientation, each saw the potential of a mass market of home users. They started a concerted research drive to bring the video recorder to that market. From its inception in 1946, Sony focused on producing innovative electronic products for the consumer market. In the mid-1950s, cofounder Masaru Ibuka set a challenge to his engineers to develop a video recorder for the home market. Just 3 months after Ampex developed its video recorder, Sony's development group, headed by Nobutoshi Kihara, made their own recorder. However, it was quite similar to the Ampex system and, in the words of Kihara, "was as heavy as an anchor."[5] Kihara thought it would be a great source of business even though it would have to sell for 20 million yen (about $55,000). However, Ibuka, whose sights were clearly on the mass market, insisted, "We are not going to make broadcast equipment; we want to make home video. If you can make one like this, you can also make one for home use. Develop one that will sell for 2 million yen."[6] When Kihara's group did so, Kihara was told, "Now make one that will sell for 200,000 yen (about $550)."[7] This target was 1 percent of the initial price, and less that 1 percent of the price of Ampex's initial video recorder.

In a similar way, research on video recorders also started at JVC in 1955. The managing director thought that Ampex's four-head scanner was too complex and expensive for the home market, and directed research on a two-head scanner. Following this directive, Yuma Shiraishi, manager of video recorder development at JVC, provided his engineers with only a few guidelines: Develop a machine that would use little tape, retain high picture quality, and sell for $500.[8] Such stringent directives were difficult to meet. Indeed it took each of these companies 20 years of research to realize their goals. But the directives were clear and firmly focused on the mass market of home users. The companies reaped enormous rewards when the mass market for their products took off in 1980 (see Figure 4-2).

Ampex did not walk away from the market without a fight. In the

Figure 4-2. Takeoff and Growth of VCR Sales in the United States

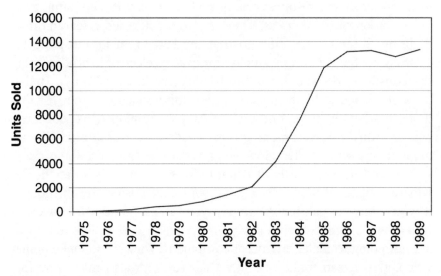

VCR Sales

Sources: Dealerscope Merchandising and Electronic Industries Association.

1950s it either refused to license its patents to the three newer competitors or did so in a very limited way. By the early 1960s, Sony and JVC had bypassed Ampex's patents to develop workable video recorders. But even then, Ampex's technological prowess was ahead of its competitors. Through the 1960s, Ampex intermittently tried to design video recorders for the consumer market. However, most of them were priced too high or had unsuitable features to elicit adequate consumer interest. Ampex's best prototype for the consumer market was the Instavideo, a battery-powered video recorder and camera that won rave reviews. The firm developed this model in the early 1970s with the intent of leapfrogging the lead of Sony and Matsushita in catering to the home market. Unfortunately, Ampex's CEO doubted its ability to mass-produce the machine and handed production to an Ampex-Toshiba joint venture in Japan. This venture failed to deliver the product. Ultimately, Ampex, engulfed by losses in the other businesses it had started, killed the Instavideo project, and withdrew from the market.

In the video recorder market, Ampex had a great deal going for it. It was the pioneer. It had a team of experienced and capable engineers and controlled all the important early patents. It had the best product on the market for years. It had a strong base of professional buyers of that product. Yet Ampex lacked one important characteristic for success: a clear vision of the mass market that could motivate a concerted effort to realize that market. As a result, it failed to focus its unique technological strengths on the market that had the most promise: home users of video recorders.

In contrast, Sony, JVC, and Matsushita set their sights firmly on the mass market. They identified the price points necessary to tap that market. To do so, these companies focused on an alternative two-head technology. This technology did not provide as good an image quality as Ampex's four-head technology, but it was simpler and less expensive to manufacture. They channeled all their efforts on achieving the targeted price at an acceptable quality. Their efforts bore fruit in the mid-1970s when Sony introduced the relatively convenient Betamax at an affordable price. The subsequent takeoff and rapid growth of the VCR catapulted these companies to dominant positions in the electronics industry. In the 15 years following 1970, video sales went from $2 million to almost $2 billion at JVC, from $6 million to $3 billion at Matsushita, and from $17 million to almost $2 billion at Sony. In contrast, total sales increased from $296 million to only $480 million at Ampex (see Figure 4-3).

With the experience and economies achieved in the consumer market, Sony was able to enter and excel in even the professional market that Ampex initially dominated.[9]

exploiting the economies of the mass market

The example of the microprocessor reveals the important dynamics along which mass markets evolve. Even at a low margin, a mass market can generate huge profits that can be invested to lower costs, improve quality, and further expand the market. Wisely exploiting these dynamics can give a firm a tremendous advantage over competitors and catapult it to leadership of the market.

The microprocessor is one of the most important innovations of the twentieth century. It is the brain, or central processing unit

Figure 4-3. Growth in Video Sales of Key Manufacturers

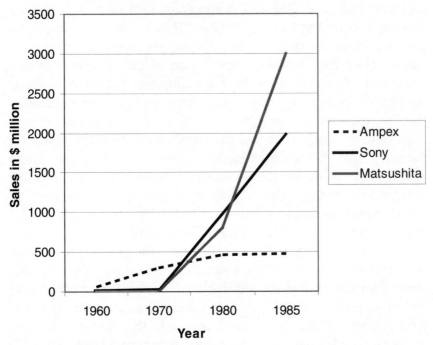

Figures for Ampex are total sales.
Source: Richard S. Rosenbloom and Michael A. Cusumano, "Technological Pioneering and Competitive Advantage: The Birth of the VCR Industry," *California Management Review*, 24, Summer, 1987, p. 66.

(CPU), of the personal computer, and is responsible for bringing computing to the mass market. It is also responsible for many of the "smart" machines we have gotten used to, such as calculators, personal digital assistants, and global positioning systems. The wonder of the microprocessor lies in what it does and what it costs. It can perform millions of computations per second and it can be mass-produced at a relatively low cost. Its performance is based on the density of a vast array of transistors that are mechanically etched on a single chip. A transistor can be configured to either allow or disallow the flow of electricity, and thus can be used to store or process information in binary form.

Intel developed the microprocessor in 1971, only 3 years after Robert Noyce and Gordon Moore started the company. Intel was a small company, living in the shadows of computer giant IBM and other semiconductor giants, such as Fairchild Semiconductor. Why was Intel at the forefront of the microprocessor revolution while these other firms passed up the opportunity to exploit the market opportunity? The answer is found in their differing vision of the mass market.

In the late 1960s, IBM was the dominant firm in the computer business. With its massive profits, large cadre of qualified researchers, and extensive laboratories, it was eminently positioned to produce either a microcomputer or a microprocessor. However, it focused on producing high-margin, high-priced mainframe computers for a small number of business users. Producing low-priced microcomputers or microprocessors for a mass market would have been anathema to the company because it would have undercut the sales and profits from its highly lucrative mainframe computers.

In the 1960s, Fairchild Semiconductor was also well positioned to produce a microprocessor. It was a leading semiconductor firm, and had some of the best minds in the electronics industry, including Noyce and Moore. Noyce and Moore initially worked for Shockley Semiconductor. They left that firm, frustrated by the lack of vision and the authoritarianism of its owner, William Shockley. They then joined Fairchild Camera and Instrumentation Company and started the Fairchild Semiconductor *Division* of the company. From the very beginning, Noyce and Moore focused on producing semiconductors for an ever-larger market. Semiconductors were used as components in other electronic products.

In the course of their research and experience with high-volume production, Noyce and Moore realized they could design semiconductors with a greater number of transistors compressed on a single silicon chip. These compressed chips were cheaper, had more functions, and were of better quality. As such, they generated greater demand and volume. The higher volume led to better experience and higher profits, which could then be channeled into research for greater compression. Their focus on volume triggered an important positive cycle of lower costs, better functions, better quality, and still higher volume and profits. Indeed, within 10 years of the start of Fairchild Semiconductor in 1957, Noyce had grown the division to become the most profitable of all the divisions of the parent company. The key to success was in producing more efficient chips in volume for a mass market.

However, managers of the parent company neither appreciated the success of the business nor understood the dynamics of semiconductor production. They were not willing to reinvest profits in the division. In particular, in 1967, Noyce wanted to branch out into producing small silicon-based semiconductor chips to replace the large magnetic cores used for storing memory in mainframe computers. But his superiors were unwilling to invest in these new directions. In frustration, Noyce, Moore, and some other engineers at Fairchild Semiconductor resigned from the division they founded to start Intel Corporation in 1968.

From its founding, Noyce and Moore decided to pursue silicon-based semiconductor technology for producing memory products. At the time, the standard technology for memory products was magnetic core technology. Intel's new approach was a bold and risky departure from the standard because semiconductor memory was initially 100 times more expensive than magnetic core memory. But Noyce and Moore strongly believed that the advantages of semiconductor memory—smaller size, greater performance, and reduced energy consumption—would convince customers to prefer it to magnetic core memory. More importantly, they hoped to exploit steady declines in costs from accumulated experience that such new technologies provided (Figure 4-4 shows Intel's dramatic decline in manufacturing costs subsequently). In its first year, Intel's sales were a mere $2672. However, Noyce and Moore were their own masters, and were free to pursue their vision unhampered by myopic managers. They first created a chip (Intel 1103) that could store memory passively. They followed with a string of superior chips so that sales reached $9.43 million in 1971.

In 1969, a Japanese company, Busicom, was planning to develop a handheld calculator that could make a large number of computations similar to those done on large computers. For this purpose, Busicom asked Intel to produce a set of at least 12 specific chips, each of which would perform the various operations of the calculator. Such tailor-made chips were common at the time. But in this case, Busicom needed 12 or more of these chips because the calculator it was developing was quite complicated. Busicom paid Intel $60,000 for the development of the design. The job was assigned to Ted Hoff, an Intel engineer. Hoff reasoned that developing so many

Figure 4-4. Decline in Intel's Manufacturing Costs of Chips in Million Instructions per Second (vertical axis is on a logarithmic scale)

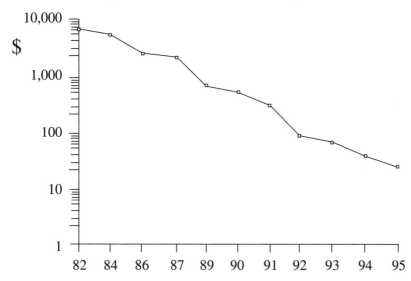

Copyright Intel Corporation. Reprinted with permission of Intel Corporation.

specific chips for a small company would be costly, be of limited use, and exceed Intel's programming capacity. Moreover, Intel's president, Moore, was not in favor of custom products for specific firms. He wanted Intel to produce generic products in high volume for a large number of firms. Yet Intel was still small enough that it did not want to turn away customers such as Busicom.

So Hoff initially suggested simplifying the Busicom design to make it more efficient. Busicom's engineers, who had already done some preliminary work, dismissed Hoff's ideas. Their general response was, "Go away, don't bother us. We know what we're doing."[10] However, Noyce, who was more attuned to the larger mass market, encouraged Hoff to proceed with his idea. So Hoff pursued his idea and came up with a visionary solution. He recommended a single, generic chip that would carry out only the logical operations. Another read-only-memory chip would contain the programs that would instruct the logic chip about the operations to carry out. When combined with two other chips for random access memory and output functions, the four-chip set could carry out all the operations for which Busicom wanted at least 12 chips. In addition to its simplicity, the advantage of such a design was that the generic chip could be fitted with other program chips to serve a variety of products and customers. Thus it would have the potential to cater to a mass market.

Hoff presented his design to Busicom's engineers. They again rejected it. Hoff had this to say of the Japanese engineers. They "had a great reluctance to change the design. I can understand it. They had already done a fair amount of coding . . ."[11] But Noyce encouraged its continued development. In the face of this impasse, Hoff's team and Busicom's engineers made competing presentations to Busicom's senior managers. Hoff argued that Busicom could use his design for other more complicated products, with changes only in the read-only-memory or program chip. This approach would greatly simplify and reduce the costs of new product development. That argument persuaded Busicom, and it accepted Hoff's design. Busicom's resistance to Hoff's design was so strong that Hoff said about the decision, "I always thought it was a coup that we managed to persuade the Japanese to choose our design."[12]

The actual execution of Hoff's design required work by a team of engineers, prominent among whom was Federico Faggin. Working at an intense pace to meet Busicom's deadline, they completed the design in about 9 months. The logic chip turned out to contain the entire processing unit on a single generic chip. Thus was born the Intel 4004 (see Figure 4-5). It was a little computer on a chip, which Intel called a microprocessor. Hoff says of the design, "The real key was . . . the organization, the architectural concept in which you take a general-purpose computer and build it"[13] into a single chip.

The calculator market turned very competitive, and Busicom asked Intel for a price cut in the chips so it could be competitive. Some within Intel, including perhaps Faggin and Hoff envisioning the enormous potential of the microprocessor, lobbied to recapture rights to the design.[14] They urged Noyce to agree to the price cut in exchange for full rights to the design. By the initial contract, Busicom held all the rights, even though Intel did the design. Intel ultimately offered to repay Busicom's initial investment of $60,000 for the design and cut prices to Busicom. Busicom agreed, and Intel gained the right to sell the microprocessor initially only to noncompetitors of Busicom and then to any firm. Lacking any vision of the

Figure 4-5. The Intel 4004

value of the design it had ordered, Busicom gave up the rights to one of the most profitable technologies of all time for $60,000 and a price cut on current supplies.

But Intel's marketing department was opposed to marketing the microprocessor. The department explained to Hoff that Intel was late entering the computer business. At the time, only minicomputers would be likely to use the product and their sales were only about 20,000 a year. Even with 10 percent of that market, sales of the microprocessor would be minuscule. Moreover, at a price of $50 to $100 a unit, Intel would not even cover its costs. Marketing was convinced only with the argument that each time Intel sold a microprocessor, it would also create demand for two supporting memory chips. That is the way the director of marketing recalls viewing the microprocessor: "Originally, I think we saw it as a way to sell more memories, and we were willing to make the investment on that basis."[15]

Many engineers were also emotionally attached to the memory business and did not quite see the potential of the microprocessor. They were concerned that the effort would distract the firm from memory chips, which were then its bread and butter business. It required the firm direction of Noyce and Moore to steer Intel in the direction of the microprocessor. With their support, Intel began marketing the microprocessor with an ad that said, "Announcing a new era of integrated electronics: a microprogrammable computer on a chip" (see Figure 4-6). Gordon Moore was bolder and more pre-

Figure 4-6. Intel Ad for the 4004

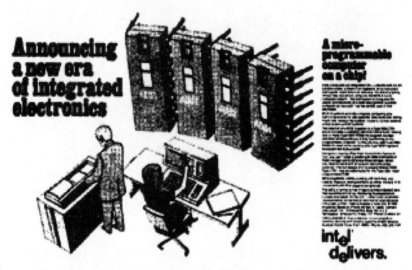

scient when he called the microprocessor "one of the most revolutionary products in the history of mankind."[16]

The 4004 made possible the production and sale of inexpensive digital watches and calculators. Its sales took off with the craze for those products. By 1973, Intel's sales reached $66 million, and the company's stock market value soared to $79 million. Eager to maintain leadership of the growing market for microprocessors, Noyce and Moore supported continued research at the firm. The fruits of that research were successive generations of superior chips, such as the 8008, the 8080, the 8088, and the 8086. When IBM wanted a microprocessor for its PC, it chose the Intel 8088, based on Intel's innovativeness and the product's competitive merits. When the PC and its clones took off, they all chose Intel chips, and the firm became an early leader in the market.

However, a number of competitors, such as Texas Instruments, Motorola, Zilog, and AMD, quickly entered the microprocessor market, leading to intense competition and rapid technological change. Market leadership in this environment required relentless innovation. A subsequent chapter addresses the problems that Intel faced and how it met these challenges to stay ahead of competitors and grow into a colossus. As a result, by the end of 2000, Intel's capitalization was about $220 billion, much higher than IBM's capitalization of about $165 billion, and dwarfing that of Fairchild Semiconductor at $1.5 billion (see Figure 4-7).

The root of Intel's success was the vision of a few men: to develop a generic chip for the mass market rather than specialized chips for market niches; to see a market for the microprocessor despite its initial meager performance; and so to quickly buy back the full rights to the 4004. Many companies that were better positioned to do so, including IBM and especially Fairchild (for whom Intel's founders initially worked), lacked the vision and missed a great opportunity.[17]

the role of price and quality in tapping the mass market

These four examples illustrate the enormous advantages of targeting the mass market rather than particular niches. They also show the powerful dynamics by which mass markets evolve. They emphasize the critical role of a clear vision in harnessing those dynamics for early success.

A common theme in these examples is the importance of low price to appeal to the mass market. While disposable diapers were available for decades before Pampers, they took off only when Pampers dropped the price to a point at which they became competitive with home laundering and diaper services. Kodak's camera was a hit because its price was just $25 plus $10 for developing 100 pictures. This price represented a huge savings from the total costs of chemicals, plates, and photographic equipment previously required to take pictures. Video recorders began to appeal to the mass market when their price fell below $1000 per unit and they became convenient for taping shows. Finally, the revolution launched by microprocessors was not merely in miniaturization but also in costs. As we shall see in subsequent chapters, the Intel microprocessor was inexpensive enough to produce the Altair, the Tandy TRS 80, and other personal computers for under $600. At the time, some main-

Figure 4-7. Comparative Growth of Fairchild, IBM, and Intel

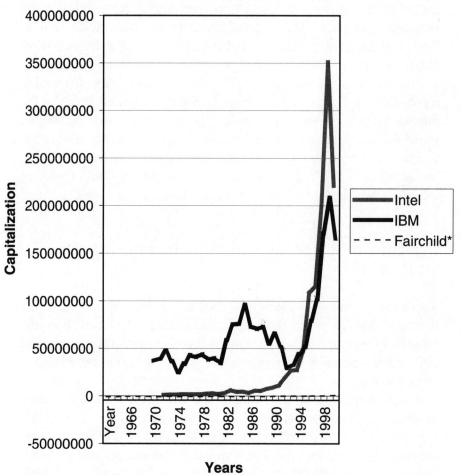

Source: Center for Research in Security Prices, Graduate School of Business, University of Chicago.
*Fairchild's capitalization peaks in 1969 at $403 million and declines thereafter.

frame and minicomputers cost more than hundreds of times as much. In these and many other cases, the price drop was critical to unleashing the mass market for these products.

Targeting a low price often prompts managers to identify and develop technologies to manufacture products at those prices. For example, the thrust of P&G's effort was to develop a manufacturing system that could produce diapers at 3 cents a unit. The efforts of Sony and JVC were geared to produce video recorders that would retail for $500 each. Thus it is the vision of the market that drives the production system and not the other way around. Perhaps, a better-known example is Ford's contribution to personal transportation. Ford's invention of the assembly line is one of the most celebrated innovations because it brought the price of a car below $500 and unleashed the mass market for automobiles. Many people assume that it was this invention that drove Ford's pricing strategy. However, the truth is the opposite, and is elegantly described by Theodore Levitt in his article, "Marketing Myopia": "Ford's real genius was marketing. . . . He invented the assembly line because he had concluded that at $500 he could sell millions of cars. Mass production was the result not the cause of his low prices."[18]

Targeting a low price is a critical issue, especially for new entrants to a market, because they often face a choice between two technologies. They can choose a superior technology that leads to a high-quality, high-priced product, or an alternative technology that delivers lower-quality products but at a substantially lower price. Typically, the incumbents have chosen the costly technology and marketed to a small niche. The above examples repeatedly show that if the price is low enough and the quality is acceptable to appeal to the mass market, then the product can become a runaway success.

For example, at the time it was initially introduced, the Kodak camera delivered inferior-quality pictures to those obtained from glass-plate technology. But consumers found their lower cost and convenience irresistible. Personal computers based on microprocessors initially offered much slower and less powerful features than mainframe or minicomputers. But their lower costs and convenience were so strong that they quickly became popular. Initially, the home video recorders based on the two-head technology produced inferior images than those from professional video recorders using the four-head technology. But their lower cost, compactness, and convenience were keys to their strong appeal for consumers. In all these cases, the substantial price reduction afforded by the new technology was an important factor in the takeoff of products for the mass market.

Once firms target and sell to the mass market, their scale of operation increases enormously, by a factor of thousands. This massive scale of operation enables firms to reap great economies in purchasing, manufacturing, and marketing, while also generating great profits. The declining costs and increasing profits enable firms to support research to improve quality and lower prices of the new products. This process can further expand the mass market, leading to a positive cycle of benefits to the firm and consumers. Over time, quality can improve so much that it can equal or surpass the high quality of the old products that served a niche market. Firms that served this niche may then be threatened with obsolescence and extinction by firms that use the new technology to serve the mass market.

summary

The lessons of this chapter can be summarized in the following key points:

- A vision of the mass market prompts a target price at which the product would appeal to the mass market. This target helps to channel all research and production efforts to achieve that price point.
- Pioneers and other early entrants often serve various market niches with high-priced, high-quality products.
- The mass market can be thousands of times larger than these niche markets.
- Serving the mass market generates massive economies of scale that lead to low unit costs and a small unit margin. However, when multiplied over the large scale, even the small margin translates into massive profits.
- Firms can reinvest some of these profits in research to improve the quality and lower costs. These changes lead to further ex-

pansion of the mass market, further declines in cost, and further increases in profit. The positive cycle continues to the advantage of the firm that exploits it.

- This positive cycle can enable even a late entrant that focuses on the mass market to surpass the technological lead of pioneers that focus on a niche. Eventually, such late entrants may better serve even the market niche on which a pioneer had focused.

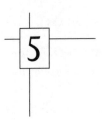

uniqueness of vision

Consider McDonald's, Gillette, Federal Express. Contrary to modern beliefs, these firms were not pioneers of their markets. In fact, they entered established markets. At least two of them were given no chance to succeed. Yet they endured and grew into great enterprises. When we trace the history of these organizations, we find that they are rooted in a unique vision. This vision distinguished these organizations from competitors, gave them their distinct culture, and is the root cause of their enduring success.

What exactly is vision? A defining component of vision is a focus on the evolving needs of a mass market as discussed in the prior chapter. But vision also constitutes a novel idea about serving the mass market. In the case of McDonald's, it was low-priced, fast food in a clean restaurant for people on the go. With respect to Gillette, it was the disposable blade for convenient and safe shaving. For Federal Express, it was fast, reliable delivery for consumers with urgent shipments. These ideas often have a paradoxical feature. They now seem quite simple, even obvious; yet at the time they were first proposed, they seemed infeasible, radical, or even foolish.

Today, the idea seems quite simple and intuitive because we observe the market in hindsight, after a visionary has pursued that idea and nurtured it into a large, successful enterprise. In so doing, that visionary has validated his or her logic of serving the market and invalidated the old way of doing things. In hindsight, the logic seems transparent to us and it needs no strong persuasion. For example, no one today would question the value of Fred Smith's idea for express mail that is picked up and delivered within a guaranteed time by a single company with a dedicated fleet of trucks and planes. However, at the time this idea was originally formulated, it ran counter to the accepted practices and beliefs of firms in the market. At that time, most firms did not buy the idea, doubted its viability, and scorned or derided its value. That was the reception that King Gillette and Fred Smith both received when they first proposed their novel ideas for serving the shaving and mail markets, respectively. That is why we describe their ideas as a *vision*—and why we describe the proponents, as *visionaries*.

The reason that firms rejected the vision at the time it was originally proposed is that they worked in an entirely different worldview. That worldview fashioned their perceptions and shaped their experiences. Whatever they saw and experienced went to further reinforce the same worldview. The visionary is an outsider or a latecomer who arrives at the scene with a different perspective. He or she observes the market and comes to a different conclusion. From that conclusion is born a new view of the world, which suggests a different way of solving the problem consumers face. However, at the time, the market sees it as a radically different way of doing things, which is neither proven nor meaningful, and probably infeasible or even foolish.

The seeds of that vision are already present in products available in the market at the time the vision is first formulated. However, firms that market those products are so immersed in their own narrow worldview that they fail to appreciate the insight in the vision even when it is explained to them.

Initially, at least, those manufacturers may be right. The visionary may not be able to realize his or her vision right away because of numerous problems in design, manufacturing, distribution, or financing. If realizing the vision were easy, existing firms would already have done so. Realizing the vision requires persistence, innovation, and financial commitment. For these reasons, the visionary not only sees the future of the market but *creates* the future by bringing that vision to fruition.

The evolution of three markets will clarify these essential characteristics of vision and show how vision lies at the very foundation of enduring market leadership.

seeing what no one else could

King C. Gillette's transformation of the safety razor business exemplifies the essence of vision. Gillette started his career in the hardware business, where he grew to be a traveling salesman. He was a restless soul, always dabbling in new inventions and designs. By the age of 35 he owned a couple of patents for gadgets he had invented. However, he failed to profit from these inventions. In 1891, he began working for the Baltimore Seal Company, and struck a friendship with the company president, William Painter. Painter invented and patented the cork-lined bottle cap, which became so popular that the company changed its name to the Crown Cork and Seal Company.

One day Painter suggested to Gillette that he think of inventing something like the bottle cap, which enjoyed repeated sales because it was thrown away after use. Gillette immediately saw the enormous value in a patented or branded disposable product sold to the mass market. After that, he developed lists of products that could be improved upon by including a throwaway part. At home and on trips, he spent hours thinking about how these products could be redesigned to include a patented, disposable component. One of the products in the list was the razor.

Men have shaved their faces since prehistoric times. They may have done so for a variety of reasons, including convenience, hygiene, youthful looks, or fashion. They may have also done so for safety. In ancient times, when hand-to-hand combat was necessary for survival, an enemy could gain a deadly hold on a man's beard. At the same time, for most of history, getting a clean shave was costly and inconvenient, if not painful and unsafe.

The obstacle to shaving has always been the same: the lack of a tool that could provide a quick, safe, and smooth shave. Cave drawings of prehistoric men show hairless chins. The men probably cut their hair or shaved with shells, bones, or flint. With advances in metallurgy, razors were made of copper, iron, and improved alloys. The Egyptians used a variety of razor shapes, while the Greeks and Romans seem to have preferred the open design like that of the cut-throat razor. The design of the cutthroat survived in Europe and else-where until the invention of a primitive safety razor in France in 1763 by a professional barber, Jean Jacques Perret. This design had a guard to protect the user from cutting too deeply into the skin. It may have been inspired by the carpenter's planer used for smoothing wood.[1] In the early 1800s, an improved design emerged in England, which was lighter and less cumbersome than the French model. In the 1880s, a T-shaped safety razor was designed in the United States. The T-shaped or rake-shaped razor had a short handle at-tached to a blade held approximately perpendicular to it. Some of these razors encased the blade in comblike teeth to ensure safety (see Figure 5-1A and B). It was the angle and protection of the blade that determined the safety of the razor.

Prior to 1903, men in the United States used the straight razor or a T-shaped safety razor for shaving. The straight razor, or cutthroat, consisted of a knifelike gadget whose length and width were de-signed to suit the dimensions of the face (see Figure 5-1C and D). The cutthroat and the safety razor required sharpening by stropping on a leather strap or a stone. Sometimes even that would not be enough to sharpen them properly, and the gadget had to be taken for honing at a cutler's shop. Some razors had removable blades to en-sure easier sharpening. Both the cutthroat and the razor blades were made from the highest-grade steel by forging and highly skilled grinding to ensure that the edge would last a lifetime of sharpening. Despite these improvements, shaving remained an expensive, incon-venient, and uncomfortable routine. One could go to a professional barber for a shave, but that was expensive. Or one could shave at home, but the tools were expensive to buy, and keeping them in good condition was inconvenient.

In particular, it was the difficulty and inconvenience of stropping and honing that triggered Gillette's invention. One day when shav-ing, Gillette found that his razor needed honing by a cutler. At that moment, the simple design of the disposable blade dawned on him: a razor with a handle, whose head encased a simple, sharp, two-

Figure 5-1. Early Designs of Safety Razors

A . An 1893 Review of The Fox Showing Razor with Safety Teeth	B. Kampfe Bros. Star Model 1 U.S. 1888
Teeth encase blade. The blade is removable to enable sharpening in the stropping device below. 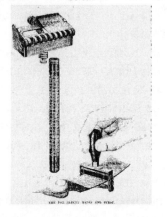	*Safety razor with nondisposable (re-sharpenable) blades, half-way stage in development of the razor between open/ cut-throat and Gillette. Nickel-plated brass shaving head, extremely ornate with lists patents etched on the back.* 
C. Plantagenet England 1830	**D. Kram Cut-throat Germany 1900**
Example of a safety cut-throat. The comblike guard fits on side of the blade and is held in place by a screw in a keyhole slot on the top. 	*Example of early cut-throat with hollow ground steel blade and ivory handle. Packaged in slim dark gray box. Handles also made from bone and, later, phenol plastic.* 

"Kampfe" and "Kram" courtesy of Paul Linnell, "Simply Switch On . . . !" Reprinted with permission from homepage.dtm.ntl.com/paul.linnell/electricity. "The Fox," from *Scientific American,* Aug. 19, 1893, p. 116. "Plantagenet" courtesy of Knife World Publications and R. Waits. Reprinted with permission.

edged blade that was inexpensive enough to be thrown away when blunt. No more stropping, honing, and scraping. The blades would be so inexpensive that the consumer would keep coming back for more. The moment of realization is described, perhaps a little colorfully, in Gillette's own words:

> I was consumed with the thought of inventing something that people would use and throw away and buy again. On one particular morning when I started to shave I found my razor dull, and it was not only dull but it was beyond the point of successful stropping and it needed honing. . . . As I stood there with my razor in my hand, my eyes resting on it as lightly as a bird settling down on its nest—the Gillette razor was born. I saw it all in a moment, and in that same moment many unvoiced questions were asked and answered more with the rapidity of a dream than by the slow process of reasoning. . . .
>
> At that time and in that moment it seemed as though I could see the way the blade could be held in a holder; then came the idea of sharpening the two opposite edges on the thin piece of steel that was uniform in thickness throughout, thus doubling its services; and following in sequence came the clamping plates for the blade and a handle equally disposed between the two edges of the blade.[2]

Many contemporary reports misunderstand or misreport what Gillette's key contribution really was. Gillette was not the first to invent a safety razor, a T-shaped razor and blade, or a two-part system consisting of a blade removable from the razor. All these designs existed before Gillette's invention (see Figure 5-1). What Gillette envisioned was a two-part razor and blade, in which the blade could be removed *and thrown away* when it became blunt (see Figure 5-2). In other words, Gillette's key innovation was a disposable blade. Indeed, early ads for the Gillette shaving system emphasized the great convenience of not having to sharpen a blade anymore (see Figure 5-2).

Gillette's vision was especially valuable, because the industry at

Figure 5-2. Ads Showing Design and Convenience of Gillette Safety Blades

A. Gillette 1904 Razor and Blades in Case

Early Gillette three-part safety razor using pioneering system of disposable blades (patented by Gillette in 1904). Silver-plated knurled removable handle, slim silver-plated snap case with floral decorative border.

B. Gillette Assembled Razor and Blade

C. Early Ad for the Gillette

Gillette's first ad appeared in the October 1903 issue of *System Magazine*. The first year, Gillette sold 51 razors and 168 blades. The next year sales reached 90,000 razor sets and 123,000 blades.

Courtesy of The Gillette Company. Reprinted with permission.

that time had an entirely different perspective. The industry believed that razors should be made of expensive, tough metal to last a lifetime of stropping and honing. Gillette envisioned using cheap sheet metal that could be thrown away after some use. Cutlers and metallurgists, people in the know, said that Gillette's idea was impossible because it embodied contrary goals. The blade had to be sharp enough to cut hair cleanly, strong enough to hold the edge without breaking, and cheap enough to throw away when blunt. According to Gillette, they were unanimous in their verdict. "Those whom I went to or consulted invariably advised me to drop it; that I never would succeed in putting an edge on sheet steel that would shave. They told me I was throwing my money away; that a razor was only possible when made from cast steel. . . ."[3]

Visionaries see what others around them do not. Indeed, people schooled in the thinking of the experts not only failed to think of the design, but ridiculed it. One inventor, whom Gillette converted to his point of view much later, said of the experts of the time, "Razor experts laughed at his scheme, called it visionary and absurd and discouraged him in every way."[4] Gillette says he got little sympathy or encouragement from friends. "The razor was looked upon as a joke by all my friends and a common greeting was, 'Well Gillette, how's the razor?' but no offering was made to take an interest."[5] He himself confessed that his thinking was that of an amateur outsider. If he knew of the technical difficulties, he said he would never have started.

Gillette's approach to market entry runs contrary to all modern dictates of strategy. He entered what was then an established market, not a new, high-growth market. He planned on a mass-market strategy, not a niche strategy. He envisioned a low-priced, low-margin product, when competitors were selling high-margin razors and blades to limited geographic and design niches. The difference is entirely due to vision. Gillette envisioned a huge, nearly limitless mass market for disposable blades, where suppliers at the time saw a limited, mature market niche for high-priced safety razors.

Gillette's vision did not come entirely out of the blue. By temperament, he was a tinkerer and inventor. Also, at Painter's suggestion, he was on an intense search for an everyday product that could be redesigned to include a disposable component that consumers would keep repurchasing. His self-described enlightenment was just a moment when his longtime quest, Painter's suggestion, and his own frustration with shaving all came together in a new design for the razor and blade.

Was he right? Not immediately. There were huge obstacles to making the disposable blade a commercial success. His initial idea was quite primitive. But Gillette stuck to his vision. In subsequent chapters we will see how that conviction was essential to sustain the enormous effort needed over many years to overcome those obstacles.[6]

a vision good for a grade of c?

Perhaps the most well-known story of Federal Express is the legend about founder Frederick Smith's term paper. Smith formulated his idea for priority airfreight service as a term paper for a course at Yale in 1965. He received a C for the paper, though the service he proposed became a billion dollar success. That grade is often used as an illustration of Smith's vision.

However, more telling about his vision is the fact that when he started Federal Express, none of the service providers ran the business the way Smith envisioned it. Neither did they think much of Smith's efforts. Airfreight service started in the United States in the 1920s. When Smith started Federal Express in 1971, the market leader, Emery Air Freight, was 25 years old. The company was the largest of the so-called freight forwarders. These companies picked up and delivered parcels in various cities and shipped them via passenger airlines. Hundreds of companies were involved in this very competitive business. Emery's CEO, John Emery, did not operate his business as Smith did, with a proprietary fleet of planes and a guarantee of overnight delivery. On the contrary, Emery was not impressed with Smith's idea. Even in 1974 and 1975 when he lost some business to Federal Express, he dismissed the company as "an expensive toy" and incapable of success.

In the early 1970s, most people in the business were not impressed with Smith's start-up. Most of the major airlines had tried an all-cargo service in the 1960s and abandoned it because of poor returns. The U.S. Postal Service, the granddaddy of all mail services, concentrated on regular mail rather than on airfreight of parcels. As a huge bureaucracy, it was comfortable with regular (relatively slower) service. Even after Smith introduced Federal Express and the firm began growing steadily, investors on Wall Street did not give the service many months to survive. Smith later said of his idea, "I just knew it was correct, but there were few believers at first. The overwhelming body of opinion said it wouldn't work, or that we couldn't raise the money."[7]

Smith came from a family with deep roots in the transportation business. His grandfather was a captain of a steamboat that plied the Ohio and Mississippi Rivers. His father started and ran a successful bus business that he sold to Greyhound Bus Lines. That heritage gave Smith some insight about transportation. After his college graduation, he served in Vietnam as a pilot and then returned to run a business for buying and selling aircraft. Those experiences probably helped to hone Smith's vision of what the market needed and what could be achieved.

At the core of Smith's vision was the belief in a huge market for priority mail. By *priority* he meant items that were high value *and* time sensitive, such as documents, medicines, and electronics. Smith criticized the current system of delivery that used passenger aircraft, with which he saw at least three problems.

To begin with, service providers did not optimize routes to ensure the shortest distance and time for priority mail. Such mail often needed to be shipped between small cities, late in the evening, to reach their destination early the next morning. However, at that time, the transportation of mail took place in the luggage compartments of passenger aircraft. Passenger service ran along routes and at times that suited passengers, typically between major cities during the daytime. As a result, as Smith described it, parcels went "hippety-hopping around the country from city to city and from airline to airline before reaching their destination,"[8] typically after several days.

Second, by using passenger aircraft, service providers did not exploit potential economies of scale from the choice, loading, and unloading of aircraft to ensure the lowest per-item cost. Smith said of this problem, "The costs would not come down with volume. It was a technical and economic impossibility. Air freight would only work in a system designed specifically for it, not as a simple add-on to passenger service."⁹ The system he envisioned would use a dedicated fleet of aircraft that would bring mail in from various cities to a central hub city, which was Memphis. After sorting and forwarding, the same aircraft would then take mail to their destinations on their return routes. Thus these aircraft would be organized in a hub-and-spoke system. In each city, a dedicated fleet of pickup and delivery trucks would support the aircraft service. Smith described people's reaction to this idea, "People thought we were bananas. We were too ignorant to know that we weren't supposed to be able to do certain things. We wanted to fly uneconomic planes and fly everything into Memphis."¹⁰

Third, service providers at that time handled both large and small packages. Smith reasoned that the fast delivery of large, heavy packages would typically be too costly for consumers. However, small packages could be delivered quickly for a price consumers might be willing to pay. This was the key insight that Smith brought to the priority mail service. At the time, neither the service providers nor the airlines shared Smith's view of things, which ensured they would leave the market for him, at least initially.

But it did not simplify the enormous task ahead. Like Gillette many decades before him, Smith grossly underestimated what it would take to develop a priority mail service using a private fleet of aircraft and trucks. He later admitted that his term paper was a rush job done at the last minute. Thus the grade may not have been entirely unjustified. Indeed, his instructor faulted the paper on just one of the many hurdles to such an undertaking—the strict regulations that government placed on the airline industry, which would hinder the development of an independent, dedicated airfreight service. That was only one of the many problems that Smith faced. The truth of Federal Express is far deeper and more complex than the superficial legend of a term paper that earned a C but launched a revolutionary enterprise.

In a subsequent chapter we will examine the problems Smith faced and how he overcame them. For the present, it suffices to say that the success of Federal Express definitely depended on vision, but not only on vision. It required persistence and financial commitment against enormous odds stacked against the concept and the company.[11]

building on the past: the vision of the web

Today the Internet is a vast network of millions of computers around the world. It consists of computer servers that store information, computer routers that relay information, client computers that post or retrieve information, and communications systems (cable, satellites, etc.) that link these computers together. A series of innovations in computers, communications, software, and protocols were responsible for developing this dynamic and powerful medium. Perhaps the most visible of those innovations for the average person was that of the World Wide Web.

The Web is a network of information sources that can be accessed through the Internet. It is just one face of the Internet through which people use or distribute information. In just a decade since its birth, the Web has become a revolutionary means of communication. Despite its recent success, the vast majority of Web users are unaware that the idea of the Web is mostly due to the vision of one man, Tim Berners-Lee. Yet at the same time, Berners-Lee did not so much as invent all the components of the Web, as merely define a context in which many past innovations could work together seamlessly for its realization. To explain this vision, we describe first the development of the Internet and then the development of the Web.

DEVELOPMENT OF THE INTERNET

The Internet owes its origin to the visionary ideas of a few individuals, such as J. C. R. Licklider and Robert Taylor. These individuals strongly believed that computers would be more effective as interactive and communication devices, rather than as remote machines computing in batch mode, as they were then used. A step in this direction would be to link computers into a network. Initially, the U.S. Defense Department's Advanced Research Projects Agency (ARPA) sponsored the development of such a network. ARPA established the first network, ARPAnet, in the late 1960s. Initially it consisted of only four nodes. But it grew steadily over time and was used by the military and civilians. In 1983, the military set up its own network, MILnet, and ARPAnet remained entirely for civilian use.

In the 1980s, the U.S. National Science Foundation developed a superior network, NSFnet, to facilitate research among scientists. This network grew over the years to link various mainframe computers at universities, research centers, defense contractors, and departments of the U.S. government. After NSF allowed commercial use of the network, several private companies set up their own national and international networks.

By 1990, the Internet progressed to being a complex system of several networks, each connecting a community of scientists and administrators. Each network used its own language and protocol. As such, communication between systems was difficult. The main functions of the Internet at that time were email and file transfers. While email worked fairly well, file transfers through the Internet were neither smooth nor flawless. Moreover, the Internet made possible the storage and distribution of vast amounts of information. Yet for any individual, the search for relevant information was quite difficult and often limited because of the variety of systems, languages, and protocols.

Two of the popular early networks were Gopher and WAIS. Gopher was the campuswide information system at the University of Minnesota, and was named for the university mascot. In the early 1990s the university opened its system to the public at large. Gopher was a menu-based system that let users search for information using hierarchical menus. It was easy to use. But once one got to the end of the hierarchy, there was nowhere else to go. Also, Gopher could only access information on its own system. As such, it was quite structured and limited. Brewster Kahle at Thinking Machines designed the Wide Area Information Servers (WAIS). WAIS had good search engines to find sources of information but no links to easily connect to those sources.

Thus in the early 1990s, the Internet had realized the dream of linking many of the world's computers. But the retrieval of information was slow and difficult because of the variety of incompatible systems.

DEVELOPMENT OF THE WEB

In the 1980s, Tim Berners-Lee, a British scientist at CERN (now the European Laboratory for Particle Physics), began thinking of a way to solve a similar problem at CERN. CERN had a number of visiting scientists who spent a few years at the center and then returned home. These scientists brought to the center their own computers and programs. Over the years, the center grew to encompass thousands of affiliated scientists all over the world, working on various computer systems, yet all needing some commonality to collaborate. In that sense, CERN was a microcosm of the world at large.

In 1980, Berners-Lee wrote a simple program, Enquire, to remember the connections among various researchers, computers, and projects at CERN. When Berners-Lee left CERN, he left the program behind. It ultimately got lost. However, the exercise of developing Enquire planted a seed that grew in his mind. When he returned to CERN a few years later, he addressed the same problem with renewed vigor. Extending the analogy of Enquire to the whole world, he wondered whether the information stored on all the computers in the world could somehow be linked. Horizontal linkages between documents based on keywords would open up a web of limitless information. Such a system would contrast with hierarchical menu-based programs such as Gopher. As Berners-Lee says of his insight, "I was excited about escaping from the straightjacket of hierarchical documentation systems." [12]

Hypertext offered a means to do that. Hypertext, initially proposed by Ted Nelson in 1965, was a text format that included links between documents. Berners-Lee realized that the marriage of the Internet with hypertext could provide a solution to the problem of scattered and disjointed information around the world. He discovered a British company, Owl Ltd, which had developed a program called Guide that could do just that. But it was not Internet based, nor was Owl interested in transporting it to the Internet.

After years of thought, discussion, and trial, Berners-Lee designed the World Wide Web, an integrated system for posting and retrieving the information in documents that resided on computers anywhere in the world. It consisted of three key components:

- Uniform addresses to locate where documents were stored (called uniform resource locators, URLs).
- Links in documents that let one get from one document to another (called hypertext markup language, HTML).
- A standard protocol for exchanging the information in documents across sites (called hypertext transfer protocol, HTTP).

All three of these elements existed before. *But they did so independently*. Berners-Lee was the first to put them together in an integrated system to share information. He explains his vision thus: "The fundamental principle behind the Web was that once someone somewhere made available a document, database, graphic, sound, video, or screen at some stage in an interactive dialogue, it should be accessible (subject to authorization, of course) by anyone, with any type of computer, in any country. And it should be possible to make a reference—a link—to that thing, so that others could find it."[13]

A key component to do so effectively was the address. In the World Wide Web, each server, or computer that stored information, had a unique address (URL). The address had three parts separated by slashes, "/", for example, http://www.cnn.com/allpolitics. The first part (http) indicated which protocol to use, such as, gopher, wais, ftp, http, and so on. Http was the one that Berners-Lee favored and the one that now is widely used. The second part (for example, www.cnn.com) indicated the name of the server. The periods further delineated type and location of servers. The third part (for example, allpolitics) indicated the specific page within that server. By using this uniform address and the standard protocol, HTTP, the Web allowed for accessing documents irrespective of the type of system, protocol, or language in which the information was stored.

Berners-Lee envisioned two pieces of compatible software that made the system run smoothly. One piece, also called the server, resided on the site's computer server and made the information available to various users or clients. The other piece, called the browser, resided on the client's computer and retrieved the information. Keywords in any document stored on the server, which had the address of any other related document (on any server), would be highlighted. By clicking on these keywords or hyperlinks, a client could access the other documents. By hopping from document to document across servers, a user had limitless access to information, without relying on any one central computer or system. Thus links between sources were continuous and unlimited, and not hierarchical and limited as in Gopher. This was the powerful logic of the World Wide Web.

Berners-Lee explains that logic: "What was often difficult for people to understand about the design was that there was nothing else beyond the URIs [as they were then called], HTTP, and HTML. There was no central computer 'controlling' the Web, no single network on which these protocols worked, not even an organization anywhere that 'ran' the Web. The Web was not a physical 'thing' that existed in a certain 'place.' It was a 'space' in which information could exist."[14] More accurately, by reconfiguring conventions and software available at the time, Berners-Lee had defined a new medium in which information could be exchanged instantaneously, all over the world.

But the world did not beat a path to his door. At least, not immediately. In 1989, Berners-Lee initially proposed a simpler version of this system as a documentation system for CERN. At that time, his system was just one of many alternative methods for documentation. He got no formal support from CERN's administration. Actually he got no response at all. In 1990, he revised his system and again submitted the proposal. Again it was shelved. Friends of his within CERN gave him a hard time, saying his system would never take off. They criticized the acronym, WWW, which required nine syllables to pronounce. Even with the help of an experienced colleague within CERN, Berners-Lee did not have much luck winning support for his system. In the meantime, Gopher and WAIS were being widely adopted, and Berners-Lee was concerned they would edge out the Web, a superior system. Thus he realized he would have to proceed quickly on his own.

He recognized that the main problem the Web faced was the absence of good server and browser software. Without a server and browser, people found it difficult to envision the Web. So in the summer of 1990, he began programming a new browser and server that would exploit his vision. He first programmed a browser to run on a NeXT computer that CERN had provided him for his research. He called the browser *WorldWideWeb* (in italics and without spaces to distinguish it from the name of the system itself). He wrote the code for URLs, HTML, and HTTP. He intentionally designed the system to be compatible with the two popular protocols of the time, Gopher and WAIS. To access and retrieve pages from these sites, the user had to include the name "gopher" or "wais" instead of "http" before the first two slashes of the address. Thus users adopting the World Wide Web could now draw from a much wider universe of information than ever before. He also wrote the software for the browser to create and edit pages. And he wrote the code for the server at CERN, which he called info.cern.ch. This server became the first site on the newly designed Web. Unfortunately, Berners-Lee worked on a NeXT computer, so both his server and the browser ran only on the NeXT computers.

In August 1991, he released on the Internet the *WorldWideWeb* for the NeXT and the basic server software for any machine. He also wrote and released a rudimentary line-mode version of the browser that would work on any machine. With these programs in place, people could actually experience the value of the Web. However, he did not get much of a response. So he took to personally promoting the system, talking about it at conferences and seminars. He still got little response. Finally, he began posting notices about the system on several Internet chat groups. That was a turning point.

He first got queries and suggestions for improvement. Then word got around. Interest began to pick up. People who liked the Web downloaded the server, posted their own information, and added links of their own. Thus the Web began to develop its own community and momentum, even without the explicit support of CERN. In August 1991 his site got 100 hits per day. The hits began increasing exponentially, doubling every few months. In a year the number had increased 10 times. This was a pattern that would be replicated on the Web with many other Web-based programs.

At that time, one constraint in the growth of the World Wide Web itself was the absence of a graphical browser that could run on the more widely owned computer systems, such as UNIX, Apple, and Windows. Berners-Lee went around encouraging others to develop such a program. He especially encouraged university students to work on the problem. At least one such effort yielded fruit—Mosaic, developed by students at the University of Illinois. With the design and release of Mosaic in early 1992, people clearly saw the superiority of the Web. From then on, the system took off. It spread so rapidly and completely all over the world that the Web became ubiquitous, and the World Wide Web became synonymous with the Internet.

Berners-Lee's design of the Web carries many lessons. Like King Gillette and Fred Smith, Berners-Lee had a distinct vision of communications in an electronic world. In hindsight, the core concept seems simple and intuitive. However, at the time, the vision was not obvious. Indeed, the majority of people immediately around Berners-Lee did not share his insight and tended to focus on its limitations rather than its benefits. Moreover, many rival systems for sharing information existed on the Internet.

At the same time, the vision does not necessarily involve a radical transformation in available tools and methods. The key components for the design of the Web were already in existence. The backbone for the Web, the Internet and personal computers, was the work of others. The essential components—addresses, hypertext, and transfer protocols—all existed before Berners-Lee. Indeed, Berners-Lee could not have proceeded and done what he did without the existence of these components. As such, his contribution rested on the achievements of thousands of others who worked over the previous three decades. Even at this time, programs already existed that exploited some of these separate components for information exchange. Indeed, some of these programs, like Gopher and WAIS, excelled at exploiting the individual parts of available technology. They took off before the World Wide Web and were quite popular.

What Berners-Lee brought to the table was a unique vision for standardizing and integrating all these elements to facilitate quick, easy, and limitless information sharing. This is perhaps the greatest paradox of vision. All the ingredients are there. In retrospect, the ideas seem quite simple. Yet at the time, only one or a few individuals seem to see how it could all fit in a new worldview. Contemporaries do not share this view, sometimes even when it is explained to them. This unique view of the world is the essence of vision.

There is an important distinction between Berners-Lee and the other two visionaries, Smith and Gillette. The latter two built huge commercial enterprises and profited enormously from their vision. Berners-Lee did not. The reason is embedded in their unique visions. Berners-Lee was interested in neither profits nor proprietary ownership. He did not patent his invention and did not charge for any aspect of it. He freely distributed the specification of the Web as well as the server and client software to use it. Indeed, it was his specific goal that the Web be free to all individuals. Such low mass-market pricing probably facilitated the rapid adoption of the Web.

Ironically, others after him had stronger commercial interests than he did, and commercialized various aspects of the Web. In particular, entrepreneurs commercialized the software to navigate the Web. Berners-Lee did develop *WorldWideWeb*, the first browser to navigate the Web on the NeXT computer. But he gave it away freely and did not develop it for other computer systems. Either he was not interested, or his vision did not encompass a market for such software. Within a few years, demand for this software grew into a multibillion dollar market with rapid changes and fierce rivalry. We will examine the battles among these parties in subsequent chapters.[15]

questions

These three examples show how visionaries have a unique perspective that is not always appreciated by their contemporaries. They also raise some important questions of a more practical nature.

DOES VISION APPLY EQUALLY TO NEW AND OLD MARKETS?

A cursory reading of these stories may suggest that vision applies only to new markets and not to old markets. However, the age of the market is irrelevant to vision. For example, Berners-Lee's vision occurred about 20 years after the start of the Internet. Fred Smith's vision of priority mail by air crystallized several decades after commercial airline service and centuries after mail service started in the United States. Gillette's vision occurred many centuries after the adoption of the cutthroat and over a century after the design of the safety razor. Indeed, a stagnant, seemingly mature market may be just the opportunity for a new way to serve consumer needs.

Vision involves a view of evolving markets that transcends the current scenario, with all its actors, products, and problems. The evolution of the market depends on technological forces and consumer tastes. A clear vision projects where the market will be several years in the future, what form consumer demand will take, and how a firm can position itself to take advantage of this evolution. But vision may also suggest how a firm itself shapes that evolution by an appropriate choice and deployment of technology or an appropriate framing of products to suit consumer tastes. That is the key contribution of Gillette, Smith, Berners-Lee, and many others, whom we will cover in subsequent chapters.

DOES VISION RESIDE WITH INDIVIDUALS OR CORPORATIONS?

Our research shows that most often vision lies with individuals. By its very nature, vision is a perspective not held by a majority. A corporation involves the social interaction among a large number of people. By its very structure, it tends to suppress individuality and encourage group thinking. So it is much harder for visionaries to thrive and succeed within a corporation. As we shall see in later chapters, sometimes such individuals may have to leave the corporation to realize that vision. This is especially true with new ideas and products.

For this reason, the enduring success of a corporation depends on its ability to attract, support, and retain the leadership of visionary individuals. This is less of a problem as long as the visionary founder is still at the helm. However, once a succession takes place, the organization runs the risk of losing its leader, and with him or her, its vision.

Still, some firms are able to build a culture which itself sustains a vision of the mass market and of the firm's role in it. Examples of such firms covered in this book are Intel, Gillette, Procter & Gamble, Sony, Matsushita, and at times, Xerox. These corporations have held leadership positions in their markets for decades. In these cases, the corporations internalized the key aspects of the vision for those markets. Most importantly, they kept their sights on the mass market, while constantly innovating and leveraging assets to serve that market effectively.

A good illustration of the complexity of this task is the development of the microprocessor at Intel. The idea sprang out of a concern for producing a generic product for a mass market, rather than custom products for a variety of market segments. This perspective was formulated and encouraged by Robert Noyce to exploit economies of learning that followed Moore's law of a doubling in chip performance every 18 months. In that environment, Hoff was able and encouraged to design the logic chip, which developed into the microprocessor. The chip was due to Hoff's unique insight. But it was also due to the environment established by Noyce and Moore. In particular, Noyce and Moore supported the design in the face of opposition from the client Busicom, Intel's own marketing department, and some of Intel's own engineers. We will examine other examples of such conflicts in subsequent chapters.

WHAT FACTORS HINDER THE DEVELOPMENT OF VISION?

Three common factors may hinder the development of vision: complacency, protection of assets, and internal focus.

Once a vision has been fully realized, it can richly reward the visionary with great market success, market power, and profits. With that success comes complacency, which may sap the motivation for continually striving for success. Or complacency might cloud the vision by falsely suggesting to the individual or corporation that its success is inevitable.

A successful individual or corporation accumulates assets. Over time, the individual or organization may forget that these assets are rewards for the successful realization of a vision. The organization or individual may make its goal the protection of those assets, rather than the continual refining of the original vision and the continual striving to realize it fully.

The problem of internal focus arises primarily because of the corporation. Corporations are social entities. They need certain structures and routines to operate harmoniously. However, the smooth operation of such structures and routines may themselves become a focus of attention. If this happens, the firm loses sight of markets and what role it should play in them. An internal focus may also result from an obsession with costs or a reactive climate that forces an organization to manage from crisis to crisis.

Any of the above factors can cloud the vision of an individual or firm. Worse still, these factors could replace vision with a myopic focus on the firm's past achievements, its current assets, or its internal working.

summary

Chapter 4 articulated one essential characteristic of vision—a focus on the mass market. This chapter describes another key component of vision, a unique way of serving that mass market. The examples of Gillette, Federal Express, and the World Wide Web illustrate this second component of vision:

- Vision often has a paradoxical feature. It is, in hindsight, a simple idea and, at the same time, a radically new worldview.
- From one perspective, the core insight of the vision seems simple and intuitive. This perspective emerges in hindsight after a business leader transforms his or her vision into a large, successful, new enterprise.
- At the time it is originally formulated, the vision runs contrary to accepted beliefs and practices. Most marketers at that time do not buy into the vision, doubt its viability, and scorn or deride its value because it involves a new way of viewing and solving consumer needs.
- The seeds of a vision are often present in available products and

markets. However, manufacturers of those products are so immersed in their own narrow worldview that they fail to appreciate the insight in the vision, even when it is explained to them.

- When such a vision is first formulated, a market for serving consumer needs not only may exist but may be quite mature. Firms in that market may be quite entrenched. The visionary may often be a late entrant into a seemingly mature market, or one struggling at the fringes.
- The visionary faces numerous problems and difficulties in realizing the vision. For enduring leadership, the visionary also needs persistence, relentless innovation, and financial commitment.

persisting—against all odds

A cursory reading of the history of highly successful new products leads many analysts to attribute the success of these products to luck: being at the right place at the right time. Others, upon examining the history of such products, might describe their design as breakthrough inventions of tinkering scientists. However, enduring market leaders rarely achieved their success through luck or sudden breakthroughs. Actually, successful products are the fruit of small, incremental innovations in design, manufacturing, and marketing over many years. Entrepreneurs and managers must have the will to persist in their efforts through seemingly insurmountable obstacles, slow progress, and long time periods. Vision of the future motivates the heroic efforts and guides the choices that these people make. On the other hand, two misperceptions about market success may discourage persistence: the belief in luck and the wait for a breakthrough.

Some reports isolate chance events in the history of enduring market leaders. They glorify these moments, suggesting that a lucky concurrence of events led to ultimate success. A good example is Bill Gates's (supposedly) lucky discovery of QDOS just when IBM wanted such a program. However, when we examine the history of markets in detail, a different picture emerges. Luck plays a minimal role. True, combinations of people and events create problems and suggest solutions. However, it requires vision to spot those solutions, persistence to work for them, and commitment to seize them promptly.

Some reports isolate and glorify the big moments of discovery in the history of science and business. In the realm of science, classic examples include Archimedes' realization of flotation in his bathtub and Newton's realization of gravity when hit by a falling apple. In the realm of business, a good example is Gillette's invention of the disposable blade. However, these stories seem to miss the long struggle with the problem prior to the vision or after its formulation. They overstate the simplicity of the solution and understate the vision necessary to envision a formula as the solution, and the persistence required to realize that vision.

Belief in luck or the search for a major breakthrough may lead to unrealistic expectations and premature termination of projects. An examination of five histories of enduring market leaders indicates that the road to success was long, hard, and trying. These firms found the will to persist through that long struggle.

naïve persistence

The development of Gillette's safety razor is a lesson on the importance of persistence in bringing innovations to market. Gillette wrote that the key components of his design dawned on him in waves at the same moment that his current razor and blade had grown blunt. He envisioned a two-part razor and blade. The blade would be flat with two edges to double its service. It would be made of some cheap metal so it could be thrown away when blunt. The razor's head would have clamping plates for the blade. The handle would be positioned at the center of the clamps, for convenient use of both edges of the blade. At that point in time, he imagined the design would be easy to implement.

Gillette became obsessed with his idea of a disposable blade. He made drawings of it, and would talk about it to anyone who would listen. He did not find much encouragement among his listeners, many of whom could barely appreciate his insight. To develop a prototype, he directed his attention to developing such a blade.

He first attempted to develop the blade from sheet steel, which was inexpensive enough for disposable blades. He tried to temper it suitably to hold a sharp enough edge to cut whiskers. However, that was one of the first major problems he encountered. Sheet metal was too brittle and weak to sustain a sharp edge. Gillette did not have much luck on his first try, nor on many subsequent attempts. He then approached professionals in the field, cutlers and metallurgists, with the hope that their expertise could solve the problem. They all gave him the same answer: Sheet metal could not hold a sharp edge. But Gillette pursued his goal doggedly. In his quest for a solution, he noted that "it went on for nearly six years, during which time I was experimenting with blades. I tried every cutler and machine shop in Boston and some in New York and Newark in an effort to find someone who knew something about hardening and tempering thin steel so it would keep its flatness and not be warped by strains. Even [the Massachusetts Institute of] Technology experimented and failed absolutely."[1] The most knowledgeable were also the most discouraging about his goal to put a sharp edge on sheet metal. Gillette also contacted his friends and financiers to provide capital for his enterprise. But he had no success. On the contrary, his attempts to develop a new razor and blade became a joke among all his friends.

The only encouragement he got was from his old friend Painter, who set him on this course. However, Painter was too old and ill to join him in his quest.

Unfortunately, Gillette could not devote his whole time to developing the blade. He was a traveling salesman and had a family to support. So in the summer of 1899, he approached a Boston machinist, Steven Porter, for help in designing a razor and blade. After much effort and with the help of Gillette's designs and supervision, Porter made three razors, and for the third he made several blades. It took 4 years for Gillette to obtain the first prototype of his invention. Gillette lathered up his face and shaved successfully with the first working model. The next step that Gillette launched was obtaining a patent to protect his invention. His first attempts in this direction met with failure. Ironically, the assistant of a patent attorney, on seeing the design, said, "No invention would be involved in making razors in the proposed manner."[2] However, Gillette persisted in the belief that he had a unique design and applied for a patent a few months later, calling his design "something new in the art of razor manufacture and use."[3] He finally got the patent he sought.

The next challenge was to develop a manufacturing system that could mass-produce razors and especially blades on a large scale. This task was something well beyond Gillette's knowledge and training. A mutual friend introduced Gillette to Jacob Heilborn, a financier of small enterprises. Gillette discussed his project with Heilborn, explaining that the only thing that separated him from realizing his dream was a metallurgist who could overcome the design problems. Unlike others around him, Heilborn saw the merit of Gillette's design and immediately thought of William Nickerson.

Nickerson was an MIT chemist by training, but had a great interest in inventing new gadgets. He had designed saws for cutting tree bark, safety devices for elevators, vacuum pumps for electric bulbs, and weighing machines for coffee plants. He had a number of patents to his name. However, due to poor planning and business acumen, Nickerson failed to make a commercial success of any of his ventures. A year earlier, a friend of Gillette had shown Nickerson Gillette's design for the safety razor. Nickerson had not been impressed. He himself used a straight razor and was unfamiliar with the safety razors of the day. He examined the model that Gillette's friend provided him and found the blade too stiff and the handle too light. He failed to see any of the potential that Gillette envisioned. Moreover, he knew nothing about cutlery, so he dropped the project.

When Heilborn broached the topic, Nickerson's opinion had not changed. However, under prodding from Gillette, Heilborn again asked Nickerson to research the design. He met with him several times to persuade him of its merits. Finally, more to stop Heilborn's badgering than in belief of the design's merits, Nickerson agreed to work on the project for a month.

It was a critical month for Nickerson, and especially for Gillette. After that month of research, Nickerson's view of the razor and blade changed completely. He thought that Gillette's design was feasible. Indeed, the more he worked with it, the better possibilities he saw. He emphasized the need to develop a blade of the highest sharpness and strength that would hold its edge without deterioration even after several uses. If the blades were made correctly, they would surpass in quality anything then on the market. He suggested that low price was a very high priority. He thought he could bring the price down with the machines he had in mind, without sacrificing quality.

Clearly Nickerson's expertise and his native inventiveness had led to a breakthrough in the quest for a new blade. However, it was Gillette's persistence that had led him to Nickerson, and Gillette's persuasiveness that had converted Nickerson into an ardent believer of his design. Indeed, Nickerson now believed in the new shaving system as ardently as Gillette did.

Some analysts may claim that Gillette's success was due to certain lucky breaks. For example, the concept of the new shaving system came to him by chance one day when his blade was too blunt to use for shaving. The successful prototype was actually designed by Steven Porter, a Boston machinist he seemed to have run into by chance. The key developer of the manufacturing system was Nickerson, whom Gillette was lucky to have met through a mutual friend. Thus Gillette's success may seem to have depended on three lucky breaks.

However, such superficial accounts of the development of the new shaving system ignore important details that were critically responsible for its success. The concept of the new shaving system came to Gillette only because he was on a persistent long-term search for some household product that would have a disposable component. He believed that if it were designed properly, consumers would keep coming back for more of the same, just as they did for the Crown cork. Without that unusual goal in mind, the concept of the new shaving system would never have occurred to him. Indeed, no other contemporary manufacturer of razors came up with the idea or regarded Gillette's idea as feasible.

It took countless hours of experimentation, travel, and search before Gillette encountered Porter, who developed the successful design. Similarly, Gillette's relationship with Nickerson was no happy accident. Gillette was on the lookout for a manufacturer of his prototype. He sought out all cutlers and manufacturers of razors in

Boston and neighboring cities for several years. Even Nickerson needed to be persuaded to work on the project on two separate occasions, 1 year apart.

Gillette wrote later of his vision, "Fool that I was, I knew little about razors and practically nothing about steel, and I could not foresee the trials and tribulations that I was to pass through before the razor was a success."[4] While acknowledging his persistence, Gillette suggests that it was his naïveté coupled with his dream for riches that kept him going: "But I didn't know enough to quit. If I had been technically trained, I would have quit or probably would never have begun. I was a dreamer who believed in the 'gold at the foot of the rainbow' promise, and continued in the path where the wise one feared to tread, and that is the reason, and the only reason why there is a Gillette today."[5] He did not think that it would take 6 years, require numerous sacrifices, and involve the labors of many other individuals. Indeed, it took a "fanatic's zeal" to surmount the difficulties in developing the Gillette safety razor.[6]

persistence for a "low-tech" innovation

In the complex world of microprocessors, genetic engineering, and space travel, the disposable diaper appears to be a low-tech product. It is just a combination of fabrics enclosing an absorbent material, designed to fit the contours of a baby's bottom. Despite this apparent simplicity, disposable diapers were only mass-produced in the early 1930s. Quality remained poor and the price high right up to 1966, the year that P&G made a successful national rollout of Pampers. Ironically, from the time P&G first considered entering this market, it took the company 10 years of persistent planning and research to achieve success. What problems did the firm face?

The first problem with producing an acceptable disposable diaper for the mass market was the conflicting goals that the product had to simultaneously meet. The diaper had to be soft enough to be comfortable, yet strong enough not to disintegrate when wet. It had to be absorbent to retain moisture, yet remain dry enough not to cause a skin rash. It had to be leakproof, yet not so airtight as to be uncomfortable. It had to be easy to put on and take off, but stay firmly in place with an active child. Coupled with these conflicting goals was the fact that babies varied greatly from one another in the amount of fluid they passed. For a single baby, that amount varied as much as 50 percent from day to day, depending on food intake and temperature. Moreover, babies' waist sizes also varied, from about 14 inches to 23 inches. The second problem with producing an acceptable disposable diaper was cost. The diaper had to be of high quality in each of the above dimensions, yet inexpensive enough to compete with diaper services and home laundering. Thus, the task for the firm was primarily one of design to resolve the first problem and one of manufacturing to solve the second problem. P&G launched a concerted research drive to solve these problems.

The first task was to identify the appropriate materials. After initial research, P&G tested a design in Dallas in 1958. The product was a pad held in place by plastic pants. A researcher describes what was learned from this test market: "From this experience we learned a little about weather and a lot about diapering. We learned that it gets *very* hot in Dallas in summer, and where there isn't much air conditioning, mothers do not subject their infants to the rash-producing Turkish bath that comes with plastic pants. So it was back to the process of discovery and invention."[7]

After research and testing, the engineers solved the problem by using a three-part design. They had an inner lining of a treated rayon fabric that stayed close to the skin. This fabric was soft, allowed moisture to pass through to the middle layer, but stayed dry itself. The middle layer was made of a soft, absorbent material like tissue or wood pulp. The outermost layer was made of a waterproof polyethylene that allowed some air but no fluid to pass through. In the next product test, this product design met with better acceptance, with one-third of the panelists rating the product better than cloth diapers.

P&G's next task was manufacturing this design on a mass scale. After 5 years of research, the lowest price it achieved was 10 cents a unit. P&G tested its disposable diaper at that price in Peoria, Illinois, in early 1962. The test market was a failure, with sales reaching only a third of their targeted 1.9 million units (2.5 percent market share). The product was rated well and found to be convenient. The main problem was price. The price of 10 cents a unit for Pampers was substantially higher than the average cost of 3.5 cents per change for diaper service and 1.5 cents per change for home laundering.

So the engineers persisted with their research. The next major task for the firm was to develop a manufacturing system that would mass-produce the design at a low price. As research proceeded to improve the quality, and especially lower the price, P&G also proceeded to test consumer acceptance of the redesigned product. To account for variation in absorbent needs among babies and across time, P&G developed three sizes of diapers: newborn, daytime, and extra-strength for nighttime use. Interspersed with the research effort, the company launched a series of test markets in Sacramento (1962, 1964), St. Louis (1964), and Indianapolis (1964). Each experiment tested an improved design, better quality, and better advertising copy. Each successive test market met with improved success. However, the price was still too high. P&G finally came up with a sophisticated machine extending for one entire city block, which could produce 400 diapers a minute at a cost of 3.5 cents each. That enabled the company to set a retail price of 5.5 cents for a national rollout in 1966. At that price, the launch was a great success.

The diaper is a fairly low-tech product. Yet it took a major corporation 10 years of persistent manufacturing and marketing research to design a product that would appeal to the mass market. In fact, according to an article in *Forbes* magazine, "P&G spent more time and money on developing and test-marketing Pampers, than Henry Ford plowed into his first automobile or Edison spent on inventing the first incandescent bulb."[8] The firm persisted with research despite numerous setbacks, many test market failures, and limited sales. The members of the research team were willing to innovate, test their changes, and learn from their mistakes. They exhibited a "dogged dedication to learning,"[9] as one of the team members put it. That fact may explain why J&J, a market leader that entered much before P&G, did not stumble onto the right design of the disposable diaper despite 30 years of experience. J&J had high margins, a secure niche, and no vision of a mass market. P&G, the late entrant, had a vision that was clear and strong enough to sustain 10 years of persistent efforts. The right design came from persistent efforts to realize a vision, not from pioneering, experience, luck, or sudden breakthroughs.[10]

the long journey of persistence

When journalists describe the advent of the Beta and VHS video recorders, they often characterize them as breakthroughs in the quest for a home video recording system. The impression one gets today is that these innovations were quick and dramatic. However, the truth is that they were painfully slow and very, very long in coming. Indeed, Sony, JVC, and Matsushita spent over twice as much time and effort in this quest as P&G did for diapers. But their persistence was unwavering.

Sony started research on video recorders in 1958. It first built a replica of the four-head Ampex video recorder in only 3 months. Senior managers encouraged a simpler technology than that used by Ampex, with the goal of producing a product for the mass market. For a brief period in 1960, Sony, then still a small company, obtained technical guidance and licensing agreements from Ampex in exchange for providing transistor technology. However, that arrangement soon broke down over disagreements on royalty payments. Sony then continued on its own to develop a recorder. It took the firm about 4 years of research to develop the PV-100, a two-head helical scanner less than one-twentieth the size of the Ampex VRX 1000 (see Figures 6-1 and 6-2). Ampex engineers, who stuck to the four-head technology, did not believe that such a model was possible. Sony introduced the product to the market in 1962. While a technological wonder, the product was still far removed in price, features, and the ability to record color to appeal to either the consumer market or the institutional market of education and business.

Sony kept up with research and introduced a CV model in 1965 at a price below $1000. This model recorded in black and white and was still a little difficult to use. The high price, lack of color, and inconvenient usage dissuaded consumers from adopting the product. However, the institutional market—schools, businesses, and hospitals—did find the device useful for educational purposes.

Sony's early failures provided valuable experience in understand-

Figure 6-1. The Ampex VRX 1000

Courtesy of Ampex Corporation. Reprinted with permission.

ing what was necessary for the product to become a hit with consumers. Chairman Ibuka kept encouraging engineers to develop a
low-priced, user-friendly machine for this market. He would plant a
seed of an idea and ask engineers to try out solutions. When they came
up with one, he would urge them to improve on it. Sometimes such
requests required minor changes, and sometimes major changes. But
Ibuka was constantly challenging his engineers to make products that
were uniquely useful. He gave the engineers "the actual target and the
dimensions of the target," and they knew they could develop the technology to achieve that.[11] Such persistence greatly helped to motivate
and direct the efforts of the engineering team.

After another 4 years of research, in 1969, Sony introduced a
"magazine-loaded" video recorder that used 1-inch tape. The new
machine provided better picture quality than the old one. The magazine was more convenient for handling than the older reel-to-reel
tape technology, but it was not as convenient as the compact cassette

Figure 6-2. The Sony PV-100

Courtesy of Sony Electronics Inc. Reprinted with permission.

that had not yet been invented. As such, it was not convenient enough for the mass market. Throughout the 1960s, Sony manufactured improved models. It marketed these primarily to the institutional market in competition with Ampex and other Japanese and European firms. Ampex at that time targeted the premium segment with a high-priced, high-quality machine. It had a reputation of superior quality and technological leadership. Sony and other Japanese firms tended to serve the low-priced segment with products that were of slightly lower quality, but less complex to produce and easier to use.

In the early 1970s, Sony began work on the Betamax. Initially, the firm focused on the design of the prototype. Once convinced of the design, it moved to development of manufacturing facilities for mass production. In April 1975, Sony offered the Betamax for sale in the market. This was the first video recorder to become popular with consumers.

JVC followed a similar path in developing its video recorder. In fact, its efforts were so slow that director Shiraishi chose to keep the project secret from his superiors for fear of losing support. But the steadfast direction of Shiraishi finally paid off. A few days after the introduction of the Betamax, JVC revealed to its parent, Matsushita, that a small group of engineers were developing a home video recorder that was almost ready. JVC introduced its product in fall 1976, 21 years after research began at the firm, 20 years after Ampex pioneered the market, and more than 1 year after Sony introduced the Betamax. Matsushita, the parent of JVC, adopted the VHS in early 1977. Even though it was introduced a little later, the VHS was more successful than the Betamax because of its longer tape limit (2 hours to 1 for the Betamax) and Matsushita's strategy to be an original equipment manufacturer (OEM) for RCA and other firms.

Sony's Betamax and JVC's VHS were responsible for stimulating the mass market for video recorders. Sales increased rapidly, and in 10 years reached almost 12 million units a year in the United States alone (see Figure 4-2). However, like JVC's VHS, the Betamax was not Sony's only product, nor its first product, nor a sudden breakthrough. The Betamax was the culmination of about 16 years of research. It came 13 years after Sony launched its first machine, the PV-100. During those 13 years alone, Sony engineers worked to reduce weight by 71 percent, increase recording density by 11 times, reduce price by 88 percent, and introduce color (see Table 6-1). Many people consider Betamax a revolutionary product that started the video recorder market. What few people realize is that the Betamax came as the evolutionary fruit of persistent research to solve diverse problems over nearly two decades.

In the 15 years from 1956, Ampex dominated the professional market with a reputation for quality and superior technology. But it had neither a coherent vision of the mass market nor a persistent strategy to succeed in it. It made only sporadic attempts to develop a product for this market. Others had what Ampex lacked, developed the mass market, and dominated it. When that market grew, they came to dominate the entire industry. Thus in the video recorder market, order of market entry, reputation, and past technological

Table 6-1. Sony's Technical Progress over 13 Years

	Sony PV-100 1962	*Sony Betamax 1975*
Tape utilization in square meters per hour	19.8	1.8
Video display	Monochrome	Color
Tape loading	Manual reel-to-reel threading	Automatic cassette threading
Weight in pounds	145	41
Price to consumer	$12,000	$1400

Source: Richard S. Rosenbloom and Michael A. Cusumano, "Technological Pioneering and Competitive Advantage: The Birth of the VCR Industry," *California Management Review*, 24, Summer, 1987, p. 66.

achievements were unimportant. Vision of the mass market and persistence to design a product for that market were critical.[12]

how vision drives persistence

The story of the Xerox 914 reveals how a small firm can grow to dominate a market through persistence. It also shows how even an entrenched position cannot protect a large incumbent that fails to innovate.

Xerox's story begins with Chester Carlson, a patent attorney, who tired of the tedious method of copying that existed in the 1930s. Having a physics background, Carlson sought a better system of copying. His library research indicated that a Hungarian scientist had made images of pictures with powder and static electricity. This principle of copying appealed to Carlson because it was clean and dry. Carlson decided to make a copier based on this principle. He started experimenting in a makeshift laboratory with the help of a German physicist. After three years of labor, they developed a dry copying machine that could make a crude image on regular paper (see Figure 6-3).

Carlson was delighted with his achievement. He took his invention to numerous firms, including the major American technology firms of his day: IBM, Kodak, RCA, General Electric, and

Figure 6-3. Copy of First Image by Carlson's Copier

Courtesy of Xerox Corporation. Reprinted with permission.

Remington Rand. He hoped the firms would commercialize his invention, but none was interested. Yet Carlson persisted in his search. He approached over 20 firms without eliciting any interest. Finally, in 1944, he found a sponsor in the head of a graphic arts division in a nonprofit institute, the Battelle Memorial Institute. Six years after his invention, and nine years after starting his research, Carlson went to work for Battelle, which bought a 60 percent interest in his invention. Carlson's invention still needed a firm that would be willing to commercialize a product based on it. It came in the form of a small company called the Haloid Corporation.

Haloid was a small manufacturer of photographic paper for large firms such as Kodak. In 1945, Joseph Wilson, the grandson of the company founder, and his staff were on the lookout for new inventions that could help the firm diversify and grow. The firm's research effort led it to the technology of xerography, then owned by Battelle. Wilson went with his chief engineer, John Dessauer, to examine the technology. The demonstration they saw involved a manual prototype, which was very messy. But it caught Wilson's attention. He exclaimed, "Of course it's got a million miles to go before it will be marketable. But when it does become marketable, we've got to be in the picture!"[13]

With keen vision, Wilson proceeded to purchase the rights to develop Carlson's technology. For these rights, he paid $25,000 down plus 8 percent of future revenues from sales based on the technology. The down payment amounted to almost a quarter of Haloid's earnings of $101,000 for the year. Wilson chose a technology that was rejected by firms such as Kodak, IBM, and RCA, which were better equipped, were better funded, and had more closely related products than Haloid. At that time, these firms were giants with deep pockets, leaders in photography, office equipment, and communications, respectively. Moreover, dry copying would have fit into the charter of any of these firms. For RCA, it would have been an alternative means of communications. For Kodak, which was already in the market, it would have been a means of making better copies. For IBM, it could have served as valuable office equipment. Indeed, when the copier market took off and became a multibillion dollar business, IBM did enter the market with its own product.

But the technology was in a rudimentary form. It required a visionary to see the potential in such a technology. Wilson was such a person. He launched a major effort to develop the technology into a viable product. A year later, his researchers called the technology *xerography*, from the Greek for dry copying. In 1948, Wilson demonstrated the technology at a national conference in Detroit and promised to produce a commercial product soon. Unfortunately, the task was too great for the available time. A year later, Haloid introduced the first product, the Model A. But the product was a failure. It was huge, consisting of three separate machines. It was manual and complicated, and it took 2 to 3 minutes for a single copy. The operator had to carry out a large number of complex operations, including carrying a heavy plate from one machine to another. Getting all of them to work well and seamlessly was a formidable task.

So it was back to research, which turned out to be much slower and took much longer than anyone expected. There were problems with the copy paper sticking to the photoreceptor, toner residue building up on the photoreceptor, paper jamming in the machine, and the machine itself periodically erupting into flames. All told, engineers had to solve thousands of problems to convert Carlson's prototype into a viable product. Wilson said of that effort, "For every technical problem that we solved, we encountered another for which we had no answer."[14] Researchers would get frustrated and discouraged. Dessauer, director of research, describes the atmosphere: "Hardly anybody was very optimistic in the early years. Various members of our own group would come in and tell me that the damn thing would never work. The biggest risk was that the electrostatics would prove to be infeasible in high humidity. Almost all the experts assumed that—they'd come in and say, 'You'll never make copies in New Orleans,'"[15] where humidity could get very high. On top of that, there were the pessimistic sales forecasts. Dessauer continues, "The marketing people thought we were dealing with a potential market of no more than a few thousand machines. Some advisors told us that we were absolutely crazy to go ahead with the project."[16]

However, Wilson championed the project. He motivated researchers to continue with research. He kept close tabs on the progress, asking his research staff for reports on past progress, decisions made, and future plans. He was content with the small successes that came along, and had the research department systematically file for all patents emerging from the research. Carlson's original patent was due to expire in 1957, and additional patents would protect the product from competitive imitations, should it become a success.

In 1959, after 13 years of research on the product, a commercially viable product began to emerge. However, to ensure he would have an unquestionable success, Wilson did not rush the product to market. The company needed funds to invest in manufacturing and marketing in order to bring the product to market, but the company was strapped for funds. It sought outside funding from a variety of sources, including IBM. The latter company asked Arthur D. Little to study the copier market and evaluate Haloid's offer. The consulting firm estimated that no more than 5000 machines would sell, so Haloid received no support. Haloid's own external consultants came up with similar estimates of a very limited market. However, analysts within the company believed that it was difficult to accurately estimate demand for such a revolutionary product.

Still convinced of his vision, Wilson persuaded the board to sell company stock to pay for the cost of manufacturing the machine. The board continued to support his vision. Wilson backed up his request with personal sacrifices. He and some executives took some of their pay in company stock. Some executives put up their savings and the mortgages on their homes to support the cause. In the meantime, employees labored on the project in rough and demanding conditions to meet their goals while keeping costs as low as possible.

The first commercial unit of the product, the Xerox 914 (see Figure 6-4), was shipped in March 1960. It earned that name because it could make copies on plain paper that was 9 inches by 14 inches. The machine consisted of 1260 components, all of which had to work in unison for a successful copy. The product took 14 years of research, during which time Haloid spent $75 million on the research effort, *twice* its operational earnings over the entire 14-year period. The list price was a phenomenal $29,500. To ensure that firms would accept the product, Haloid decided to lease the product for $95 a month. That cost included service and 2000 free copies. Additional copies cost 4 cents each. The product had to compete with copiers from 30 other companies, including those from Kodak and 3M. However, it was simpler, faster, and easier to use than its competitors. It did not use messy liquids but a dry toner. Most importantly, it could produce copies on ordinary paper. Business analysts initially saw that as a disadvantage because competitors at that time made their profits by supplying special paper for their proprietary machines. This is akin to Gillette's strategy of supplying disposable blades for his proprietary razors.

The Xerox 914 was a huge success. By the end of 1961, within 2 years of introduction, Xerox installed 10,000 copiers. In 1961 alone, sales totaled $59 million, almost double that of the previous year. The company changed its name to the Xerox Corporation. In 1962, sales almost tripled those of the previous year. By 1966, sales crossed a half billion dollars and Xerox held 61 percent of the copier market. The firm had grown to be one of the nation's largest corporations. Wilson savored the success, but did not sit still. He developed a huge research center at Webster, a suburb of Rochester, New York. He motivated his researchers to continue improving the product and develop others for different market segments. Indeed, in 1966, Xerox spent $40 million on research, almost 8 percent of its revenues. That year it won its 500th patent. The research effort paid off in a stream of valuable new products that helped Xerox

Figure 6-4. The Xerox 914

Courtesy of Xerox Corporation. Reprinted with permission.

dominate the copier market for years. By the end of the 1960s, Xerox had grown to 38,000 employees and a stock market value of $8.2 billion. That value was *66 times* its value of about a decade earlier, when the Xerox 914 was first introduced.

Xerox was not the pioneer of copying. Rather it entered a crowded field with giant competitors. The success of the firm can be fairly attributed to Wilson. Specifically, it was his vision of the potential of dry copying that was the driving force behind the firm's great endeavor. That vision enabled him to persist with innovation over a great many obstacles, 14 years of research, and an investment of $75 million. Few if any people outside the company shared that vision. Indeed, there were no buyers for Carlson's technology before Haloid invested in it. Ironically, even after Haloid researched the product for 13 years, developed a prototype, and was ready to manufacture it, the product had no other commercial investors. Even a leading consulting firm completely misjudged the potential market for the product. These facts clearly underscore how unique Wilson's vision was among contemporary managers and entrepreneurs.[17]

"luck" of the persistent visionary

One of the greatest legends of the personal computer age is the story of the origins of DOS, and Bill Gates's supposed luck in being in the right place at the right time.

In 1980, IBM had decided on producing its own personal computer in response to the success of the Apple and Tandy personal computers. In an attempt to rush to market, IBM put together the computer from off-the-shelf components available in the market. IBM needed an operating system for the PC. Gary Kildall, owner of (Intergalactic) Digital Research, then was the leading provider of operating systems for the personal computer market. His CP/M was the standard. So IBM contacted Kildall for his operating system.

However, when IBM's managers called at Digital Research, Kildall was supposedly out flying his plane. So IBM then contacted Gates for an operating system. Gates did not have one. But he licensed the software from Seattle Computer Products, a small company in Seattle. Tim Paterson, a programmer at Seattle Computer, had created a program called QDOS (Quick and Dirty Operating System). QDOS is supposed to have been a clone of Kildall's CP/M. The structure of the two systems seems similar, and some commands appeared identical. Gates paid the company a fee of $10,000 for the unrestricted right to license the software to any number of clients, with an additional royalty of $15,000 per licensee. (A year later he bought the entire rights to the software from the company for $50,000.) He then turned around and licensed the software to IBM for a huge up-front fee plus a per-unit fee while retaining the rights to the software.

When the PC and its numerous clones took off, DOS became the standard operating system for all personal computers. Sales of DOS rose rapidly, making Microsoft a large, profitable company. Microsoft's ownership of the DOS copyright was a major factor in transforming the small Seattle company into the market leader and near monopolist in operating systems for PCs. Casual commentators often describe Gates's success as a stroke of perfect luck. He was in the office ready to sign with IBM while Kildall was away. His clever purchase and license of QDOS appears as the deal of the century, perhaps of all time. And Kildall was just naive and unlucky, like the biblical Esau, cheated out of his rightful inheritance.

However, a close study of the historical detail reveals a substantially different picture. At the time that IBM came knocking, Bill Gates and Paul Allen, cofounders of Microsoft Corporation, had embarked on an ambitious plan to be leading providers of software for personal computers. They had already built a reputation as young but knowledgeable and trustworthy software developers. They had done so through a decade of experience with programming, and 5 years of total involvement in programming for personal computers. Gates and Allen actually began programming in high school, where they would spend hours writing programs, playing games, and learning different computer systems. They used whatever computer they could access through neighborhood firms and institutions. They even did odd jobs programming for firms that needed specific programs to computerize payroll and other accounting tasks. Gates was obsessive about computing and ran contests with friends to see who could spend 3 or 4 days programming continuously. The same passion for programming accompanied him to college.

In early 1975, Gates was in his second year at Harvard. Allen, 2 years his senior, told him about the MITS Altair, a primitive personal computer that was featured on the cover of *Popular Mechanics*. The machine lacked a keyboard, monitor, and software programs. Until then, there was no such machine and therefore no programs that would run on it. Gates and Allen were fascinated by the machine and immediately perceived its enormous significance. At that time they were experts at BASIC, a simple, publicly available language, that enabled people to write programs on minicomputers. Allen called up Ed Roberts, the owner of MITS, and promised a program before he had written it. Roberts told him he would license the software from the first person who provided a working program. At least one minicomputer firm insisted that it was not possible to write a high-level language to run on a personal computer.[18] But Allen and Gates were confident of their abilities and focused all their efforts on quickly adapting BASIC for the Altair.

They plunged into this task, hardly sparing time for food or sleep, to design a program before anyone else. They were paranoid that others would beat them to the task. As Gates recounted, "We realized that the revolution might happen without us. After we saw that article there was no question where our life would focus."[19] Ironically, they did not have a model of the Altair. So they programmed their minicomputer at Harvard (a Digital Equipment PDP 10) to simulate the Altair, whose description they found in a magazine. Less than 2 months of intensive work bore fruit. Allen flew to New Mexico to demonstrate their new program to MITS without even a test run. On the first try it failed. But on the second try, it printed out the word "ready." Gates describes the moment as related to him by Paul Allen: "And they were amazed that this thing worked. Paul was amazed that our part had worked, and Ed was amazed that his hardware worked, and here it was doing something even useful. And Paul called me up and it was very, very exciting."[20] It impressed Roberts so much that he hired Paul Allen as an employee, and licensed the program for $30 a unit shipped.

In the summer of 1975, Gates and Allen founded Micro-Soft, which earned $16,000 the first year (they later dropped the hyphen in the name). From the time that the Altair came out, Gates believed the personal computer would be the wave of the future. It was that belief that motivated him to put programming above studies at Harvard. After their first version of BASIC ran successfully on the Altair, Gates remained captivated by the enormous potential of personal computers. He could not take his mind off the project to concentrate on studies at Harvard. Ultimately, he dropped out of school and joined Allen, working full time for Microsoft. His parents were not "all that excited that their son was dropping out of a fine University to start a business almost nobody had heard about called microcomputers."[21] Indeed, the Altair soon failed, but Gates and Allen continued adapting their programs for the large number of rival PC firms that entered the market. One of these rivals was Tandy, whose computer, the TRS-80, was the next hot personal computer in the market.

When IBM wanted a language and operating system for its PC, it contacted Microsoft because of the reputation the young firm had developed. Gates offered IBM a version of BASIC for the PC but directed IBM to Kildall for the operating system. However, when the latter failed to sign a contract with IBM, Gates took over. He did not have an operating system ready for the personal computer. He was not even in the market for selling operating systems. Nevertheless, he immediately grasped the value of working with IBM, then the largest manufacturer of computers in the world, with revenues exceeding $50 billion. Eager for the IBM contract, and confident in his abilities, Gates promised to deliver an operating system to IBM in 3 months.

He purchased the rights to QDOS and hired its creator, Tim Paterson. They modified the program and changed its name to Microsoft DOS. Most importantly, Gates shrewdly held the right to license the program to other manufacturers of personal computers, thus retaining a proprietary hold on the market. Eventually, when over 100 million computers were using the operating system, Microsoft eclipsed IBM in power, profitability, and market capitalization. Gates became a multibillionaire.

A superficial read of the facts may suggest that Gates was just the right man at the right place. However, a closer study of the events suggests that vision and persistence, rather than luck, were key to the success of DOS. Indeed, the first contract between IBM and Microsoft in 1980 was neither solely nor primarily due to luck. The reason that IBM signed with Microsoft was because the latter firm had the best version of BASIC for personal computers and had developed a solid reputation for hard work, innovative solutions, and timely deliveries. Gates and Allen were so involved in their tasks and so much in demand for their skills that they often worked late into the night and over weekends. As Allen remarked, "We would just work until we dropped."[22] Indeed, an intense work ethic is a hallmark of life at Microsoft even today. The hard work and many risks paid off for Microsoft, which by that time had a unique position as a leading provider of programming languages for personal computers. Indeed, the hard work of Gates and Allen had grown the start-up into the biggest supplier of applications for the personal computer market. It was that position that attracted the confidence of IBM, as it did that of other firms before and after. True to style, Gates then matched this position by a bold move: promising to deliver to IBM an operating system in 3 months without any design in hand.

Contrast their style with that of Gary Kildall. Although he missed the first meeting with IBM, he later had talks with IBM. However, he failed to negotiate a deal due to a disagreement with the fee structure IBM offered. The real reason for the failure was that Kildall was overconfident of his worth and undervalued a contract with IBM. At that time, Digital Research was one of the largest computer software companies in the world. Kildall had become a millionaire with the widespread use of his CP/M. Secure in his dominance of the market for operating systems, he underestimated the impact IBM would have on the personal computer market and refused to work with the firm.

When he learned of Microsoft's deal with IBM using QDOS, Kildall was furious. He believed that QDOS was a knockoff of his CP/M. He was ready to sue. Yet he probably believed that Microsoft was too small and its owners too young for him to battle in court. Moreover, he had plenty of other clients. So he settled with a promise from IBM to also offer a version of Kildall's CP/M for the PC. Kildall did bring out a version of CP/M for the PC. However, there again he misjudged the market. His version carried a price tag of $240, compared with MS DOS's price of $40. The choice for consumers was clear. They invariably preferred DOS to his program. When DOS became a standard, Kildall's CP/M and Digital Research faded from the scene.

Thus, the root cause of Gates's success and Kildall's failure was not a matter of luck. Events would not have been different if Kildall had been there for the first meeting with IBM. At the root of the matter lay the radically different visions and styles of two men, Kildall and Gates. Kildall was content with his achievements and confident of his position. He failed to see the role of IBM. He did not see the value of fighting for his rights to the software. He let a rival strike a lucrative deal on a product for which he was the market leader, using a version that he thought was a knockoff of his own. He did not envision the price that would appeal to the mass market. In contrast, Gates always had his sights on the mass market. He was relentless in his quest to dominate that market fully. From his earliest days, Gates would take every competitive advantage he could. In the business world he pursued every perceived infringement of his copyrights with legal suits. When IBM came knocking, he saw the opportunity and grabbed it. He did not hesitate to sell IBM a product that he did not even own and may not have been an original.

In hindsight, Gates's purchase of QDOS for $50,000 seems like the deal of the century. However, at the time, it was primarily an intuition of Gates that was shared neither by Kildall nor even by Gates's colleagues at Microsoft. The company was still small with minimal resources. These resources were stretched out trying to meet the current demand for its products and services. Its expertise revolved around BASIC, and not necessarily operating systems. Moreover, Microsoft signed on to supply an operating system in just 3 months, without having any program in hand or any ongoing effort to develop one. At the same time, IBM had a reputation for flirting with the personal computer business without any real vision or commitment. It had already not completed three previous personal computer projects. The firm was primarily committed to its main business in mainframe computers. If the firm lost interest in the personal computer market, Microsoft's investment in QDOS would be for naught. Indeed, the IBM executive negotiating with Gates warned, "I've been at IBM a long time, and I make a lot of proposals, but not many of them get implemented. Don't get your hopes up."[23] Moreover, IBM entered into fairly strict nondisclosure and other agreements with suppliers. These agreements appeared threatening to small firms and could prove costly should suppliers lapse in service or confidentiality.

Thus, hitching onto the IBM bandwagon, with minimum security, was initially an act of faith—faith in a vision of pervasive home computing. Gates had plenty of vision, together with an unwavering determination to realize that vision whatever the costs. When the Altair first came out, Gates commented, "MITS didn't understand the importance of it. Nobody did. But we knew people in schools everywhere would have these computers."[24] Even in the mid-1970s, when there were barely a hundred personal computers, Gates claimed his vision was to have "a computer on every desk and in every home."[25] This vision was born of the realization that "the PC, along with great software, can become sort of the ultimate tool dealing with not just text, but numbers and pictures, and eventually, even difficult things like motion video. Paul and I would . . . always say that there were no limits."[26]

Nevertheless he believed that software was more critical than hardware. He said of this difference, "When you have the microprocessor doubling in power every 2 years, in a sense you can think of computer power as almost free. So you ask, why be in the business of making something that is almost free? What is the scarce resource? What is it that limits being able to get value out of that infinite computing power? Software."[27]

Finally, MS-DOS was not just a carbon copy of CP/M. To begin with, Tim Paterson had already designed QDOS to run on a 16-bit processor. At that time CP/M was not available for such processors. Gates recruited Paterson to work on modifying the program for IBM. With Paterson's help, Microsoft made numerous modifications to the software that made it more intuitive and provided a better file storage system. DOS succeeded over CP/M not only because of the IBM contract but also because it was more user-friendly, more timely, and lower priced than CP/M. In this market as in so many others, market leadership went not to the pioneer of operating systems, Kildall, nor even to the inventor of the DOS framework, Paterson, but to the one who envisioned and persisted in exploiting the mass market, Gates.

Gates's vision of the mass market for computers so consumed him that his entire life revolved around Microsoft, programming new software for new personal computers. His subsequent success with DOS, Windows, Microsoft Office, and other programs was due to his wholehearted determination to be the world leader in providing the best software for personal computers. Like Gillette, Eastman, Ford, and other persistent visionaries before him, Gates was successful due neither solely nor primarily to luck—nor was Gates a pioneer of operating systems. As in the other examples described earlier, pioneering and luck had little to do with ultimate success. Vision and persistence played the major role.[28]

how long to persist?

At this point, an entrepreneur or manager may ask a highly pertinent question. How long should one persist in an effort? It is a pervasive question that managers constantly face when dealing with both major and minor responsibilities. When exactly should one start or stop a task, enter or quit a market, buy or sell a stake? On the one hand, this is the million dollar question. There is no simple, general answer that serves for all times and places. The right answer depends on good judgment in a particular situation. However, consideration of several issues may enlighten the answer to this difficult question. Here we discuss three of these issues: role of vision, product takeoff, and the dynamics of technological change.

ROLE OF VISION

Consider some of the histories reviewed above. Many of the visionaries we studied believed so passionately in the market potential of their vision, that they would not entertain the idea of quitting. Conviction in their vision motivated their persistent endeavors. Specifically, they saw the mass need for a particular product and believed that a technology, if fully realized, would serve that need. For example, Gillette saw that a disposable blade would completely obviate the tedium and inconvenience that millions endured while personally sharpening their razors. P&G realized that an inexpensive disposable diaper would be much more convenient and comfortable than the cloth diapers then in vogue. Sony's cofounder, Masaru Ibuka, realized that a convenient, inexpensive video recorder would find wide appeal among households. In these and other cases, overcoming technological hurdles was the challenge that these people faced. Their vision suggested what solution to strive for, while strong belief in that vision provided the motivation and the reason to persist.

PRODUCT TAKEOFF

For radically new products, three factors can influence the time and likelihood of the product's takeoff and success: price relative to introductory price, market penetration, and time since introduction. To understand this, we explain the concept of takeoff and the results obtained from our analysis of over 40 consumer durables, such as cell phones, camcorders, and satellite TV systems.[29]

Our historical analysis of these products shows that most products pass through a life cycle with typical patterns (see Figure 6-5). Initially, when the category is first introduced, sales are low. They stay low for several years, growing only slowly. The main reason is that the new category does not offer superior benefits per dollar relative to alternative, typically mature products that consumers use for similar needs. During this time, the new product's quality improves and the price drops steadily. The price and quality of rival mature products in the market may not have similar improvements in quality or decreases in price.

As this process continues, the new category reaches a point at which it offers superior performance to any other product in the market. At that point, its sales soar and the product takes off. The product's sales grow more than 400 percent in a single year and continue to grow dramatically for several years. The product rapidly penetrates the market. After several years of growth and market penetration, improvements in product quality are no longer substantial, market penetration tapers off, declines in price level off, and growth slows down. The new product enters the early maturity stage of its life cycle.

While some of these features of the product life cycle are well known, our analysis gives some precise statistics about the dynamics between these stages, and provides a formal model to estimate the time to takeoff. Of the various stages in the product life cycle, the time to takeoff is one of the most critical because the product seems inferior to competing products, growth is slow, and profits are often negative. There may be enormous pressure on managers to pull the plug on the new product. Knowing how similar products have fared may provide managers with some indices with which to evaluate their own performance.

Our historical analysis of more than 40 consumer durables provides the following indices of performance:

• Time to takeoff has been declining substantially over the decades. For example, prior to World War II it was 18 years, but after World War II it was about 6 years. In recent years it has dropped to 5 years.
• Market penetration at takeoff is about 3 percent. Here again

Figure 6-5. The Product Life Cycle

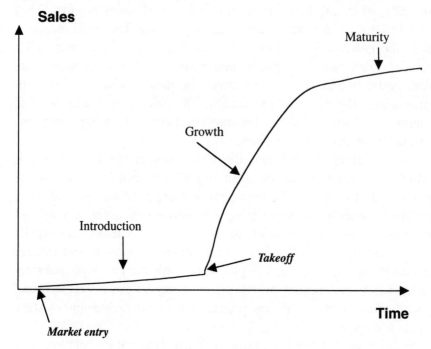

this number has been declining over the decades. It was 4 percent before World War II but about 2 percent after.
• Prices fall steadily with time, even prior to takeoff. As such, in
more recent decades, the price at takeoff is about 63 percent of
the price at introduction.

Using this information, we have developed a model that can estimate the likelihood of a new product category taking off, and the
year and price at which that might occur. Figure 6-6 provides an
illustration of the model's output for one category, depending on the
price drops that the manager implements. Managers can estimate
this model for a sample of products that resemble the one they are
handling. They can then include the values of price, penetration, and
year of introduction into this model, and determine the likely date
and probability of its takeoff. If the new product does not take off
several years past its predicted time, managers should seriously consider pulling the plug on the venture.

Figure 6-6. Marginal Probability of Takeoff for Three Annual Price Reductions

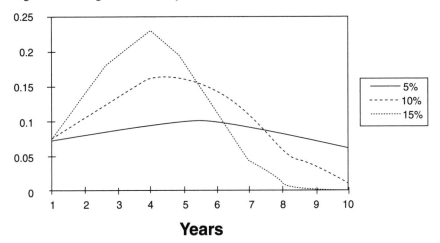

Years

Source: Peter N. Golder and Gerard J. Tellis, "Will It Ever Fly? Modeling the Take-off of Really New Consumer Durables," *Marketing Science*, 16, 3, 1997, 267.

Discussions with managers suggest that they are frequently under pressure to show early results for new products, typically in the form of an early product takeoff. However, radically new products take an average of 5 to 6 years to take off *after market introduction*. It may take many more years to *develop and introduce* a new product, as the examples we discussed illustrate. Under pressure, managers might prematurely pull the plug on new products. Thus for new products, use of historical experience from similar products may provide guidelines in determining when to persist and when to stop.

DYNAMICS OF TECHNOLOGICAL INNOVATION

Historical research over the last two decades has shown that the technology that underlies products may itself pass through life cycles with certain distinct patterns. In particular, these patterns may appear as sequential S-curves when one plots improvement, in benefits per dollar against time, of an older and newer technology.

To appreciate this phenomenon, consider Figure 6-7 in which the older technology is T_1 and the new technology T_2. T_2 emerges at some point (*a*) during the maturity of the older technology, T_1. Initially, because of problems implementing the technology, T_2's bene-

Figure 6-7. Dynamics of Technological Innovation

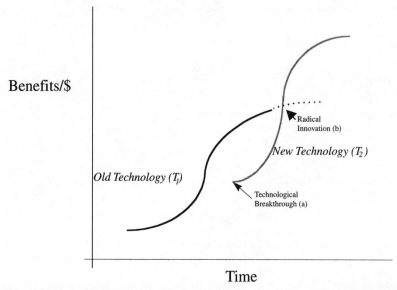

Benefits/$

Radical
Innovation (b)

New Technology (T₂)

Old Technology (T₁)

Technological
Breakthrough (a)

Time

Adapted from Rajesh Chandy and Gerard J. Tellis, "Organizing for Radical Product Innovation," *Journal of Marketing Research*, 35, November, 1998, p. 474–487.

fits per dollar are inferior to those of T_1. However, as researchers learn about T_2 and begin to work with it, T_2 begins to improve rapidly in consumer benefits per dollar. It then ascends its own S-curve. A point comes (*b*) when T_2 may pass the existing technology, T_1, in benefits per dollar. If a new product is introduced into the market, its sales may take off at or a little after this point. Sales of the old products based on the old technology begin a corresponding decline. As time passes, T_2 ceases to improve substantially, and sales based on the new product slow down. If another technology emerges, the cycle may repeat itself.

When a technology is old, it may initially appear much superior to a new technology in terms of benefits offered. That would be any point to the left of *b*. This situation occurs because of the decades of research into and experience with the old technology. But the older technology may not be improving much with further research. In contrast, a new technology may appear inferior, but it may be improving much faster.

For example, consider the case of razors and blades at the turn of the century. Initially, the blades made of sheet metal were much inferior to those made with the old technology. But the old technology was also quite mature, and despite decades of experience, could not solve the problem of consumers having to sharpen their blades every so often. Nickerson's research on the new technology using sheet metal showed steady improvements in the quality of the blade. Because such blades were inexpensive, they did not have to be preserved and regularly sharpened. Thus investments in the new technology seemed to be more rewarding per dollar invested than investments in the old technology.

The S-curves of technological change suggest some important practical principles for managers. They need to consider (1) whether their products are based on an old or a new technology and (2) whether improvements per dollar invested in research are more productive with the old or new technology. Persistence with a technology is particularly relevant when a technology is newer, seems inferior to, but is improving faster than an existing technology. On the other hand, persistence may be imprudent when working with a technology that is old, improves slowly, or does not improve at all, even if it appears superior to a newer rival technology.[30]

In conclusion, while persistence is a subjective trait, it is not one that managers or entrepreneurs need to exhibit blindly, pursuing their goals with equal intensity in every situation. Persistence must be guided by a vision of the mass market and motivated by belief in that vision. It can be specifically informed by research on the histories of similar new products and the dynamics of technological change. While it is impossible to know the right decision with certainty, in general, it is better to err on the side of persistence, especially if it is for a new product with a potentially large mass market. When new products do take off, sales increase many times over several years. The profits from such increases are huge, and can sustain innovation and investment for greater rewards in the future. Overall, the downside of failure in such cases tends to be several times smaller than the upside of success.

summary

The examples in this chapter underscore the following important principles:

- At the root of enduring market leaders lies a vision of serving the mass market. However, realizing that vision is quite uncertain and fraught with many hurdles and setbacks. The road to realization is extremely hard and often very long.
- Two problems inhibit persistence and may lead to premature termination of projects: a misplaced belief in luck and a futile hope for a major breakthrough.
- In casual observation, successful projects often appear to be the result of chance events that favored lucky entrepreneurs.
- Detailed studies of market evolution suggest that luck plays a minimal role. True, combinations of people and events create problems and suggest solutions. However, it requires vision to spot those solutions and persistence to work for them.
- After many decades, new products may appear to be the fruit of one or a few major breakthroughs.
- Detailed study of the path of success suggests that success is the fruit of a series of minor solutions often made by numerous people over time. Each of these solutions builds on a previous one. Progress occurs from step to minor step, from day to day, and from hour to hour.
- Market leaders are firms that have the will to persist in their efforts through seemingly insurmountable obstacles, slow progress, and long time periods.

the need for relentless innovation

In the world today, technology is constantly changing. Consumer tastes, too, are constantly changing, sometimes triggered by new technology. Changes in technology and consumer tastes cause markets to be in a state of constant flux. Old markets die out, new markets emerge, or multiple markets merge into a new one. Thus markets today are constantly evolving. In this context, enduring market leadership is not guaranteed. Rather, long-term leadership requires continuous innovation. Firms must have the will to change their products, their attitudes, and their marketing to maintain leadership.

Innovation is important when a firm plans to enter a market with a new product. The product may not yet fully realize the firm's vision and may need many improvements. But innovation is equally important when a firm is successful and dominates its category. The more successful and profitable a firm, the more competitors try to get a share of its market. Competitors may develop innovations of their own or try to improve on the dominant firm's design. Unless a firm is vigilant and innovative, it will soon lose its leadership to more innovative competitors.

Two attitudes within firms restrict the relentless pursuit of innovation: complacency and fear of cannibalizing existing products.

First, the very success that attracts competitors may lull a dominant firm into complacency. Managers of a dominant firm might begin to believe that their current products are beyond the reach of competitors or that their technological prowess is unassailable. This attitude may limit innovation. The more dominant a firm's position, the more complacent it may get, and the more likely it is to be surprised by innovative competitors.

Second, fear of cannibalizing existing products can become a major hindrance to innovation. New products, especially if they are based on new technology, render a firm's current products obsolete. But firms are reluctant to see their current products die, because of their emotional and financial investments in building up those products. Even when a firm has successfully developed a promising new technology, it may be reluctant to deploy it because the firm fears it will cannibalize the sales and profits from its existing products. Such an attitude may delay important innovations. Worse still, it may kill off the innovation process necessary for new products and sustained leadership.[1]

Yet firms must be willing to innovate relentlessly to maintain their market leadership. Successful innovation comes from a culture that must be deeply ingrained in the firm. Senior managers must strongly support if not primarily instill this culture. They must also make sure that the culture permeates throughout the organization, even to the lowest levels. A strong component of this culture is the fear of obsolescence. Indeed firms that thrive on innovation are acutely aware of their vulnerability to technological change.

The dynamics of three markets illustrate these principles. In particular, various epochs in Gillette's history provide dramatic proof of the need for relentless innovation, the hindrances to innovation, and the costs that must be borne to make innovations successful. Gillette's experience prior to the 1930s illustrates how complacency with early success can result in arrogance and almost in a loss of market leadership. In contrast, Gillette's modern experience shows how willingness to cannibalize leading brands can lead to a series of successful innovations. The second example shows how Intel cannibalizes current products to generate a positive cycle of lower prices, higher quality, and better profits. The third example—the case of the web browser market—shows how constant rapid innovation is more critical than early market entry.

stagnation from complacency and arrogance

Once William Nickerson mastered the design and production of the Gillette disposable blade, sales increased rapidly every year. Nickerson kept improving the design, while supervising the expansion of manufacturing facilities to keep up with demand. Numerous competitors jumped in to get a share of this fast-growing market. However, because the Gillette Company controlled the original patent as well as patents on subsequent improvements, it stopped imitators by threat of or actual legal action. Thus, rivals could not match the basic Gillette design until its initial patent expired in 1921. Even World War I did not stop the company's growth. On the contrary, the Gillette Company popularized self-shaving by having the U.S. government buy Gillette's razors and blades for its troops. When soldiers came back home from the war, they took the habit of self-shaving national, spurring further growth in sales. Through 1926, Gillette's growth was so strong that an investment in the initial company stock would have grown more than 100 times. Moreover, Gillette dominated the safety razor market without any serious competition. Unfortunately, such success seems to have led to complacency.

In 1926, Henry Gaisman designed and patented a disposable two-edged blade called Probak. Gaisman was no amateur in the shaving market. He was chairman of the Autostrop Safety Razor Company and had filed his first patents for safety razor systems even before King C. Gillette. While Gillette's innovation took off, Gaisman persisted in the market, competing as an underdog. By the mid-1920s, his company was about one-tenth the size of the Gillette Company. He also kept developing novel innovations in this and other categories. Gaisman's latest innovation, the Probak blade, was like Gillette's, except that its center was a little less brittle so the blades did not crack when tightened in the razor. Shrewdly, he designed the Probak blades to fit Gillette's razor handle as well as his own. However, the Gillette blade could not fit into the Probak razor (see Figure 7-1). With this innovation, Gaisman proposed a merger of the companies. When negotiations over the next few years failed, Gaisman threatened to market the Probak.

Gillette's directors ordered a new blade design to combat the Probak threat. However, through foresight or spying, Gaisman co-opted elements of the Gillette design and patented his own improved design for the Probak. With that move, Gaisman upped his demand to 25 percent of Gillette shares for a merger of the two companies. When Gillette introduced its new product, Gaisman threatened to sue for patent infringement. Gillette's directors were so confident of their market position and their technological leadership that they challenged him to do so. In a public letter in March 1930, Gillette's chairman boasted, "If anyone feels that our company has infringed on his patent rights, we suggest he come into court. We are not only prepared for any legal controversy, but we invite it."[2] Perhaps complacency had given way to arrogance.

Gaisman sued. He also introduced Probak to the market, where it fared well. The financial markets sent a clear signal, as they saw that Gillette now had competition. The price of Gillette's stock dropped 40 percent despite the efforts of Gillette's directors to boost it, while the price of AutoStrop's stock rose. As the case dragged on, Gillette's directors grew wary of letting a judge rule on what no longer seemed a clear-cut case. They agreed to settle for a merger of the two companies. However, in the course of reviewing each other's books, Gaisman learned that Gillette had inflated the company's performance for several years. Gillette had a policy of billing goods to foreign subsidiaries at higher than cost price and treating these sales as completed transactions even though the subsidiaries had not yet sold them to the public. As such, the company's dividends and the director's bonuses were based on inflated sales. By leveraging that damaging information, Gaisman forced Gillette's directors to settle on far more favorable terms to him than what he had earlier proposed. One result was that Gaisman won a controlling share of the company. A year later, under threat of a shareholder lawsuit, Gillette's directors resigned, and Gaisman took over as chairman of the Gillette Safety Razor Company.

This early history of the Gillette Company reveals a fascinating

Figure 7-1. Gillette and Probak Competition over Blade Designs

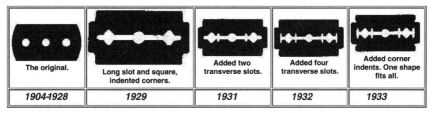

Gillette vs. Probak Timeline

1928	April 1929	Nov. 1929	Dec. 1929	Mar. 1930	May 1930	July 1930	Oct. 1930
Probak Company formed.	NEW GILLETTE patent filed (3-hole blade).	Probak blade Trademarks filed.	Probak razor patent filed - includes slotted blade.	New Gillette Razor announced. Gillette slotted blade patent filed.	Revised Gaisman (Probak) patent filed.	NEW GILLETTE patent filed (slotted blade).	Merger of Gillette and AutoStrop.

Gillette Blade Evolution

The original.	Long slot and square, indented corners.	Added two transverse slots.	Added four transverse slots.	Added corner indents. One shape fits all.
1904-1928	1929	1931	1932	1933

Source: Robert Waits, (1990), and http://www.geocities.com/safetyrazors/blades/ DEBladePage.htm. Reprinted with permission of Robert Waits.

angle to the corporation's psychology. Growth, near monopoly, and immense success created an aura of invincibility among the directors of the company. They grew complacent and slackened off enough on innovation so that a lowly competitor was able to take the innovative lead, patent a clever design, and then sue Gillette for patent infringement. Seemingly, complacency led to arrogance, to careless decisions, and ultimately to management's loss of control. Subsequently, the Gillette Company itself survived through the vision, persistence, and leadership of Gaisman and the people he chose to run the company.[3]

cannibalizing leading brands

Gaisman took over just when the United States was entering the Great Depression. During that difficult economic time, price became a major criterion for consumers' choice of shaving systems. While Gillette continued its research into better products, it focused on producing low-priced blades to keep low-priced competitors at bay.

The Depression was followed by World War II, and when the war ended, Gillette's sales flourished. With improving sales and profits, the company's focus turned again to research to develop innovative products and stay ahead of the competition. In particular, sales of electric razors were growing rapidly and threatened to severely reduce the wet shaving market. Competitors within the wet shaving market were preparing superior products, while one in particular, Schick, launched a vigorous advertising campaign that attacked Gillette's position.

Gillette's research in the 1950s revealed that silicone coating on a carbon-steel blade reduced pressure against the skin and whiskers. As a result, it gave a shave vastly smoother than current blades. Some company executives thought this innovation was the most important since that of King Gillette's double-edged disposable blade. In 1960, Gillette introduced the innovation as the Super Blue Blade to differentiate it from its then leading brand, the Blue Blade. Despite modest claims in its advertising and a premium price, the introduction was a hit. Sales soared. In 6 months, Super Blue accounted for a quarter of the company's sales. By the end of 1961, Gillette captured 70 percent of total blade sales and almost 90 percent of the double-edged blade market. Gillette had reestablished its complete dominance of the market and seemed invincible. Once again, success seems to have led to complacency.

In 1962, Wilkinson Sword introduced a stainless-steel blade, Super Sword-Edge, that lasted three times longer than Gillette's carbon-steel blade. Wilkinson Sword was a British company that was originally in the cutlery and garden tools business. In fact, Wilkinson first introduced its stainless-steel blade to promote its line of premium-grade garden tools. The company introduced the stainless-steel technology because it provided more long-lasting blades than those produced from carbon steel, as were Gillette's. To overcome the problem of roughness with stainless steel, Wilkinson Sword also coated its blades with a synthetic compound as Gillette did for the Super Blue. The Super Sword-Edge was a tremendous hit. Consumers rushed to try it, and the supply was easily consumed wherever the blade was available. In the United Kingdom, the blade quickly captured 15 percent of the market. Worldwide, Gillette's market share fell 20 percent due to Wilkinson's entry. But Wilkinson could not keep up with market demand. At one point, Wilkinson even limited blade distribution in the United States to retailers who also purchased at least one unit of its entire line of garden tools. Moreover, Wilkinson saw no need to advertise in a market where it could not even supply the current demand. Once established competitors saw the potential of stainless-steel blades, they entered too. Gillette's share fell to 50 percent in little over a year. Gillette was shaken.

The irony was that Gillette was aware of the stainless-steel technology all along. Indeed Wilkinson had to license the technology for coating the stainless-steel blade from Gillette, which held the patents. Gillette had considered introducing the stainless-steel blade, but had not done so for three strategic reasons. First, it would have rendered obsolete much of its manufacturing capacity for carbon-steel blades like the Blue Blade and the Super Blue Blade. Second, the material and production costs of stainless-steel blades were twice as high as that of carbon-steel blades. Third, the blades lasted more than three times as long as carbon-steel blades, thus reducing consumers' frequency of blade purchases. So it did not make sense to managers to introduce a costlier technology that yielded lower profits. Being an outsider, Wilkinson Sword faced no such drawbacks and challenged Gillette with the most serious competition it faced in the postwar era. Wilkinson Sword did not destroy Gillette because it had not developed sufficient manufacturing capacity to fully exploit the demand. Also, it seemed to be more concerned with using stainless-steel blades to promote the company's high-margin garden tools, rather than building a business selling blades.

The Wilkinson experience galvanized Gillette to innovation even at the cost of cannibalizing its own established products. Gillette introduced its own stainless-steel blade in 1964 to stem further losses in market share. Gillette's stainless-steel blade did cannibalize Super Blue's sales, but it could not easily win back customers it had lost to rivals. So the company had to look into more advanced technologies to regain market share and prevent another debacle like that of the stainless-steel blade.

Following many years of research, Gillette introduced the Trac II twin-head blade and razor in 1972. This time the company proceeded with the launch even though it led to its older successful brands losing share to the twin-blade technology. Then, while Trac II was still in its prime, Gillette introduced ATRA pivoting head razors in 1977, knowing that this product in turn would cannibalize Trac II sales. In 1976, Gillette was threatened by the imminent entry of Bic disposable razors. Gillette continued to innovate by introducing the Good News twin disposable razor, even though the cheaper disposable cut into short-term profits. Each of these moves was expensive but well rewarded, with Gillette retaining dominance of the razor and blade market and even expanding its share.

In 1989, Gillette introduced the next big innovation, Sensor, a razor with twin blades that move independently. This innovation gave such a good shave that it began to reverse the loss of market share from less profitable disposables. Finally, even though Sensor was not threatened, in 1998, Gillette introduced Mach 3, a new shaving system that had three pivoting blades. Each of these new introductions cannibalized sales of older brands. However, by innovating ahead of competitors, Gillette maintained its dominance of the razor and blade market (see Figure 7-2).

In retrospect, most of these innovations were huge successes. At the time though, each innovation was a risky venture. If it succeeded, it ran the risk of cannibalizing Gillette's older brands without guaranteeing a higher overall market share, or a higher profit margin in the case of disposable razors. If it failed, it ran the risk of wasting huge expenditures in research and development. For example, Gillette spent $740 million in research and development for the Mach 3. This amount does not include the hundreds of millions of dollars spent to effectively market the product. Such huge investments can heighten the fear of failure and easily dampen the spirit of innovativeness within a firm. That is not what happened at Gillette.

The atmosphere within Gillette reveals how it succeeds at innovation. There is a passion for the product, while innovation is almost an obsession. At any time Gillette has over a dozen shaving products in the works. The company uses hundreds of its employees to personally test its new shaving systems. They analyze the consumers' shaving style, the number of strokes used, the smoothness of the shaved skin, and the output in terms of shaved hair. One manager working on prototypes told a reporter of his dedication to product

Figure 7-2. Interbrand Cannibalization of Gillette's Products

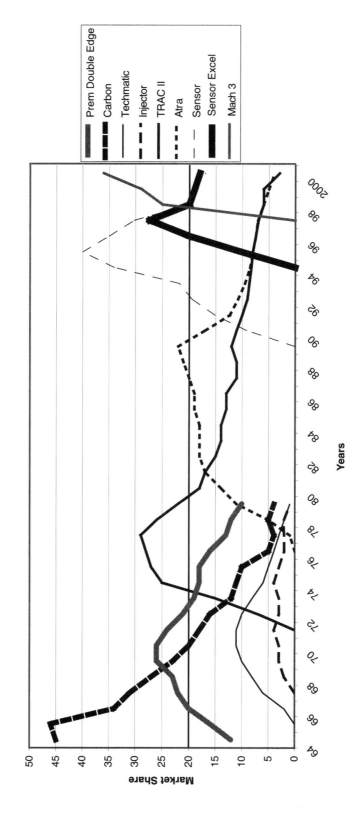

Gillette Razors Market Share

Sources: Charles M. Kummel and Jay E. Klompmaker (1982), "The Gillette Company"; Case No. 9-581-619, Boston, MA: Harvard Business School International Case Clearing House; Pankaj Ghemawat and Benjamin Esty (1992), "Gillette's Launch of Sensor," Case No. 9-792-028, Harvard Business School Publishing Division, Boston, MA; Prudential-Bache Securities Analyst Reports; Information Resources Inc., Chain Drug Review; Drug Store News; and authors' estimates.

testing, explaining, "We bleed so you'll get a good shave at home. This is my 27th year. I came here my first week. Haven't missed a day of shaving."[4]

A vice president of the technology laboratory described Gillette's attention to detail in the research for a better product, saying, "We test the blade edge, the blade guard, the angle of the blades, the balance of the razor, the length, the heft, the width. What happens to the chemistry of the skin? What happens to the hair when you pull it? What happens to the follicle? We own the face. We know more about shaving than anybody. I don't think obsession is too strong a word."[5] Indeed, there is perhaps no laboratory in the world that knows more about facial hair than Gillette's.

This emphasis on research and development promotes Gillette's sustained dominance of this market and its high profitability. It has diversified into numerous other markets so that razors and blades now account for only a third of its sales, but they still account for almost two-thirds of its profits.

Figure 7-2 reveals an amazing phenomenon. On the surface, Gillette's market share would appear stable at around 65 percent. Beneath the surface, turmoil is rife, as a constant stream of new brands introduces new technologies, creates new brand identities, and renders older, successful brands obsolete. The casual observer may see great stability in market shares. If such an observer were to mistake Gillette as a pioneer, he or she may easily conclude that pioneers have long-lived advantages. But the truth is that firms in this market face intense competition, insecurity, and a constant flux in market shares. Success stays with the firm that can keep ahead through relentless innovation. Through past missteps, Gillette learned that complacency with success is a formula for disaster. Continued success lies in its striving to find innovative products that make existing products obsolete. Relentless innovation must be its lifeblood. It is the engine that enables it to sustain its dominance of the market for shaving systems.[6]

feedback loop for continuous innovation

Intel's experience shows how constant innovation not only keeps competitors at bay, but generates profits for further innovation. The market for microprocessors is much more dynamic than that for shaving systems. Figure 7-3 shows the pattern of sales for successive generations of Intel's chips. Each time Intel introduces a new generation of chip, sales of the older generation begin to level off and then decline. This sales history shows that each new generation of chips cannibalizes sales of the old one. Also, in every case, Intel controls the timing and characteristics of the chip that it introduces. The invention of each chip requires the research effort of a large number of scientists and engineers over many years. Intel must retool, if not entirely redesign a factory, for the production of new chips. Moreover, especially at the start, Intel was almost a monopolist in the market for computer chips. So why does Intel cannibalize its own products?

The most obvious reason is the pressure of competitors. This is the same reason that motivates Gillette to embark on innovation. Because of Intel's highly profitable business, various competitors have entered the market and worked hard to steal market share from the firm. They too invest resources to make chips that may have comparable or superior attributes to those of Intel. For example, Motorola and IBM have been long-term giants in the industry. In addition, AMD is a smaller though a little older competitor that has striven to exactly duplicate the capabilities of Intel's chips through licensing, reverse engineering, or innovations of its own. Reverse engineering is a process by which a follower designs a new product to perform the same functions as the patented product designed by the technological leader in the field, without infringing on any of the leader's patents. To do so, the follower recruits engineers with no knowledge of the leader's design, to develop a fresh design by observing only the inputs and outputs of the leader's product. By using this process, it took AMD 9 years to copy Intel's 286 chip, 6 years to copy Intel's 386, 4 years to copy the 486, and less than a year to introduce the AMD-K6, a competitor to Intel's Pentium. More recently, AMD has even introduced chips that are superior to Intel's on some performance dimensions.

Throughout its history, Intel has known that failure to innovate will allow competitors to take the lead in introducing new chips. The company will then fall behind in market share and sales. With loss of sales comes the loss of the revenue and profits necessary to drive the innovation to stay ahead of the competition. This market

Figure 7-3. Life Cycles of Successive Generations of Intel's Chips

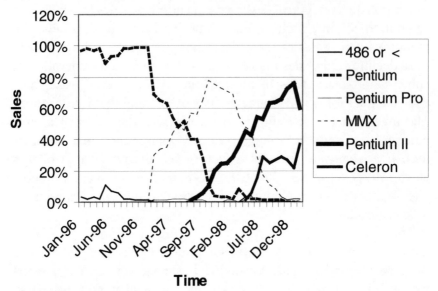

Source: Pacific Crest Securities.

is so competitive that failure to lead with the next generation of chips could doom a firm to obsolescence and rapid decline. As an oft-repeated quote in the industry says, "We must eat our own lunch before others do so." Or perhaps more apt is Andy Grove's description of the phenomenon, "Only the paranoid survive."[7]

However, there is another equally compelling reason for relentless innovation in this market. Intel grew from the vision and intensity of its founders, Noyce and Moore, to compress more transistors onto a single chip. Moore predicted that the computing power of chips would double every 12 months. (Later he revised this prediction to every 18 months. The prediction has turned out to be fairly accurate, and is known as Moore's law.) This activity leads to many important benefits. First, each new chip becomes more powerful. More powerful chips can do the same tasks as before in less time. More powerful chips can also perform more complex tasks such as graphic displays, 3-D visuals, video, or voice recognition. Second, as chips become smaller, the products in which they are used also become smaller, more portable, and more useful. Third, smaller chips use smaller amounts of costly, high-purity raw materials, such as silicon wafers. Thus, product costs come down steadily with greater compression of transistors. Fourth, smaller chips also use less electricity, thus lowering the cost of operation. Fifth, as single chips incorporate multiple functions, there is less need for workers to manually wire together multiple chips. Thus the entire assembly takes less time and products are more reliable.

Thus compression of transistors leads to smaller, faster, more powerful, better-quality, and cheaper chips. As a result, computers that use these chips are much more valuable than an older generation of computers. These improved attributes attract a new set of consumers, expanding the market for computers, and thus for chips. In the past, as Intel introduced new chips, its revenues increased rapidly. At the same time, its costs per unit also declined. Thus Intel's managers realized that innovation provided the twin benefits of increasing revenues and decreasing costs, leading to rapidly increasing profits. Rather than relax in their success, the managers decided to reinvest the profits into more research to maintain the tempo and productivity of innovation. These profits helped support more research for better designs, in particular, greater compression. Thus the cycle of progress continued at a faster pace, turning Intel into a colossus.

Similarly, from Noyce's and Moore's launch of Fairchild Semiconductor in 1957 through 1967, sales had grown to $130 million and the work force to 15,000 employees. When Noyce and Moore founded Intel, the company's sales grew from $2672 in 1968 to $66 million in just 5 years. Rather than pay high dividends, Intel's founders reinvested the profits into research and development and production. The research enabled Intel to produce three new generations of chips, the 8008, the 8080, and the 8086/8. Impressed by the quality of Intel's products and its innovative spirit, IBM chose the 8088 as the microprocessor to power its first personal computer. When sales of personal computers took off, so did Intel's sales. Fired by the spirit of its founders, Intel continued to invest profits into research on ever-more valuable chips, for an ever-growing mass market. It stayed ahead of competitors, always leading the industry with a new generation of chips every few years. Indeed, it was these successive generations of chips that triggered lower prices, higher power, and increasing sales of personal computers. By early 2001, Intel's stock market value exceeded that of IBM and dwarfed that of Fairchild Semiconductor.

The irony of Intel's history is that it grew in an industry dominated by giants that existed for decades before Intel was even formed. Moreover, the founders of Intel, Noyce and Moore, worked for some of the firms it displaced. They left only because senior managers lacked vision and failed to appreciate the importance of relentless innovation. Those managers were blind to the pace of innovation, even though the founders of Intel impressed on them its value by argument and results. This chronology of events shows that prior position in an industry is not a key determinant of enduring success. But single-minded devotion to innovation and a determination to pursue it relentlessly are critical.[8]

speedy response to innovation

Markets involving the Internet, electronic commerce, or high-technology products evolve very quickly. Analysts believe that if speed is so important, then entry timing must be equally important. They think firms must enter quickly, if not first, to get a strong position in these markets. Thus, such analysts believe that order of market entry is even more critical in the new economy.

In fact, there is a big difference between strategic speed and order of entry. Technology changes fast. Firms move quickly. Competitive dynamics is measured in weeks or days, not in months or years. But that does not mean a firm must be first to market or it will lose everything. In these fast-moving markets, consumers' loyalties also change fast, and so do market shares. Indeed, a late entrant that supplies distinctly superior goods could see its market share rise quickly, even to 100 percent. Conversely, a pioneer that does not keep up with the pace of innovation could see its market share evaporate overnight. A case in point is the Web browser market. The example shows the speed with which product innovation erases a pioneer's initial leadership and the futility of being first with an inferior product.

As described in Chapter 5, after Berners-Lee designed the Web, he had neither the time nor the resources to systematically improve the browsers he had developed for it. His first browser, called *WorldWideWeb*, was graphically based. But it ran only on the NeXT personal computer, which was not popular. His second browser, a line-mode program, would work on any computer. But it was hard to use and never took off. Wishing to speed the adoption of the Web, Berners-Lee encouraged the development of better browsers, primarily among university students. As a result, in the early 1990s, developing browsers became the favorite research project of computer science students at various universities. Several browsers became available to the public, including the Lynx 2.0 (University of Kansas), Cello (Cornell University), Erwise (Helsinki University), and Viola (Berkeley) (see Table 7-1).

In 1992, the Software Development Group at the National Center for Supercomputing Applications (NCSA), at the University of Illinois at Urbana-Champaign, was developing software to enable researchers to collaborate over networks. Dave Thomson, a member of the group, discovered the CERN site on the still small World Wide Web, and its available browsers. He brought it to the attention of his boss, Joseph Hardin, who ran the software group, and to Marc Andreessen, a student worker in the group.[9] Andreessen, suspecting that user-friendly Web programs would have wide appeal, immediately immersed himself in the task of improving upon the available browsers. He enlisted the help of Eric Bina, a superb programmer at the center. Both worked at an intense pace to accomplish their goal quickly. They worked well together, playing complementary roles. Andreessen served more as an architect, evaluating available programs, tapping into public discourse on these programs, and recommending new features. Bina, on the other hand, served as the programmer who wrote code and solved various technical problems.

Their collaboration is colorfully described by author George Gilder:

> Every Gates has to have his Paul Allen (or Jobs, his Steve Wozniak). Andreessen's is Bina—short and wiry where Andreessen is ursine, cautious where he is cosmic, focused where he is expansive, apprehensive where he is evangelical, bitwise where he is prodigal with bandwidth, ready to stay home and write the code where Andreessen is moving on to conquer the globe. Wildly contrasting but com-

Table 7-1. Selected Early Browsers

Date Available	Program	Firm	Network System	Platform	Mode
1989	Lynx	University of Kansas	Web	UNIX	Screen
		Programmer: Michael Grobe and associates			
1991	WAIS	Thinking Machines Corporation	Local	UNIX	Line
		Programmer: Brewster Kahle			
1991	Gopher	University of Minnesota	Local		Menu
		Programmer: Paul Linder and Mark McCahill			
March 1991	*WorldWideWeb*	CERN	Web	NeXT	Graphical
		Programmer: Tim Berners-Lee			
May 1991	Line-mode browser	CERN	Web	UNIX, DOS	Line
		Programmer: Nicola Pellow and Tim Berners-Lee			
1991	Viola	University of California, Berkeley	Local	UNIX	X-Windows
		Programmer: Pei Wei			
April 1992	Erwise	Helsinki University	Web	UNIX	X-Windows
		Programmer: Ari Lemmke			

Date	Name	Institution	Author	Type	OS	Interface
May 1992	ViolaWWW	University of California, Berkeley	Pei Wei	Web	UNIX	X-Windows
July 1992	Midas	Stanford Linear Accelerator Center	Tony Johnson	Web	UNIX	X-Windows
February 1993	Mosaic	National Center for Supercomputing Applications, University of Illinois	Marc Andreessen and Eric Bina	Web	UNIX	Screen
December 1992	Samba	CERN	Robert Cailliau and Nicola Pellow	Web	Macintosh	Mac-Windows
1992–1993	Cello	Cornell University	Thomas Bruce	Web	Windows	PC-Windows
March 1993	Lynx 2.0	University of Kansas	Lou Montulli	Web	Web	Screen
1993–1995	Arena	Hewlett-Packard	Dave Raggett	Web	UNIX	Graphical
November 1993	Mosaic Final 1.0	National Center for Supercomputing Applications, University of Illinois	Andreessen et al.	Web	Windows	PC-Windows

pletely trusting and complementary, these two—in an inspired siege of marathon code-writing between January
and March 1993—made Mosaic happen.[10]

Together, the two first rewrote the code of Berners-Lee's line-mode
browser to make it run faster. They then greatly enhanced it by in-
corporating a screen mode that allowed for graphics. In a further
refinement they included multimedia capabilities, to produce a new
browser they called Mosaic.

Mosaic represented an advance over available browsers for several
reasons. First, it made a Web page lively, with colors, fonts, and full-
page formatting. Multimedia capabilities allowed links to pictures,
sound, and video. Second, Mosaic allowed users to easily navigate
among Web sites. By positioning a mouse over a hypertext entry,
users could switch to a new Web page with just a click. Third, Mosaic was easy to download, install, learn, and use. Fourth and most
importantly, Andreessen was passionate about improving the program and expanding its adoption to the mass market. He kept in
touch with users, incorporated features people wanted, and improved the program in response to criticism.

Later in 1993, other students were recruited to adapt Mosaic to
the two prevailing major desktop systems, Windows and Macintosh.
The team's efforts paid off, with the rapid and phenomenal success
of Mosaic. Six months after introduction, a million users had downloaded the free software. A year later, 10 million copies of the program were thought to be in use.

Analysts often misstate the reasons for Mosaic's success. Mosaic
was not the first browser. Many browsers preceded it, some such as
Gopher and Lynx by several years. Mosaic was not the first browser
to run off the Web. Berners-Lee's *WorldWideWeb* and his line-mode
browser were the first. Mosaic was not the first browser to run on
the UNIX. Erwise and Viola preceded it. Mosaic was also not the
first Web browser with graphics. ViolaWWW had the ability to do
graphics, animations, and embedded applications (later called ap-
plets). Finally, Mosaic may not even have been the first browser to
run on Microsoft Windows. Cello may have preceded it (see Table
7-1). Indeed, in correspondence to Berners-Lee, Andreessen admitted his disadvantage, noting "I'm starting the game late."[11] Mosaic
succeeded, not because it was the first, but because it was better.

Moreover, Andreessen was committed to constantly improving the program to better serve users.

Many analysts also misstate Andreessen's key role in developing Mosaic. He may not have introduced the idea of developing a browser to NCSA. Thomson probably did. He was not the head of the group that developed Mosaic. Hardin was. He was not the principal programmer. Bina probably was. And he did not run a secret project with other students. Mosaic's development was overt and sanctioned by NCSA. What Andreessen brought to the project was passion about product improvement so as to achieve mass adoption. He kept in touch with newsgroups to incorporate features that people wanted. He listened to criticisms by users and quickly made changes to the program in response. What Andreessen represented at NCSA was a market researcher, innovator, and planner, all in one. Berners-Lee had this to say of Andreessen's passion: "People say that the key innovation in Mosaic was the addition of images, but what I think Marc did really well was make it very easy to install—and he supported it by fixing bugs via e-mail, anytime night or day. You'd send him a bug report, and then two hours later he'd mail you a fix."[12] Competing programs lacked a leader with the same passion for speedy innovation and product improvement.

And speed was important. In the browser market, change rather than permanence became a pattern. Market popularity went from WAIS to Gopher to Mosaic in about 2 years. Moreover, in the next 4 years, market leadership passed from Mosaic to Netscape to Internet Explorer. All these shifts in leadership came swiftly. The unambiguous reason for three of these four shifts was the superior features born of rapid innovation. In the fourth case, the shift from Netscape to Internet Explorer was caused by innovation together with Microsoft's skillful leverage of assets, as we will see in another chapter. Order of market entry seems quite unimportant. On the contrary, it may have been an impediment, hindering a leader from perceiving or attempting to implement the next great change in browser design.[13]

the cycle of innovations

There is an important commonality in the evolution of the three markets described here: the cycle of innovations. No single brand lasts forever. New brands emerge, become popular, lead the market for some time, and then give way to better brands. Figure 7-3 and Table 7-1 illustrate this phenomenon. If data were available, we could draw similar curves for the early razor and browser markets too. Indeed, as we will see in a later chapter, this cycle of innovations holds for the browser market in subsequent years.

The most obvious implication of this phenomenon is the need for relentless innovation. Any wavering in innovation could lead to loss of leadership. Probak and the Super Sword-Edge got a foothold because Gillette hesitated in innovating promptly. Failure to innovate can lead to loss of share and ultimate demise. Intel and Gillette maintain their leadership, not from any pioneering advantage, but primarily from their relentless innovation.

The striking feature is that this pattern holds across substantially different markets in substantially different decades. Blades are a hundred-year-old disposable product that uses moderately sophisticated technology. Microprocessors are a highly sophisticated modern durable product. Browsers are a recent product that belongs to the relatively unique software category. A vast number of categories follow this pattern, including appliances, electronics, detergents, drugs, and medical devices.

The major difference among these categories is in the duration of the cycles. For blades, the cycle lasts about a decade. For microprocessors and software, the cycle lasts just a few years. Moreover, there is scattered evidence that these cycles are becoming shorter in some markets.[14] Thus the need for innovation is greater in more recent times. The strategic issue of speed raised by analysts of digital and electronic markets may be somewhat misplaced. The issue is not so much of being first to a new market. Whatever advantage such pioneering may bring will be inevitably short-lived. The issue is one of innovating relentlessly because the market is constantly changing.

The pattern of life cycles also exposes the futility of one of the major barriers to innovation: complacency. As some of the examples here show, even dominant firms with abundant resources—such as Gillette, Intel, and Microsoft—cannot afford to be complacent. Similarly, fear of cannibalizing one's products is completely misplaced. If a leading firm will not cannibalize its own products, some competitor quickly will.

summary

This chapter makes the following key points:

- Technology and markets change constantly, rendering obsolete once successful products. The positions, even of entrenched firms, are quite susceptible to such changes. Thus a dominant firm must be willing to innovate relentlessly in order to sustain its success.
- Two attitudes hinder the relentless pursuit of innovation: complacency with past success and fear of cannibalizing existing products.
- Complacency with past success may lead a firm to believe that it is superior to competitors or has a winning formula that will last forever. Such an attitude leads a firm to ignore or deny promising innovations.
- Fear of cannibalizing existing products arises especially when new products are created to serve markets or functions that are already being served by the firm's current products. Firms are reluctant to see their current products become obsolete because of their emotional and financial investments in building up those products. Such an attitude delays or kills the innovations necessary for new products.
- In contrast, successful innovation comes from a culture that is deeply ingrained in the firm. Senior managers must strongly support this culture and ensure that it permeates throughout the organization.
- A strong motivator for innovation is fear or paranoia that changes in technology or customer tastes can render current products obsolete. Indeed firms that thrive on innovation are acutely aware of their vulnerability to technological innovations introduced by competitors.

organizing for innovation

The previous chapter highlights the need for relentless innovation to maintain market leadership. It shows how attitudes within a firm can be important drivers of such innovation. This chapter describes how key organizational initiatives can greatly enhance the speed and success of a firm's innovation: using autonomy to break up bureaucracy, focusing on emerging markets over current customers, and fostering talent over institutions.

Bureaucracy can be a formidable barrier to innovation. Large successful firms tend to have a large staff to manage their current business. Especially during times of growth and increasing profits, firms tend to hire freely. Management of a large number of employees requires establishing rules, routines, and procedures for evaluating innovations and making decisions, resulting in bureaucracy. Bureaucracy slows the review processes and delays or kills innovations.

Autonomy can be a great antidote to bureaucracy. Autonomy results from the creation of small units with an independent mission, goal, and budget. When entrusted with research, development, and the introduction of new products, these units can quickly identify and respond to emerging markets without interference from central bureaucracies. However, the firm still needs vision to guide the setup and direction of such units.

An important hindrance to radical innovation is managerial pre-occupation with current customers and competitors. As competition in a market heats up, it can create enormous pressure for managers to do their best with the current technology. As a result, managers might get preoccupied with the present technology and customers at the cost of emerging mass markets. This can cause them to overlook promising innovations that enable a firm to leapfrog competitors by harnessing new technologies for emerging mass markets. Thus pre-occupation with the present may lead to loss of a promising future.

An important organizational hindrance to innovation is a firm's emphasis on the institution over individual talent. Such an emphasis may emerge especially after a firm has had a history of success with past innovation. However, institutions do not create successful ideas, people do. A firm's talent is the strongest force it can marshal in pursuit of innovation. Especially in high-technology markets, a firm needs to hire and retain the best talent it can, and motivate them to work together productively. To begin with, a firm can sustain the flame of innovation by regularly hiring fresh talent from the market. It then needs to provide an autonomous and supportive atmosphere to stimulate the fusion and cross-fertilization of ideas. Such an en-vironment is essential to the development of novel ideas for suc-cessful innovation. An equally important challenge for all organi-zations is retaining creative talent. As individuals become famous for their creations, their demand in the market rises, sometimes ex-ponentially. Organizations need to retain them with adequate credit, rewards, and autonomy.

The continuing history of some markets we covered previously illustrates these problems and opportunities in organizing for inno-vation.[1]

innovation to break the bureaucratic mold

The story of Xerox's Palo Alto Research Center (PARC) shows the bureaucratic mold that hinders innovation and the organizational design that can help a firm break out of this mold.

By the late 1960s, Xerox's success with copiers had transformed the firm into a giant, highly profitable corporation, with a virtual monopoly on the copier market. Since copiers were the key product responsible for its growth, Xerox strove to ensure that its copiers remained the very best in the market. Research at the laboratory at Webster, New York, and other facilities focused on fine-tuning the current portfolio of copiers to make them faster, more reliable, and less costly. In its quest to achieve these goals, the firm as a whole did not fully appreciate a maxim of its CEO, Wilson, that initially motivated his adoption of xerography: A firm can only advance so far with its current technology; further growth must come from new technologies. Having seen how xerography rendered coated paper and carbon copying obsolete, Wilson feared that some new technology would arise to make xerography obsolete too. He was particularly concerned about the potential of digital technologies replacing optical imaging.

Wilson expressed this fear to Xerox's president at that time, Peter McColough:

> Look, we're only communicating graphic information. Things that have been written down that you can copy and send from one person to another so they can share that information. But in looking at the future, all information is not going to be graphic. The computer is coming along. The computer handles information in a totally different way, in digital format. And if we're going to be big ten years or twenty years out we've also got to be able to handle information in digital form as well as graphic form.[2]

As such, Wilson was articulating the vision of the paperless "office of the future."

Within Xerox, however, success with copiers had brought a large measure of complacency, bureaucracy, and short-term thinking. Such an atmosphere was more conducive to business as usual than to a creative search for new technologies for the office of the future. The atmosphere at Webster, in particular, was not inspiring. The laboratory was under pressure to meet the goals of bringing to market improved copiers and accessories. So its scientists were narrowly trained and were involved in narrow research pursuits. Nearly all of the research was geared to improving current products. There was little attempt to bring in new research ideas or methods. There was also little exchange of ideas, in the form of visits from outside scholars or visits to other research centers. As such, the center had become insulated from the pace and tempo of research on the outside.

McColough had captured some of Wilson's vision of the future and was eager to get the company into new technologies. He was concerned that Xerox's reliance on perfecting the old technology of optics, for its current line of copiers, would not enable it to withstand competition for more than a decade. Indeed, in 1970, IBM introduced its first copier, ending Xerox's near monopoly of the market, and initiating a period of intense competition. IBM itself had grown to be a giant corporation from its success with computers. At that time, digital and computer technologies held great promise. The market for computers was growing very fast as they were rapidly becoming a key component of the office. Office equipment was Xerox's core market, with its strength in copiers. Thus an entry into computers promised a foothold in another fast-growing market as well as technology to develop innovative products for the office of the future.

To initiate this change, McColough wanted to hire a visionary head for Xerox's research. He had identified such a leader in Peter Goldman, then at Ford. However, Goldman refused to accept the job until John Dessauer, Xerox's current head of research, resigned. Now Dessauer was the first and only "chief scientist" at Xerox. He was the one who had advised Wilson to purchase the rights to dry copying, when the company was still small and was called Haloid. He was also the one who had overseen the research that created the Xerox 914 and helped the company sustain its leadership in the copier market. Thus Dessauer was a celebrated leader and an icon at Xerox. Removing him was no easy task. However, success and age had made him less sensitive to change in the market and the needs of the future. McColough was eager to revitalize Xerox's research climate with new talent and ideas. So he orchestrated Dessauer's retirement. To make the change palatable, McColough requested that the current CEO, Wilson, also resign, together with

Dessauer. Wilson stayed on as chairman of the board, McColough took over as CEO, and Peter Goldman came on board as senior vice president for research and development. This change at the top brought in a new era of research at Xerox. It contained an odd mixture of revolutionary ideas for the future, with a continuation of the incremental improvements for the present.

In order to enter the computer market quickly, McColough made two major investments. First, he decided to purchase a current computer manufacturer. But every one of his offers to major computer manufacturers of the time was rejected. Finally, in seeming desperation, McColough purchased Scientific Data Systems (SDS) for $920 million in 1969. This was a fast-growing but small manufacturer of computers in Southern California. SDS operated in a profitable niche for time-sharing computers. However, it had neither the resources nor the innovativeness to compete with market leaders such as IBM or Digital Equipment Corporation. Moreover, the company was in decline, though McColough did not realize it at the time. In fact, SDS turned out to be a dog. After 6 years of losses and gaining no more than 1 percent of the computer market, Xerox folded the company. That year it took an $84.4 million write-off and recorded its first loss since introducing the Xerox 914.

McColough's second investment was dramatically different in scope, content, and success. He established the Palo Alto Research Center, a research laboratory dedicated to basic research and the development of leading-edge products for the computer age. The idea for the lab came from Goldman after he became unhappy with the purchase of SDS. He conceived of a research lab richly funded and wholeheartedly devoted to advanced research in the basic science of digital technologies. He felt that McColough's goals would be better achieved with such a lab than with the purchase of another second-class computer business. Now Xerox already had an extensive research facility at Webster, employing about 400 people and supported by a large budget of about $70 million. Goldman, however, saw it as a narrow research environment focused on improving current products. He envisioned the new lab as a prestigious center of pathbreaking research, such as AT&T's Bell Labs and IBM's Watson Research Center in Yorktown Heights. Managers at Xerox yearned to have a prestigious research lab such as these well-known ones. So McColough bought into Goldman's proposal. He was impressed not only by the need for research but also by the prestige and publicity that would come from a center devoted to state-of-the-art research. The research center was approved and officially opened on July 1, 1970, in Palo Alto, California. For the next 10 years, Xerox management supported it generously but let it operate independently from any other part of the corporation.

Was the experiment a success? PARC was a tremendous success in terms of the sheer creativity of its innovations. It pioneered many of the greatest technologies of the personal computer age. The list of innovations at PARC is impressive. In hardware, the laser printer, mouse, key elements of personal and portable computers, and computer networking were developed at PARC. In software, PARC engineers developed the graphical user interface (GUI), overlapping windows, pop-up menus, a graphical word processor, color graphics, and an object-oriented programming language. Moreover, these innovations were developed many years, sometimes more than a decade, before other companies developed and commercialized comparable products. In many cases, competitors who did commercialize such products got ideas from PARC, lured away its inventors, or were formed from engineers who left PARC. Thus, in developing products for the office of the future, the center's productivity easily surpassed that of older research centers at top universities and major corporations. Indeed, PARC was far more productive in developing innovations than any of its founders may ever have envisioned.

What led to this enormous productivity? Four important features of the design of this center distinguished it from nearly all others across the country and enabled it to become the most highly innovative and productive frontier of computer research at that time.

First, Xerox located the center in Palo Alto, California. The region's proximity to both Stanford University and the University of California at Berkeley enabled it to benefit from the talent and ideas emanating from these top engineering schools. Indeed, some of PARC's talent and ideas came directly from Doug Engelbart's productive research project at the Stanford Research Institute nearby. The region was also becoming a hotbed for start-ups that developed components and accessories for computers. Because of its geographic and research climate, the area easily attracted talent from other parts of the country.

Second, Palo Alto was far from Xerox's main research laboratories at Webster, New York. Research at the latter center was tightly focused on improving current products (copiers) using current technology (optics), and was immersed in Xerox's highly bureaucratic culture. Locating the new center in Webster had the advantage of linking the center's work to Xerox's current products and markets. However, it ran the risk of being stymied by the bureaucratic culture of the parent, if not destroyed by outright interference and control by Webster's researchers. As Peter McColough described the situation, "These people here in Rochester have had a heady success with xerography. But I'm not sure they're adaptable enough to take on new and different technologies. If we're going to bring new technologies into Xerox, it would be better to do it in a whole new setting."³ By locating the center in Palo Alto, Xerox freed it to embark on whatever path its researchers thought fruitful. Without any preconceptions at the outset or any ties to the parent, it was free to develop its own innovative culture.

Third, Xerox provided the new center with a generous budget for research. It increased that budget over the years, even though senior managers did not immediately see the fruits of that investment. Indeed, the first director of PARC, George Pake, on being hired by McColough, told him that "it would be too soon to expect research results in five years, but that there certainly should be some useful commercial output before ten years had elapsed."⁴ Xerox's hugely profitable copier business did help in providing the cash for such a long-term venture. But Goldman was also careful to ensure that the center had adequate funds to achieve its original goals. He proposed an initial staff of about 25 on a budget of $1 million, growing over the years to about $5 million. In fact, by the end of the decade, PARC's budget reached about $30 million with a staff of about 400.

Fourth, Xerox supported the director's policy of hiring the best minds in the country. Goldman was successful in hiring a core of visionary directors, scientists, and engineers for the center. One of the early hires was Robert Taylor, who became the associate manager of the computer science laboratory at PARC. Taylor was the former director of the computer research division of the Advanced Research Projects Agency during the time it launched ARPAnet. Taylor was neither a Ph.D. nor an engineer. His formal education was in psychology rather than computer science. Through his experience at ARPA, he had become a firm believer in networking and interactive computers. He had a vision of the computer being most effective as a communications device, rather than a number-crunching machine. He believed that the future of computers lay in their ability to enable *interaction* among a network of users. This was the vision that inspired the ARPAnet and that Taylor brought to PARC. Taylor was also a great judge of talent and a motivator of employees. As a director in ARPA, he was familiar with the best researchers in the field. Thus in a short time, he brought many outstanding researchers to PARC, and continued to motivate and direct them during the next decade. In doing so, he was helped by Xerox's generous financial support of the lab, the uninhibited culture within the lab, and the attraction of the mild Palo Alto climate. This mix of characteristics made the center a highly desirable place for young innovative researchers. Moreover, as the core group of scientists assembled and began their work, their productivity and presence attracted even more talent.

This review of the late 1960s and early 1970s shows that Xerox boldly invested its resources to get new technologies, products, and markets. The purchase of SDS with its promise of immediate products and markets was a billion dollar disaster. In comparison, Xerox's more risky investment in an entirely new research facility turned out to be enormously productive, at far lower cost. In PARC, Xerox created the ideal atmosphere for radical innovations: a stimulating environment, minimal structure, generous funds, and outstanding talent recruited and directed by visionary leaders. This combination of essential ingredients made PARC the most productive computer science laboratory in the world at that time. What is commendable in both investments is that the firm took a huge risk and committed great resources to try to enter a promising new market.[5]

However, enduring market success requires that a firm transform these innovations into products that serve the mass market. In this regard, Xerox was much less successful. The following example indicates the organizational characteristics that hinder commercialization of innovations and describes what firms can do to overcome them.

innovation in hostile and supportive environments

Xerox was the first firm to develop a working model of the laser printer. Yet IBM was the first firm to commercialize a laser printer, and today Hewlett-Packard is the market leader. What happened behind the scenes? Why was Xerox so slow to commercialize this innovation? The story of Xerox's laser printer is a dramatic lesson of the stifling of an innovation by a bureaucracy—and, conversely, the flourishing of an innovation in a supportive environment. It confirms McColough's fears of the stifling culture of Xerox's Webster laboratories and his hope in the new facility at PARC. Some highlights of this case, as recounted by Michael Hiltzik in his book, *Dealers of Lightning*, and other sources, bear important lessons about the environment for innovation.[6]

In the 1960s, Xerox's core technology for making copiers was based on traditional light optics. However, earlier that decade, lasers emerged from Bell Labs as a promising new technology. Relative to the traditional light beam, the laser was a powerful, concentrated beam of single-wavelength light, which had all its photons in phase. As such, it had many promising uses in the fields of surgery, manufacturing, communication, and computing, besides any other area that relied on traditional optics. In particular, when properly developed, lasers could replace regular light as a means of copying.

However, at that time, it took a visionary to see such potential. Gary Starkweather was such a person. He worked as a researcher in Xerox's main research laboratories in Webster. Starkweather saw that traditional light was too feeble and distorted to take copiers to the next level of speed, reliability, and accuracy that the company wanted. He realized that lasers held a promise for the future. He figured that because of their unique characteristics, lasers could be altered in intensity (modulated) to carry information. This information could be harnessed to make copies that were superior to those made with the current technology. At that time, lasers were expensive and dangerous and burned out fast. Some of Starkweather's colleagues and supervisors at Xerox could not visualize how lasers could be harnessed for use within a small inexpensive office copier. Moreover, the Webster facility was under immense pressure from management to keep improving current products to better meet the needs of current customers. Thus there was absolutely no support for research on laser technology at Xerox.

Starkweather's only recourse was to experiment on his own. He scraped together time and equipment to work out a prototype of a copier based on lasers. However, his machine was too primitive to make good copies. His effort met with the scorn of colleagues and superiors. They claimed that Starkweather would never be able to modulate the laser beam adequately for a workable copier. They also believed that the beam would be so intense that it would burn out the selenium layer used for conducting the image. Starkweather's efforts met with the same derision and disbelief that Chester Carlson faced some 35 years earlier. The irony was that Starkweather faced such disbelief within the very organization that had grown successful from the persistence of lone visionaries such as the inventor of xerography, Carlson, and the supporter of the copier, Wilson. What kept Starkweather going? It was his strong belief in the potential of lasers coupled with the simple realization that the images from his prototype were no worse than those from Carlson's prototype.

So Starkweather persisted in his research to develop a laser printer. He said of his motivation, "There's a feeling down in your stomach where you're sure the thing has potential. You have to believe against all odds that the thing will work."[7] He discovered that the laser would not permanently etch or destroy the selenium conductor because it had to hit the conductor for only a fraction of the time that a regular light beam needed. His research also showed that it was possible to modulate the laser beam. He realized that if he could match these modulations to digital information, he could use the laser beam for printing. In that case, instead of actually scanning a page in, as is done in xerography, he could also create the image from a computer. This is indeed the essence of a laser printer.

However, his colleagues and supervisors thought his efforts were "lunatic" and a huge waste of expenditures. On hearing of his persistent experiments, his manager ultimately threatened him with serious consequences, saying to him, "Stop, or I'm going to take your people away."[8] Frustrated with the lack of support, Starkweather asked for a transfer to the PARC facility, which he had read about in a newsletter. He went to Palo Alto to interview for a transfer. PARC researchers were fascinated with his work. However, PARC's director did not want to cause friction with Webster and so was unwilling to intervene on his behalf. His boss was totally opposed. "Forget it, Gary," he said. "You're never going to be moved to the West Coast. And you're to stop playing with that laser stuff."[9]

At that point, totally frustrated and dejected, Starkweather went to George White, head of advanced product development who reported to the vice president of research, Peter Goldman. White had never heard the story before. However, he had a Ph.D. in nuclear physics and had done some work on laser technology in the mid-1960s. So he sympathized with Starkweather's faith in laser technology. He realized that Starkweather and his colleagues at Webster lived in two different worlds, due to entirely different mindsets. "Webster could spend an infinite amount of money doing their prissy little chemistry and fine-tuning second-order effects in copiers," he said. "But they would never find their way to the new world"[10] of laser technology. If Starkweather stayed in his department, even with support, the atmosphere would stifle if not destroy him. White concluded, "Gary's project at best would have limped along without enough power to allow his full productivity. At worst it would have got canceled, and if he wasn't willing to just design lenses and illuminators for classical copiers he'd have had to look for another job."[11] Indeed, that is close to what Starkweather's boss had threatened.

White took the case to Goldman himself. Both of them realized that the attitude of the research group at Xerox was precisely the one they wanted to eradicate. So they willingly agreed to Starkweather's transfer to PARC.

Starkweather got to PARC in January 1971, just 6 months after the center opened. Initially, he was shocked at the primitive state of buildings and equipment at PARC. But he soon realized that the center was free from the stifling culture and rules of Xerox's research headquarters at Webster. Unlike at Webster, funds for his research flowed freely, without his having to beg and plead his case. Most importantly, he was in the company of fellow visionaries, excited by the potential of new technologies and eager to build innovative products for the office of the future. The laser printer fitted in neatly with other products being developed at PARC, aimed at making computers more personal and easier to use. The whole atmosphere was highly supportive of radical innovations such as his. He got his life's opportunity to pursue his dream project. In 2 years, through intense efforts and with the help of like-minded researchers, Starkweather developed what others thought impossible, a working prototype of a laser printer. It was soon put into service at PARC.

Despite its revolutionary technology and its similarity to Xerox's current business in copiers, the company did not immediately embrace the laser printer. The product remained in development for several more years before being launched in 1977 as the Xerox 9700. But when it was introduced, it became one of Xerox's most profitable products, more than paid back Xerox's investment in PARC, and ensured Xerox's continued presence in printing and especially copying, which increasingly used lasers, for at least two more decades. Even then, Starkweather's boss at Webster never seemed to grasp its significance, as is the case with people immersed in a different worldview. Starkweather recounts, "Years afterwards I went back there. I ran into my old boss, the one who had tried to keep me from leaving. His last words to me were, 'Are you still playing around with that laser stuff?' By then the laser printer was a $2 billion-a-year business."[12]

The story of Xerox's laser printer shows the roadblocks that large bureaucracies set up to radical innovations. These roadblocks are a firm's preoccupation with its current products and its reluctance to consider rival technologies. This atmosphere can prevail even within a research laboratory apparently dedicated to innovation. Such an atmosphere can stifle creative scientists, discourage experimentation, and cripple the innovative process. Some individuals may still succeed in developing radical innovations. However, to do so, they need vision to see through the opacity of bureaucratic procedures and rules, and determination to persist against the inertia and stubbornness of such bureaucracies. Nevertheless, the need for resources and feedback is so great that even such gifted individuals must have a supportive environment. Such an environment can come from an independent laboratory outside the organization, such as PARC, a move to an entirely different firm, such as Fairchild Semiconductor, or a fresh start-up, such as Intel. Fortunately for Xerox, PARC provided such a supportive environment for Starkweather.

how talent drives innovation

The importance of investing in human talent is borne out by the brief but dramatic browser battle between Netscape's Navigator and NCSA's Mosaic. NCSA had the indisputable lead with the enormous popularity of Mosaic in 1993. By the end of 1993, NCSA claimed 2 million users and thousands of downloads of the software per week. Late in 1994, NCSA's sole licensee, Spyglass, claimed it had licensed 10 million copies of Mosaic. The success of Mosaic prompted Spyglass to go public with an initial public offering (IPO) that was valued at $24 million in June 1994. As of March 1994, Netscape was not yet born, and may never have been had NCSA been more protective of its talent. Yet by December 1995, Netscape was the clear leader of the browser market. It had rendered Mosaic obsolete. Today, most Internet users have not even heard of the name Mosaic.

How did this dramatic change occur? What was the key to one's success and the other's failure? One important difference between the two organizations was their investment in creative talent. This difference grew from a dramatic difference in vision, philosophy, and management styles established within Netscape by cofounder Jim Clark and within NCSA.

Larry Smarr founded NCSA in 1986, at the University of Illinois, to be the premier center in the world for computer research. The center was supported by grants from the National Science Foundation, the state of Illinois, the University of Illinois, various private corporations, and some federal agencies. Over the years, the center attracted talented researchers and students, and produced some profitable software. By the 1990s, NCSA's reputation matched its founder's goal. It provided high-performance computing for about 6000 users at more than 380 universities and corporations. It came to be known as the "Midwestern hub of the information superhighway."[13] In 1990, two researchers from the center started Spyglass to commercialize the software that emerged from NCSA. However, NCSA's most well-known success was Mosaic.

Joseph Hardin was the head of the group that developed Mosaic at NCSA, at the University of Illinois. However, Marc Andreessen was probably the spiritual leader. Student workers at NCSA had enviable jobs with the latest computers, their own office space, and the opportunity to work on cutting-edge programming tasks. But they also worked at students' wages of about $6 per hour. When Mosaic took off in 1993, the university was swamped with requests for the software, licensing, and support. It realized that it was neither capable of serving the tremendous demand for the product nor positioned to exploit its commercial potential. So it contracted with Spyglass to handle all licensing of the software.

A related challenge for NCSA was to appropriately deal with the talent responsible for creating Mosaic. The treatment of creative talent differs between universities and business firms. Universities tend to allow individuals to retain the copyright to their creations, but the universities take credit for hiring and retaining creative individuals. Business firms typically retain the copyright of creative works carried out in their laboratories and with their resources. But they credit and reward, at least internally, the talent responsible for those works. Institutions, such as NCSA, organized within universities, run the danger of falling between these two approaches. They may both claim the rights and take the credit for creative works produced by their employees. At least, that seems to be the behavior of NCSA toward the team that created Mosaic.

When Marc Andreessen graduated in December 1993, Joseph Hardin asked him to stay on as an employee. However, he was not given the leadership of the ongoing research project on Mosaic. On the contrary, Hardin supposedly asked him to leave the Mosaic project. Such an arrangement may have been to ease difficulties with managing Andreessen, or it may have been an attempt to distance Mosaic from its initial creators and emphasize NCSA's authorship of the program. Indeed, in a much publicized *New York Times* story on Mosaic, reporter John Markoff interviewed Bina and Andreessen but neglected to describe their role in developing the software.[14] Instead of a picture of the programmers, the article included a picture of Smarr and Hardin. The article triggered bad feelings among the programmers, which led ultimately to a breakdown in communication between them and NCSA's managers. Moreover NCSA's managers tended to portray Mosaic as the culmination of NCSA's research program, which began with its founding in 1986 and proceeded with the development of a multimedia hypertext system called Collage. For example, Smarr positioned the Mosaic project as follows: "The underlying pieces of what later became Mosaic started here in 1986."[15] Overall, Andreessen and some of his coworkers did not feel adequately rewarded and acknowledged for their contributions to Mosaic. In frustration, Andreessen left the center, left Illinois, and moved to Silicon Valley. While there, he met Jim Clark.

Jim Clark was the founder and former CEO of Silicon Graphics Inc. (SGI). The company became famous as the producer of high-end three-dimensional graphics workstations. These machines helped bring to life the dinosaurs in the movie Jurassic Park. The company owned a niche, selling its workstations for around $50,000 a piece. However, it lost its position as workstations from Sun Microsystems and Hewlett-Packard improved and provided similar features at much lower prices. Jim Clark left the company in frustration with the politics and strategy of management that led to its decline. He was bent on starting another company that would be more attuned to the rapid changes that new technologies brought to the mass market. In particular, he was looking for young talent that he could lead in the formation of such a company. An old friend from SGI suggested he contact Marc Andreessen.

It was a meeting of complementary talents. Clark had a keen insight into market trends; Andreessen, into software capabilities. The former was a master of business entrepreneurship; the latter, a master of tailoring software for consumers' easy use. Once they met, the two decided to pool their skills in a new company devoted to developing innovative software.

After some weeks of brainstorming, Andreessen impressed upon Clark that their best prospect lay in developing a superior browser, a Mosaic killer. With his former coworkers, Andreessen could design an entirely new program that would completely outdo his former creation Mosaic, the current killer application on the emerging World Wide Web. His goal was probably driven not merely by frustration at NCSA, but also by a vision of the burgeoning market, confidence in his abilities, and awareness of the limitations of Mosaic. It was not clear to Clark, at that time, how exactly one could make money with browsers. But he was keenly aware of the intuitive appeal and rapid growth of Mosaic. From his experience at SGI, he was also acutely aware of the importance of the mass market. He realized that a product like Mosaic, which could attract millions, did not have to sell at a premium. Even a small margin would ensure ample profits for investors.

Once Clark had Andreessen's knowledge and connections on his side, he felt confident of the marketability of the product. He strongly believed that in this market the key to success was the talent that could do the job. The obvious choice was the original programmers of Mosaic who were also disenchanted with NCSA. On Andreessen's advice, the two immediately flew to Illinois to recruit this team. Four of the team members, who were close to graduation, enthusiastically signed on. They were happy to do what they always wanted to do, but now for a real salary. Another team member, Eric Bina, decided to join but stay back and work from the Illinois campus. One team member had this to say of the contract, "I always thought Marc was a businessman, that he would start something big. And I hoped he would include us when he did."[16] The founders also recruited Lou Montulli, one of the key programmers who developed Lynx 2.0. Thus in a few rapid moves, Jim Clark signed up the key talent responsible for creating the major browsers at the time, Mosaic and Lynx. He thus swiftly and shrewdly grabbed the initiative in the battle of the browsers.

It is ironic that NCSA and Spyglass, which benefited enormously from Mosaic, let their original programmers slip away. Even more ironic is that Jim Clark, the person who hired these programmers, had only recently heard of Mosaic, and barely had a company. Indeed, NCSA seemed to assist the departure of this talent by its indifferent attitude and behavior. Consider the differences in the treatment of the talent by Jim Clark and by NCSA.

The students working on Mosaic at NCSA earned $6.85 an hour. When the product became successful, NCSA earned tremendous publicity and royalties. In 1994, Spyglass earned $1.3 million on revenues of $3.6 million, and gave the university 7.5 percent of its

Mosaic revenues. The university patent and copyright income totaled between $2 and $3 million, a substantial part of that from Mosaic. Yet the two organizations shared none of this wealth with the original programmers. NCSA assigned them neither royalties nor bonuses for their work. Academic institutions may be prone to this behavior, at least toward their student employees. Further, Andreessen felt the university tried to take credit due to his team. Now NCSA's managers acknowledged the creative work of the Mosaic team. But they emphasized that the center was ultimately responsible for Mosaic. Such claims implied that the institution, not talent, was primarily responsible for innovations.

While NCSA overlooked its talent, Jim Clark perceived its true value. In NCSA's seeming rebuff of its bright students, he saw a golden opportunity. He set up Netscape with himself and Marc Andreessen as cofounders. At 50 he took the title of president, but gave the 22-year-old Andreessen the title of vice president of technology. Although Clark alone invested in the company, he split ownership of the company with Andreessen and his team. He magnanimously valued the collective expertise of Andreessen and his team at $3 million. Though the company did not have any income, he offered the students a generous starting salary of $65,000 a year (in 1994), plus 100,000 shares of the company's stock. At that point, Clark's start-up had no research center, no structure, and no customers. All he had was a firm belief that the group of six had sufficient talent to create a browser that would definitely outdo Mosaic.

At the time, numerous individuals and organizations all over the world were working on a better browser, including NCSA, Spyglass, and students of computer science at universities around the world. The competition was intense. However, Clark's swift and bold moves were decisive in this battle. He won the talent that was intimately familiar with Mosaic and most capable of improving on it. Moreover, his generous investments and contracts won their dedication and enthusiasm. As soon as they graduated at the end of spring 1994, the team plunged into work on the project. As we will see in the next chapter, that combination of talent was to radically change the browser market and the shape of the Internet.[17]

living by innovation

Microsoft today is a giant corporation with a market value of several hundred billion dollars. It has the dominant market share for spreadsheets and word processors and almost a monopoly on operating systems for personal computers. It is a leader in many other markets, and is constantly buying up smaller firms with innovative products. Indeed, competitors and the U.S. Justice Department accuse Microsoft of monopolizing or attempting to monopolize various markets for software products. If these accusations are true, then Microsoft is in a very strong and an almost invulnerable position.

Yet paranoia pervades the firm. Says an employee of this mentality, "It's etched in our brains: Don't get complacent."[18] This paranoia is born of the belief that if the firm does not constantly innovate, it will stagnate and die. Jim Clark, who competed with Gates in the browser market, has this to say of him: "There's nothing that can't be and won't be dramatically improved upon or rendered obsolete in the space of a given year. No one in American business understands this better than Bill Gates. The fact that his company absolutely dominates its industry and has the cash and capability to dominate other industries, too, has never slowed him down or cooled his fierce ambition for a minute. . . . Gates's Microsoft constantly operates as if it's under siege by enemies that threaten its existence."

Such paranoia has made constant innovation part of life at Microsoft. Unlike many other corporations before and around it, Microsoft survives and indeed thrives on innovation. The whole organization revolves around innovation. Microsoft's unique nature of innovation is not to come up with radically new products that no one has ever thought up before. Their innovation is one of constantly and relentlessly enhancing products to better serve consumers' needs.

The spirit of innovation does not come naturally to the firm just because it is in the computer software business. Indeed, one has only to look at the cycle of successes and failures that have beset many of Microsoft's predecessors to realize this point. A small entrepreneur has a big idea. He or she starts a small company. It brings out an innovative product. Sometimes the innovative product is a huge success. The company then becomes very successful, its stock price soars, and the entrepreneur becomes wealthy. The company grows to be huge and rich, yet becomes complacent. Complacency breeds stagnation and decay. Smaller firms or new entrepreneurs, at the fringe of the market, are quick to introduce innovations. Some of the innovations catch on and make yesterday's winners obsolete. The once successful firm declines rapidly.

Examples abound. Consider the market for word processors. In the 1970s the leading machine for creating manuscripts was the IBM typewriter. Many of these were conventional electric typewriters, but many others included magnetic memory and electronic word processing capabilities. IBM, a giant, was also in the computer business and could have foreseen the computerization of word processing. Yet by the late 1970s, Wang had introduced its dedicated word processors, which began to make the memory typewriter obsolete. Wang grew to be powerful and dominant, but missed the next wave of innovation. Personal computers became cheap and popular, and with suitable software, they could do what Wang's machines did plus many other things. WordStar replaced Wang as the most popular program for creating documents. However, WordStar in turn failed to innovate with each successive generation of PCs, and was soon replaced by WordPerfect as the leading software. Failure to innovate in time led that product in turn to yield market leadership to Microsoft's Word. Today, one important reason why Word is still the dominant product is because Microsoft constantly innovates, regularly bringing out new versions with superior features for consumers. Similarly, in spreadsheets, market leadership went from VisiCalc to Lotus 1–2–3 to Microsoft Excel.

Gates had witnessed this pattern in these and many other categories. So he knew the dangers. Indeed, despite Microsoft's enormous resources and many successes, he expressed his fear of obsolescence: "We've done some good work, but all of these products become obsolete so fast. . . . It will be some finite number of years— and I don't know the number—before our doom comes."[19] What fires Gates is not only the demise of once-successful firms that failed to innovate. It is also his own vision of the future, and his tremendous desire to realize that vision, to be the dominant force in software solutions for the future. He knows that innovation is key to realizing that vision. So constant innovation is Microsoft's creed.

Gates sustains this atmosphere of innovation through a strategy consisting of three crucial components: hiring "very smart people," keeping a loose structure, and organizing workers in small, intense, task-oriented groups.

One crucial component of the strategy is Gates's great investment in intellectual talent. He strives to hire the brightest minds in the industry. He says, "The key for us, number one, has always been hiring very smart people. There is no way of getting around that, in terms of IQ, you've got to be very elitist in picking the people who deserve to write software. . . ."[20] Hiring the brightest has several benefits. Bright workers find solutions to problems. A software company is foremost a provider of solutions for people's information problems. Smarter workers ensure faster, better, or more efficient solutions. As Steve Ballmer said, "Smart people can learn to do most things. Workaholic smart kids is what we're after."[21] Thus an investment in the best minds ensures that Microsoft can discover innovative solutions to future problems. Gates has commented, "Take away our 20 best people and I tell you that Microsoft would become an unimportant company."[22]

Gates also favors graduates fresh out of the top research universities. The hiring of young, fresh university graduates has numerous advantages. Such people are most likely to have the time, inclination, and motivation to work the long hours required of Microsoft's workers. More importantly, fresh graduates are least likely to be set in their ways, and most likely to be open to new ideas. Thus an influx of fresh graduates is likely to keep alive an atmosphere of innovation and dynamism in the firm. Moreover, graduates who have come from the best research universities in the country have learned from the leading researchers in their respective fields. Thus they are likely to bring with them the latest research ideas, in addition to an ethic of hard work, research, and innovation.

The second component of Gates's strategy is an informal work structure. A tight structure is good for an operational organization such as an army or a sales force. However, it is deadly for a creative organization. Tight structure inhibits creativity. Rules, whether for work routines, project approval, or project change, sap valuable energy while also dampening initiative and creativity. In contrast, openness and spontaneity foster creativity. Thus employees, especially research employees at Microsoft, do not have fixed or formal work hours, attire, schedules, or work habits. Employees dress casually, frolic on the job, and have many opportunities for exercise on the Microsoft campus.

The third component of Gates's strategy is an intense goal-oriented work ethic. The Microsoft environment demands solving tough problems, in short time frames, with limited staff, in an intense work environment. Employees are organized in small groups with a leader and assigned to specific programming tasks. Groups tend to be intentionally understaffed. Gates believes that small groups are better able to communicate with each other, while the challenge of meeting seemingly impossible goals with limited staff motivates people to give their very best. Gates leads by example and demands of his employees total dedication to solving an assigned problem. Employees often work long hours during the day, into the night, and over weekends. Caffeinated drinks are free, and food is heavily subsidized or free on the Microsoft campus. As Gates says, "I like pushing things to the edge. That's often where you find high performance."[23]

These components of management were diametrically opposed to those existing at the time in the other giant of the computer world, IBM. This was especially true during the crucial years when Microsoft grew rapidly and overtook IBM as the leading force in the computer software industry. IBM relied on large numbers of employees organized in huge networks. Its task forces tended to be overstaffed rather than understaffed. Many of IBM's employees were hired and trained to carefully serve existing accounts and bring in new ones. Creative problem solvers composed a much smaller portion of the work force. IBM staff operated under a huge burden of rules and procedures, with the smallest innovation requiring extensive approval. Status and perks were the motivators for hard work.

The differences in performance of these two firms are dramatic. Microsoft has come forward with a string of software products across a wide spectrum of uses. Even when a particular version of a product is unsuccessful, Microsoft persists with innovation, introducing new versions of the program, until it designs a formula that appeals to consumers and becomes a market success. And despite success, the company never stops innovating. It keeps bringing out improvements to its successful products, to make them more useful to consumers. In contrast, IBM was slow to enter the PC market, and with the exception of the XT and AT, it was slow to bring out newer versions of PCs.

Microsoft has not been a pioneer in any market in which it currently leads: operating systems, browsers, graphical user interfaces, word processors, or spreadsheets. Consumers do not buy Microsoft products merely because they have bought other products from the company or because other consumers do so. If that were the case, Microsoft would make a success of every product it introduced, and would do so with the very first generation of each product. But the first few generations of Windows, Excel, and Word were flops. Similarly, current versions of many products, such as Money and the Microsoft Network, are still not market leaders. But once Microsoft has won market leadership of a category, it has not lost that leadership, despite constant change in the market. Thus its policy of innovation has been fruitful. In contrast, IBM has lost leadership of some important markets it once dominated. Good examples are the initial word processing typewriters and personal computers.

Microsoft's successful leadership of several software markets is due, not to being first in those markets, but to following a policy of relentless innovation that comes from recruiting, motivating, and retaining outstanding talent.[24]

creating innovative organizations

Examples in this and prior chapters emphasize the absolute imperative of innovating relentlessly to maintain market leadership. The driving force of innovation is talent. Talented individuals can quickly solve difficult problems, generate new ideas, and further develop one another's ideas to create a stimulating environment for innovation. Xerox's success with PARC was primarily the fruit of great talent in an organization committed to pursuing new ideas. To keep Microsoft innovative and ahead of competitors, Gates relies on the talent of brilliant, fresh graduates. Especially in the realm of high-technology products, such talent is critical for effective innovation. In this respect, the major error a manager can make is to believe that the institution is more important than creative individuals who produce innovations. NCSA's Mosaic yielded to Netscape's Navigator primarily because Netscape's Clark shrewdly recruited the talent responsible for Mosaic.

Talent alone may not be enough. To be productive, individuals need an atmosphere of independence, freedom, and financial support. The hindrances to such an atmosphere in business organizations are bureaucracy and preoccupation with current products and customers. The experiences of Starkweather and Andreessen are illuminating. Despite working in a research laboratory at Webster, Starkweather's boss could not appreciate the enormous value of his work with lasers. Webster's research environment was so tightly focused on refining current products for current customers that it allowed little room for a radical innovation such as laser technology. Indeed, that restrictive research environment could well have ended Starkweather's career and Xerox's profitable venture in laser printing, had senior management not transferred him to the supportive PARC environment. Similarly, the independence and freedom that Andreessen initially enjoyed at NCSA and later at Netscape were instrumental in his hugely successful innovations. Conversely, the subsequent bureaucratization of the effort that produced Mosaic led to its demise and ultimate downfall.

Thus exceptional talent that is supported in an autonomous environment and focused on emerging mass markets constitutes a powerful organizational force for pursuing innovations relentlessly.

summary

- A firm's organization plays a critical role in innovation. Three organizational factors affect the speed and responsiveness of firms with innovation: bureaucracy versus autonomy, a focus on institutions versus a focus on individual talent, and a preoccupation with current customers versus an emphasis on emerging mass markets.
- Bureaucracy tends to sap a firm's energy, diffuse its focus, and cloud its vision. Innovation becomes a casualty of this process.

Bureaucracies either stifle innovation or, when confronted with it, often fail to see its value.

- In contrast, a great facilitator of innovation is providing an autonomous, supportive, and stimulating environment for research. Autonomy enables innovation to flourish without interference.
- A subtle yet strong hindrance to innovation is managerial preoccupation with serving current customers better than the competition. Such preoccupation may blind managers to promising innovations that enable a firm to leap ahead of competitors by harnessing new technologies for emerging mass markets. Champions charged with the task of serving such new markets can break this preoccupation with current problems and crises.
- The foremost component of innovation is talent. Institutions and structures do not create successful new products. Creative, talented individuals do. A firm needs to hire, motivate, and retain the best minds it can. The stimulation, fusion, and cross-fertilization of ideas occur spontaneously once such talent is assembled in an autonomous and supportive environment.

9

raising and committing financial resources

F inancial commitment is critical for all firms trying to refine new-product ideas, create interest among a mass market of consumers, and establish dominance in a new market. It can be especially important for firms entering a market later without any established position or profitability. Such late entrants often face earlier entrants with established positions. To gain merely a foothold in such markets against established rivals, the new entrant requires substantial financial resources. But to be a market leader, the entrant needs enormous financial resources. External observers of evolving markets may not sense the importance of this factor. However, every entrepreneur or new-product manager is acutely aware of the need for financial resources. Why the need for such resources? There are several reasons.

One of the advantages of the mass market is that the product can be manufactured and sold on a large scale, thus lowering costs per unit. However, targeting the mass market implies operating on a large scale. The firm needs to invest in large plants or equipment, hire many employees, build big research facilities, and buy supplies in bulk. Costs for marketing can also be quite large. The firm needs to set up a distribution system and build a sales force to serve these distributors or to win new clients. In many markets, the firm may also need heavy advertising to develop the market for its product or to differentiate it from that of established competitors. In some markets, the firm may need to finance sales to its consumers. All these activities require enormous financial resources.

At the same time, until the new product becomes successful or achieves market dominance, it does not generate enough revenues to cover these costs. Sometimes, the lag between investments and sales may be only a few months. At other times, the lag could be several years. Thus, late entrants have to commit enormous resources without the luxury of adequate sales in the near term or a guarantee of any sales in the future.

Specifically, this need for financial resources has two components: access to financial resources and willingness to use those resources. Failure in either area can lead to a failure of the entire effort. Entrepreneurs and small entrants may be more than willing to invest all their resources to attain their dreams. However, they may have meager resources or their resources may not match up with the needs. Large established firms may have adequate financial resources. However, layers of bureaucracy may hinder their committing those resources. Alternatively, the pressures from their current obligations may make committing financial resources to the new market risky or even unwise.

This problem becomes more acute if the new entrant comes in with a radically new concept. The more radical the innovation, the greater the need for resources. At the same time, the more radical the innovation, the more uncertain its payoff. Outside investors view the radical idea with skepticism, making it difficult for the firm to raise the financial resources from the capital markets. Thus entrants with radically new ideas must be able and willing to make a clear, firm commitment of resources to implement their idea.

Where does this commitment come from? Unquestionably, it must arise from the vision of the new entrant. It is the unique vision that provides the entrant with the motivation to embark on this journey when competitors are using a different business concept and financiers on the outside do not see the merits of the approach. Enduring success comes to those firms that have a vision that is clear and strong enough to enable them to commit their own resources or motivate others to do so to realize that vision.

In hindsight, after an entrant has made a success of a new undertaking, the payoffs seem to dwarf the risks. Thus an observer may not appreciate the great uncertainty that the entrant had to face and the difficulty it had in raising or committing funds for the task. Often, this commitment must proceed in the face of general skepticism about the merits of the enterprise. As a result, managers faced with such a situation may tend to prematurely pull the rug out from under a new enterprise.

The following four examples show the critical role that financial commitment plays in enduring market success, along with the difficulties encountered in making that commitment and the importance of vision in sustaining the commitment.

a huge gamble that almost failed

The origin, early struggles, and ultimate success of Federal Express reveal the importance of vision and persistence in achieving enduring market leadership. But they especially underscore the need for financial commitment.

After his graduation from Yale, Fred Smith enlisted in the Marine Corps and served in Vietnam. He excelled in this service, rising to captain and winning the Silver Star, Bronze Star, two Purple Hearts, the Navy Commendation Medal, and the Vietnamese Cross of Gallantry, within two short years. His experiences in Vietnam sharpened his will and fashioned him into an aggressive competitor. His accomplishments there made it easy for him to raise capital early in his business career. After his discharge in 1969, on returning to the United States, Smith went into private business, aided by his personal wealth. He inherited several million dollars, in addition to being a cotrustee of the Frederick Smith Enterprise Company, a holding company created by his businessman father. His share of the trust was 38.5 percent, while his half-sisters shared the rest. In 1971, he became president of the board of the Enterprise Company. With his half-sisters' support, he sought to transform the enterprise from a passive to a more aggressive investor.

In August 1969, he took a controlling interest in an aviation company in Little Rock, Arkansas. He turned this company into an aggressive business buying and selling used corporate jets. Smith used his own money for some of these transactions and made a lot of money. His successful management of this business established his creditworthiness with local banks. More importantly, it sensitized him to the need for priority mail service. Smith said of his experiences, "I became infuriated that I could not receive on any timely and reliable basis air freight shipments from places around the United States. Sometimes it might be two days, and sometimes five days before you could get a part delivered in Little Rock. It was unpredictable."[1]

The problem reassured Smith of the merits of a priority mail service, on which he had written his Yale term paper. Smith decided to do something about it. He proposed to start a company to serve the demand that he believed was widely shared among U.S. businesses. The company would be totally dedicated to reliably delivering priority mail. He was confident that firms would pay for such a service, commenting, "If you offer two services . . . the shipper will always take, if it is time-sensitive, the more reliable method, rather than the cheaper method. This is the essence of time-sensitive."[2]

Smith assembled the board of the Enterprise Company to gain their support for an investment of $250,000, promising to match that amount with his own money. The board willingly agreed. With that money, he founded Federal Express in June 1971. He envisioned starting off by winning a contract from the Federal Reserve System to move its checks on an overnight basis. At that time it took two or more days for checks to reach the appropriate destination. Smith asked the company board to guarantee a loan for $3.6 million to buy two Falcon 20 Fan Jets from Pan American World Airways. He claimed that purchase of the jets would prove to the Federal Reserve Board that he was earnest. With that contract he was confident of getting other loans to buy more jets. Pan Am had given him an option to buy those jets at a very attractive price. The board of the Enterprise Company agreed to his request and purchased the two jets. But Smith received his first setback soon after. The Federal Reserve Banks could not agree on a common shipper, and each bank decided to go its own way.

Smith persisted with his idea. To convince financiers of the merit of his idea, he commissioned two independent market research firms to determine the demand for the priority mail service. The duplication was not only to reduce risk but also to increase credibility in the findings. Both studies agreed about the demand for such a service. They estimated that the market was worth about $1 billion, that start-up costs would be $7 million to $16 million, and that a new start-up would be profitable in 1 year. They also indicated that clients wanted an integrated service with the provider owning both planes and delivery trucks.

Even before he received the results of these studies, Smith signed an option with Pan American World Airways to purchase 23 Falcons for a price of $29.1 million. Earlier Smith bought 8 Falcons in the open market with short-term loans from a local Arkansas bank. He was getting the Pan Am jets at a very low price, and figured that even if he failed with Federal Express, he could sell the jets on the open market at a profit. He again persuaded the board of the Enterprise Company to guarantee a loan of about $1 million to secure this option. Together with 10 Falcons he had purchased on earlier occasions, Smith had at his discretion a total of 33 Falcons, a sizable fleet. He was elated with his deal.

However, when the time came to take possession of the planes, Federal Express had not yet taken off and Smith lacked the financing to close the deal. Pan Am itself was having tough financial times and needed the cash badly. In September 1972 and November 1972, and again in January 1973, it put tremendous pressure on Smith to purchase the planes as contracted. Each time Smith was concerned that Pan Am would sell the planes to someone else. He then not only would lose the option of buying the fleet of planes at favorable terms but also would not be able to get an equivalent fleet to launch his service. Yet each time Smith managed to revise the terms of the option, at the cost of tough negotiations and a painful price increase on the jets.

A counsel for Federal Express describes the third of those meetings: "One of those senior vice presidents at Pan Am was a real S.O.B. I spent 23 days in New York trying to work out a deal to keep Pan Am from selling the Falcons out from under us. This guy was unyielding and unpleasant. We had to play real hardball to keep the agreement alive. At times it was all but dead. Federal Express almost died at these bitter meetings."[3] Finally, Smith agreed to take the planes by a drop-dead date of May 15, 1973. That date became a critical do-or-die date for the company. In addition, for every day after March 31 that he had not taken possession of the planes, he would have to pay $1500 per plane per day.

At the end of January 1973, the company was broke. Smith later said that at that time "just a little push" and the company would have collapsed. Two months earlier he had contracted with a New York investment banker, White, Weld & Company, to raise $20 million in long-term loans to ease the company's financial situation. However, in February, White, Weld & Company suggested that Smith put another $1.5 million of the family's funds into the company to secure the loan. Desperate for the loan, Smith borrowed $2 million from a bank in Little Rock, Arkansas. To get that loan, Smith obtained a statement signed by a Memphis attorney and an Enterprise board secretary that he had a net worth of $7.2 million. The statement also said that the bank loan would be secured by an assignment of stock from the company. In fact, Smith forged the statement, and the assignment of stock itself was fictitious. When the forgery was discovered a year later, it created a crisis in the company and fresh problems for Smith. But at the time, Smith was under extreme pressure. Even with that guarantee, by April-end 1993, White, Weld & Company failed to obtain the long-term loan for Federal Express. The deadline to purchase the Falcons was drawing near.

Early in May 1993, White, Weld & Company arranged for Smith to meet Henry Crown, an industrialist and financier, who held a controlling interest in General Dynamics. Smith was able to impress on Crown the merits of Federal Express. After careful scrutiny and intense negotiation, Crown agreed to arrange the loan that Smith needed to buy the Falcons. Finally, just 3 days before the deadline, General Dynamics guaranteed loans totaling $23.7 million to Federal Express. But Smith had to pay a steep price. General Dynamics demanded the option to purchase 80.1 percent of Federal Express for the price of $16 million. Smith's share of the company was reduced to 8 percent. Not having any alternatives, Smith agreed, and was able to take possession of the Falcons. However, his problems did not end there.

Federal Express had started business in March 1973. Initially, business was very slow. On the very first day of business, despite a network of 11 cities, Federal Express handled only 6 packages! While the number increased steadily with time, it was still below the cost of operations. Federal Express had to maintain a minimal crew and a minimum number of trucks and planes to guarantee service, irrespective of the traffic. By the end of September 1973, Federal Express had suffered losses of $7.8 million from operations. Moreover, the company had to modify each of the planes to carry freight. Taking into account the cost of the planes, cost of modifications, losses from operations, and interest charges, by September 1973, the company had piled up massive debts totaling about $47 million. Fred Smith and the Enterprise Company had seen all their investments swallowed in these losses. The loans from the Little Rock banks were in default. One lender, the Worthen Bank of Little Rock, was the uneasiest of all the lenders. It had loaned $8.7 million, and had partialed out the loan to other small banks to reduce its exposure. Every week it sent a representative to Smith to talk him into reducing his exposure to so much debt. If it foreclosed, Federal Express would have to go to bankruptcy court, pretty much destroying the undertaking. To make matters worse, the loan from General Dynamics was also overdue. Moreover, General Dynamics was unwilling to exercise its option to turn its loan guarantee into equity. Federal Express was in a dire situation.

So Smith started another search for financing, with the usual expectations and dashed hopes. A consortium of banks including the First Bank of Chicago and Chase Manhattan Bank were willing to extend new loans, but they demanded more collateral from the Smith family. Smith convinced the Enterprise board to make an equity investment of $1.5 million plus an additional loan of $2.5 million. As a result, Enterprise's total investment was $5.4 million, and Smith's total investment was $2.5 million of personal funds, not counting his 38 percent share of the Enterprise funds. With these investments, in November 1973, Smith managed to get a loan of

$52 million from the consortium of banks. With that loan he was able to pay off the company's earlier creditors.

However, the company was still not out of the woods. Shipments grew steadily through 1974 and 1975. But the company failed to turn a profit. Until May 1975, the company suffered cumulative losses of about $29 million. It also had an outstanding debt of $49 million. To cover the losses, Federal Express had to undergo two more difficult rounds of financing involving tough negotiations. In one of these rounds, his earlier forgery was discovered, which brought threats on the tenure of Smith himself. However, lenders realized that Smith was Federal Express, and without him the company had no chance to survive. Moreover, he was able to motivate his managers and employees with his unending faith in the vision of the company and his strong belief in its ultimate success.

With shrewd changes to its personal selling and advertising strategy, Federal Express's shipments kept increasing through 1975. Then in July 1975, the company had its first profitable month. That was 4 years after Smith founded the corporation and 9 years after the famous term paper. The next year, it became the dominant shipper in the small-parcel airfreight business. The year 1976 also marked its first profitable year. From then on, shipments and profits increased rapidly (see Figure 9-1). The competition began to take note, but Smith was ready for them and responded aggressively with changes in pricing and services. By 1983, Federal Express had become the dominant firm in the market in terms of shipments and profit. With annual revenues reaching a billion dollars, Fred Smith became an industry captain. The Yale term paper became a legend.

Between July 1972 and November 1973 when Smith won the $52 million financing package, his entire time was consumed trying to gain funding and ward off previous financiers demanding payments or threatening foreclosure. Describing this time to attorneys during a hearing, Smith said:

> No man on this earth will ever know what I went through during that year, and I am lucky I remember my name much less the details that you are trying to ask me. With the trauma that year, the pressure was so great on me, and

Figure 9-1. Early Growth of Federal Express

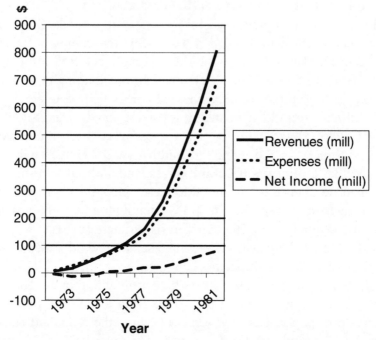

Source: Robert A. Sigafoos, *Absolutely, Positively Overnight!*, St. Luke's Press, Memphis, TN, 1983.

there were so many events that went on, and so much travel and so many meetings with investment bankers, General Dynamics, and a hundred different people who came down to Memphis, I just don't recall specifics of virtually anything during that period of time, in addition to trying to run a company at the same time.[4]

Besides negotiating the funding for the enterprise, Smith had to undertake the numerous tasks of a start-up, all in a short period of time. To begin with, he thrice had to negotiate with government agencies for relief from regulations: in 1972 to reduce the weight limitations that prevented his Falcons from transporting freight; in November 1973 to get an adequate gasoline quota during the oil embargo; and in summer 1975 to obtain permission to fly larger jets. He also had to negotiate with local officials and develop a new hub for the routing of his aircraft at Memphis. He had to modify the Falcon jets, which he did through the purchase of a small aircraft shop in Little Rock. He had to supervise the recruitment and training of pilots, truck drivers, sales staff, office staff, and managers. He had to recruit all these employees, promising them a bright future rather than offering high-paying jobs, and get them to stay on when times were rough and salaries were late. Most importantly, he had to win new business for his service.

Early in 1974, when his half-sisters and the banks found out that Smith had forged the signature of his attorney, they filed suit. Smith was indicted for forgery and had to face a court trial with a maximum penalty of 5 years in jail. The board was ready to oust him and at one time did actually find a new CEO. But Federal Express's senior managers and immediate employees threatened to resign en masse if Smith were fired. Smith also vigorously defended his actions in court. He argued that he and the Enterprise board were one and the same, and the banker handling the loan knew that he had signed for his attorney. The jury at his trial ruled in favor of Smith. Perhaps the jury was also swayed by his service in Vietnam, his heroic attempts to keep Federal Express alive, and his tenacity under extreme duress.

Indeed, the hype surrounding Smith's ultimate success often omits the great difficulties of establishing Federal Express. Smith's term paper did not come close to providing details about the new system or outlining these difficulties. It did not provide much detail of the new system and did not foresee most of the difficulties that the implementation of such a system would entail. Thus, at the time, it could have seemed to a knowledgeable reader quite infeasible on several grounds. Making a success of Federal Express was a massive undertaking fraught with numerous difficulties, which Smith himself never foresaw when he started the business. Even the market research studies barely covered the difficulties of the task, and they grossly underestimated the financing required. Indeed, the project was close to failure several times. Success emerged only through his dauntless efforts.

Art Bass, who was Federal Express's president from 1975 to 1980, says of Smith's contributions to the company: "This company should have died five or six times in its first three or four years, but

Fred refused to give up. Boy, was he tenacious. With sheer bull and courage he pulled off a miracle. That's the only way to express what he did."[5]

Ironically, at the turn of the millennium, when Internet businesses took off, their success threatened many old-economy companies. But it actually stimulated the business of Federal Express and other companies in the priority mail business. Improvements in technology and economies of scale had made such deliveries much more efficient. In addition, consumers' higher disposable incomes increased their willingness to pay for such services. While Smith could not have foreseen this twist in the economy, the development underscored his insight that people would always be willing to pay for high-value time-sensitive delivery.[6]

surviving an incumbent's financial squeeze

Netscape was incorporated as Mosaic Communications on April 4, 1994. It released the beta version of its first product, Netscape Mosaic, just 6 months later. The first version of the browser, released in December 1994, was a tremendous success. By the end of the month the browser had 10 million downloads. In about a year from incorporation, consumers had downloaded 35 million copies of the product to make it the market leader. That quick takeoff led the founders to issue an IPO just 16 months after starting the company. The IPO was a great hit, representing one of the most successful IPOs of the 1990s. That day alone, 40 of the company's employees became paper millionaires. Founder Jim Clark's share was worth $663 million, representing a paper return of more than 132 *times* his initial investment. The casual observer may attribute this meteoric rise of a company to the luck of the founders and the general boom that benefited Internet and high-tech start-ups in the 1990s. However, this superficial account masks a deeper truth. In fact, the company succeeded because its founders and early employees had a clear vision of the mass market for browsers, undertook innovative efforts to realize that vision, and had a willingness to risk all they had to make it happen.

The immense early success of the organization may blind one to the many risks involved at the outset. One has to put oneself in the shoes of the founders in order to understand the challenges facing the company. When Jim Clark and Marc Andreessen started, they had no organizational support. Arrayed against them were numerous competitors, some of whom were much better equipped and funded and more successful.

The most formidable of these was the University of Illinois' National Center for Supercomputing Applications. NCSA had over 10 years of history in computer and software design, a reputation for being a premier computer research center, and a record for producing innovative software. It had deep funding resources such as the U.S. Defense Department, the University of Illinois, the state of Illinois, and the National Science Foundation (NSF). It had experienced employees and could draw from a large pool of motivated and inexpensive labor in the form of computer science students. Most importantly, it already owned the rights to Mosaic, which then was leading in the browser market, growing rapidly in popularity, and already generating a stream of royalties.

Another rival, Spyglass, had a short but successful history commercializing software that emerged from NCSA. It could draw from the pool of talent at the university and at NCSA. Spyglass had the rights to sublicense Mosaic to businesses. It already had signed on nine large licensees for Mosaic, including such well-known names as Microsoft, IBM Network Systems Division, Digital Equipment Corporation, AT&T Corporation, FTP Software Inc., and NEC Systems Laboratory Inc. Microsoft had agreed to bundle Mosaic with Windows 95 for a license fee of $2 million. Other large institutions that were potential rivals were departments where similar work had already been done, such as at the Universities of Kansas, Minnesota, and California (at Berkeley) and at CERN. Because these were continuing centers of research, and because software at that time was distributed for free, any of these organizations could develop a new, improved browser and distribute it for free. That could undercut and preempt the potential browser from Jim Clark's Netscape. Beyond these organizations, there was the looming danger of any of the commercial software giants, especially Microsoft, getting into the fray, once these giant firms realized the potential of Web browsers.

An article in *Business Week* summarized the situation facing

Clark as follows: "Unlike SGI's early days, Clark faces immediate competition. At least 10 companies have bought licenses to commercialize NCSA's Mosaic. SPRY Inc. in Seattle is already shipping its AIR Mosaic, and well-heeled computer and software makers, including IBM and Novell, are creating competing Web browsers."[7]

To get his company moving quickly and retain control over its destiny, Clark funded the company with $3 million of his own money. The resources were necessary to attract and retain the talent from the original Mosaic software program. Because of the success of this program, these researchers could have easily obtained other offers. For example, before he joined forces with Clark, Andreessen was earning $80,000 per year at his first job after graduation. Because Spyglass continued to license a new version of NCSA Mosaic to large software and hardware companies, Clark was eager to catch up with Spyglass and surpass it as soon as possible. So he launched a rapid expansion of the fledgling company. He hired programmers, office staff, sales staff, and managers. Within 2 months of its start, the company had grown to 100 employees. These people needed salaries, stock options, office space, and office equipment. In particular, engineers needed costly workstations to do state-of-the-art programming. All these expenses resulted in a rapid burn rate of his initial investment.

Clark describes the anxiety this outflow of cash created. "The funding of a new venture resembles an hourglass," he stated. "At first, there seems to be an unlimited supply of sand (or time, or money), and though there's a steady trickle, you can't really see the whole amount changing. Then, when you get down to about one fourth of that amount, the outflow seems to be going at an incredible rate."[8] By midsummer 1994, Clark feared that he would be soon out of cash. Indeed, he was so worried about expenses that staff had to hide purchases of new equipment from him so that their arrival would not prompt him to excessive worry. Without any source of revenue, he had to worry about raising additional capital in order to keep the business going. So he embarked on a quest for external funds, with the risk of losing control to a group of opportunistic venture capitalists.

He first contacted two venture capital groups that had financed his undertaking at Silicon Graphics Inc. His experience with them had not been entirely positive, in that they took a major share of the company and did not support him in his battle with its more recent managers. This time around, Clark asked them to pay the unusually high rate of three times as much as he had paid for shares when starting Netscape. Both groups promptly turned him down. The power of the venture capitalists and their experience with Clark at SGI, where he was far more accommodating, led them to reject this offer. Time would show that that was a major misjudgment on their part. At that point, Clark was unfazed with the rejections. He was confident about his vision for Netscape and the value of that vision. He persisted with his search, and found a positive response with the venture capital firm Kleiner Perkins Caufield and Byers (KPCB). KPCB agreed to invest $5 million for a share of the company at the rate offered by Clark. Clark himself put in another $2 million at the same rate to avoid dilution of his share. Thus by the middle of 1994, Clark had invested $5 million, one-third of the equity he had earned from his severance from SGI.

One of Clark's most harrowing experiences occurred during a copyright dispute with Spyglass, NCSA, and the University of Illinois. While there were many individuals and groups working on improving Mosaic, the work of Netscape drew the attention and ire of NCSA and its associates for several reasons.

First, Clark and Andreessen called their company Mosaic Communications and called the software Netscape Mosaic. Andreessen and his colleagues felt strong ownership of the name Mosaic, given that they wrote the initial code for it. However, they developed Mosaic as employees and with the funding of NCSA. The use of the name *Mosaic*, then owned and licensed by NCSA, seemed to the latter a clear infringement of copyright.

Second, Netscape Communications did not license the Mosaic software from Spyglass, as all the other commercial users at the time had done. NCSA and Spyglass expected a license fee from Netscape as well.

Third, throughout the summer and early fall of 1994, Netscape received great publicity in the press. Reporters were always alert for promising start-ups in Silicon Valley. In Netscape they saw much promise. Jim Clark and Marc Andreessen founded the company. Clark had been the founder of the current multibillion dollar SGI.

Andreessen was portrayed as the wonder kid who led the team that designed Mosaic. He appeared on the cover of leading magazines such as *Time*. NCSA's role was often underrepresented, and sometimes it was unfairly presented as an obstructionist and exploiter of its brilliant students.

Fourth, Netscape's beta release in October 1994 was very successful. It won the admiration of the press and achieved thousands of downloads a day. The main reason for the success was that Netscape was 10 times faster than Mosaic. As servers began offering richer material on the Web, with graphics, sound, and video, download speed became a key criterion for consumer choice of browsers. Then as now, it was no fun waiting endlessly for a page to download. Netscape's superior speed would pretty much kill Mosaic. Spyglass and NCSA could see their steady stream of royalties soon drying up.

The University of Illinois and NCSA took several steps to protect their perceived rights. They informed the press to refer to their software by its trademark name, NCSA Mosaic. They made public statements about intellectual property rights and the need for students to be loyal to the university. They threatened legal action against Netscape and demanded an appropriate and fair resolution of the apparent infringement of copyright.

However, Netscape saw the situation quite differently. When Netscape first started, Clark gave very clear instructions to the programmers he hired from the Mosaic project that they should start completely afresh. They could not use any code from the Mosaic program even though it was publicly available. As far as possible, they had also to expunge from their memory any recollection of lines of code that they themselves had created for Mosaic. This way, Clark believed, the fledgling firm had insulated itself from any claims of infringement. The former student programmers felt that the university owed them at least some credit for their design of Mosaic. But they probably erred in believing they had a right to the name merely because they worked on the code. So Clark offered the university the opportunity to examine Netscape's code, plus 10,000 shares of stock in the new company to assuage any concerns.

Without examining the details of the Netscape code, NCSA insisted that its former employees used proprietary knowledge to develop the new program. So NCSA and the university did not budge from their major request that Netscape should pay a royalty on every copy of the program that was downloaded, sold, or licensed. Netscape planned to give the program away free, and make revenues from advertising on its site and sales to business users. Thus a fee on every copy downloaded would have cost the company a bundle besides hurting the strategy. On the other side, Netscape's first six employees felt the claims of the university were outrageous and unjustified because they themselves had written Mosaic's original code. They were bitter about NCSA's public relations threats of legal action. Said Andreessen, "They basically tried to shut us down. They started a campaign in the press to make us look like thieves. It was bizarre."[9]

The standoff lasted through the fall of 1994, severely hurting Netscape's prospects. At that time there was tremendous interest in the software and a growing stream of contracts from firms that wanted to license it. Any word of a copyright infringement battle would immediately put a stop to such contracts. The company would not have been able to implement past sales contracts or raise any fresh capital. If the case went to court, it could drag on for months, if not years. At the rate the market was progressing and Netscape was using up cash, that situation would pretty much kill the start-up. Legal fees were an added drain on company resources. As Clark sums up the situation, "We were burning around $1 million a month by this time, and a lot of that was my money."[10] The firm could not survive the cash drain with no income or resources.

In this sense NCSA had the upper hand. The mere threat of legal action was enough to jeopardize the sales and funding opportunities of the start-up. NCSA could drag the case on while Netscape slowly bled to death. Thus NCSA had no direct incentive for a compromise. Clark and his lawyers tried reasoning and negotiating with university officials. Over the strong opposition from company employees who were attached to the name *Mosaic*, he finally went ahead with a name change. The firm changed its name to Netscape Communications (from Mosaic Communications) and changed the name of the browser to Netscape Navigator (from Netscape Mosaic). Tense with anxiety and eager for a solution, Clark offered 50,000 shares of the company. NCSA turned it down.

Finally, in sheer desperation, Clark decided to serve a suit the company had filed months earlier in California for declaratory relief, requiring the university to examine Netscape Navigator's code for infringement. The suit risked angering his opponents and initiating a long, drawn-out, and public court case. In effect, because Netscape's code was written from scratch and the name change had already been completed, the suit neutralized NCSA's leverage with the company. University and NCSA officials saw the limits of their position and the futility of a court case. Late in December 1994, they agreed to settle for a one-time royalty fee of about $3 million. Netscape accepted the demands and was free to pursue the browser market unimpeded.

Netscape introduced the first version of the browser in December 1994. Downloads of the software took off, initially hitting 10 million copies a month. By June 1995, total downloads and sales had reached 40 million copies. The same year it earned $75 million in revenues, about seven times the total investment of the previous year. This strong performance led the company to issue an early IPO on August 9, 1995. That day, the stock opened at $28, peaked at $74.75, and closed at $58.25. This price gave Netscape a market capitalization of $2.2 billion. By December 1995, the company's value had grown to $7 billion. Kleiner Perkins's share was worth $256.3 million, over 51 *times* its initial investment.

According to Clark, within 2 weeks after the settlement with Netscape, the university gave Microsoft a license to Mosaic on favorable terms. About a year later, Spyglass sold Microsoft the lifetime rights to the PC version of Mosaic for $8 million. Ironically, the university may have ended up giving a rich out-of state corporation what it held back from a start-up created by its own former students. Thus, the university succeeded in alienating a wealthy group of entrepreneurs who could have been grateful and generous alumni. Moreover, had the university agreed to the original settlement terms offered by Netscape, its share on August 1995 would have been worth much more than the approximately $3 million it received. Due to its shortsightedness, NCSA, the leader in the early market, lost not only its talent, but also the market, a great profit-sharing opportunity, and the gratitude of some alumni.

While reports often highlight the rapid and enormous success of Netscape, they tend to underplay the equally enormous financial risk involved in the venture. A major reason for Netscape's success was Clark's courageous gamble on the company and his determination to stick it out through the threat of a costly and potentially fatal lawsuit. In contrast, a major cause of Mosaic's failure was the NCSA's focus on capturing royalties rather than on investing in the software to improve its performance.[11]

scrambling for funds

King C. Gillette's efforts to find a metallurgist to develop his shaving system describes only half the struggle to launch the Gillette Company. The other half has to do with his struggle to finds funds to commercialize the product.

Gillette's quest for a metallurgist led him to the chemist and inventor, William Nickerson. Once the skeptical Nickerson studied Gillette's designs, he became enthusiastic about the project. He knew that its success lay in the low-cost production of a high-quality blade. He was convinced he could develop the machinery for such production, but estimated it would cost almost $5000. That estimate was in 1901. Now Gillette, who then was a traveling salesman, had limited resources and had already used up his savings for his experiments. He said, "Though I always received a fair salary, I had saved very little, not because I was improvident, but because I was experimenting on something whenever I could find time, or had the money."[12]

So Gillette and Nickerson, with three other supporters, began to raise the funds for building the manufacturing equipment. In September 1901, they incorporated the firm, with Gillette as president and the others as company directors. Gillette wanted the firm to have the name Gillette Safety Razor Company. However, Nickerson objected since he felt he was making at least as much of a contribution as Gillette. In deference to Nickerson, the board of directors called it the American Safety Razor Company. The board optimistically set the company's capitalization at $500,000, based on 50,000 shares for $10 each. Gillette, the patent holder, received 17,500 shares, while Nickerson and the other four split 12,500 among themselves. They attempted to sell the rest to raise capital at a discount price of $0.50 per share, to be bought in blocks of 500 shares.

However, there was no rush for shares of the company, which then had no sales, no manufacturing facilities, not even a working prototype.

Over the rest of the year, through dint of persuasion, the owners were able to sell 13 blocks of shares, at $250 a block, to raise $3250. Investors were wealthy contacts of the founders, who bought the shares as much as a personal favor as a realistic investment. Finally, a board member, Henry Sachs, bought seven blocks to bring the round of financing to the $5000 that Nickerson needed. In gratitude, Gillette gave Sachs 2500 shares from his own allotment.

In the meantime, Nickerson had already started part-time work on the project. Instead of a larger share of company stock, he worked for a salary of $40 per week. He rented a small workshop close to a garbage loading dock in Boston. He determined the size and shape of the blade pretty early. The major task he faced was to harden sheet metal to produce a blade that would hold its cutting edge over many shaves. This was the crux of Gillette's invention, and the same problem that confounded others who studied Gillette's designs. After 8 months of intense efforts, Nickerson solved this problem and claimed the blade was ready for manufacture.

Nickerson's efforts quickly consumed the initial $5000, and the company had to survive on debt, typically from small loans. Nickerson was able to get an offer of $150,000 from his former New York business partners, in exchange for a controlling interest of 51 percent of the company. However, the offer seemed similar to previous business deals from which Nickerson had failed to earn any substantial profits for himself. Gillette's board of directors promptly turned down this proposal. Yet they had no alternatives. The company's stock was not selling even at a discounted price of $0.25 per share. The company was out of funds, and Gillette could see his dreams fading with the company's weakening financial position.

During much of that year, as the company was close to bankruptcy, the founders struggled to raise more funds. At one point they were close to considering liquidation. At that point, Gillette ran into a wealthy friend and client of his, John Joyce. Now Gillette had already led Joyce into a failed previous venture, for which Gillette still owed him almost $20,000. So until then, he had not asked Joyce to join him in this venture though he had given him a razor and blade to try out. At this meeting, Gillette told him about his latest venture, which was close to collapse because of its desperate need for funds. Joyce, who had risen from poverty through shrewd investments in brewing and utilities, had the means to support the company. He had tried the razor and blade and told Gillette he was pleased with it. So he offered to help Gillette out in this venture. However, because of the failure of his past venture with Gillette, he was more wary this time.

Joyce agreed to buy $100,000 worth of bonds at 8 percent. But he demanded a steep price. He would buy the bonds at a 40 percent discount, in addition to company stock equivalent to the face value of the bonds. He would also take the bonds only in installments, with the option to call off the deal after $30,000 worth of purchases if he did not see satisfactory progress. While the terms were stiff, the company had few alternatives, and the directors accepted the deal in October 1902. By December of that year, Joyce had pumped $9500 into the infant company and assumed an active role in company operations.

With this fresh infusion of cash, Nickerson began to tool up for commercial production. But he now had to keep up with not only his own expectations, but also those of Gillette and Joyce. It was a tough time for Nickerson. However, by April 1903, and after a total of $18,000 from Joyce, Nickerson was able to produce sample razors and blades for testing. Commercial sales started that same year, together with limited advertising. While commercialization was a big relief, by the end of 1903, the company had sold only 51 razors and 169 blades!

Just when his decade-long dream was coming to fruition, Gillette's fortunes changed. He was still working full time for the Crown Cork and Seal Company as a traveling salesman. In response to his good performance, the company gave him a raise and a transfer to London. Gillette was loath to take that offer. He was the key founder of the Gillette Company. He was its president (albeit without salary). Indeed, the company's name had been changed to the Gillette Razor and Blade Company. So he asked the board for a salary so he could forgo his transfer to London, stay back at this critical time, and work full time for the company. However, Joyce, whose funding had saved the company, would have nothing to do with that. Gillette recalled bitterly, "I was president of the company, but those in control refused to meet my wishes, giving as a reason the need of every dollar for development of the business."[13] So Gillette resigned the presidency of the company, though he stayed on as a director, and moved with his family to London. He would soon have even more serious misgivings about the move.

A few months after his departure, testimonials began coming into the company attesting to buyers' great satisfaction with the product. Consumers raved about the smoothness of the shave, the freedom from nicks and cuts, and, most of all, the saving in time from not having to sharpen the blades. One consumer was so pleased, he claimed that if the Gillette razor were no longer available, he would not part with his for thousands of dollars. These testimonials kept pace with a steady increase in sales. Nickerson could barely keep up with the demand. Unfortunately, because of a problem in manufacturing, the production level fell from a projected 2000 razor sets a week to below the breakeven number of 1250 sets per week. Nickerson had to then work to correct the problem, causing a further financial burden on top of continued debt servicing and the cost of operations. Thus, despite the sales pickup, the company was in another cash crunch. Joyce thought up some clever schemes to cross this hurdle.

One proposal was for shareholders to turn in half their shares. The company would first offer them to existing shareholders for at least $1.50 a share. Unsold shares would be sold on the market at $1.50 per share. To Gillette this seemed like a sellout and a further dilution of his holding. He was already left with only 9000 shares, after turning in the rest to compensate Joyce for his purchase of bonds. Together with Gillette, Joyce was now a major shareholder of the company. Gillette also suspected that this was an attempt by Joyce to take control of the company under the pretense of fundraising. Fortunately, the proposal required the approval of all shareholders. Gillette promptly vetoed the proposal.

Another proposal was to sell the foreign rights of the Gillette shaving system. Friends of Joyce from Chicago were willing to manufacture and market Gillette razors and blades all over the world in return for a royalty and an investment of $100,000 in the foreign business. On August 29, 1904, the board voted to give the company president full powers to execute this agreement with Joyce's friends. When Gillette heard about it, he was outraged. Intrinsic to his vision was the manufacture and sales of Gillette's shaving system all over the world. He had no reason to doubt that what consumers in the United States liked so much about the system, consumers in other parts of the world would like as well. He believed that the proposed contract was a giveaway that just could not be justified. He immediately set sail for the United States.

Gillette arrived in Boston just in time to convince the president and members of the board to reverse their decision. Near the same time, Nickerson was able to iron out the production problems as well as develop a method for superior blades. Sales began to soar. In December 1904 alone, the company sold almost 20,000 sets of razors and blades. Sales for the whole year totaled almost 91,000 sets with more than 10,000 packages of extra blades. The company was on a roll. Gillette's persuasion had saved the lucrative foreign market for the company's expansion. His persuasion, together with the improving fortunes of the company, afforded him some additional benefits. The board voted to make Joyce the new president, make Gillette vice president, and give each of them a salary of $18,000. Gillette relocated his family to Boston and oversaw the company's expansion into foreign markets. The company opened a sales office in London in 1906, a manufacturing plant in Paris the same year, a distribution center in Germany in 1906, another plant in Canada that year, and a sales operation in Mexico. The same vision that had launched the company was now instrumental in launching a multinational enterprise.

Gillette's vision had at last begun to pay off. Persistence and financial commitment through many dark years had begun to bear fruit. With the rapid growth of the company, Gillette's personal fortunes improved dramatically. In addition, by shrewdly trading on the company's stock, Gillette was able to amass 14,000 shares of company stock. He had become rich well beyond his expectations.

Unfortunately, tension between Joyce and Gillette worsened over the years as both men struggled for control of the company. Then in 1910, Joyce bought out Gillette and the other directors to become principal shareholder in the company. He held that position until 1916. Gillette became a millionaire and moved to California. However, he stayed on as a company director, and held the honorary title of president almost until his death in 1932. He took an active interest in company affairs, and freely gave his advice, which was not unwelcome. Most importantly, the company firmly internalized his vision of serving the global mass market for shaving.[14]

sacrificing profits for full service

While some readers may be familiar with Amazon's pervasiveness and success on the Web, many may not know the reasons behind its success. Some may assume that the firm is successful because it was the first Internet bookseller. But Amazon was not the first. Yet it quickly surpassed earlier Internet booksellers on its way to becoming the top online retailer of any kind. That success can be directly tied to a "relentless reinvestment in new markets in lieu of banking premature profits."[15] Consider what Amazon has achieved since opening to the public in 1995. Annual sales have grown from nothing to nearly $3 billion. Its stock market value is about $5 billion (even after the tremendous decline in Internet stocks). And in 1999, *Advertising Age* ranked it as the third-leading brand on the Internet and the sixteenth most reputable company in the whole world.[16]

How did it achieve so much in such a short time? The rapidly growing Internet provided opportunities for many firms, and Amazon captured those opportunities. From the beginning, there was never anything small about Amazon. Jeff Bezos saw an opportunity to sell books on the Internet; yet he was far from the only person to recognize this business opportunity. What set Bezos apart was his unique vision and his financial commitment. Initially, he envisioned a mass market for selling books on the Internet. His vision focused not only on the United States but on the whole world. Later, his vision expanded to include music, electronic products, software, and many other items. That vast vision inspired a massive commitment of financial resources that repeatedly sacrificed profits for growth.

When Bezos first incorporated Amazon as Cadabra, Inc., in 1994, many others had already recognized the potential for building business on the Internet. In fact, Bezos first explored Internet business opportunities as part of his work for an investment management company in New York. In that exercise, he identified bookselling as the best potential business for the emerging Internet. That conclusion sparked his vision. He realized that a good Internet book retailer needed a wholehearted commitment to selling on the Web, including a dedication to speed, convenience, full service, and wide appeal. He gave up his seven-figure income to build this radically different retail model from scratch, which required great financial resources. Bezos's vision, persistence, and financial commitment bore strong similarities to that required for the development of Federal Express.

When Bezos got started, other Internet booksellers already had a head start. Computer Literacy had registered its domain name (clbooks.com) in 1991 and became perhaps the first bookseller on the Internet. Its selling process relied on email, which was the current technology of the time. As Web browsers became more commonly available, at least two other companies established Web sites for selling books. One of these sites, books.com, was already offering over 400,000 titles by 1994, the same year Amazon started. If you asked analysts in 1994 whether books.com or Cadabra, Inc., would become the leading online bookseller, there would have been nearly unanimous support for books.com. Yet the current undisputed leader is Amazon. What is the root cause of Amazon's success? Financial commitment inspired by a vision of the mass market played the critical role.

Success from financial commitment requires access to financial resources and the willingness to use those resources. The history of Amazon clearly illustrates both factors. In the early days of the company, most of the money funding Amazon came directly from Bezos and his family. In 1994 he made personal investments and loans of over $50,000, while his start-up lost much more than that. When the company needed funds in 1995, Bezos convinced his family to invest $250,000. Access to his family's financial resources helped Amazon survive in the early days as it worked toward launching its Web site. Even though Amazon could have started to sell books quickly, it took its time to build a Web site that was easy to use and packed with information. To support the site, it provided customer service that set a new standard for Internet retailers. However, by quickly using his family's investment to get ready for a very large market without generating any revenue, Bezos put the entire company at risk.

When Amazon was finally ready to launch its Web site in July 1995, it met with some early success. Yet sales for the year totaled only $511,000 despite an investment of $200,000 in marketing and $171,000 in product development. These and other expenses led to a loss of more than $300,000 in its first year of operation. Had Amazon failed at this time, the loss would have been borne almost entirely by Jeff Bezos and his family. To continue to pursue his vision, Bezos had to inspire others to commit resources too. Toward the end of 1995, Bezos secured about $1 million from several individual investors. Bezos's willingness to use this additional capital to build his business was never in doubt. "We are taking what may be the profits and reinvesting them in the future of the business," said Bezos. "It would literally be the stupidest decision of any management team to make Amazon profitable right now."[17]

The following year, Amazon acquired even larger financial resources and continued to increase its investments in the business. The top venture capital firm, Kleiner Perkins Caufield & Byers, committed $8 million in return for about 13 percent equity in Amazon. With this additional capital, marketing expenses increased dramatically to $6.1 million in 1996. Major ads appeared in the *Wall Street Journal, New York Times Book Review*, and *USA Today*. Amazon continued to spend money on its Web site and computer systems by investing $2.4 million in product development. Over time, customers were given nearly instantaneous access to inventory and shipping status. They could read and write online reviews, and eventually, Amazon developed the capability to provide personalized book recommendations for all its customers. Amazon wanted to provide these features to delight its customers and keep them coming back to buy more. These investments slowly began to pay off. For example, in 1996, *Time* magazine recognized Amazon.com as one of the 10 best Web sites.

Amazon's willingness to commit resources to fully satisfy its customers even extended to the shipping department. Amazon developed a reputation for overpacking shipments so books would always arrive in good condition. Perhaps more importantly, Amazon ex-

panded its warehouse capacity from 50,000 to 285,000 square feet so it could deliver books to its customers faster. All these investments meant that even though Amazon's sales increased from $511,000 to nearly $16 million in 1996, its net loss grew 20-fold to over $6 million. From these stark figures, one can see that immediate profitability was not important to Bezos; investing to please consumers and become the leading supplier of books was.

Amazon took the next step in acquiring the necessary financial resources with its initial public offering in May 1997. It raised $45 million in a single day and continued to invest heavily throughout the year. Marketing expenses increased from $6.1 million to $40 million. Product development expenses increased from $2.4 million to $13 million. Amazon paid to have visitors from 6 of the 10 most heavily trafficked Web sites directed to its own site. Deals with Yahoo, AOL, Netscape, Geocities, Excite, and AltaVista gave Amazon's logo prominent placement on these companies' home pages and provided direct click through to Amazon's Web site.

During 1997, Bezos's vision was again put to the test. For the first time, Amazon faced a competitor that was able and willing to make large investments too. When Barnes and Noble opened its Web site, it planned to use its buying power to offer dramatically lower prices on best-selling books. But Bezos promptly vowed to match its low prices, again forgoing immediate profits to invest in the future of his company. He said, "We will continue to make investment decisions in light of long-term market leadership considerations rather than short-term profitability considerations or short-term Wall Street reactions. We will make bold rather than timid investment decisions where we see sufficient probability of gaining market leadership advantages."[18]

Even though sales for the year expanded dramatically to nearly $150 million, the lower prices and massive investments led to a net loss of $31 million.

By 1998, Amazon was ready to expand beyond bookselling in pursuit of Bezos's larger vision of becoming a broad-based Internet retailer. Amazon invested in music sales and quickly leveraged its established customer base into becoming the leading online music retailer in only its first full quarter of business. It expanded into videos and became the leading online video retailer in only 6 weeks.

Even though all of Amazon's sales were expanding rapidly and would reach $610 million in 1998, Amazon continued to build the infrastructure for an even larger business. Making his intentions clear, Bezos explained, "We plan to invest aggressively to build the foundation for a multi-billion-dollar revenue company serving tens of millions of customers with operational excellence and high efficiency."[19]

As part of this commitment, Amazon doubled its warehouse capacity in 1998. It invested in several other areas as well. For $55 million, it purchased leading book retailers in the United Kingdom and Germany, as well as an Internet database full of movie information. This investment increased the entertainment value of Amazon's Web site and encouraged customers to stay there longer and come back more frequently. In August, Amazon acquired an online price-comparison shopping service for $180 million. This move signaled its interest in moving far beyond selling just books, music, and movies. Finally, Amazon acquired an online address and calendar service for $90 million in order to provide an even broader set of services to its customers. Clearly, Amazon thought of itself as much more than an Internet bookseller.

In 1999, Amazon took advantage of its high stock price to access even greater financial resources. It sold $1.25 billion in bonds that could be converted to stock at a later date. This infusion of capital provided the firm with the resources to continue investing aggressively in building its business. Marketing and selling expenses grew to over $400 million, and product development expenses grew to $160 million. Its warehouse infrastructure expanded from 300,000 to 5 million square feet in just 12 months. This expansion provided the ability to ship up to $10 billion annually. Bezos was planning to make Amazon a very large Internet company.

He continued to broaden Amazon's product offerings by adding auctions, toys, consumer electronics, home improvement, video games, software, and access to a broad network of local merchants who sold all kinds of products. In addition, Amazon made multi-million dollar investments in several companies and provided links to these affiliates on its own Web site. To support this broad portfolio of products, advertising expenses grew from $17 million in 1998 to $75 million in 1999. Today, it continues to invest in mar-

keting and was the top online advertiser as recently as the 2000 holiday season.

The critical role of financial commitment in Amazon's success becomes clearer when compared with another online bookseller, the Internet Bookshop. In 1994, Darryl Mattocks in the United Kingdom had the same idea as Jeff Bezos had in the United States: Use the capabilities of the Internet to offer more books than the largest physical stores possibly could. Both men established what each claimed to be the world's largest bookstore. But they had different visions of the market and substantially different styles.

Bezos saw the whole world as his market, and wanted to serve this market fully. On the other hand, Mattocks focused on the smaller U.K. market and developed his business cautiously. While Bezos raised $11 million to "get big fast,"[20] Mattocks used an $80,000 loan and his own credit cards to build his business. According to an article in *The Economist*, "Unsurprisingly, the better-funded Mr. Bezos has comprehensively outmarketed Mr. Mattocks."[21] Both companies went public around the same time. The Internet Bookshop had a value of $10 million, while Amazon was valued at about a half *billion* dollars. From there, Amazon continued to build on its dominant position. When Amazon opened its own U.K. Web site in 1998, it immediately became the leading online bookseller in that market too.

The financial commitment of Bezos and other early investors in Amazon has reaped massive rewards. Amazon is the leading online retailer. Its brand is well known and respected, and it has a reputation for excellent customer service. The firm now has sales of almost $3 billion and customers in more than 160 countries. Although the stock market decline of all Internet stocks in 2000–2001 significantly lowered Amazon's stock price, it still has a stock market value of about $5 billion. Bezos himself is a billionaire. His family's share is worth tens of millions of dollars, and many other investors are multimillionaires.

While Amazon's future success is certainly not guaranteed, Bezos's vision of the mass market on the Internet, his strong financial commitment, and his willingness to risk assets to realize his vision put the company in the best position of any Internet retailer to succeed in the long run.[22]

committing resources in practice

The development of great new ventures almost always requires tremendous financial resources. A good idea alone is never sufficient. Good ideas require persistence over many years to get established and continuous investments in product research, manufacturing development, and marketing. During this period, costs exceed revenue, so these new ventures do not become self-sustaining for years. A pervasive belief among economists is that financial markets are efficient. By this they mean that good ideas will ultimately get the funds to support them, while bad ideas will be weaned out by lack of financial resources. This principle may hold in the general economy over thousands of investment choices. However, as the above examples illustrate, individual entrepreneurs or managers face a great struggle for funds to establish new markets because they must constantly persuade skeptical investors of the merits of their proposals.

For individuals or small firms with limited resources, the challenge to get the needed funds can often be insurmountable. These individuals need a clear vision of the mass market they wish to pursue and strong commitment to realize that vision. They must then inspire others who have financial resources to share that vision. Gillette's struggle described in this chapter illustrates the great lengths an individual must go alone to succeed. The efforts of Haloid (later Xerox) described in an earlier chapter illustrate the challenge that small firms undergo to succeed.

From a distance, it might appear that access to personal funds may somehow ease this burden. However, such resources do not resolve the problem entirely. For example, even though Jim Clark, Jeff Bezos, and Fred Smith had access to substantial personal and family funds, they required even greater resources. In the case of Fred Smith, the need arose from the sheer scale of operation that he visualized. In the case of Jim Clark, the need arose from the speed with which the Internet start-up consumed funds. In the case of Jeff Bezos, the need arose from the massive investment required to quickly implement a new form of retailing while also providing high-quality customer service. Their acute need for funds forced these individuals to seek external funds from private investors and ultimately the financial market. In all these cases, the use of personal resources increases the risk of the total venture to the individual, who then has time, employment, and savings invested in the same business. Thus the need for commitment on the part of wealthy individuals is as great as for an individual or small firm with limited financial resources.

Similarly, it may seem that large corporations with deep pockets may be able to easily deploy resources for a promising venture. However, cases in this book reveal that the battle for funds is no less intense even in these corporations. There are always competing uses for funds. Moreover, the really promising ventures are typically apparent to only one or a few individuals. Others in the corporation need to be convinced of them. Additionally, large successful corporations are often burdened with bureaucracy. Thus the challenge to commit the necessary resources remains great. A few visionary individuals need to convince the bureaucracy or senior management of the merits of a new venture. Aspects of the history of Xerox and Microsoft, which we cover in the next chapter, illustrate how intense this battle for funds can be.

Throughout this struggle, the great temptation facing the visionary is to "sell out" to a larger firm or a team of investors. The danger in such a sale is that other investors who have the funds but not the vision may take over. They may then steer the venture in short-term profit-yielding directions that compromise the original vision and fail to tap the mass market or attain market leadership. For example, Gillette's reliance on Joyce led Joyce to control the fortune of the early Gillette Company. He was then ready to sell the international rights of the innovation for a small short-term gain. It was Gillette's prompt return and articulation of his vision of a global mass market that saved the tremendous international opportunity for the company. Today, Gillette's international operations are the major source of sales and profits for the company. Similarly, Fred Smith had to fend off nervous banks and investors for years in order to keep alive and realize his vision of a national priority mail service.

summary

- Financial commitment is important to firms when they first enter a market, especially if they face entrenched competitors or huge start-up costs.

- The primary need for financial resources is to pay for research, manufacturing, and marketing in order to operate on the large scale necessary to meet the needs of the mass market.
- At the same time, until a firm's new product becomes successful, it does not generate enough revenue to cover the cost required for these expenditures.
- Financial commitment consists of both the availability of monetary resources and the willingness to commit them to the task.
- Entrepreneurs and small entrants may be willing to invest all their resources but may lack sufficient resources.
- Large entrants may have adequate financial resources but may lack the willingness to commit them to the new task.
- The more radical the innovation or the larger the scale of operation, the greater the need for financial resources. At the same time, the more radical the innovation, the more uncertain its payoff, and the less willing are internal or external financiers to invest.
- Enduring success comes to those firms that have a vision that is clear and strong enough to motivate themselves or others to commit financial resources to realize that vision.

leveraging assets despite
uncertainty

Firms that hold dominant positions in a product category are often able to become leaders in a new related category or market even if they enter late (see Figure 10-1). For example, IBM's dominance of the mainframe computer market enabled it to quickly enter and lead the PC market, even though it did so late. Microsoft's dominance of the PC operating systems market helped its late entry and dominance of the browser market. Other categories where a dominant firm has entered late and succeeded are Coke in diet colas and Tide in liquid laundry detergents. In all these new categories, once the late entrant got into the market, the pioneering brand or the existing market leader quickly lost its position.

What specific advantages enable established firms to succeed with a late entry into a related category? The advantages come from the assets firms accumulate from their established position in the old category. We can classify these assets into two groups, generalized assets and specialized assets.

Generalized assets are those that a firm can transfer relatively easily from one category to another, without the assets necessarily losing value. A firm's brand name, reputation, customer base, or talent represents generalized assets. For example, when word pro-

Figure 10-1. Role of Specialized Assets in Entering New Categories

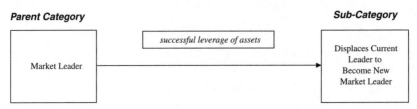

cessors became popular, Microsoft used its brand name well known for its operating system to label its own new program *Microsoft* Word. The key characteristic of generalized assets is that they can be transferred with minimal change. In the same context, Microsoft could transfer its talented programmers from working on the operating system to working on the word processor with only minimal reeducation.

The ability to transfer generalized assets easily does not make the decision to do so an easy one. Such transfers involve risks and must be carefully managed. For instance, the sale of a mediocre word processor could tarnish the reputation of Microsoft in the parent category. The shift of programmers from designing an operating system to designing a word processor could jeopardize the firm's technological leadership in the operating system's market. Thus we use the term *leverage* to suggest that the firm needs to wisely transfer generalized assets without jeopardizing its position in the old category.

Specialized assets are those that may not transfer easily to the new category, such as current products, technology, manufacturing facilities, sales force, or distribution systems.[1] For example, when IBM planned to enter the personal computer market, it could not easily use its current sales force and distribution system, which were based on servicing large businesses. The market for PCs was much broader. They were being sold to large and small businesses as well as to consumers for their home use. Similarly, when typewriters became primarily electronic, more reliable, and less expensive, IBM's dedicated sales and service personnel were not suitable for the retail distribution channels that started selling the newer typewriters. In such situations, a firm may have to sacrifice its specialized assets when entering a new category or when trying to stay competitive in an existing category. As another example, when IBM designed and introduced its personal computer, it bought components from the outside rather than from other divisions of the company, and developed a new manufacturing facility, sales force, and distribution system. In some cases, such moves may cannibalize specialized assets. For example, when Microsoft planned to introduce Internet Explorer, potential marketing strategies would have led to a decline in sales of their existing products such as Microsoft Network. Thus, entry into a category extension by leveraging current assets requires either transferring generalized assets or sacrificing specialized assets.

As the above examples suggest, a major hindrance to leveraging assets is the extent to which the new category does or appears to threaten the old category. For example, does the advent of personal computers threaten sales of mainframes? Do sales of computer printers threaten sales of copiers? The greater this threat, the harder for the firm to enter the new category. If the firm has specialized assets in the old category, and the new category threatens the old, then the firm runs the risk of losing much or all of the value it accumulated in these specialized assets. To enter and dominate the new category, the firm must be willing to cannibalize its specialized assets. For example, once personal computers became popular, Wang would have had to cannibalize the assets it had invested in developing dedicated word processors if it wanted to enter and compete in the new word processing market. Such an attitude is always difficult, especially when managers have spent a lifetime building these assets, or have come to associate the assets with the firm itself. Nevertheless, failure to do so can lead to the loss of a large opportunity in the new category and loss of the strong position in the current category if it goes into decline.

A second related hindrance to asset leverage is a strict focus on costs. Market entry invariably involves risks. Such risks are greater for the firm with a dominant position in an established market because it could damage or sacrifice some of the assets it developed to establish that dominance. A narrow, rigid cost analysis will often lead a firm to the highly defensive posture of defending its accumulated assets and not venturing into new markets. While managers must not ignore costs, they must also fully assess the benefits of tapping a potential mass market that may lie dormant within a new and related category. They must also take into account the enormous benefits that arise from new technologies in servicing this mass market. As previous chapters have demonstrated, such benefits include declining manufacturing costs, improved quality, and increased product features. Thus, a proper assessment of new market opportunities requires a full analysis of future costs and benefits rather than a narrow focus on current costs. Examples in this chapter will detail the difference between these two approaches.

A third hindrance to asset leverage is a myopic view of markets. By myopic view, we mean that managers are so constrained by their focus on current products and current customers that it is difficult or impossible for them to see new opportunities due to changes in customers or technology in evolving or emerging markets. This problem can afflict firms that are dominant in the old category as a result of years of effective management and successful defeat of competitors. Success and domination can lead to complacency and short-sightedness. When managers in such firms see the start of a new category, they may ignore it, doubt it will grow, or just deny its importance. Thus, success in the old category leads to a myopic view of market evolution and a premature denial of the potential of the new category. Such myopia runs contrary to the vision that is so essential in entering markets and achieving long-term dominance.

A fourth hindrance to asset leverage is bureaucracy. This problem is especially true for firms that have a long period of sustained and unchallenged leadership in the old category. Such firms often become large and bureaucratic. The organization incorporates more departments and many more hierarchical levels of management. Managers from various parts of the organization often make decisions by committee. This process of decision making takes time and tends to exclude bold or radical decisions. Thus the firm may become slow, cautious, and indecisive. In contrast, new categories in their infancy evolve rapidly. Firms competing in the new category need to demonstrate independent thinking, quick decisions, and rapid moves. Because of the category's newness, it may require bold or radically different technologies, designs, organizational structures, or strategies. Thus bureaucracy may hinder a dominant firm from entering a new category successfully or dominating it for very long.

One way to overcome these problems is for dominant firms to develop independent departments or business units under the leadership of entrepreneurial managers. Such units need independent authority to enter the new market with minimal interference from managers serving the established category. Another approach is for firms to develop product champions and assign them resources to identify market opportunities and enter those they think are promising. A third approach is for some senior managers to have sole responsibility for surveying market changes and exploiting new market opportunities. Such managers need to be future and externally oriented. They need to distance themselves from the travails of current businesses. They can then communicate this vision to employees of the firm to provide them with the direction and motivation to boldly enter new markets and aggressively compete to succeed in them. For example, Bill Gates recently gave up his CEO duties at Microsoft in order to concentrate his attention on articulating his company's vision for the future.

The start of a new market poses great challenges to a firm that dominates an older related category. The new category can serve as an immense opportunity for the firm to extend its dominance. Such dominance has generally enabled the firm to accumulate many generalized and specialized assets. However, success in the new category often depends on the firm's skillful leveraging of these assets to extend its dominance into the new category. Entry into this market runs the risk of damaging generalized assets or cannibalizing specialized assets.[2] Thus the firm can be torn between exploiting the opportunity or succumbing to the fear of losing current position by moving aggressively into the category extension. A detailed look at some cases reveals the intensity of this challenge. We focus on four cases in particular: Charles Schwab's entry into online brokerage, Xerox's potential to market products for the office of the future, Microsoft's entry into Web browsers, and IBM's entry into the PC market. We return to some familiar companies from previous chapters by introducing new aspects of their experiences that demonstrate the benefits and risks of asset leverage. We begin our discussion with the completely new example of a company that epitomizes success through asset leverage.

sacrificing current position to dominate online trading

During the late 1990s, online stock trading exploded onto the national spotlight. These new trading systems gave individual consumers the ability to trade stocks like professionals, by using their own computers and paying substantially lower commissions on trades. Early on, several companies moved aggressively into this new market. The first firm to offer Internet trading on its Web site was K. Aufhauser & Co. in 1994. Ameritrade acquired Aufhauser in 1995, as Ameritrade began to push into the new online market. In the same year, another early entrant, Lombard, introduced Web-based trading. Within 4 months, 12 percent of Lombard's trades were being done on its Web site. E*trade entered the Web-based online market dramatically in early 1996 by offering stock trades for the low price of only $14.95. Prior to that, E*trade had offered online investing services through America Online and CompuServe as early as 1992. By May 1996, E*trade was already doing more than 35 percent of its trades on the Internet. In 1997, Ameritrade intensified the competition in this market by offering Internet stock trades for as little as $8.

During this period, several analysts drew parallels to the mid-1970s when fixed commissions were abolished in the stock brokerage industry. At that time, several discount brokers emerged as formidable competitors to the traditional full-service brokers. Foremost among these firms was Charles Schwab. The new Internet brokers posed similar challenges to both discount brokers and traditional full-service brokers. Since these new online brokers used the Internet, many thought that they would possess unique skills that would enable them to dominate this new and rapidly growing market. Consider the following quote from *Business Week* in 1996: "What Schwab did to the full-service firms, Lombard and E*trade will do to Schwab and the full-service firms."[3]

When discount brokers became popular with investors, traditional full-service firms faced the dilemma of either losing market share to the discount brokers or losing margin by matching their prices. In 1996, Charles Schwab faced the same threat from online brokers.

Now, fast-forward to 2001. Charles Schwab executes the majority of its trades online, accounting for nearly 25 percent of all online trades. With 4.1 million online accounts, "Schwab is still the undisputed king" of online brokers.[4] How did Schwab go from being severely threatened in 1996 to the king of online brokers today?

Schwab's history is a strong example of the benefits of asset leverage. By transferring its existing strengths to the growing online market, the firm was able to enter later than other online brokers and quickly dominate this new market. That move was not without risks or costs. Schwab ran the risk of alienating its current customers by offering apparently better deals to online customers. The firm also faced the potential of lower margins and severe price competition by entering the online business.

But Charles Schwab, the founder and still leader of the company bearing his name, had a vision of the emerging market in online trading, and of how he could leverage his firm's current assets to serve that market. Schwab (the company) made use of assets in four key areas: a large customer base, a strong brand name, technological proficiency, and a reputation for excellent customer service. Schwab's history reveals several important lessons in how a firm can apply the principle of asset leverage to transfer strengths into a new market that is related to a firm's current market. By exploring Schwab's history, we will see how Schwab's strengths as a traditional discount broker enabled the firm to become the dominant player in the new online brokerage market.

Charles Schwab & Co. emerged from the deregulation of the brokerage industry in the mid-1970s and established itself as a technological leader and innovator in the discount brokerage business. Its application of technology enabled it to provide superior customer service at low cost, thus offering high value at reasonable prices. However, Schwab never tried to compete solely on the basis of low prices. It focused on superior service at a fair price, rather than trying to offer the lowest price alone.

Although Schwab was rarely first with innovations, it continually improved several innovations during the 1980s and 1990s. In 1985, Schwab introduced Equalizer, a DOS-based software program that provided online transactions and research via personal computers. This program used a dial-up service that let customers use telephones to connect their PC to Schwab's computers. In 1989, Schwab introduced Telebroker. This new low-cost channel enabled Schwab to expand its service by adding automated telephone capabilities. This allowed Schwab to offer a price discount to customers who executed trades through this new system.

In 1993, Schwab introduced its StreetSmart software for Windows. This software program expanded the features of the Equalizer software and made it compatible with the next-generation Windows operating system. In addition to these technological innovations, Schwab differentiated itself from other discount brokers by opening an extensive network of retail stores. These physical stores enabled Schwab to provide services that its competitors could not match since many customers preferred to do at least some of their transactions in person. Also, the physical presence of these stores made many customers feel more secure about having their money invested with Schwab in the first place.

In total, Schwab's innovations in these and other areas helped establish it as the dominant discount broker by the time Internet trading began to emerge. To many brokerage firms, the Internet was a serious threat. To Schwab, the Internet became a great opportunity because the company was able to transfer its assets to this new market.

When other firms began to offer online trading via the Internet in 1994, Schwab did not rush into the new market. But it did begin to make some careful moves. In early 1995, it launched a Web site, but only to provide information to current and prospective customers. An immediate move into online trading posed considerable risks for existing brokerage firms. Since trades were priced much lower online, quickly converting customers to online accounts could mean a large and immediate decrease in revenue and profit. By one estimate a fast conversion by Schwab could have led to an immediate 50 percent reduction in revenue. Therefore, Schwab was in no rush to encourage a fast transition among its customers, especially while online trading was still in its infancy. In addition, Schwab's formidable strengths meant that it could enter later and still become quite successful.

By late 1995, new Internet brokers continued to add accounts at a fast pace. Meanwhile, traditional brokers continued to resist the move to the Internet. They couldn't really see where this market was heading. Even the vice president of marketing for Smith Barney's Web site didn't foresee the changes ahead. When asked about Internet trading, he said simply, "Our clients don't want it."[5]

However, by late 1995 Charles Schwab himself had begun to develop a vision for what Internet-based brokerages could become. He directed his company to move quickly. He now believed that the Internet represented the future for the brokerage industry. And this future rested on many of the assets that Schwab already possessed. First, a strong brand name would attract new customers to Schwab's Web site. Second, a large group of existing customers provided a large pool of potential customers for Internet trading. Third, Schwab's technologically skilled employees were ready to build the computer systems necessary to move to the Internet. In fact, Schwab initially received bids from outside vendors to build its Web site for $2 million in 9 to 12 months. Since Schwab was committed to moving faster at this point, it developed its Web site internally for only $1 million in just 3 months. Fourth, Schwab's existing retail locations gave it a unique advantage over the new online brokers. Even though customers might require in-person service very rarely, this asset provided Schwab a reassuring physical presence relative to its virtual competitors.

Charles Schwab's vision of what the Internet could become was consistent with what his company had been doing for many years. The Internet provided a means of dramatically expanding the services and features he could offer to his customers. Importantly, these services could be provided at much lower cost than if they were provided through traditional telephone or retail store channels. Thus, Schwab could continue to offer high-quality service at fair prices. While established competitors waited to move, Schwab's vision of what the market could become led him to now move quickly and decisively. Schwab compared his market foresight to the greatest hockey player of the time: "Like Wayne Gretzky, we want to skate where the puck is going to be."[6] In late 1995 and 1996, Charles Schwab had the vision of where this market was headed. According to *Fortune* magazine, "Chuck Schwab has a vision of how people will handle their personal finances a few years out."[7]

Schwab's vision spurred his firm into action. He began by establishing a group within Schwab to offer online trading through a service called e.Schwab. In January 1996, e.Schwab went national. This service enabled customers to open accounts that would be handled over the Internet. Customers would interact with Schwab through email and were allowed one phone call to a telephone representative per month. The lower-service features of e.Schwab were more than compensated for by the much lower commissions. Within the first 2 weeks, 25,000 customers signed up. By the summer, the price for trading 1000 shares through e.Schwab had been reduced from $39.95 to $29.95. By the end of 1996, Schwab had 600,000 online accounts. During 1997, this number doubled to 1.2 million online accounts, with more than half coming from its existing customer base. Schwab's ability to leverage its existing customer base meant that it had more than three times as many accounts as its next closest competitor, DLJdirect. It was even further ahead of other firms like E*trade, Ameritrade, and Lombard.

However, trouble soon began to emerge. Some online customers did not like the fact that they received a lower level of service than offline Schwab customers. Frontline employees on the telephone and in the stores had to continually explain to some customers why they could not get the same level of service. This situation put Schwab's vision to the test. But Charles Schwab and his co-CEO David Pottruck were thoroughly convinced that the Internet was fundamentally and irreversibly transforming the brokerage industry. According to *Fortune*, "co-CEOs Schwab and Pottruck were willing to bet their company's future on the Web's transforming technology."[8] So rather than offering online accounts for only a small portion of their customers, they decided to thoroughly embrace the Internet. In late 1997, Schwab offered all of its customers online trading through the Internet for only $29.95 per trade along with Schwab's full range of services.

Many customers began to move to this new and vastly improved online account. In the first 5 months, 500,000 new online accounts were opened, bringing in $40 billion in assets. Schwab and Pottruck foresaw an immediate negative impact on the firm. And it did occur. Since so many people were now trading at a lower price, the average commission dropped from $63 in the fourth quarter of 1997 to $57 in the first quarter of 1998. Schwab's experience told them that online customers would trade more frequently, but this increase did not materialize right away. Schwab's 1998 first-quarter revenue was 3 percent lower, and pretax profit declined by 16 percent relative to fourth-quarter 1997. The stock price suffered too, by dropping 20 percent from its previous 52-week high. Yet Schwab persisted in building its online business.

By the end of 1998, Schwab began to see the rewards of this persistence. Schwab's strong brand, superior technology, and excellent customer service paid off. Annual revenue increased 19 percent, and pretax profit increased 29 percent. The stock market also began to recognize Schwab's vision. Between June and December, Schwab stock appreciated 158 percent, and its market cap topped that of Merrill Lynch, even though Merrill Lynch managed nearly three times the amount of assets.

Today, Schwab has more than 4 million online accounts. The majority of its trades are executed on the Internet versus just 36 percent 3 years ago. The low-cost Internet channel has enabled Schwab to continue to offer superior service at fair prices. It beat the online upstarts at their own game by leveraging its strengths in brand name, technology, customer service, and an existing customer base. Even though Merrill Lynch has become more valuable than Schwab again, Schwab's market cap has nearly quadrupled since 1996.

Charles Schwab's vision to leverage his existing business and turn it into the dominant online brokerage has been very rewarding for him personally. In just 5 years since he began to move his business to the Internet, Schwab's personal net worth has grown about five times and today stands at over $6 billion.[9]

squandering assets in turf battles

Xerox founded the Palo Alto Research Center to develop the office of the future. As with all such futuristic projects, Xerox's managers at the time had no idea what innovations to expect or what shape that future office would take. PARC was an astonishingly successful experiment. The center developed a host of radical innovations that revolutionized the concept of the computer and what it could do for people. Key among these innovations were the following:

- The laser computer printer, the forerunner of desktop laser printers and laser copiers, was operative in 1971. That was 4 years before IBM introduced its own laser printer. Laser printing itself became a major category, and one that is still closely related to paper copiers.
- Smalltalk, an object-oriented programming language, which was a precursor to Java, was developed in 1971.
- Alto, an early personal computer, was operational in 1973. That date is 2 years before MITS commercialized the Altair and launched the massive new category of personal computers.
- Bit-mapped graphics that allowed overlapping windows, pop-up menus, and graphics on a desktop monitor was developed in 1974. This date was 8 years before Apple included these features in its Lisa, and 11 years before Microsoft included them in its first version of the Windows operating system. Operating systems for personal computers became another huge new category.
- The Ethernet, a system for networking personal computers, was developed in 1971, and was used to support a network of computers and printers by 1975. As computers became increasingly linked in the 1990s, networking itself becoming another major category.
- Gypsy, a graphical word processing program with true fonts (and what-you-see-is-what-you-get display), was ready in 1975. A user could prepare the entire document on screen with a keyboard, navigate through it with a mouse, edit, cut and paste as necessary, and print it out on a laser printer. Such software that predated Microsoft's Word by more than a decade ultimately replaced typewriters and dedicated word processors.
- Notetaker, a suitcase-size portable computer, was ready in 1978. That was 3 years before the market introduction of the Osborne I.

Thus with its successful copier business and its rich portfolio of innovations, Xerox was probably the most asset-rich company in the world at the time. It could have become a giant by dominating any one of five new categories: word processors, operating systems, laptop computers, laser printers, or personal computers.

However, Xerox did not leverage those assets effectively. PARC itself was so successful that the parent company barely understood its creations, had no idea of their commercial value, and rejected or delayed most of them. Xerox only reluctantly brought to market three of the major innovations developed at PARC: the laser printer, Ethernet, and Star (personal) Computer System. The first was a partial success, the second became an industry standard, and the third was a failure because it was too late and too high-priced. Thus, Xerox made a big commercial success of only one of these innovations.

Why did this happen? Xerox's failure really arose from the reluctance on the part of senior managers to leverage the firm's current assets to embrace and commercialize the new innovations. Xerox's CEO at the time, Peter McColough, chose the easy path of deferring to these managers rather than leading them in this task. In order to appreciate this explanation, we review how Xerox handled just two of its promising innovations, the laser printer and the Alto personal computer.

DELAY OF THE LASER PRINTER

By the end of 1971, Gary Starkweather's persistence and PARC's supportive environment enabled the successful completion of a working model of the laser printer. PARC's engineers had installed one to work with the distributed computing system based on Altos that they had established in their labs at PARC. To encourage their efforts, the Lawrence Livermore National Laboratories ordered five laser printers. The researchers at PARC and also vice president of research, Peter Goldman, were eager to fill the order. However, the final decision rested with James O'Neil.

O'Neil headed the Information Technology Group that was responsible for introducing new products and technologies. He came to Xerox from Ford, where cost management was an important means of ensuring profitability. In the auto industry, small savings in cost, when multiplied over millions of units, can amount to major savings. During the successful decade of the 1960s, Xerox earned massive profits, grew rapidly, and spent lavishly. By the late 1960s, costs were completely out of control. So McColough brought finance managers from Ford, IBM, and other major corporations to control costs at Xerox. Cost control became such an obsession at Xerox that O'Neil, a finance manager, rose to head the Information Technology Group. An engineer or market visionary would have been better suited for such a critical leadership position. As two analysts assessed his role, O'Neil "understood neither the science of xerography nor the discipline of engineering."[10]

O'Neil applied the same rigorous cost management principles at Xerox that he had developed at Ford. O'Neil reasoned that the laser printer was so new and untested that filling and servicing the Livermore order would suck up a great deal of maintenance staff as Xerox technicians were called to service potential problems with the machine. He estimated that the laser printers would cost Xerox $150,000 over the life of the contract if the printers needed repair as often as the copiers on which they were based. Moreover, O'Neil did not see any market for the laser printer, at least immediately.[11] It was a typical myopic, cost-oriented analysis. It lacked vision of the emerging market for printers that would be driven by decentralized personal computers. It failed to envision how Xerox could leverage its existing customer base, manufacturing facilities, and sales force to grow and dominate this emerging market.

In particular, there were two flaws with O'Neil's argument. First, because the laser printer had fewer moving parts than traditional printers and copiers, it needed less maintenance and was more reliable. Indeed, engineers at PARC already had good experience with the product. Second, even if it were costly, installing five machines on a small scale would be a worthwhile market experiment. It could serve to test what improvements were necessary for a full-scale market launch. Indeed, Xerox's former CEO, Wilson, made just such a gamble when he introduced Haloid's first copier based on xerography, the Model A, in 1949. That model was a failure for the intended market. Every machine sold to businesses was returned. However, the machine found another niche. It was a good way to make paper masters for offset printing presses then in use. That provided a small source of revenue for further research to improve the product. More importantly, Haloid learned from the experience how to improve the product for the mass market. It was those efforts that led to the successful model 914 more than a decade later.

In the case of the laser printers, O'Neil vetoed their sale to the Livermore Laboratories. Goldman was outraged. He felt that Xerox lost a great opportunity to beat the competition with its innovative technology. It also lost a great opportunity to test-market the product. So the laser printer languished in the laboratory for another 2 years. Then in 1974 Xerox's product review committee was considering the technology that Xerox should support for a future generation of copiers. The choice had come down to two options: PARC's laser printer or a super printer based on the traditional technology. The committee, based on the East Coast, was leaning toward the super printer. At that point, Goldman got wind of the deliberations and fumed, "A bunch of horses' asses who don't know anything about the technology were making the decision."[12]

Goldman felt that the super printer was quite inadequate for the level of speed that the market would demand. So he again interceded on behalf of the laser printer. He obtained a company plane and, 2 days before the final decision, flew two members of the product review committee to PARC to see the machine. The members were sufficiently impressed to decide in favor of the laser printer. Unfortunately, it was an empty victory for the printer. Although the committee accepted laser technology, it refused to assign the product for commercial launch, as Goldman wanted. That decision would have allowed Xerox to market the laser printer in a year. Instead, the committee wanted the laser printer to be marketed after Xerox's introduction of its next generation of high-speed optical copiers, the 9000 series. This introduction did not occur until 1977. Perhaps members of the committee situated on the East Coast were too attached to the products they already knew about to back unfamiliar products developed on the West Coast. Or perhaps they found it politically difficult to kill the new 9000 series on which researchers and engineers had labored for so long. Moreover, since his hire, Goldman was viewed as hasty and idealistic, and his influence in Xerox had slowly ebbed.

The laser printer was finally launched in 1977 as the 9700 printer. That was 6 years after Starkweather and his associates had a working model, and despite at least two major decisions that almost killed the product. It was 2 years after IBM introduced its own laser printer, the IBM 3800. Canon in Japan and Siemens in Germany were close to or had already introduced laser printers. Xerox's delay was the outcome of petty battles fought inside a bureaucracy that seemed primarily concerned with protecting its established products. As a result, Xerox lost the opportunity to lead in serving this massive new market and reap the financial rewards of its innovative research.

THE BIRTH AND DEATH OF THE ALTO

The Alto was a highly innovative, relatively powerful personal computer. It was the fruit of PARC's engineering abilities and Taylor's vision that the future of computing lay in "personal distributed computing." By this term he meant that each person had his or her own computer, which was linked to similar computers of others. As such, the computer would also be a communications device rather than only a computing device. Taylor believed that an essential characteristic for this purpose was the presentation of information. He pressed for a video display, which allowed for instantaneous and easy communication between the computer and the user. In contrast, at that time, time-sharing of minicomputers or mainframes was gaining in importance from the earlier mode of batch processing. In time-sharing and batch processing, users had to rely on a single large, remote, expensive computer.

By using materials already available and drawing on the experience of PARC's earlier minicomputer, PARC's engineers built the Alto in about 4 months (see Figure 10-2). It was an immediate hit in the lab. It was small enough to fit under a desk, yet allowed for independence and networking. It rivaled the minicomputer in its power and functions (though not in speed), yet was inexpensive enough for each person to have his or her own machine. By one estimate, the cost per Alto was less than the per-user cost of building PARC's minicomputer. The Alto had an Ethernet port that allowed it to be networked with other Altos and to the Xerox laser printer. Perhaps its most attractive feature was its monitor, which could display text and pictures. That display allowed navigation with a

Figure 10-2. Children Playing with the First Prototype of the Alto

Courtesy of Xerox Corporation. Reprinted with permission.

mouse, also developed in the lab, based on earlier work done at Doug Engelbart's lab.

The Alto was operational in April 1973. This date was nearly 2 years before MITS commercialized the relatively basic Altair, 3 years before the Apple I computer was introduced, 8 years before IBM's first PC came into the market, and 11 years before the Macintosh, whose graphical user interface was inspired by the one developed at PARC, made its debut. The Alto became an even more useful machine by 1975, with the completion of PARC's bit-mapped graphics, overlapping windows, and the Gypsy word processor. It then had more user-friendly features than the minicomputers of the time. People who saw the Alto immediately wanted one, but PARC was not allowed to fill that demand. Two units were produced at PARC in 1973. The next year, small-scale production commenced at Xerox's SDS unit in Southern California. That unit produced about 60 Altos, which were mostly used at PARC. However, lacking a champion, no large-scale production of Altos took place.

In the mid-1970s, Xerox assigned a PARC manager, John Ellenby, to supervise the manufacture of the machine on a limited scale. Ellenby redesigned the machine for this purpose. The redesign reduced costs and enabled easier maintenance. The new machine was called the Alto II and began coming off the assembly line in 1976. It was a great computer according to its users. Ellenby supervised the production of about 1500 Altos, which were distributed to users in Xerox and at select research centers and universities.

Given the successful reception of the Alto, the issue of commercialization seemed appropriate, especially for the engineers who designed the machine. The first opportunity came in the mid-1970s.

At that time, the word processing market was changing and growing rapidly. IBM was the dominant player in the market, with memory-based typewriters. Adding memory to typewriters enabled the user to store, edit, and make original copies of text without having to retype documents. Because of the popularity of these machines and their potential to increase office efficiency, a number of companies were interested in the business, including HP, 3M, and Wang. Of all these companies, Xerox seemed to be in the best position to enter and compete against IBM, because of its strong position in copiers. So in January 1975, Xerox set up the Office Products Division with the mission of entering the word processing market. For this division, Xerox had to make three key choices in management, location, and products.

The first choice was of an executive to head the division. At the time, PARC had already developed hardware and software that would define word processing two decades into the future. So a reasonable choice would have been an engineer or scientist from PARC, like Ellenby, who could get the job done. However, Xerox chose Bob Potter, who came from the technical side of Xerox and earlier had come from IBM. Unfortunately, Potter was less familiar with the potential of the emerging technologies in office automation. His decisions were based not on a vision of the mass market but on his ability to communicate with Xerox's senior managers about sales, costs, and profit targets. Costs had become an obsession at Xerox with the ascendancy of finance managers such as James O'Neil.

The next concern was the location of the unit's manufacturing facilities. Xerox rightly decided on locating the unit far away from the influence and constraints of its East Coast copier business. The choice of location came down to Palo Alto and Dallas, Texas. Locating the new facility close to PARC would have allowed the unit to draw on the expertise and technology developed there. However, the issue was decided on costs. Xerox chose Dallas because it offered distinctively lower costs for facilities and labor.

The third issue was choosing a product to introduce. Potter decided to develop typewriter-based word processors. In doing so, he focused entirely on the prevailing technology in the market. However, that technology was changing rapidly. Moreover, PARC's Gypsy program, which ran on the Alto, had already rendered such word processors technically obsolete. Senior managers at Xerox did not fully appreciate that fact. Neither did Potter even though he visited PARC. By the time it came out, Potter's first memory typewriter, the 800, was overpriced and outdated. Competitors had already moved to machines with better features, such as a cathode-ray display, and lower prices than the 800 had. As a result, the 800 was a complete failure. As one former salesman described it, "We had one of the oldest products on the market. It's tough when you have to look a customer in the eye and say 'Yeah, I agree. There's really no reason you should buy this machine.' In my seven years at Xerox, I can think of no product more rejected by major accounts than the 800."[13]

Not grasping the deeper cause of the failure, Potter planned a better model, the 850, with a cathode-ray display, but one still rooted in the old technology. At about that time, happy with his success with the Alto II, Ellenby planned the Alto III, a personal computer to be mass-produced for the national market. He naturally identified Dallas as the location for production, given its focus on word processing. But the Dallas unit had already invested in the typewriter technology and was already committed to the 850. Its manufacturing facilities, sales force, and distribution system were all specialized assets tied to the old typewriter technology. So the two groups each pressed for their own product and rejected that of the other. Xerox faced a choice between the 850 and the Alto III. On the surface it may have seemed a minor conflict between two Xerox units in the western part of the United States. In effect, it was a major clash in managing assets for the future of the company. Xerox commissioned a task force to suggest a solution.

There was some agreement within Xerox and among members of the task force that the Alto III was superior to the 850. The key issue again was cost. Potter claimed that the 850 could be produced for $5000, while the Alto would be much more expensive. Initial estimates for the Alto were as high as $15,000, based on the prior limited production. However, Ellenby argued that the Alto III could be produced for $5000, given the rapid reduction in costs typical for computer components and the economies of scale from producing for a mass market. A panel of independent Xerox engineers agreed with him. The task force initially concluded in favor of the Alto III. However, PARC lacked the political clout at headquarters. Under pressure from Dallas, their own lack of vision of evolving markets, and their obsession with costs, Xerox's executives decided in favor of the 850.

Even if Ellenby's estimates were a little optimistic, at the time, the market was willing to pay top dollar for innovative features. For example, in mid-1976, Wang introduced its dedicated word processor, with a CRT screen for viewing and editing text. Despite a huge price tag of $30,000, it was an instant hit. At the trade show, Wang could not keep up with the enormous demand from visitors wanting to see the new product. In 2 years, the product propelled Wang to leadership of the category, destroying demand for traditional memory-based typewriters.

Moreover, price itself need not have been a hindrance to introduction. For example, when Xerox under Joe Wilson introduced its first highly successful copier, the 914, in 1960, the product had a phenomenal price of $29,500. To resolve the sticker shock, the company devised the clever scheme of leasing the machine and charging for each copy made. Not only did that approach stimulate sales, but it provided a steady stream of profits for several years. Thus, one could reframe the price to make it suitable for the mass market.

However, it would have required considerable vision and courage to sacrifice the typewriter for the personal computer when typewriters were still popular. Moreover, it would have required bold decision making, given the Dallas unit's strong commitment to typewriters. Those qualities seem to have been lacking among senior managers. So Xerox approved the 850 and rejected the Alto III. Ellenby realized that the Alto was dead. What could have been the world's first commercial personal computer had been killed for cost considerations and for the sake of protecting a mediocre typewriter line. In this sense the firm was consistent: the location, management, and product choices of the Office Products Division were decided on cost criteria rather than on leveraging Xerox's enormous assets for the highly dynamic and emerging market in word processing and personal computers.

By the time the 850 came out, it too was overpriced and under-featured, just as its predecessor had been. Indeed, in the first 6 years of its existence, the Office Products Division was profitable in only one quarter. Its attachment to specialized assets led it to products that were too costly and too late for their times.[14]

ANALYSIS OF THE FAILURES

Xerox was the first firm to produce and use personal computers within its own firm. It was also the first to produce and use a host of related products that went with the personal computer, including the laser printer, the mouse, the graphical user interface, word processing software, and the Ethernet. In PARC, Xerox controlled access to all these great technologies for the office of the future. It had filed and owned patents to protect some aspects of these technologies. It had generalized assets such as its brand name, reputation, and research staff to easily introduce these innovations to market. It also had specialized assets such as manufacturing facilities, sales force, and distribution systems, which it could have adapted to introduce the innovations to the market. Moreover, given its current focus on office products such as copiers, commercializing the innovations of PARC would have been a natural implementation of McColough's vision of the office of the future.

Yet the firm failed to leverage nearly all of these assets and convert them into marketable products. In addition, it was slow in commercializing even the laser printer. Apologists have suggested several reasons or defenses for Xerox's failure: culture clash, justified focus on copiers, and large size. We need to look at these explanations a little closer to see if they are valid reasons or superficial excuses for the failure of Xerox to leverage its assets.

One defense of Xerox's performance is the culture clash between PARC in California and the corporate headquarters and research laboratories on the East Coast. All the above innovations came from PARC, while the responsibility for new product introduction was vested with senior staff at the corporate headquarters. The two groups were at loggerheads and rarely worked together. The scientists at PARC scorned the scientists and staff at Webster, New York, whom they considered narrow, obsessed with obsolete technologies, and devoid of a good understanding of the future. People at Webster found PARC's scientists arrogant, opinionated, and unapproachable. Lack of meaningful dialogue between these two groups prevented any productive planning.

However, that is a superficial view of the problem. A difference in culture between the two groups is understandable given their radically different missions. Such tensions also exist in other large organizations between scientists who create new technologies and executives who manage established products. A firm's senior executives need to manage such tensions for productive output. That is the mark of leadership. In this case, senior executives not only failed to provide leadership, but invariably chose to protect current products at the cost of delaying or rejecting new, innovative technologies. Xerox's CEO at the time also failed to take a clear stand. He himself had given PARC a charter to develop new technologies and was aware of the revolutionary products invented there. But when push came to shove, he deferred to senior corporate executives. In this respect, McColough turned out to be quite the opposite of Xerox's previous CEO, Wilson. The success of the Xerox 914 was due to Wilson's leveraging Haloid's meager resources, manpower, and facilities to develop xerography over a 15-year period. In contrast, McColough failed to direct any of the senior managers to leverage Xerox's assets to exploit the new products PARC had developed.

Some analysts propose another defense of Xerox's performance—that most of these innovations were too far from Xerox's primary business in copiers. They would constitute a diversification from Xerox's core business in copiers and could weaken its hold in that market. Such thinking is consistent with the business maxims popularized in the 1980s and 1990s such as "stay close to your knitting" or focus on "core competencies." Indeed, case histories of diversification efforts of firms during the last three decades show that many of them turned out to be failures. Diversification into unrelated markets can distract management, disperse company focus, take firms into areas in which they are not strong, and often not realize promised synergies. Moreover, the copier market was far from dead in the mid-1970s. Indeed, copiers still constitute a multibillion dollar market. Would Xerox's adoption of PARC's innovations be an unrelated and harmful diversification? Wasn't Xerox better off focusing on copiers?

The problem with this argument is that the new technologies developed at PARC were closely related to Xerox's current business. They were closer to Xerox's copying business than xerography was to Haloid's original business in photographic supplies. For example, printers could be considered the replacement of copiers in an age of word processing on personal computers. Printers and personal computers would gain importance as manuscripts were prepared on and disseminated via computers. Indeed, most of PARC's innovations were the direct fruit of McColough's goal to position Xerox for the paperless office of the future. Moreover, Xerox no longer had a lock on the copier market. It was facing tremendous competition from large companies like IBM and from inexpensive copiers coming from Japan.

A third defense of Xerox's performance, put forward by analysts, is that its large size prevented successful commercialization of these innovations. According to this view, Xerox was a large corporation and all large corporations inevitably grow lethargic and die. The latter argument is easy to dismiss. Numerous large corporations remain highly innovative, dynamic, and responsive to market changes. Examples detailed in this book include Microsoft, Intel, and Gillette.

Culture, focus, and size are superficial defenses for Xerox's failures in the 1970s. The above review of the critical decisions affecting some of these innovations indicates that the real reason for Xerox's failure was a strong attachment to or a fear of cannibalizing its specialized assets. This attitude arose from an inward-looking bureaucracy preoccupied with costs and immersed in organizational turf battles.

In this respect, Xerox contrasted sharply with Microsoft in the late 1970s. Whereas Xerox was bureaucratic, risk averse, and inward-looking, Microsoft was zealous, risk seeking, and driven by the potential mass markets for new technologies. Gates was a hands-on leader, who was acutely aware of Microsoft's vulnerability to changing market conditions, and drove the entire organization with his vision for Microsoft. An image of this difference comes from Charles Simonyi, who left Xerox to join Microsoft. At Xerox PARC, Simonyi had developed Bravo, a graphical word processing program with what-you-see-is-what-you-get display. By 1980, after the departure of talent from PARC, and after Xerox shelved a number of PARC's innovations, Simonyi became disenchanted with the company. On a tip from a friend, he visited Microsoft and interviewed with Bill Gates. Under pressure from PARC's director, he also visited Xerox's headquarters to consider a senior technology position at the central office, in lieu of joining Microsoft. Simonyi had this to say of the two companies: "We are talking about a sunset industry and a sunrise industry. It was like going into the graveyard or retirement home before going into the maternity ward. I could smell it and feel it. You could see that Microsoft could do things one hundred times faster, literally, I'm not kidding. Six years from that point we (Microsoft) overtook Xerox in market valuation."[15]

Thus Xerox retains the distinction of having the vision, entrepreneurship, and willingness to commit financial resources to develop some of the twentieth century's greatest innovations. At the same time, it suffered enough from myopia, bureaucracy, and fear of cannibalizing its specialized assets, as not to have capitalized on nearly all of its innovations. A study of Microsoft after it became large and successful reveals the atmosphere that enables a company to act decisively to establish itself as an enduring market leader.[16]

sacrificing current investments for future gain

On June 7, 2000, U.S. District Judge Thomas Penfield Jackson (Circuit Court, Washington, D.C.) issued an order demanding the breakup of Microsoft Corporation. Even though the verdict was widely anticipated, the news made headlines. At that point, the company was one of the best-known brands, one of the largest corporations in terms of capitalization, and one of the most famous success stories in U.S. business history. The verdict hinged on whether the company had a monopoly of the operating system market and tried to illegally monopolize the browser market. Whichever way the case finally settles, it will be a landmark decision because of the sheer size, enormous success, and notoriety of the key defendant. Legal scholars will debate its subtleties for decades. The root cause of the case was Microsoft's bundling of its new Web browser, Internet Explorer, with its dominant operating system, Windows.

Due to the drama and hype surrounding the case, reporters may have missed the whole strategy that launched Internet Explorer. Controversy over that bundling decision cast a shadow over and clouded the important lessons in Microsoft's strategy. The basic strategy was bold, clever, and atypical of a successful giant. The strategy involved the company's leveraging of its name, technology, and distribution assets for a foothold in the rapidly emerging and uncertain Internet market. The strategy was very aggressive. Aside from the potential illegality of specifics, which may still be overturned by an appellate court, the overall strategy carries important lessons for incumbents. Our focus here is on Microsoft's strategy rather than on legal issues.

Bill Gates initially misjudged the revolution unleashed with the development of the World Wide Web in the early 1990s. The prior 15 years belonged to the desktop computer. The three major components of the desktop computer revolution were the microprocessor, the operating system, and software applications. Microsoft had grown to dominate the market for operating systems and software applications. With single-minded focus, Gates and Microsoft strove to deliver the best software in the market for PCs. As Gates stated, "Our vision of the last 20 years can be summarized in a succinct way. We saw that exponential improvements in computer capabilities would make great software quite valuable. Our response was to build an organization to deliver the best software products."[17] The explosion of PC sales and Microsoft's superior products in operating systems and applications transformed the company into a colossus.

The Internet represented a new revolution in personal computing. The browser was a sort of operating system by itself, while sufficiently powerful servers with rich content and numerous applications threatened to render traditional applications obsolete. By the mid-1990s, the World Wide Web was growing rapidly, creating new products and markets. Most people did not know which direction it would take, or how one could profit from it. Neither did Gates or Microsoft. According to Netscape's founder Jim Clark, Gates is supposed to have stated, "If I could push a button and blow up the whole Internet, I would do it, because I do not know how to control it."[18] Gates's misjudgment cost him the browser market early on. By March 1996, Netscape had 85 percent of the browser market, compared with only 4 percent for Internet Explorer. Indeed, drawing on the theory of pioneering advantage, many analysts believed that Netscape's early lead was insurmountable. For example, one analyst with Cambridge, Massachusetts–based Forrester Research thought that despite Microsoft's efforts, Netscape had "already sewn up the browser market."[19] A computer center director thought "Microsoft started too late. Netscape owns the market and won't sit by and watch Microsoft—or anybody else—take it away."[20]

Observing Netscape's rapid growth, some at Microsoft saw the potential of the Internet and the danger of ignoring it. Moreover, the rapid increase in Web users and the media attention surrounding Netscape's success underscored the importance of the World Wide Web. These developments convinced Gates of the importance of exploiting the Internet instead of fighting it. In April 1994, Gates had a retreat with his key lieutenants about the Internet. At that meeting, according to Gates, the firm resolved to address the challenge of the Internet. About a year after that meeting, Gates stated in a memo titled "The Internet Tidal Wave": "I have gone through several stages of increasing my views of its importance. Now I assign the Internet the highest level of importance. In this memo I want to make clear that our focus on the Internet is critical to every part of our business."[21]

The change in Microsoft's approach to the Internet says much about large successful corporations in general and Microsoft in particular. Like any other large incumbent facing a radically new technology, Microsoft initially ignored the Internet. This is not different from the way IBM, with its dominance of mainframes, initially downplayed the importance of the PC. With its huge research budget and researchers at its disposal, IBM could easily have produced both the microprocessor and the operating system for its own PCs. However, myopia, born of success and fear of cannibalizing the lucrative mainframe market, led its managers to veto or delay the changes needed to win and hold the PC market. So also did Xerox, with its dominance of the copier market, deny and delay its commercializing of the laser printer. Similarly, Microsoft initially downplayed the new frontier of the Internet.

However, Microsoft is not only a large company, but also an innovative one, on the lookout for technological innovations, and paranoid about competitors. Thus, as the importance of the Internet became clear, Microsoft jumped into the market wholeheartedly. To be meaningful, this change must take place right at the top, permeate the organization, and involve genuine sacrifices. Microsoft really only started on the Internet when Gates himself was convinced about its inevitability. The change in emphasis then easily permeated the whole corporation. Gates's new strategy involved two components: 1) embracing and extending protocols adopted by Internet users and the competition and 2) focusing wholeheartedly on the Internet. He explained the change in his thinking and his new strategy in December 1995: "So the Internet, the competition will be once again, embrace and extend, and we will embrace all the popular Internet protocols. . . . For Windows it's very simple. We want to be the best Internet client. A major way that we'll do that is through integration. . . . (For) MSN, we're going to talk about how an Internet online service can fully embrace the idea of the Internet. . . . So this is my summary of Microsoft and the Internet. . . . We are hardcore about the Internet. Anything we're focused on, we're hard-core, and we are focused on this and therefore, very hard-core."[22]

This change must involve sacrifices that the firm and its managers endure to implement the new strategy. Gates showed his commitment to the Internet and his willingness to leverage assets with four radical moves. These moves sacrificed some specialized assets of the firm and transferred other generalized assets for the benefit of the new browser it developed.

First, it sacrificed the prospects of a relatively new product, the Microsoft Network (MSN), for the benefit of Internet Explorer. Up until then, Microsoft had expected that Internet service providers were the major business opportunity that arose from the growth of the Internet. The growth and success of America Online earlier in the decade convinced the company of the need to have a similar service. That decision resulted in the birth of MSN. By 1996, Microsoft had invested hundreds of millions of dollars in building MSN and was pouring $500 million a year into supporting it. Steve Ballmer, Microsoft's executive vice president, predicted that MSN would lose over $1 billion in the next 3 years of operation.[23] One strategy for promoting MSN was to put the MSN icon as a permanent fixture on the Windows desktop and to offer consumers the option of signing up for the service with every new installation of Windows. At that time, the Windows desktop represented some of the most expensive real estate on consumers' PCs. Microsoft reserved a corner of that space exclusively for MSN, not for any other Internet service provider. Thus while rivals had to aggressively market their services through costly promotions, MSN got wide exposure for free.

However, Gates believed that Internet Explorer represented a better opportunity for Microsoft than did MSN for two reasons. One, Microsoft was a software company more than a media-access company. In this sense Internet Explorer fit its profile better than did MSN. Two, Internet Explorer offered the opportunity for setting a software standard, just as Microsoft had done for operating systems and applications software. The world of Internet access was inherently too fragmented for Microsoft to play such a role with MSN.

Once it decided that the future lay in the browser market, Microsoft put bite into its decision. On March 12, 1996, it signed a contract with AOL, offering the latter the option of an icon on the Windows desktop in exchange for AOL making Internet Explorer its preferred browser. The deal offered Internet Explorer a good chance of being the choice of AOL's subscribers, who then numbered over 10 million. In return, AOL won immediate presence on the desktop of 90 percent of all new PCs sold, and all old ones that upgraded to Windows 95. As a result, MSN lost its exclusive presence as the only Internet service provider on the Windows desktop. The manager of MSN, and its original champion, resigned rather than continue under these circumstances. In effect, Gates had made the fortunes of MSN entirely secondary to those of Internet Explorer. In a move unusual among large corporations, Microsoft sacrificed a promising new product, MSN, for one that was even newer and more risky, Internet Explorer. In contrast, as Xerox, IBM, and many other examples illustrate, large bureaucracies rarely sacrifice current products for newer ones.

The importance of the strategic alliance with AOL was not lost on Wall Street. By mid-March 1996, Netscape's stock lost about half of the value it had from its December 1995 high, with most of that loss occurring in the last month.

MSN was not the only product that Microsoft sacrificed for Internet Explorer. Gates mentioned that his strategy was to "embrace and extend." By that he meant embracing current standards and protocol and extending them, rather than coming out with his own. Such a strategy was critical to successfully entering the market late. Microsoft embraced HTML that was developed by Berners-Lee and further developed by Netscape. It also contracted with Sun Microsystems to license its software, Java. In so doing, Microsoft gave up its own product, Blackbird, which it was developing for multimedia software applications.

A second way Gates showed his commitment to the Internet was that immediately upon planning to develop Internet Explorer, Microsoft organized to invest heavily in the new product with people and resources. Talent was Microsoft's greatest resource. To speedily develop Internet Explorer, Microsoft formed a browser task force. This task force was headed by Benjamin Slivka and included 80 programmers. This group included the brightest and strongest of its talented programmers. As in the case of Netscape Navigator, such talent was critical to developing a strong and innovative version of Internet Explorer. Overall, Microsoft invested about $500 million in the development of the first few versions of Internet Explorer. The fruit of its investment was evident. Several independent agencies rated Internet Explorer 3.0 equal to or better than Netscape Navigator 3.

Third, Microsoft freely distributed both Internet Explorer and the accompanying server software. This is an unusual strategy for a large corporation. Initially, Netscape gave the browser away free but licensed the software for servers. Later, it began to charge $49 for the browser too. Moreover, until that time, Microsoft sold all its products for a fee. This strategy applied even to software, such as

Windows, where the marginal cost of each unit was close to zero. Microsoft also charged for the Microsoft Network, where the fee was on the monthly service and not on the software per se. By setting a price of $0 for Internet Explorer, Microsoft showed that it was willing to leverage its strong position in operating systems and applications to build market share in the browser market.

Fourth, Microsoft leveraged its most valuable asset, Windows 95, for Internet Explorer: It bundled Internet Explorer with Windows 95. Because Windows was the dominant operating system and because Windows 95 was very popular, this new method of distribution represented a major strategic coup. Whether or not consumers were explicitly going to choose Internet Explorer over Netscape, making Internet Explorer available through the operating system greatly increased the probability of consumers choosing it as their default browser. Moreover, Microsoft began integrating Internet Explorer with Windows, so that the linkage between the two programs would be seamless. To appreciate the importance of this move, one has only to consider the size of the respective markets. Around March 1996, Netscape had about 10 million users. In comparison at the time, Microsoft licensed about 50 million new copies of Windows per year, while it could access a worldwide market of about 150 million users of Windows. By bundling Internet Explorer with Windows, Gates reached out to a market that was *15 times* bigger than Netscape's. Gates also indicated that all other Microsoft software applications would be Web-ready.

In contrast to the atmosphere in Xerox in the 1970s, Microsoft in the 1990s was quick and decisive. The CEO himself was actively involved in new-product decisions. He had a clear vision of where he wanted to take the corporation. That vision permeated the whole organization and focused resources in critical areas. In particular, it prompted Microsoft to transfer generalized assets such as its brand name and talent to the new product, Internet Explorer. At the same time, it sacrificed specialized assets, such as MSN and Blackbird, for the benefit of Internet Explorer. This strategic leveraging of assets played a critical role in the fast rise of Internet Explorer, and the corresponding decline of Netscape Navigator (see Figure 10-3). By December 1996, just 1 year after announcing the strategy, Internet Explorer's market share had risen from 4 to 24 percent. In that year,

Figure 10-3. Browser Market Shares over Time

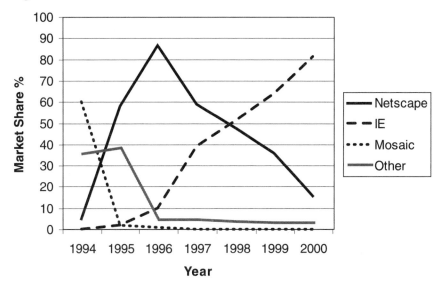

Sources: Authors' estimates based on reports by IDC, Dataquest, Zona Research, NUA Internet Surveys, Scripps Research Institute.

Netscape's market share declined from a peak of about 87 percent to 70 percent. Thereafter, Internet Explorer's share grew rapidly until it dominated the browser market.

autonomy versus bureaucracy

The development, introduction, success, and decline of the IBM PC is a dramatic example of the struggle for effective asset leverage amid vigorous attempts by a bureaucracy to protect its own turf. In this case, an autonomous group was initially able to circumvent the bureaucracy to leverage some of IBM's assets for a remarkably successful entry into a new category. However, the sacrifices necessary for such an entry and the staying power of the bureaucracy finally engulfed the autonomous unit and stymied the new entry.

Initially IBM ignored the personal computer market. The company had become a behemoth with its highly profitable sales and service of large mainframes. The mainframe market had two characteristics that distinguished it from the personal computer market. First, each machine cost over a million dollars, which, together with IBM's strong market position, enabled the firm to collect a huge premium per unit. Those premiums, when aggregated over the annual sales or leases of thousands of units, contributed to a comfortable profit level. In contrast, personal computers sold in the price range of $600 to $3000 a piece. IBM's managers did not see the mass market for personal computers, and thus did not envision how that business could be as profitable as the mainframe business. Second, the expensive machines required extensive maintenance and service. IBM had a large, well-trained, and exemplary sales force for this purpose. With this professional sales force, an impeccable brand name, and a massive R&D budget, IBM developed an almost impenetrable position in the mainframe market. As a result, the firm became complacent, bureaucratic, and lethargic and focused myopically on its mainframe market.

In contrast, the personal computer market was characterized by fast-moving companies, rapid innovations, and an intensely competitive climate. Moreover the market was strongly driven by Moore's law. Performance of components, especially microprocessors and memory chips, doubled every 18 months. Thus every 18 months or less, a company had to be ready with a new product. Companies that kept up with this pace of innovation had a competitive advantage, while those that were slow to innovate died out.

With its huge research laboratories, teams of researchers, and extensive experience, IBM had the technical expertise to develop a personal computer from scratch. It had the personnel and facilities to develop both hardware and software for such a machine. But technical expertise aside, the company lacked the entrepreneurial climate to make a success of such an endeavor. At IBM, each new design had to be approved by numerous committees. Decisions were rarely the responsibility of one manager, but had to be made by committee, often by several committees. In this respect, it bore similarities to Xerox in the 1970s. A former IBM executive describes the situation this way: "IBM is like Switzerland—conservative, a little dull, yet prosperous. It has committees to verify each decision. The safety net is so big that it is hard to make a bad decision—or any decision at all."[24]

Besides slowing development time, the long and convoluted approval process eliminated bold or radical innovations. An IBM programmer, giving his view of what such decision making did to the company, commented: "I mean it's like getting four hundred thousand people to agree with what they want to have for lunch. You know, I mean it's just not going to happen—it's going to be lowest common denominator you know, it's going to be you know hot dogs and beans. At one point somebody kind of looked at the process to see well, you know, what's it doing and what's the overhead built into it, what they found is that it would take at least nine months to ship an empty box."[25]

Besides needing state-of-the-art hardware, the success of personal computers also depended a great deal on innovative software. But software development was even more of an individualistic, entrepreneurial task than hardware development. A few programmers worked intensely, sometimes round the clock, to create a new program. The whole process sometimes took only a few months. In contrast, IBM assigned huge teams of programmers to software development tasks. Each of these teams worked on different aspects of the code, sometimes with differing and even conflicting goals. The work could drag on for years with little resolution.

Thus the IBM of the 1970s was too bureaucratic and slow to succeed in the world of personal computers. During this time, IBM had already made three attempts to develop a personal computer. However, none of them had borne fruit. One project in particular, to add computer operations to its dedicated word processor, had gone on for 4 years without yielding a new product. A key problem in these failures was the inability to produce good software, especially the operating system.

BIRTH OF THE PC

In the meantime, the personal computer market raced on. In 1975, MITS commercialized the first personal computer, the Altair. The $300-plus Altair and machines like it appeared to senior IBM managers as hobbyists' toys that posed no real threat to the billion dollar business of the company. The year 1977 saw the introduction of three new personal computers: Commodore's PET, Radio Shack's TRS-80, and Apple's Apple II, which quickly became popular. The success of these machines impressed IBM that the personal computer market had potential. By 1980, the personal computer market crossed a billion dollars in sales. Managers who were used to IBM's success in the mainframe market began to take note. A few engineers within IBM had toyed with components available in the market and had developed some prototypes of personal computers. Apple machines also penetrated IBM's own offices and were used by its managers for office reports. To the world's biggest computer company, that was an embarrassment. IBM's chairman Frank Cary was known to say, "Where's my Apple?"[26]

William Lowe, a manager of a small IBM unit in Boca Raton, Florida, decided to take up the challenge. He solicited the help of an engineer who had been working on designs for personal computers. With his help Lowe made a proposal to IBM's corporate management committee for an IBM personal computer using readily available parts and software. The committee was skeptical. Managers cited the problem of low margins, a sales force that was used to big computers, and the limitations of its research and manufacturing resources. Most of all, the committee claimed IBM lacked financial resources to devote to this seemingly unimportant project. However, with his eye on the market, Cary was really interested. He realized that going through the routine approval process would mean getting mired in IBM's bureaucracy, as had past efforts. So he offered Lowe a deal. He would approve Lowe's proposal, but only if Lowe could complete the project in 1 year.

Now finishing anything in 1 year would be a revolutionary undertaking at IBM. But Lowe probably realized, as did Cary, the importance of moving fast. So Lowe accepted the deadline and got the mandate. IBM entrusted the design and manufacture of the new personal computer to Lowe's unit, at Boca Raton. That location was far from the scrutiny and influence of IBM's headquarters in Armonk, New York. Moreover, Lowe reported directly to Cary, and was freed from IBM's stifling bureaucracy. In a few months, Lowe accepted a promotion and transfer to Rochester, New York, and Don Estridge took over the project in Boca Raton.

Estridge was strongly independent, and relied heavily on the direct line of contact he had with Cary. He said of this arrangement, "IBM acted as a venture capitalist. It gave us management guidance, money, and allowed us to operate on our own."[27] A member of his team compared the atmosphere between the rest of IBM and his group in these words, "Before I went to work on the team, I helped develop a printer at IBM. That printer was in development for seven years! I kept telling myself, 'It's coming . . . it's coming.' But the printer was hopelessly mired in design changes and bureaucracy. After a while, those layers and layers at IBM really get to you. . . . It's no exaggeration to say that I made more decisions in my first 30 days with that PC group than I made during my first 14 years with IBM."[28]

In this respect, the Boca Raton project bore similarities to Xerox's PARC facility in Palo Alto, California, each being far removed from the company headquarters. It was entrepreneurial, free from bureaucracy, and goal driven. However, unlike the PARC facility, the Boca Raton facility was primarily a production unit, not a research center. It had a clear mandate—to introduce the personal computer in 1 year. That 1-year deadline proved to be a key factor in the product's initial success—and the underlying cause of its ultimate demise.

One of the first decisions that Lowe faced was whether to make or buy the various components of the personal computer. IBM had the laboratories, technical personnel, and facilities to produce most, if not all, of the components for the personal computer. Also, IBM's tradition was always to make rather than buy. That gave the company proprietary control over the product and enabled it to maintain its fabled quality standards. However, in this case, Lowe had a tight deadline to meet. Moreover, attempting to make components within the corporation would have risked dependence on other departments as well as potential scrutiny and reviews by various committees. That would certainly delay the project if not kill it outright.

So Lowe chose to buy almost all the parts of the PC from components readily available in the market. IBM's departments could bid to supply parts in competition with outside vendors. In particular, Lowe used Microsoft's DOS as its operating system and an Intel chip. Lowe chose Intel's 16-bit processor, the 8088. This chip was not as fast as Intel's 8086, but it cost a little less and made the personal computer less threatening to IBM's minicomputers. Consistent with this move to buy parts, Lowe designed the machine with an "open architecture" and many expansion slots. That way outside vendors could easily sell peripherals for the personal computer, without depending on IBM's other departments, increasing the product's usefulness. He even encouraged manufacturers to supply such peripherals.

The only exception to this "buy" policy was the machine's BIOS. BIOS stands for Basic Input Output System and is a piece of code that connected the hardware and software. Ironically, it was designed originally by Kildall to make it easy to make one generic version of his CP/M work on the variety of machines then available. IBM's BIOS was proprietary, protected by IBM copyright. It was the only component that made the PC unique.

A team of dedicated engineers and staff worked feverishly at the Boca Raton unit, all through the fall of 1980 and the first seven months of 1981. Then in August 1981, almost a year since Lowe got the mandate, the unit met its deadline. IBM introduced its own personal computer, the IBM PC. The product was an instant hit. Supported by a massive advertising campaign, retail distribution, and a competitive price, sales exceeded all expectations. By the end of 1981, the company had sold 13,000 units. In a year the company's sales totaled almost 200,000. It could barely keep up with demand. In a few years, IBM captured 25 percent of the personal computer market, with sales totaling $1 billion. Personal computer revenues soon equaled those of mainframe and minicomputers combined. The company's market value almost doubled to $75 billion. IBM followed up with two successful product line extensions, the PC XT and the PC AT.

While several factors contributed to the PC's success, the primary one was the brand name. The personal computer market was already growing rapidly. However, businesses were wary of investing in such equipment for their offices. They wondered why the granddaddy of all computer manufacturers, IBM, had not entered the market. They waited to see what the firm had in terms of an alternative. When IBM entered the market, it gave the new category legitimacy. Moreover, the new PC had the IBM name. It assured businesses that they could count on the quality and superior service of IBM. In this respect, IBM successfully used its name established in the mainframe market to guarantee its own personal computer. At the same time, by procuring all components from other companies, and establishing a completely new production facility and sales force, IBM sacrificed many of its other, strong specialized assets. Thus IBM's initial success with the PC was due to skillful leverage of generalized assets and a willingness to move away from established specialized assets and build new specialized assets.

DECLINE OF THE IBM PC

Unfortunately, the dramatic success of the IBM PC taught the company no lasting lessons. Indeed, the corporation hardly changed. As a result, IBM's success in the personal computer market turned out to be a blip on the radar, rather than a new management model for the company to emulate.

Determined to meet the 1-year deadline and secure in the belief of IBM's continued dominance of the computer market, Lowe entered into fairly generous licensing agreements for the software. For example, he licensed the software from Microsoft, then a small company, on very generous terms. IBM allowed Microsoft to hold the copyright for the software and to license the same software to IBM's competitors in the personal computer market. Similarly, it used Intel's microprocessor without seeking any exclusive rights to the chip. So Intel was free to sell the same chip to other firms. IBM did not use its own chip initially, nor did it make any serious attempt to develop one internally once the PC took off. Thus Intel and Microsoft got a foothold in the personal computer market, while IBM had only the BIOS protecting its uniqueness.

The open architecture ensured healthy competition in components and accessories for the PC. But it also encouraged competitors to clone the PC and introduce models of their own. Within a few years, Compaq reverse-engineered IBM's BIOS. Soon after, Dell, Hewlett-Packard, and a host of other companies entered the personal computer market by doing the same. At first, they were content to follow IBM's lead with new models. IBM introduced two new successful models, the XT and the AT, based on Intel's 286 processor. However, when Intel introduced the 386 chip, IBM failed to bring out a new model right away, hoping to milk its old model based on the Intel 286 chip. Competitors like Compaq used the 386 chip to grab the lead, and IBM soon lost its position in the personal computer market. After that, the hardware market moved too fast, with too low an overhead structure for the slow giant to retake the lead.

In a final attempt to gain a proprietary advantage over this market, IBM tried to enter the market for PC operating systems. However, there it was in competition with Microsoft. In the early 1990s, IBM still had as many engineers and as much financial resources as Microsoft, if not more. So it was confident that it could assert its supremacy with the design of a new graphical operating system, called OS/2. IBM contracted with Microsoft for the development of OS/2 but retained sole rights to license the program, unlike its policy for DOS. Unfortunately, here too it was unwilling to cannibalize or threaten its older mainframe market.

First, IBM insisted that OS/2 be compatible with its mainframes. That way, owners of PCs could easily hook up to IBM's mainframes, extending the usefulness of the latter, while potentially increasing IBM's hold on the market. Unfortunately, ensuring compatibility with mainframes made OS/2 a huge, clumsy, and slow program. At the same time, inexpensive microprocessor-based servers further eroded the importance of mainframes and reduced the need for such compatibility. Second, IBM entrusted the design of this system to Microsoft, because of concern with its own slow bureaucratic development of software. Microsoft did develop OS/2, but not any faster than it developed its own graphical operating system, Windows. Windows was free of any baggage requiring compatibility with mainframes. As such, it turned out to be a faster and more reliable system. When Windows and OS/2 were finally launched, the former proved to be far more useful and quickly took over the market. Thus IBM finally lost both its hardware and software positions in the personal computer market.

The root cause of this loss was IBM's bureaucracy, along with its eagerness to protect its mainframe business. This attitude arose from an unwillingness to sacrifice the assets of the mainframe business for the promise of the personal computer business. Despite the success of the Boca Raton unit, the company neither spun off the unit as an independent business nor gave its leaders independent control. Rather, as the unit grew with success, IBM tried to absorb the unit back into the corporate fold, while saddling it with new layers of bureaucracy. Early in the history of the unit, IBM assigned the entrepreneurial Lowe to another part of the bureaucracy. Later, most of the original design team left. Some joined smaller companies. Others asked for transfers. They found the task of working on the PC too demanding and the rewards too scant. IBM had a problem rewarding performance and individual contributions. At one point, even Estridge seemed resigned to this philosophy, saying, "We want to fit into IBM, because it is the right thing for our customers."[29]

Moreover, many suppliers of hardware and software realized that the personal computer represented a revolution in computing. The personal computer gave each individual computing power and freedom from dependence on the limitations and the vagaries of one central mainframe. Even when its own PC had begun to realize this revolution and the PC market quickly rivaled and then surpassed the mainframe market (see Figure 10-4), IBM seemed to lack a vision for the new market. Instead, deep within IBM's bureaucracy, the personal computer market still seemed secondary to the mainframe business.

Many IBM managers saw the personal computer as a threat to the mainframe business, not as an opportunity to exploit. They sought to slow the personal computer market in order to protect the mainframes business. Attempts to develop a more powerful personal computer were saddled with the burden of not rendering IBM's mainframe or minicomputer businesses obsolete. The concern was that no personal computer could ever command the premium that IBM got from a mainframe. If businesses replaced the mainframe machines with personal computers, it would ultimately eat into IBM's mainframe business and wipe out its profit base. In a guarded criticism of this policy, IBM's former CEO, Thomas J. Watson, Jr., who grew the company into a colossus, wistfully declared, "Didn't I read an article that John [Akers] felt we had hung on too long to the mainframe philosophy because of the high profits we were making there?"[30]

the promise and burden of assets

A firm that dominates a market is typically in a strong position to expand its dominance into new markets that are related to its prin-

Figure 10-4. Evolution of Personal and Mainframe Computer Sales

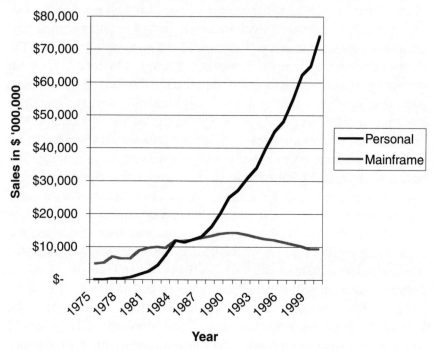

Source: Computer and Business Equipment Manufacturer's Association, The Information Technology Industry Data Book, Dataquest Inc., IDC Twice Market Research, Sanford C. Bernstein & Co. Inc., Alexander & Associates, and authors' estimates.

cipal business. We call these new markets *category extensions*. The keys to the firm's ability to expand dominance are its generalized and specialized assets. However, as the above examples show, assets are a two-edged sword that can help or hinder a firm's market expansion.

For example, Xerox and IBM failed to effectively leverage their enormous assets in their respective core businesses of copiers and mainframes to dominate the personal computer market. On the other hand, Microsoft and Charles Schwab were able to leverage their current assets to dominate the newly emerging markets of web browsers and online trading, respectively. Tracking the evolution of these markets shows some interesting reversals in asset leverage, even within these four firms. For example, under Wilson, Haloid leveraged its limited assets to develop xerography and dominate the copier market for decades. Yet under McColough, Xerox failed to leverage its enormous assets to enter the related markets of printing, personal computing, and word processing, even though it developed the basic technology and initial products for all three markets. The reasons for the differences across firms and also within firms are differences in the willingness of managers to effectively leverage assets.

Generalized assets may be easily transferred to the new market, though the firm runs the risk of diluting those assets or weakening its position in the old market. Specialized assets do not transfer easily. Because the new market may appear to threaten the old market, firms may fail to even enter the new market for fear of cannibalizing these specialized assets. In addition to this fear, myopia, bureaucracy, and cost orientation may also hinder the effective entry and dominance of new markets.

For example, Haloid's CEO Wilson himself envisioned the potential of xerography and steered Haloid's heroic effort to bring that technology to market. However, Xerox's CEO McColough let bureaucracy, cost orientation, and the fear of cannibalizing assets in its copiers slow or stymie Xerox's entry into the printing, personal computing, and word processing markets. Similarly, by creating an independent unit and entrusting its managers with introducing a personal computer in record time, IBM effectively leveraged its brand name and talent to quickly dominate that market. However, by later enveloping that unit in its bureaucracy, IBM equally quickly dissipated its advantage and lost its dominance of the new market. IBM's managers were reluctant to advance the personal computer market, lest they further the demise of the company's own mainframe business. Such unwillingness to sacrifice specialized assets also afflicted Xerox's senior managers, who were reluctant to introduce the laser printer lest it jeopardize sales of their copiers. These examples are diametrically opposite to the attitude of Microsoft, which readily sacrificed MSN and Blackbird to further the market for Internet Explorer, and of Charles Schwab, which risked its established business model to embrace the market of online trading.

summary

- Firms that dominate a category can become leaders in a new related category even if they enter late. To do so, dominant firms must be willing to leverage current assets for future gain even though that gain is uncertain.
- Firms' assets can be broadly classified as generalized assets and specialized assets.
- Generalized assets are those that a firm can transfer relatively easily from one category to another, with minimal loss in value. Examples of these are the firm's brand name, reputation, customer base, and talent. Firms need to be willing to skillfully transfer these assets to the new category.
- Specialized assets are those that firms may not transfer easily to the new category. Examples of these are current products and technology and, frequently, manufacturing facilities, sales force, and distribution systems. Firms need to be willing to sacrifice these assets to enter a promising extension of their current market.
- A major hindrance to leveraging assets is the extent to which the new category does or appears to threaten the old category. Sales growth in the new category may come at the expense of the old category. Moreover, the dominant firm's entry in the new category may promote the latter's growth and hasten the demise of the old category. Such fear hinders prompt and effective asset leverage.
- A second hindrance to asset leverage is a narrow and obsessive focus on costs. A firm needs to evaluate its costs together with the benefits that emerge from marketing in the category extension. These benefits can be huge when the firm taps into the mass market for a new product. Also, future costs can be dramatically lower than current costs by exploiting the benefits of new technologies and the economies of large-scale production.
- A third hindrance to asset leverage is myopia, which arises from a focus on past achievement or current successful products. This attitude prevents a firm from seeing the opportunity in a new category and responding to it in a timely way.

- A fourth hindrance to asset leverage is bureaucracy. Dominant firms develop a large cadre of employees, many committees, and a number of operating rules and routines. These structures slow the decision process, eliminate bold initiatives, and foster inertia.
- To overcome these problems, dominant firms need to develop independent units with the authority to enter the new market with minimal interference. Another method is for firms to develop product champions and assign them resources and talent to identify market opportunities and enter the most promising ones. A third approach is for senior managers to take over the responsibility for surveying market evolution and directing the company to exploit the best new market opportunities.

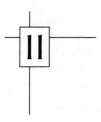

assessing the new thesis

C asual observation of markets leads many people to conclude that the first firm to enter a market is the enduring leader of that market. Much empirical evidence, especially in the last two decades, has supported this conclusion. Economists and psychologists have developed elaborate theories to explain why this first mover may become the enduring market leader. The concurrence of observation, formal theory, and empirical evidence on the great rewards of market pioneering has led some authors to claim that it is the first law of marketing.

However, this book argued that the empirical data contain three serious flaws. First, past studies have ignored pioneers that failed. Second, both reporters and some firms themselves have wrongly labeled current market leaders as pioneers. Third, some analysts have defined markets too narrowly, thus making the concept of pioneering less meaningful. These three problems lead to serious biases or errors in the same direction—an exaggerated or upward estimate in the survival, success rate, duration of leadership, and steady-state market shares of pioneers.

We argued that a historical analysis of markets *as they evolved* would provide an accurate estimate of the true rewards of pioneers.

Based on our extensive study over many years, we found that pioneers mostly fail, have a low market share, and are rarely market leaders. In particular, about two-thirds of the pioneers in our sample failed. On average, pioneers have an equilibrium market share of only 6 percent. And only 9 percent of these pioneers endure as market leaders.

These results suggest that entering a market first does not confer enormous benefits. Instead, we found five factors that were key determinants of enduring market leadership: vision, persistence, innovation, financial commitment, and asset leverage. Our thesis is quite different from the one that is widely held in the business and academic worlds. Since our results run counter to conventional wisdom, we have faced many questions about our method and findings. This chapter attempts to answer them.

What about the stability in market shares that is easily observed and often reported?

Casual observation suggests that leading brands do not lose their market leadership very quickly. Rather, market leadership tends to persist. Many articles attest to this stability in market shares. For example, the *Advertising Age* article discussed in Chapter 1 found that 19 of 25 market leaders maintained their leadership for at least six decades (see Table 1-1). Recently, an article in *Harvard Business Review* claimed that "many brands that were market leaders half a century ago are still market leaders today."[1]

Since pioneers are market leaders upon entry, these reports of long-term leadership may seem to undercut our findings that pioneers are not successful. We researched these reports in an attempt to better understand our own findings. Although many reports make claims about long-term leadership, we find that these claims all tend to refer to the same *Advertising Age* article.[2] So it became critical to thoroughly research the study reported in this article. Our research raised several concerns. First, the study is far removed from the time of the 1923 data on which its results depend. Second, the choice of the first year, 1923, appears arbitrary and suspicious. Third, no author is listed for this article. The source of the article's findings is the president of a small communications design and marketing research firm; beyond that, there is no information about his expertise in this area.

The *Advertising Age* article does provide one lead that we investigated further: a 1923 book that provides the original data on brand leaders. Our investigation of this original source revealed a startling finding about the commonly referenced "fact" that 19 out of 25 market leaders maintained their leadership for at least 60 years. Although this finding of long-term leadership has been widely reported in marketing textbooks, marketing journals, and mass-market publications, it is based on a biased sample of categories. The original 1923 study was not done on 25 categories, but rather, on *100 categories*.[3] The sample of 25 categories seems to have been selectively chosen to demonstrate long-term leadership. Therefore, this particular article is dramatically flawed and unable to generate conclusions about the long-term stability of market leaders.

But what is the *real* occurrence of long-term leadership? How stable are the market shares of leading brands over prolonged periods of time? To address these questions, we took the original data *of leading brands in all 100 categories* in the 1923 sample and compared those data with new data on the current market shares of those brands.[4] We used the combined data to determine the actual percentage of former leaders that have maintained leadership. Table 11-1 presents a sample of the 100 categories with the leading brands in 1923 and today.[5]

Our complete data provide several ways to evaluate long-term leadership and market share stability. First, we can assess the frequency with which firms maintain market share leadership. Table 11-2 compares the current belief about the frequency of maintaining market leadership based on the biased sample with our new findings based on the full sample. The difference in the findings is striking.

Leading brands maintain their leadership at a rate less than one-third of the rate that is currently believed. Table 11-3 presents many more detailed results from these data.

Overall, our analysis yields the following specific results:

- More of the leading brands in 1923 failed than remained leaders.
- More of the top three brands in 1923 failed than remained among even the top five brands.

Table 11-1.   A Sample of Leading Brands in 1923 and 1997

Product Category	1923 Leaders	1997 Leaders
Cleanser	Old Dutch	Comet Soft Scrub Ajax
Chewing gum	Wrigley's Adams	Wrigley's Bubble Yum Bubblicious
Motorcycles	Indian Harley-Davidson	Harley-Davidson Honda Kawasaki
5-cent mint candies	Life-Savers	Breath-Savers Tic Tac Certs
Peanut butter	Beech-Nut Heinz	Jif Skippy Peter Pan
Razors	Gillette Gem Ever Ready	Gillette Bic Schick
Soft drinks	Coca-Cola Cliquot Club Bevo Hires	Coca-Cola Pepsi Dr. Pepper/Cadbury
Coffee	Arbuckle's Yuban White House Hotel Astor George Washington	Folger's Maxwell House Hills Bros.
Laundry soap	Fels Naptha Octagon Kirkman Ivory Babbitts Crystal White	Tide Cheer Wisk
Typewriters	Underwood Remington Oliver Corona	Smith Corona Brother Lexmark
Cigarettes	Camel Fatima Pall Mall Murad Lucky Strike	Marlboro Winston Newport

Table 11-1.   A Sample of Leading Brands in 1923 and 1997 (Continued)

Product Category	1923 Leaders	1997 Leaders
Hosiery	Holeproof Onyx Phoenix Luxite	L'Eggs Hanes No Nonsense
Shoes	Douglas Walkover Hanan	Nike Reebok
Candy	Huyler's Loft Page & Shaw Whitman	Hershey M&M/Mars Nestle
Jelly or jam	Heinz	Smucker's Welch's Kraft

Source: Peter N. Golder, "Historical Method in Marketing Research with New Evidence on Long-Term Market Share Stability," *Journal of Marketing Research*, 37 (May 2000), p. 164.

- Market shares over this prolonged period are not stable.
- For durable goods, the rate of maintaining leadership is lower than that for nondurable goods, and the rate of failure is higher than that for nondurable goods.
- In product categories of clothing, no brand maintained leadership over this time period, and 67 percent of the 1923 leaders failed.

These results underscore the theme in this book, that long-term market leadership is not an automatic reward for market pioneering or for past leadership.

how generalizable are the results?

The various chapters of this book highlight specific examples. Our purpose in doing so was to show the rich and complex way in which

Table 11-2. Long-Term Success Rate of 1923 Market Leaders

Percentage of 1923 Market Leaders at Each 1997 Market Share Rank

	% of 1923 Leaders	
1997 Market Share Rank	*Based on Advertising Age Article (Using Selective Sample of 25 Brands)*	*Based on Authors' Research (Using Complete Sample)*
First	76	23
Second	16	8
Third	4	9
Top 5	4	8
Top 10	0	7
Below 10	0	16
Failed	0	28

firms achieve enduring market leadership instead of the simplistic notion that such leadership comes from pioneering. On perusing these examples, a reader might wonder how generalizable or widespread our findings really are.

Generalizability of the results has been a major concern of ours. For that reason we proceeded to research the causes of enduring leadership in a number of markets. Over the years, our research has extended to 66 markets. Chapter 3 describes our quantitative results for pioneers, based on this sample of 66 markets. Our findings about the real causes of enduring success are also based on the same sample of 66 markets.

To determine the frequency of the five factors, we reviewed each of the markets to see to what extent each of these factors was responsible for enduring market success. Because some of these categories are older or information is scarce, we could not determine the role of these factors in *all* 66 categories. Thus, these results are based on the categories where we have reasonable confidence in our identification of each factor. Table 11-4 presents the results of this analysis. Note that the first four factors were important for the enduring success of the market leader in almost all the markets for

Table 11-3. Comparison of Market Share Positions in 1923 versus 1997

1923 Rank Based on Market Share	Sample Size	1997 Rank Based on Market Share						
		No. 1	No. 2	No. 3	Top 5	Top 10	> 10	Failed
Number 1 brand	97*	23%	8%	9%	8%	7%	16%	28%
Number 2 brand	70	11%	9%	3%	4%	9%	26%	39%
Number 3 brand	43	5%	7%	2%	5%	9%	14%	58%
Number 4 brand	26	4%	4%	4%	4%	8%	42%	35%
Number 5 brand	12	0%	0%	25%	0%	17%	42%	17%
Number 6 brand	5	0%	0%	0%	0%	20%	20%	60%
Number 7 brand	1	0%	0%	0%	0%	0%	0%	100%

*The authors of the 1923 study determined that three categories had names mentioned that were not actual brands. The remaining 97 categories include 45 durables, 51 nondurables, and 1 service.

which we had information. The fifth factor, asset leverage, was responsible for the enduring success of the market leaders in about half of the cases in which we had sufficient evidence.

The reason for the lower occurrence of asset leverage is due to the smaller number of category extensions and the nature of this factor. It requires that a dominant firm in one category leverage its assets from that category to achieve dominance in a related second category. As discussed in Chapter 10, there are a number of serious hindrances to such entrepreneurial behavior by dominant firms. Thus we find that this particular factor may not be as common a cause of enduring market success as the first four factors. However, many firms have been able to leverage assets from one category to establish enduring leadership in a related category.

Thus, firms use these five factors quite frequently to establish enduring leadership. Some have suggested that we could have gone a step further by developing specific scales for each of these factors, measuring the organizations in terms of these scales, and testing our model statistically. However, we feel that the strength of our thesis comes from our ability to examine the details of so many cases.

Table 11-4. Generalizability of Causes of Enduring Market Leadership

Cases	Vision	Persistence	Innovation	Financial Commitment	Asset Leverage
% with confirming evidence	55%	56%	56%	52%	30%
% with disconfirming evidence	6%	5%	5%	6%	32%
% with insufficient evidence	39%	39%	39%	42%	38%
Total	100%	100%	100%	100%	100%

Wringing the cases through a set of scales and statistical models would lose much of the richness without yielding new insights. Indeed, these five factors direct today's managers and analysts to the important determinants of enduring leadership.

Finally, we could have evaluated the importance of the five factors in more than 66 categories. This large number of categories that we do consider is the result of more than 10 years of work. The size of our sample is larger than that used in nearly all business books with which we are familiar. If we had considered more categories, perhaps some other factor may have turned up to be also relevant. However, we believe it is highly unlikely that the five factors we identified would have ceased to be important no matter how many categories we considered. The similarity in results across a number of subsamples provides good confidence in our results and conclusions.

are the five causes of enduring leadership related?

We believe that the five causes are structurally related in a causal chain (see Figure 3-1). The root cause and the driving force for enduring market leadership are the same: vision of the mass market. However, the market is a changing target. Consumers' tastes change, and technology changes how these tastes can be met. Thus vision involves understanding where the mass market is headed and how best to serve it. Yet vision should not be a purely reactive force. Visionaries do not merely read the future well. Actually, true visionaries create the future by striving to implement solutions for the mass market that previously did not exist.

Vision provides the inspiration for entrepreneurs to persist in the difficult task of setting up a new business and overcoming obstacles. It also suggests how long and how hard one needs to persist. For example, Gillette's conviction of the merits of disposable blades led him to seek out an engineer who could manufacture such blades from sheet metal. He did not stop till he found Nickerson, and continued to badger Nickerson till he agreed to try for a month to make a blade from sheet metal. Vision also provides entrepreneurs and managers with the courage to commit huge resources to what many people at the time consider impossible ventures. Thus, Fred Smith's vision of overnight mail throughout the United States inspired him to risk enormous financial resources to realize that vision.

Innovation, especially of a radical nature, needs resources. The willingness of entrepreneurs or firms to commit resources enables them to finance such innovation. For example, it was Jim Clark's commitment that brought the resources to enable the fledgling Netscape to develop a browser in just 6 months. Such innovation frequently provides the solutions to achieve enduring leadership.

These factors are not isolated characteristics, characteristics that occur separately in different situations. Rather one leads to another. The starting point is vision, which then drives the willingness to persist against great odds, commit financial resources, innovate relentlessly, and leverage current assets. One of these factors alone will rarely be enough. But several of these factors working together will magnify the impact of any individual factor. Thus, it becomes critical to adopt the mindset associated with these five factors rather than adopt any one factor alone.

do moderators influence the role of the causes of enduring leadership?

We find that the importance of the five factors of enduring success varies by firm and market characteristics. In particular, three types of firms affect the relative importance of these factors: new firms, established firms competing in established markets, and established firms entering new, yet related markets.

Vision, persistence, and financial commitment are most important for a new firm. This situation holds whether the firm enters a new or established market. Such a firm invariably faces established competitors in the new market or from related markets. Also, the difficulties of a start-up are myriad. In this context, the firm needs to have a clear vision or understanding of the mass market and what unique contribution it will provide to this market.

Relentless innovation is particularly important for an established firm competing in an established market. Often, in the mature stage, such markets may appear quite stable, while the position of an established firm may appear strong and invulnerable. However, this appearance can often be quite deceptive. In reality, changes in consumers' tastes and in technology are constantly refashioning markets and shaking up firms' positions. To maintain its position and keep ahead of competition, an established firm needs to innovate relentlessly despite the ever-increasing cost. For example, the cost of innovation kept increasing over the history of the Gillette Company, as the product became more complex. Innovation for the introduction of the first Gillette blade cost $10,000, while for Mach 3 it was $740 million. Not only is this strategy of relentless innovation the best defense, but it is also a means to grow in strength and market share. In this context, the goal of the firm is not so much to read the future as to strive to create the future.

Asset leverage is especially important for established firms that dominate in a related or parent category. Such firms accumulate a large number of assets through years of success in the parent category. These assets may be general ones such as brand name reputation and talented employees, or specialized ones such as products, sales force, distribution systems, or manufacturing facilities. Over the course of its history, a firm is likely to face the start of a new category that is related to or an offshoot of its current market. The new category may appear threatening, tempting the firm to deny it or defend against it. Instead, the firm needs to transfer its general assets and sacrifice its specialized assets in order to enter and dominate the related category. For example, when Apple entered the personal computer market, it had few assets to leverage. The founders worked in a garage, and initial investments came from individuals rather than a large company's cashflow. However, when IBM entered the same market, it relied on its enormous brand name and reputation to gain good distribution, widespread acceptance by businesses, and quick adoption of the product. The importance of assets, such as brand name, increases as a product's attributes are more ambiguous, and consumers rely on the reputation of the brand. For example, the success of Diet Coke probably had more to do with the name *Coke* than with any precise formula for the product based on innovation. Indeed, ambiguity itself may be negatively related to technical complexity, as in the case of soft drinks. Thus a firm's newness, the ambiguity of product attributes, and the technical complexity of product design appear to moderate the causes of enduring leadership.

does the early albeit short leadership of pioneers provide adequate rewards to pioneering?

There may be some truth in the fact that some market pioneers reap enough rewards to meet their goals or reduce their motivation to continue in the market. However, in most cases market pioneers fail even when future profits in the category far exceed past profits.

On average, market pioneers lead their respective category for about 12 years. During that time they may well reap substantial rewards. For example, in the mid-1970s, Gary Kildall's CP/M was so successful that in 1981 alone his small firm totaled $6 million in revenues. Yet his success in operating systems is minuscule compared with the eventual success of Microsoft. In another case, the McDonald brothers sold their business to Ray Kroc for $2.7 million in 1961. At the time it had already grown to 200 units. This price represents good success for most entrepreneurs. Yet by 1977 Ray Kroc estimated that their share in McDonald's restaurants would have been worth $15 million *a year*. When asked in 1991 about their decision to sell out, one of the brothers, Dick McDonald, had this to say: "We weren't kids anymore. We had three homes and a garage full of Cadillacs and we didn't owe a dime to anyone. . . . I have no regrets. Yachts on the Riviera were not my style at all."[6]

However, most of the pioneers we studied were completely unsatisfied with the limited rewards they achieved, for several reasons:

- Sales increase exponentially following the tapping of the mass market [e.g., note the market growth of VCRs (Figure 4-2) or PCs (Figure 10-4)]. Pioneers often fail at this growth stage and forgo potentially huge rewards. Examples are Ampex relative to Matsushita or Digital Research (owner of CP/M) relative to Microsoft (owner of DOS).
- Pioneers *fail at this stage despite efforts to succeed* because they lack vision, persistence, commitment, or innovation. So their failure is the result of behavior, not intentions. For example, Gary Kildall complained about how DOS seemed to be a knock-off of his program CP/M. He did develop a new version for the IBM PC, and contracted with IBM to let the new version be sold as an option. It failed because of its high price and inferior features to DOS.
- Some pioneers fail so soon that the small rewards they achieve may be inadequate to recover even a minimal investment. Examples are MITS in personal computers and Trommer's Red Letter in light beer.
- The failure of pioneers may be accompanied by big losses in the market value of their stock, as witnessed by the demise of many Internet pioneers.

Thus the failure of pioneers is neither planned nor necessarily satisfying to the managers or entrepreneurs involved.

do the conclusions change if we focus on profits rather than on market leadership?

Our research has focused primarily on market measures of success, such as survival, market share, and market leadership. It does not explicitly address profits because such accounting data are reported at the company level and are not possible to obtain for individual product categories except in rare instances.

Profit considerations may change the conclusions a little, but not substantially. The main reason is that the increase in sales following the opening of the mass market is so large and rapid that firms that survive or make this breakthrough enjoy huge profits, even when these future profits are discounted. Pioneers suffer a huge loss of this financial opportunity by failing at or before the massive increase in sales. Moreover, financiers, venture capitalists, and shareholders who invest in pioneers do so with the hope that their targets will be hugely successful rather than merely meet some limited short-term profit goals. A pioneer's emphasis on short-term profits itself may be inappropriate.

Moreover, a strong principle of business strategy has been to strive for enduring leadership rather than for short-term profits. A focus on short-term profits is more likely to be appropriate as a hedge against declining markets. It is completely inappropriate in most high-growth markets.

is regulation necessary?

Throughout the last century, U.S. laws have consistently discouraged monopolies. This policy has led the government to file antitrust cases against large firms when they seemed to have established a monopoly in certain markets. Three well-known and controversial cases are those against IBM, Xerox, and Microsoft. These cases lasted for a long period of time, cost millions of dollars to both the government and the firms, and have been major distractions for the senior managers of the firms involved. (In two of the cases, Xerox and IBM, the cases may have also increased the bureaucracy within these firms, and limited their initiative in new markets.)

Thus a reasonable question is, is the aggressive pursuit of antitrust policy, especially in fast-moving high-technology markets, worthwhile? It is well beyond the scope of this book to fully assess the merits of the antitrust and monopoly laws. However, it is possible to comment briefly on their merits in the three well-known cases that come within the domain of our research: IBM, Xerox, and Microsoft.

We first need to restate the logic of antitrust policy. Free markets serve the public interest because competition among firms, as an invisible hand, works to serve consumers with ever better products at ever lower prices. However, these benefits accrue to consumers only if markets are reasonably competitive. Such markets are characterized by utility-maximizing consumers and by profit-maximizing firms that are numerous enough so as not to influence the market, are free to enter and exit the market, and have good information about the functioning of the market. In the United States, antitrust policy is enforced when there is a real or perceived failure in two of these assumptions—that no firm has undue influence and that market entry is free. When a dominant firm seems to exert undue control over prices and features so that new firms cannot enter the market freely, potential entrants are seriously disadvantaged and consumers suffer with high prices, inferior quality, and limited choice. This assessment has motivated the government's antitrust cases against IBM, Xerox, and Microsoft.

While the complexity of the issues prevents any simple, clear statement of right and wrong in these cases, we think that, on the whole, the implementation of the policy in these cases may be more costly than beneficial to consumers for four reasons.

First, market positions of dominant firms exhibit great instability. Even when firms have an entrenched position, new technology and firms emerge that can threaten that position and quickly render obsolete the advantages of the dominant firm. This phenomenon is particularly true of high-technology markets, such as computers, copiers, and software. These are the very markets in which the government launched its biggest and most famous cases. For example, the advent of PCs and workstations greatly weakened IBM's hold on the computer market. The advent of personal computers and printers greatly weakened Xerox's hold on copiers. The rise of the Internet has threatened even Microsoft's hold on the software market.

Second, the cases impose a great monetary cost on the firms that are defendants in the case. To the extent that these costs are passed on to consumers as higher prices or forgone quality improvements, consumers suffer. Moreover, the cases also impose a huge direct cost on consumers, who as taxpayers must foot the government's legal bill. In all three of these cases, the benefits if any seem small relative to the costs.

Third, the cases turn out to be a great distraction to managers, who must devote valuable time to analyzing legal briefs, instead of envisioning the future of markets and developing solutions to better serve consumers. In several cases, the distraction may be so great as to immobilize companies and turn them into sterile bureaucratic environments. For example, some analysts believe that the government's legal cases against Xerox and IBM greatly increased the bureaucratic environment within those firms. This bureaucratic culture is the antithesis of the innovative culture that creates the really new products that bring tremendous benefits to consumers.

Finally, we strongly believe that the success of firms is due to vision, persistence, financial commitment, innovation, and asset leverage. It is not due to a prior established position. The market share, profits, and high stock prices that result from these five principles of firms are strong motivators for the sacrifices made by those managers and entrepreneurs who practice them. This reward system is the essence of the free market and the underlying motivation for entrepreneurs and managers. Thus lawyers' and economists' attacks on such rewards as pernicious returns of an entrenched market position seem unjustified on the basis of empirical evidence, economic rationale, and benefits to consumers.

what are the practical implications of our results for managers and analysts today? should firms enter late rather than enter early or first?

Our findings have many important implications for today's managers and analysts.

First, in general we are not recommending that a firm should enter late simply for the sake of entering late, any more than we would recommend that a firm should pioneer a new market simply to be the pioneer. However, we sincerely hope that we have moved readers away from the simplistic notion than pioneering by itself has much at all to do with enduring leadership.

Second, the small rewards for the typical pioneer in our sample of 66 categories should cause all observers of new markets to think twice before claiming a pioneering or first-mover advantage in any market. While market leaders have some advantages, these advantages tend to be proportional only to the size of the *current* market, not the size of the *potential* market. Some leadership advantages reside in production efficiencies. However, these only become meaningful once volume is high. Other advantages can come from brand name reputation and word-of-mouth effects. However, this set of advantages relies on the assumption that the leader sells a high-quality product. If the leader or pioneer does not sell a high-quality product, the reputation of the brand will be poor and word-of-mouth effects will be negative. Thus, a high-quality pioneer really benefits from being high quality, not from being a pioneer.

Third, not only have we shown that pioneers have very limited rewards from their initial leadership, but leaders in established markets tend to be much less enduring than previously believed. Whether a firm leads its market simply because it is the pioneer or it captures leadership in a mature product category, the advantages from leadership tend to be somewhat static. The five causes that we identify tend to create enduring leaders because they are dynamic and help the firm to establish and maintain its leadership as markets evolve over time.

Fourth, the advantage ensuing from these five factors dominates any of the effects associated with market pioneering or market leadership. Thus, whether a firm pioneers its market is not the critical issue. The critical issue is whether a firm embodies these five factors. Later entrants need not fear to challenge a pioneer. Yet they should be cautious in challenging any firm that is an exemplar of these five factors.

Fifth, in theory, an earlier entrant embodying these five factors may beat a later entrant also embodying these five factors. In this imaginary scenario, earlier entry may seem to be an advantage. However, in all 66 markets we studied, we did not find any situation where two firms were both exemplars of these five factors. Therefore, the effect of the five factors always dominated any effect from earlier entry. The only pioneers in our study that achieved enduring success also embodied these five factors.

Finally, there are actually several market situations where later entrants have advantages just from entering late. This situation occurs when markets are very new and uncertainty abounds. Here, later entrants can learn from the successes and mistakes of pioneers. Later entrants can learn at little or no cost about consumer tastes, the potential size of the market, and innovations in product features and manufacturing design. Later entrants can benefit from pioneers who spend money to educate consumers about a new product. Also, later entrants have a relative advantage over pioneers that rush an inferior product to market and consequently suffer negative effects from brand reputation and word of mouth. In all these cases, later entry by itself is an advantage.

conclusion

Managers and entrepreneurs frequently adhere to the motto of being first to market. Academic research provides strong support for this motto with findings that market pioneers rarely fail, have high market shares, and dominate their markets. Market pioneering came to be perceived as the magic step to enduring leadership, and the business press trumpeted the simplistic virtue of first-mover or pioneering advantage. However, as we pointed out, the research supporting this belief suffers from problems of survival bias, self-report bias, and loose definitions. Our research, which corrects these problems, shows that market pioneers tend to have very limited rewards, whereas firms that enter much later than pioneers tend to dominate markets. We have devoted this book to try to answer the question of why these latecomers are so successful while pioneers are not.

Our effort to address this question led to many years of studying the historical evolution of 66 product categories. Contrary to common belief, we found that market pioneering is neither necessary nor sufficient for long-term success and leadership. Instead, enduring market leaders embody five principles more critical to success than pioneering. Actually, a strategy for market entry is much like one for battle. A first strike may be desirable. But careful preparation for attack, counterattack, penetration, and consolidation are critical for success. Such preparation requires answers to five key questions:

1. *How will the entrant exploit the potential market?* **Vision.** Many an innovation initially appears too crude, costly, and limited in appeal. Market leaders are firms that can envision the mass market for these primitive innovations. Firms that can define that vision have the opportunity to assemble resources and inspire people for the task ahead.

2. *Can the entrant stick it out?* **Persistence.** The road to success is rarely easy; otherwise many a competitor would have taken it earlier. Technological blocks, legal constraints, consumer misperceptions, and competitive threats are some of the obstacles that new entrants face. Market leaders are those that persist through these challenges in quest of the vision.

3. *Does the entrant have the resources to put to the task?* **Commitment.** The mass market cannot be tapped cheaply. Many innovations hinge on new-product technologies, which develop slowly with costly research and development. Others require expensive process technologies and large-scale production to achieve the low costs necessary for the mass market. Still others require massive promotion to alert consumers to the innovation or clear away misperceptions. Market leaders are firms that can commit the resources to the vision of the mass market when sales are a trickle but costs loom large.

4. *Can the entrant change even at the cost of current position?* **Relentless innovation.** Markets, consumers, competitors, and technology change constantly. Stagnation in this environment leads to erosion of share or quick failure. Market leadership belongs to firms that innovate relentlessly even at the risk of cannibalizing or rendering obsolete their own products.

5. *Can the entrant transfer its strengths to the new market?* **Asset leverage.** Leaders in a mature category often dominate with a well-known brand, extensive distribution, or unique expertise.

These strengths constitute a relatively easy means to enter and dominate a new and related category. Market leaders are firms that can nurture these strengths while extending them discreetly to dominate new markets.

The first four factors are especially important in emerging new categories. They are not independent, but related; their interplay constitutes, within the firm, a driving force for success. It is the vision that inspires persistence and the willingness to commit huge resources. Relentless innovation provides the solutions to realize the vision and maintain leadership. Order of market entry, on the other hand, is not crucial. The rush to enter new markets often hinders a firm's ability to establish enduring leadership. For example, IBM's rush to enter the personal computer market in the early 1980s led it to use Intel's chip and Microsoft's operating system rather than develop its own. That decision to enter quickly meant that IBM lost the opportunity to capture at least some of the stock market value of Intel and Microsoft today.

Be first to enter new markets? Without these five factors, a first entrant is merely an alarm for competitors. By embodying these factors, a late entrant can easily outpace a more lethargic pioneer. An earlier entry along with these five principles may be an advantage. But being first to market by itself is neither necessary nor sufficient for enduring market leadership.

appendix I
the historical method

introduction

All the findings and conclusions in this book are based on applying the historical method to the study of pioneers and later entrants. In this appendix, we elaborate on this method and describe how we applied it in our research. This discussion should provide a better understanding of how we reached our findings and conclusions. Using the historical method, we evaluated successful and unsuccessful firms in 66 product categories. This evaluation enabled us to identify those factors that differentiate winning firms from losing firms in each category. This process led to identifying the five factors that were most common across all the categories we studied.

As we discussed in Chapter 2, the historical method provides four unique advantages for studying market pioneers, as well as identifying the causes of enduring leadership. First, the historical method is the best approach to uncover contemporaneous reports about firms and their strategies in new markets. We collected and evaluated evidence that was recorded at the same time important events actually occurred in each category. These contemporaneous reports enabled us to take a *prospective* look at pioneering because information is written as each new market develops. In contrast, surveys or interviews with current survivors are *retrospective* because people recall events that occurred many years or decades previously. A prospective look at pioneering is more similar to the way today's managers view their own product categories. A second major advantage is that evidence is collected and presented by independent reporters. These records reflect an unbiased perspective, in contrast with company reports that tend to promote an individual company's interests. While many firms claim to be the pioneer, only one firm in a market can be the actual pioneer. Since we must identify the actual pioneer in each category to assess its performance, use of these independent reports is critical. A third advantage is the rich detail of events uncovered through the historical record. These details enable us to evaluate the relative success of multiple firms: pioneers, early entrants, and late entrants. More importantly, we come to understand how each firm's actions and strategies contributed to its success or failure. We did not begin our study with a predetermined notion of the causes of success and failure. The insights from our application of the historical method led us to uncover our five causes of enduring leadership. Finally, the matched-sample benefit of historical research sets our study apart from nearly all other studies of business success. Most business books try to identify principles of success by looking at selected firms. In many cases these firms are only the successful ones. In contrast, we began by selecting markets, and then we evaluated multiple firms in each of these markets. These firms include pioneers, late entrants, some firms that failed miserably, some that succeeded spectacularly, and others that had moderate success. Our investigation of multiple firms in 66 markets leaves us confident that the five factors we identified are the primary causes separating the winners from the losers in each new market.

The following discussion elucidates how the historical method is uniquely suited to provide the four primary benefits that were so important in our study of market pioneers and enduring leadership. We now present a detailed review of the historical method and then describe how we applied each stage of the method in our research.

description of the historical method

Research using the historical method seeks to develop accurate descriptions of social phenomena after a careful consideration of all relevant and available data. The social phenomena of our research are the actions of business executives seeking to establish and maintain long-term leadership in new markets.

Historical research tries to uncover generalizations that emerge from an examination of events viewed in their broad context. These generalizations are developed with the following principles in mind: They are founded on all facts and contradict none; they are plausible and do not contradict the accepted laws of nature; they are capable of disproof and verification; and they are as simple as possible. Acceptable proof for historical generalizations is similar to the proof required in a legal case, where events are established beyond a reasonable doubt. Just as jurors might do in a legal trial, historians approach all evidence with a critical or skeptical attitude.

The historical method is conducted in five stages. We will describe each stage and discuss its specific application to our research.

STAGE 1: SELECT A TOPIC AND COLLECT EVIDENCE

Historians can study a wide range of topics from the distant past as well as the more recent past, as long as sufficient records of these events are available. Fortunately, our research focuses primarily on twentieth-century events where data are plentiful.

After selecting a topic, historians prepare questions of interest rather than develop hypotheses from established theory. They approach sources attempting to find their answers. The general approach is that the "material must precede the thesis."[1] Once some evidence has been evaluated, working hypotheses can be developed. However, these hypotheses should be prepared as questions rather than declarative statements to help maintain a noncommittal position.

Potential data sources include published materials, interviews, and company archives. Initial research for most questions begins in the library, where books and periodicals are available on most topics. Electronic databases are extremely useful for more recent articles.

Older articles can be found using the *Business Periodicals Index, Readers' Guide to Periodical Literature, New York Times Index,* and *Wall Street Journal Index.*

With so much data available, a common mistake of researchers is to spend too much time collecting unnecessary data. Researchers must be vigilant to maintain their focus on relevant data, rather than merely interesting data; otherwise they can be overwhelmed. Researchers' questions of interest and working hypotheses must be used to focus their data collection efforts. Researchers should constantly ask whether the data being collected support or refute their propositions.

When compiling evidence, notes are often sufficient. Carefully recording quotes is important, especially in cases where that information may contradict the accepted story. We have found that making copies of all relevant articles is the most efficient approach. Important information can be highlighted rather than transcribed, and the entire text is readily available for further analysis.

Although historical research may end up confirming established beliefs, it may be more important for generating new findings from new data. Because this method enables researchers to study phenomena that cannot be studied with other methods, it has the potential to generate novel results and sometimes even results that directly contradict current beliefs.

Our Application of Stage 1. We began by identifying our general topic of interest: the causes of enduring success or failure in new markets. We began with one simple question:

- What are the true rewards of market pioneers, after controlling for survival bias and misidentification of pioneers?

After discovering that the rewards of pioneers were much less than believed, we expanded our study by asking several additional questions:

- Why do pioneers fail so often?
- Why are early leaders so successful?

- And most importantly, what are the real causes of enduring market leadership, if not being first in the market?

After establishing our research questions, we selected a sample of product categories to evaluate. We wanted a large sample of categories so that our results would be likely to generalize across a wide variety of industries and contexts. We selected four samples.

Sample 1 is based on three criteria. First, the sample includes only consumer goods because we believed that these categories would be more likely to receive significant press coverage in widely available periodicals. Second, the sample includes more recent product categories because reports on these categories are more easily available. Third, the sample contains very new product categories (e.g., camcorders) and moderately new categories (e.g., light beer) so that we could evaluate any potential differences in the causes of enduring leadership between these types of categories. We found 19 product categories satisfying these criteria. The first sample is not biased toward or against the theory of pioneering advantage.

Sample 2 consists of 24 categories from the *Advertising Age* report of long-term leaders. We chose these categories because many authors have used this study as evidence of enduring market leadership and of pioneering advantage. Including these categories in our study was important because these categories include long-term leaders, and pioneers are believed to be long-term leaders. Thus, this sample is biased toward the prevailing view of a pioneering advantage.

Sample 3 consists of 8 product categories with famous firms that are widely believed to be (although may not be) market pioneers, e.g., Xerox, Polaroid, and Coca-Cola. Thus by definition, sample 3 is strongly favorable to the prevailing hypothesis that market pioneers are successful.

Sample 4 consists of 15 categories that are representative of the new economy. For this purpose we chose categories of high-tech or digital products. Many authors believe that because these markets evolve very fast, market pioneering or early entry is critical for long-term success. Here again, this sample is biased in favor of the prevailing view of pioneering advantage.

Overall, our total sample of 66 categories is more likely than a random sample of categories to include pioneers with strong rewards. Since we found that these pioneers' rewards were actually quite low on average, our results are likely to understate the challenges facing pioneers.

We sought specific data on 17 key variables in each product category: the firms classified as product pioneer, market pioneer, early leader, and current leader; parent company, date of market entry, and current market share of each of the four firms from these classifications; and duration of leadership of pioneers. In addition to these data, we recorded information on many other variables and events, especially those that were related to the long-term success or failure of the multiple firms in each market. These data led to our determination of the five causes of enduring market leadership. Since we studied multiple firms within each category, our conclusions about long-term leadership are based on an examination of over 250 different firms.

The sources of our data are all publicly available documents. We considered a myriad of sources of two types: periodicals and books. First, we examined over 2000 articles in 30 different periodicals. Some of the most helpful and commonly used periodicals were *Business Week, Advertising Age, Forbes,* and the *Wall Street Journal.* Second, we analyzed information from over 300 books. In addition to periodicals and books, we reviewed the annual reports of many firms. The large number and wide variety of sources helped us satisfy several important criteria specified in the second and third stages of the historical method.

STAGE 2: CRITICALLY EVALUATE SOURCES OF EVIDENCE

The primary purpose of this stage is to evaluate the *authenticity* of documents and to exclude all unauthentic evidence. During this stage, researchers seek to determine who wrote each document, and where, when, and under what circumstances. Historians sometimes criticize other social scientists for not sufficiently applying the criteria of external criticism and accepting data too easily.

There are three steps in this stage. The first step is *textual criticism,* which calls for examining documents to see if they are original or the best copy available. The next step is *investigation of authorship*, which calls for determining who wrote the document, where it came from, and when it was written. Finally, there is a *classification of sources*, in which verified documents are arranged according to several principles. Documents are considered more authentic if they are written with the following characteristics:

- Close to the event being researched (or rely on records written close to the event)
- For making a public record (newspapers and magazines)
- By experts with broad knowledge of the events of interest
- For the sole purpose of making a record (e.g., legal documents)
- For confidential communication
- For communicating with a small number of people (personal correspondence)
- For a personal record or memory aid (diary)

Newspaper or magazine reports are usually rated high on authenticity because the time between events and their reporting is short. In addition, reporters generally have a vested interest in reporting events accurately, and the public nature of the reports leaves them open to correction. Of course, the reputations of these sources must be considered too.

Anachronisms within a document may uncover reports that are low on authenticity. Therefore, it is important to have a broad knowledge of events during each period of interest. Examples of modern documents that must be scrutinized for authenticity are press releases and some private correspondence.

Another useful classification is whether documents are based upon primary or secondary sources. Primary sources are eyewitness accounts of an event. They also could be based on audio or video recordings of an event. Secondary sources are testimony from witnesses who were not present at the event of interest. These secondary sources can provide important corroboration or add missing details that are consistent with the testimony of primary sources.

After completing external criticism, researchers should have established the testimony of their witnesses (as recorded in documents most often) and have an understanding of each witness's capability to report that testimony. The next stage analyzes the particular content of each witness's testimony.

Our Application of Stage 2. It was fairly straightforward to establish the authenticity of our documents. All documents were obtained from major university or city libraries. Articles from periodicals were read primarily from microfilm or microfiche copies of the original publications. The same was true for companies' annual reports. Information from books was read from original copies of each book.

STAGE 3: CRITICALLY EVALUATE EVIDENCE

The primary purpose of this stage is to evaluate the particular contents of a document and extract *credible* testimony from it. Documents must be evaluated for two types of errors, deliberate and unintentional.

Three steps are part of this stage. One step is *interpretive criticism*, which seeks to determine what the author meant. Special attention is required if the author's account was written many years ago since reporting styles and conventions have changed over time. Also, a witness's testimony must be considered in its full context rather than in isolation. Otherwise, some statements may be misunderstood.

A second step is *negative internal criticism*, in which the veracity of the author's or witness's statements is evaluated. What a witness expressed may not be what he believed since he may have lied; and what he believed might not have actually happened since he may be mistaken. Therefore, historians do not feel obligated to accept all the testimony of even authentic witnesses. An important consideration in determining veracity is a witness's objective in presenting evidence. Personal interests may distort a report for the witness's benefit. An author with a literary style may recount hearsay without the proper disclaimer. Egocentrism may increase the witness's role. A desire to please may cause omission of important details or a less harsh presentation of events. Conditions that promote veracity include the witness being indifferent to the subject or event, the witness being harmed by his own testimony, and the witness relating events that would most likely have been common knowledge among his audience.

The final step is evaluating the *independence of observations*. Obviously, testimony from multiple, independent witnesses is valued highly.

Since evaluating credibility is central to internal criticism and also important to external criticism, there are four criteria for this critical task:

- *Competence*. Is the witness able to report correct information? Important factors are nearness to the event and nearness to the recording of the event (geographical and temporal) and familiarity with the subject (expertness).
- *Objectivity*. Is the witness willing to report correct information? Important factors are assessing personal interests, biases, and a desire to please.
- *Reliability*. Is the witness accurately reported? Does the reporter have a reputation for integrity? Does the document lack internal self-contradictions?
- *Corroboration*. Is there confirmatory evidence from equally credible witnesses?

Evidence is considered credible if it passes all four criteria. In particular, the final criterion is vital for developing confidence in the data. Conformance with other facts and witnesses is a critical test of evidence. Uncorroborated evidence should be reported accordingly. When secondary evidence is evaluated, credibility is determined for the primary evidence on which it is based. Doubts about the particulars of an event usually arise from the lack of testimony based on primary evidence.

The goal of internal criticism is to verify the events on which the historical record will be based. In a multitude of cases, these events are straightforward, well documented, and rarely disputed among historians. These cases typically do not involve value judgments, do not involve contradictory evidence, and are logically acceptable. These conditions apply to pure descriptions of many events. Fortunately, in much business research, these types of descriptions provide the basis for generating and testing theories, models, and frameworks.

Our Application of Stage 3. We asked several questions in evaluating and establishing the credibility of our evidence. First, who wrote each document? In most cases, writers were business journalists who worked for very reputable publications. Most of the authors of the books that we used fit into three categories: business journalists, academics, and independent researchers. All evidence from books was considered more credible if it was based on primary material written close to the time of the events being described or if it relied on eyewitness testimony of events. In the case of annual reports, we viewed this evidence more skeptically since the writers of these documents had an obvious self-interest bias. However, financial data from annual reports was considered credible.

A second factor we considered was the circumstances surrounding each publication. Documents were considered more credible if they satisfied the following criteria:

- Written close to the event being reported
- Relied on eyewitness accounts of events
- Written by disinterested third parties
- Written by experts with broad knowledge of surrounding events

Throughout our research, we gave much thought to the quality of the evidence we collected. In the end, we relied extensively on the four critical criteria for evaluating the credibility of evidence: competence, objectivity, reliability, and corroboration.

The competence criterion was satisfied by relying on highly regarded sources that were written or based on information written at the time each firm made an important move in a new market. The objectivity criterion was satisfied by relying on sources of information written by disinterested third parties. The reliability criterion was satisfied by using information from sources that were, and continue to be, highly respected for balanced, accurate reporting. The corroboration criterion was satisfied by using information from multiple data sources for each product category.

The final criterion of corroboration is a cornerstone of historical analysis. All the major themes in this book are based on at least two independent accounts of events. Although we are not able to corroborate every piece of data (like nearly all historical research), all the evidence we present is consistent with each of the broader themes that have been corroborated with independent sources of evidence.

STAGE 4: ANALYZE AND INTERPRET EVIDENCE

Only evidence that has passed the stringent tests in stages 2 and 3 is qualified for further analysis and interpretation. At this point, many historians organize their data chronologically within each subject area (e.g., person, institution, country). This arrangement has two advantages. Contradictory evidence can be viewed in the appropriate context, and potential explanations are more easily recognized since causes precede effects. Proper synthesis of evidence usually requires multiple readings of documents.

Historians may use inferences at this stage to complete information that is not specifically provided. However, these inferences are usually restricted to situations where they are much more precise than educated guesses. Inferences beyond what the data specify should be clearly delineated.

After organizing their data, historians analyze and interpret the information. This process is straightforward, with simple descriptions of common events. Often, there is little dispute among historians in these cases. The process of interpretation sometimes becomes complicated when historians try to provide a higher level of meaning to a collection of events. Since most historians seek to understand the meaning of events and not just report facts, multiple potential causes should be considered. These explanations can be the source of disagreement among historians. Yet these disagreements tend to focus on the relative degree of importance rather than the existence of certain evidence or causes. In terms of the data on which their theories depend, historians have an advantage over most other social scientists. The evidence of historical events is generated independently of any effort to study them. Therefore, data or evidence is not generated by researchers, as it is in laboratory research.

Finally, with an adequate understanding of specific events, many historians try to develop generalizations and interpret events in a way that is relevant to present times and circumstances.

Our Application of Stage 4. After compiling and evaluating all our evidence in the preceding stages, we sought to understand our data in stage 4. Some of our data were easy to understand, and the results could be presented as simple descriptive statistics. For example, it did not require extensive interpretation to determine the high percentage of pioneering firms that failed. However, significant analysis was required to uncover our five factors of enduring leadership. To do so, we found it important to consider all events in each category in chronological order. In this way, we could identify the strategies that led to long-term leadership. Conversely, we could also see how unsuccessful firms did not adopt similar strategies. By considering a large number of categories, we could identify those success factors that were most common across all the 66 product categories we studied. We strongly believe that these five factors differentiate the winners from the losers in the new markets we studied. While additional factors were also important in some individual categories, the five factors we identified were the most common factors across all our categories.

STAGE 5: PRESENT EVIDENCE AND CONCLUSIONS

When presenting their research, historians must rely on their judgment to make many decisions. A thesis developed from analysis and interpretation of evidence often guides these decisions. Historians must select evidence to present, arrange it, and decide how it should be emphasized or minimized. While it is rarely possible to present all the evidence that has been collected, historians include the most important evidence in relating their results and conclusions.

The form of presentation depends on the data that were collected to address the research objectives. Different types of evidence may be presented as chronologies, descriptive statistics, or model parameters. Most commonly, historians present their evidence, analysis, and conclusions in narrative form. This type of presentation enables historians to communicate a rich understanding of events, especially when the evidence collected is primarily qualitative. It links events together in a way that is not possible with simple chronologies.

Our Application of Stage 5.   In the final stage, we selected the best means of presenting our evidence and conclusions. In Chapter 3, we presented many descriptive statistics that came from our data. These statistics enabled us to document the long-term performance of market pioneers, early leaders, and other entrants. Similarly, in Chapter 10, we presented descriptive statistics about the long-term success of established leaders in more mature markets. Both sets of statistics confirm how difficult it is to establish enduring leadership. Therefore, it is vital for firms to understand and implement the five causes of enduring leadership that we have identified.

We identified these five causes of enduring leadership by comparing successful and unsuccessful firms in many product categories. After identifying these five factors based on an examination of more than 250 companies in 66 product categories, we selected multiple examples to support these factors. It is not possible to present even a small portion of the evidence that we collected and evaluated from hundreds of books and thousands of articles. Therefore, we selected examples of the causes of enduring leadership that would most clearly illustrate and illuminate each of the five factors. We hope that you found these examples compelling and instructive.[2]

appendix 2
key firms and dates
in samples studied

Category	Pioneer/Earliest Known Brand (Date Entered)	Current Leader (Date Entered)
Sample 1:		
Video recorder	Ampex (1956)	RCA/ Matsushita (1977)
Dishwasher	Crescent Washing Machine Co. (1900)	GE (1935)
Laundry dryer	Canton Clothes Dryer (1925)	Whirlpool (1950)
Personal computer	MITS (1975)	Dell (1984)
Camcorder	Kodak/Matsushita (1984)	Sony (1985)
Color TV	RCA (1954)	RCA (1954)
Laundry detergent	Dreft (1933)	Tide (1946)
Disposable diaper	Chux (1934)	Huggies (1978)
Liquid dishwashing detergent	Liquid Lux (1948)	Dawn (1976)

Light beer	Trommer's Red Letter (1961)	Bud Light (1981)
Diet cola	Kirsch's No-Cal Cola (1952)	Diet Coke (1982)
Liquid laundry detergent	Wisk (1956)	Liquid Tide (1984)
Dandruff shampoo	Fitch's (1919)	Head & Shoulders (1961)
Beer	Breweries in North America as early as 1637. Schlitz was interim leader	Budweiser (1876)
Toilet tissue	Sold by Joseph Gayetty in 1857	Charmin (1928)
Microwave oven	Derived from Raytheon's WW II radar technology. Sold commercially in 1950s. Sold to consumers by Amana (1966)	Sharp
Fax machine	Early twentieth-century news wire services could transmit photos. Xerox introduces in 1964	Sharp
Frozen dinner	Swanson (1946)	Stouffer's/ Lean Cuisine
Wine cooler	Introduced by California Cooler in 1981. Seagram and Bartles & Jaymes entered in 1984 and dominated. Recent sales are dramatically lower as category proves to be more of a fad	

Sample 2:

Cereal	Granula (1863)	Cheerios (1946)
Camera	Daguerrotype (1839)	Kodak (1888)
Canned fruit	Libby, McNeill, Libby (1868)	Del Monte (1891)
Chocolate	Whitman's (1842)	Hershey (1903)

Vegetable shortening	Crisco (1911)	Crisco (1911)
Canned milk	Borden (1860)	Carnation (1899)
Chewing gum	Black Jack/American Chicle (1871)	Wrigley (1892)
Safety razor	Star (1876)	Gillette (1903)
Sewing machine	4 firms (1849)	Singer (1851)
Soft drink	Vernors (1866)	Coca-Cola (1886)
Tire	Hartford Rubber Works (1895)	Goodyear (1898)
Bacon	Largest hog packers sold from Cincinnati prior to Civil War; Armour largest in Chicago in 1870s	Oscar Mayer
Crackers	Cracker bakery in Massachusetts in 1792; first brand to become no. 1 for Nabisco was Uneeda, and Ritz later became leader	Nabisco
Flour	Largest flour mills in New York City and Chesapeake Bay area in 1700s	Gold Medal (1880)
Mint candy	Large-scale U.S. production from mid-1800s; Life Savers (1913) was long-time leader	Breath-Savers (1978)
Paint	Sold for hundreds of years	Sherwin-Williams (1870)
Paper	Rittenhouse Mill in Philadelphia in 1690; Hammermill (1898) is long-time leader	
Pipe tobacco	Bull Durham, Lone Jack, and Killickinnick brands since 1860s; Prince Albert (1907) is long-time leader	
Shirt	Ready-made clothing in United States since late 1700s	

Soup	Dates back hundreds of years	Campbell (1897)
Soap	Dates back hundreds of years; Pears since 1789; Colgate Cashmere Bouquet since 1872	Dove
Tea	Sold in Boston by two dealers in 1690; forerunner of Great Atlantic and Pacific Tea Co. (A&P) formed in 1859	Lipton (1893)
Toothpaste	Used in ancient civilizations. Branded products available in 1800s. Alternating leadership of Colgate and Crest in recent decades resulting from product innovations	Colgate
Battery	Bright Star (1909) overtaken by Eveready (1920)	Duracell

Sample 3:

Telephone	Bell/AT&T (1877)	AT&T (1877)
Instant photography	Dubroni (1864)	Polaroid (1947)
Cola	Coca-Cola (1886)	Coca-Cola (1886)
Video game	Magnovox Odyssey (1973)	Sony (1995)
Rubber	Goodrich (1869)	Goodyear (1898)
Personal stereo	Panasonic (1970)	Sony (1979)
Copier	3M Thermofax (1950); Xerox (1960) was long-term leader	Canon
Urgent mail	Pan Am delivered mail by air as early as the 1920s	Federal Express (1971)

Sample 4:

PC operating system	CP/M (1975)	Windows (1985)
Word processor	IBM Magnetic Tape Selectric Typewriter (1964)	Word (1983)
Spreadsheet	VisiCalc (1979)	Excel (1985)

Personal finance software	Managing Your Money/ Dollars and Sense (1983)	Quicken (1984)
PC database software	dBase (1981)	Access (1992)
Presentation software	Harvard Graphics (1986)	PowerPoint (1987)
CD players	Sony (1983)	Sony (1983)
Online stock trading	K. Aufhauser (1994)	Charles Schwab (1996)
Online bookseller	Clbooks.com/books.com (1993)	Amazon (1995)
Web browser	*WorldWideWeb* (1990)	Internet Explorer (1995)
Microprocessor	Intel (1971)	Intel (1971)
Laser printer	IBM (1975)	Hewlett-Packard (1984)
Personal digital assistant	Amstrad PenPad/Apple Newton (1992)	Palm Pilot (1996)
Cellular phone	Motorola (1983)	Nokia
Online/Internet service provider	CompuServe (1979)	America Online (1985)

endnotes

chapter 1

1. "Study: Majority of 25 Leaders in 1923 Still on Top," *Advertising Age,* Sept. 19, 1983; p. 32. Joe S. Bain, *Barriers to New Competition,* Cambridge, Harvard University Press, 1956; Frank M. Bass and T. L. Pilon, "A Stochastic Brand Choice Framework for Econometric Modeling of Time Series Market Share Behavior," *Journal of Marketing Research,* 17:486–497 (1980); Gregory S. Carpenter and Kent Nakamoto, "Consumer Preference Formation and Pioneering Advantage," *Journal of Marketing Research,* 26:285–298 (August 1989); Marnik G. DeKimpe and Dominique M. Hanssens, "Empirical Generalizations About Market Evolution and Stationarity," *Marketing Science,* 14 (Number 3, Part 2 of 2):G109–G121 (1995); Andrew S. C. Ehrenberg, *Repeat Buying: Facts, Theory and Data,* 2d ed., New York, Oxford University Press, 1988; Andrew S. C. Ehrenberg, "New Brands and the Existing Market," *Journal of the Market Research Society,* 33:285–299 (1991); Philip Kotler, *Marketing Management: Analysis, Planning, Implementation, and Control,* 9th ed., Prentice-Hall, Upper Saddle River, NJ, 1997; Rajiv Lal and V. Padmanabhan, "Competitive Response and Equilibria," *Marketing Science,* 14 (Number 3, Part 2 of 2):G101–G108 (1995).

2. Andrew S. Grove, *Only the Paranoid Survive: How to Exploit the Crisis Points That Challenge Every Company and Career,* Currency/Doubleday/Bantam Doubleday Dell Publishing Group, New York, 1996, p. 51.

3. *Sources:* Derek F. Abell and John S. Hammond, *Strategic Market Planning: Problems and Analytical Approaches,* Prentice-Hall, Englewood Cliffs, NJ, 1979; Gregory S. Carpenter and Kent Nakamoto, "Consumer Preference Formation and

Pioneering Advantage," *Journal of Marketing Research*, 26:285–298 (1989); Alfred D. Chandler, "The Enduring Logic of Industrial Success," *Harvard Business Review*, 68:131–139 (March–April 1990); Robert G. Cooper, "The Dimensions of Industrial New Product Success and Failure," *Journal of Marketing*, 43:93–103 (1979); George S. Day and Jonathan S. Freeman, "Burnout or Fadeout: The Risks of Early Entry into High Technology Markets," in Michael W. Lawless and Luis R. Gomez-Mejia, eds., *Strategic Management in High Technology Firms*, JAI Press, Greenwich, CT, 1990, pp. 43–65; George S. Day, Allan D. Shocker, and Rajendra K. Srivastava, "Customer-Oriented Approaches to Identifying Product-Markets," *Journal of Marketing*, 43:8–19 (Fall 1979); R. J. Gilbert and D. M. G. Newberry, "Preemptive Patenting and the Persistence of Monopoly," *American Economic Review*, 72:514–526 (June 1982); A. Glazer, "The Advantages of Being First," *American Economic Review*, 75:473–480 (June 1985); J. L. Guasch and A. Weiss, "Adverse Selection of Markets and the Advantages of Being Late," *Quarterly Journal of Economics*, 453–466 (May 1980); Fahri Karakaya and Michael J. Stahl, "Barriers to Entry and Market Entry Decisions in Consumer and Industrial Goods Markets," *Journal of Marketing*, 53:80–91 (April 1989); W. J. Lane, "Product Differentiation in a Market with Endogenous Sequential Entry," *Bell Journal of Economics*, 11:237–260 (Spring 1980); Marvin B. Lieberman and David B. Montgomery, "First-Mover Advantages," *Strategic Management Journal*, 9:41–58 (1988); Barbara Loken and James Ward, "Alternative Approaches to Understanding the Determinants of Typicality," *Journal of Consumer Research*, 17:111–126 (September 1990); E. Prescott and M. Visscher, "Sequential Location among Firms with Foresight," *Bell Journal of Economics*, 8:378–393 (1977); S. Ratneshwar and Allan D. Shocker, "Substitution in Use and the Role of Usage Context in Product Category Structures," *Journal of Marketing Research*, 28:281–295 (August 1991); F. M. Scherer, "Editorial: Post-Patent Barriers to Entry in the Pharmaceutical Industry," *Journal of Health Economics*, 4:83–87 (March 1985); Richard Schmalensee, "Entry Deterrence in the Ready to Eat Breakfast Cereal Industry," *Bell Journal of Economics*, 9:305–327 (Autumn 1978); Richard Schmalensee, "Product Differentiation Advantages of Pioneering Brands," *American Economic Review*, 72:349–365 (June 1982); M. Spence, "The Learning Curve and Competition," *Bell Journal of Economics*, 12:49–70 (1981); M. Spence, "Entry, Capacity, Investment, and Oligopolistic Pricing," *Bell Journal of Economics*, 8:534–544 (1977); Mita Sujan and James R. Bettman, "The Effects of Brand Positioning Strategies on Consumers' Brand and Category Perceptions: Some Insights from Schema Research," *Journal of Marketing Research*, 26:454–467 (November 1989).

4. Al Ries and Jack Trout, *The 22 Immutable Laws of Marketing*, HarperCollins, New York, 1993, p. 4.

5. Gregory S. Carpenter and Kent Nakamoto, op. cit., p. 286.

6. *Sources:* Frank H. Alpert, Michael A. Kamins, and John L. Graham, "An Examination of Reseller Buyer Attitudes toward Order of Brand Entry," *Journal of Marketing*, 56:25–37 (July 1992); R. S. Bond and D. F. Lean, *"Sales, Promotion, and Product Differentiation in Two Prescription Drug Markets,"* U.S. Federal Trade Commission, 1977; Robert D. Buzzell and Bradley T. Gale, *The PIMS Principles: Linking Strategy to Performance*, Free Press, New York, 1987; Gurumurthy Kalyanaram and Glen L. Urban, "Dynamic Effects of the Order of Entry on Market Share, Trial, Penetration, and Repeat Purchases for Frequently Purchased Con-

sumer Goods," *Marketing Science,* 11(3):235–251 (1992); Fahri Karakaya and Michael J. Stahl, "Barriers to Entry and Market Entry Decisions in Consumer and Industrial Goods Markets," *Journal of Marketing,* 53:80–91 (April 1989); Mary Lambkin, "Order of Entry and Performance in New Markets," *Strategic Management Journal,* 9:127–140 (Summer 1988); Mary Lambkin and George S. Day, "Evolutionary Processes in Competitive Markets: beyond the Product Life Cycle," *Journal of Marketing,* 53:4–20 (July 1989); W. J. Lane, "Product Differentiation in a Market with Endogenous Sequential Entry," *Bell Journal of Economics,* 11:237–260 (1980); Gary L. Lilien and Eunsang Yoon, "The Timing of Competitive Market Entry: An Exploratory Study of New Industrial Products," *Management Science,* 36:568–585 (May 1990); Michael J. Moore, William Boulding, and Ronald C. Goodstein, "Pioneering and Market Share: Is Entry Time Endogenous and Does It Matter?" *Journal of Marketing Research,* 28:97–104 (February 1991); Mark Parry and Frank M. Bass, "When to Lead or Follow? It Depends," *Marketing Letters,* 1:187–198 (November 1990); William T. Robinson and Claes Fornell, "Sources of Market Pioneer Advantage in Consumer Goods Industries," *Journal of Marketing Research,* 22:305–317 (August 1985); William T. Robinson, "Sources of Market Pioneer Advantages: The Case of Industrial Goods Industries," *Journal of Marketing Research,* 25:87–94 (February 1988); Steven P. Schnaars, "When Entering Growth Markets, Are Pioneers Better Than Poachers?" *Business Horizons,* vol. 29, March–April, 1986, pp. 27–36; Mary Sullivan, "Brand Extension and Order of Entry," Marketing Science Institute Working Paper, Report No. 91–105, Marketing Science Institute, Boston, 1991; Glen L. Urban, Theresa Carter, Steven Gaskin, and Zofia Mucha, "Market Share Rewards to Pioneering Brands: An Empirical Analysis and Strategic Implications," *Management Science,* 32:645–659 (June 1986); Ira T. Whitten, "Brand Performance in the Cigarette Industry and the Advantages of Early Entry," U.S. Federal Trade Commission, 1979; George S. Yip, *Barriers to Entry,* Lexington Books, D. C. Heath, Lexington, MA, 1982.

7. Ries and Trout, op. cit., p. 2.

8. For example, see Phillip Robinson, "HP LaserJet 4 Introduces a New World of Printing," *Austin American-Statesman,* Dec. 28, 1992, p. E2.

9. Stephen Roberts, "Early Laser Printer Development," http://www.printerworks.com/Catalogs/CX-Catalog/CX-HP LaserJet-History.html and personal correspondence (1994).

10. "Will Microsoft Catch Netscape?" *Computerworld* Apr. 29, 1996, pp. 80–81.

11. For example, see Sandra Jones, "Net Browser Spyglass Plans 2-for-1 Stock Split," *Chicago Sun-Times,* Nov. 29, 1995, p. 69.

12. "Mosaic Quest Closes in Redmond Original," *Computer Business Review,* Feb. 1, 1997.

13. Tim Berners-Lee, "Spinning the Web: A Place for Everything, and Everything on the Web?" *Data Communications,* Oct. 21, 1997, p. 48; Hal Berghel, "Who Won the Mosaic War?" *ACM,* 41 (10):13–16, (1998).

14. Psychologists also describe a similar problem that occurs when they ask managers to describe their own attributes. Managers tend to exaggerate their positive attributes and underreport their negative attributes. They call this problem positivity bias.

15. Procter & Gamble, *Annual Report,* 1977.

chapter 2

1. Paul Freiberger and Michael Swaine, *Fire in the Valley: The Making of the Personal Computer*, Osborne/McGraw-Hill, Berkeley, CA, 1984; Amar Gupta and Hoormin D. Toong, "The First Decade of Personal Computers," in Amar Gupta and Hoormin D. Toong, eds., *Insights into Personal Computers*, IEEE Press, New York, 1985; Gerald E. Nelson and William R. Hewlett, "The Design and Development of a Family of Personal Computers for Engineers and Scientists," in Gupta and Toong, eds., op. cit.; Paul E. Ceruzzi, *A History of Modern Computing*, MIT Press, Cambridge, MA, 1999.

2. "Personal Computers: And the Winner Is IBM," *Business Week*, Oct. 3, 1983, pp. 76–95.

3. Gupta and Toong, op. cit.; Jack M. Nilles, *Technology Assessment of Personal Computers: Volume 2, Personal Computer Technology, Users, and Uses*, University of Southern California team sponsored by National Science Foundation, document available from National Technical Information Service, U.S. Department of Commerce, 1980, p. 2-5.

4. "Microcomputers Catch on Fast," *Business Week*, July 12, 1976, p. 50.

5. Ray Kroc and Robert Anderson, *Grinding It Out: The Making of McDonald's*, Regnery, Chicago, 1977.

6. Ellen Graham, "McDonald's Pickle: He Began Fast Food but Gets No Credit," *The Wall Street Journal*, Aug. 15, 1991, p. A1.

7. Kroc and Anderson, op. cit., p. 9.

8. Ibid., p. 11.

9. "Out to Crack the Copying Market," *Business Week*, Sept. 19, 1959, p. 86.

10. Sources corresponding to order of quote are "Howard Johnson—Highway Host," *Financial World*, May 20, 1964, p. 5; "Proliferating Drive-Ins," *Financial World*, Apr. 5, 1967, pp. 6–7; ibid.; ibid.; "Franchise to Growth," *Financial World*, Sept. 8, 1965, p. 6.

11. For example, see Peter N. Golder and Gerard J. Tellis, "Pioneer Advantage: Marketing Fact or Marketing Legend," *Journal of Marketing Research*, 30:158–170 (May 1993); Gerard J. Tellis and Peter N. Golder, "First to Market, First to Fail? Real Causes of Enduring Market Leadership," *Sloan Management Review*, 37(2): 65–75 (1996).

chapter 3

1. These results are based on a wider sample and are also more recent than what we had reported in academic peer-reviewed journal articles: Peter N. Golder and Gerard J. Tellis, "Pioneer Advantage: Marketing Logic or Marketing Legend?" *Journal of Marketing Research*, 30:158–170 (May 1993); Gerard J. Tellis and Peter N. Golder, "First to Market, First to Fail? Real Causes of Enduring Market Leadership," *Sloan Management Review*, 37(2):65–75 (1996).

2. William T. Robinson, "Sources of Market Pioneer Advantages: The Case of

Industrial Goods Industries," *Journal of Marketing Research,* 25:87–94 (February 1988); William T. Robinson and Claes Fornell, "Sources of Market Pioneer Advantage in Consumer Goods Industries," *Journal of Marketing Research,* 22:305–317 (August 1985); Glen L. Urban, Theresa Carter, Steven Gaskin, and Zofia Mucha, "Market Share Rewards to Pioneering Brands: An Empirical Analysis and Strategic Implications," *Management Science,* 32:645–659 (1986); Gurumurthy Kalyanaram and Glen L. Urban, "Dynamic Effects of the Order of Entry on Market Share, Trial, Penetration, and Repeat Purchases for Frequently Purchased Consumer Goods," *Marketing Science,* 11(3):235–251 (1992).

3. Al Ries and Jack Trout, *The 22 Immutable Laws of Marketing,* HarperCollins, New York, 1993, p. 7.

4. Ibid., p. 5.

5. J. C. Louis and Harvey Yazijian, *The Cola Wars,* Everest House, New York, 1980, p. 14.

6. Bill Gates, "They're Talking, We're Selling," *The Wall Street Journal,* Mar. 16, 1995, p. A22.

7. Amy Cortese, et al., "America Online's Global Push," *Business Week,* April 3, 1996, p. 78; Swisher, *Aol. Com,* Random House, New York, 1998.

8. Masaru Ibuka, "How SONY Developed Electronics for the World Market," *IEEE Transactions on Engineering Management,* 22(1):16 (February 1975).

chapter 4

1. Harry Tecklenburg, "A Dogged Dedication to Learning," *Research Technology Management,* July–August 1990, p. 14.

2. "Disposable Diapers," Internal Report and Planning Document, Johnson & Johnson Archives, New Brunswick, NJ, 1969, p. 3.

3. *Other sources:* "Diapers," *Consumer Reports,* August 1954, pp. 160–164; "Disposable Diapers," *Consumer Reports,* March 1961, pp. 151–152; "For Babies Only—Chux Throw-Away Diapers," *Delineator,* August 1935, p. 6; "The Great Diaper Rash," *Forbes,* Dec. 15, 1970, p. 24; "All Those Leaky Diapers," *Forbes,* Feb. 15, 1975, pp. 49, 50; Lawrence G. Foster and F. Robert Kniffen, Press Release 81B11, Johnson & Johnson, New Brunswick, NJ, 1981; Michael E. Porter, "The Disposable Diaper Industry in 1974," Harvard Business School Case 380–175 (1980); Procter & Gamble, *Annual Report,* 1977; Tecklenburg, op. cit., pp. 12–15; "The Great Diaper Battle," *Time,* Jan. 24, 1969, pp. 69–70.

4. *Sources:* Brian Coe, *Cameras: From Daguerreotypes to Instant Pictures,* Crown Publishers, New York, 1978; "Polaroid Cameras," *Consumer Reports,* January 1968, pp. 44–46; Vrinda Kadiyali, "Eastman Kodak in the Photographic Film Industry: Picture Imperfect?" in David I. Rosenbaum, ed., *Market Dominance: How Firms Gain, Hold, Or Lose It and the Impact on Economic Performance,* Praeger, Westport, CT, 1998, pp. 89–108; Eaton S. Lothrop, Jr., *A Century of Cameras,* Morgan & Morgan, Dobbs Ferry, NY, 1973; Beaumont Newhall, *The History of Photography,* Little, Brown, Boston, 1982; J. Utterback, *Mastering the Dynamics of Innovation,* Harvard Business School Press, Boston, 1994.

5. Nick Lyons, *The Sony Vision,* Crown Publishers, New York, 1976.

6. Ibid., pp. 150–151.

7. Ibid.

8. Richard S. Rosenbloom and Michael A. Cusumano, "Technological Pioneering and Competitive Advantage: The Birth of the VCR Industry," *California Management Review,* XXIX: 63 (Summer 1987).

9. *Other sources:* "Agencies Eye Sony Home TV Recorder for Storyboard Uses," *Advertising Age,* June 21, 1961, p. 101; "Agency Dilemma: Kin Sue Clients," *Advertising Age,* July 18, 1966; "RCA SelectVision Bows; Home Sports Fans Become TV Producers in Early '70s," *Advertising Age,* Oct. 13, 1969, p. 57; Ampex, *Annual Reports,* 1969–1976, 1980; "More Gear for Home Movie Fans," *Business Week,* July 16, 1966; "Hotter Competition in Video Recorders," *Business Week,* Apr. 25, 1977, p. 36; "A Flickering Picture for Video Recorders," *Business Week,* Aug. 21, 1978, p. 28; "Color TV," *Consumer Reports,* November 1961, pp. 612–613; "Home Video Tape Recorder," *Consumer Reports,* June 1966, p. 280; "The Betamax: How Well Does It Work?" *Consumer Reports,* May, 1977, p. 291; "The Greatest Thing Since the Nickelodeon?" *Forbes,* July 1, 1970; James P. Forkan, "Video Cassette Man Prognosticate Unit Sales Up to 60,000 in '72," *Advertising Age,* Oct. 2, 1972; James P. Forkan, "Sony Begins Roll of Video Cassette Unit in N.Y. Market," *Advertising Age,* Nov. 3, 1975; Sumantra Ghoshal and Christopher A. Bartlett, "Matsushita Electric Industrial (MEI) in 1987," Harvard Business School Case 9-388-144 (1988); Masaru Ibuka, "How SONY Developed Electronics for the World Market," *IEEE Transactions on Engineering Management,* 22(1):15–19 (February 1975); Lawrence Lessing, "Stand By for the Cartridge TV Explosion," *Fortune,* June 1971, p. 80; Mark R. Levy, "The VCR Age: Home Video and Mass Communication," Sage Publications, Newberry Park, CA, 1989; Ralinda Young Lurie, "The World VCR Industry," Harvard Business School Case 9-387-098 (1987); Lyons, op. cit.; Matsushita, *Annual Reports,* 1971–1973, 1975, 1977, 1979, 1981, 1985; Peter Nulty, "Matsushita Takes the Lead in Video Recorders," *Fortune,* July 16, 1979, pp. 110–116; Richard S. Rosenbloom and Karen Freeze, "Ampex Corporation and Video Innovation," in Richard S. Rosenbloom, ed., *Research on Technological Innovation, Management and Policy,* Vol. 2, JAI Press, Greenwich, CT, 1985; Richard S. Rosenbloom and Michael A. Cusumano, op. cit., pp. 51–76; Scott R. Schmedel, "Sony TV Tapes Stir U.S. Firms to Act; Separation Spreads to Canada's West," *The Wall Street Journal,* Mar. 28, 1977, p. 6; Sony, *Annual Reports,* 1973–1974, 1976–1982, 1984; "VCR Owners," *The Wall Street Journal,* May 1, 1986, p. B5; David B. Yoffie, "The World VCR Industry," Harvard Business School Case 9-387-098, rev. Jan. 23, 1990.

10. Robert Slater, *Portraits in Silicon,* MIT Press, Cambridge, MA, 1987, p. 178.

11. William Aspray, "The Intel 4004 Microprocessor: What Constitutes Invention?" *IEEE Annals of the History of Computing,* 19(3):10 (1997).

12. Ibid.

13. Ibid., p. 179.

14. Both Faggin and Hoff claim a role in gaining back the rights to the 4004 and urging Intel to market the chip. But Faggin claims Hoff was opposed to marketing it. William Aspray, op cit., 1997.

15. "The History of Intel, 30 Years of Innovation," http://www.intel.com/pressroom/archive/backgrnd/cn71898a.htm

16. Tim Jackson, *Inside Intel,* Dutton/Penguin Putnam, New York, 1997, p. 73.

17. *Other sources:* Robert A. Burgelman, "Fading Memories: A Process Theory of Strategic Business Exit in Dynamic Environments," *Administrative Science Quarterly,* vol. 39, 1994, pp. 24–56; Gene Bylinsky, "How Intel Won Its Bet on Memory Chips," *Fortune,* November 1973, pp. 142–147, 186; Dennis Carter and Robert Burgelman, "Intel Corporation: The Evolution of an Adaptive Organization," Academy of Management Conference, Chicago, August 6–11, 1999, http://www.aom.pace.edu/meetings/1999/INTEL1.htm; Paul E. Ceruzzi, *A History of Modern Computing,* MIT Press, Cambridge, MA, 1999; George W. Cogan, "Intel Corporation (A): The DRAM Decision," Graduate School of Business, Stanford University, Palo Alto, CA, 1989; Robert X. Cringley, *Accidental Empires,* Addison-Wesley, Reading, MA, 1993; Elvia Faggin, "Faggin Contributed to First Microprocessor," *San Jose Mercury News,* Oct. 3, 1986, p. 6B; Paul Freiberger and Michael Swaine, *Fire in the Valley: The Making of the Personal Computer,* Osborne/McGraw-Hill, Berkeley, CA, 1984; Andrew S. Grove, *Only the Paranoid Survive: How to Exploit the Crisis Points That Challenge Every Company and Career,* Currency/Doubleday/Bantam Doubleday Dell Publishing Group, New York, 1996; Amar Gupta and Hoormin D. Toong, "The First Decade of Personal Computers," in Amar Gupta and Hoormin D. Toong, eds., *Insights into Personal Computers,* IEEE Press, New York, 1985; Marcian E. Hoff, Jr., "Patents Don't Tell Whole Microprocessor Tale," *San Jose Mercury News,* Oct. 12, 1986, p. 10B; Gerald E. Nelson and William R. Hewlett, "The Design and Development of a Family of Personal Computers for Engineers and Scientists," in ibid.; Joel N. Shurkin, *Engines of the Mind: A History of the Computer,* Norton, New York, 1984; Albert Yu, *Creating the Digital Future: The Secrets of Consistent Innovation at Intel,* Free Press/Simon & Schuster, New York, 1998; Rob Walker, Interview with Marcian (Ted) Hoff, Oral Histories of Semiconductor Industry Pioneers, Program in History and Philosophy of Science, Department of History, Stanford University, March 3, 1995.

18. Theodore Levitt, "Marketing Myopia," *Harvard Business Review,* September–October, 1975, pp. 1–13.

chapter 5

1. The planer consists of a small rectangular block of wood that has an adjustable blade that protrudes at a forward angle through the bottom. By adjusting the depth of the blade and repeatedly passing the tool over a piece of wood, the carpenter can get that piece to a desired level of smoothness.

2. King C. Gillette, "Origin of the Gillette Razor," *The Gillette Blade,* February 1918, p. 6.

3. Ibid., p. 7.

4. William E. Nickerson, "The Development of the Gillette Safety Razor," *The Gillette Blade,* May 1918, p. 5.

5. Gillette, op. cit., p. 7.

6. *Other sources:* Russell B. Adams, Jr., *King C. Gillette: The Man and His*

Wonderful Shaving Device, Little, Brown, Boston, 1978; George B. Baldwin, "The Invention of the Modern Safety Razor: A Case Study of Industrial Innovation," *Explorations in Entrepreneurial History,* vol. 4(2), December 1951, p. 73–104; Anne Bezanson, "The Invention of the Safety Razor: Further Comments," *Explorations in Entrepreneurial History,* vol. 4(4), May 15, 1952, pp. 193–198; King C. Gillette, "Origin of the Gillette Razor," *The Gillette Blade,* March 1918, pp. 7–14; William E. Nickerson, "The Development of the Gillette Safety Razor," *The Gillette Blade,* December 1918, pp. 5–13; William E. Nickerson, "The Development of the Gillette Safety Razor," *The Gillette Blade,* January 1919, pp. 6–18.

7. Robert A. Sigafoos, *Absolutely, Positively Overnight!,* St. Luke's Press, Memphis, TN, 1983, p. 31.

8. Ibid., p. 32.

9. Ibid., p. 31.

10. Winston Williams, "Overnight Delivery: The Battle Begins," *The New York Times,* Jan. 1, 1979, Sec. 3, p. 9.

11. *Other sources:* "A New Kind of Flight Plan for Small Freight," *Business Week,* Nov. 3, 1973, p. 3; "Why Airlines Fear the 'Federal Express Bill,'" *Business Week,* Sept. 13, 1976, p. 116; Christopher H. Lovelock, "Federal Express (A)," Harvard Business School Publishing, 9-577-042 Boston, 1976; Christopher H. Lovelock, "Federal Express (B)," Harvard Business School Publishing, 9-579-040 Boston, 1976; John D. Williams and Steve Frazier, "Federal Hustles to Keep Ahead of Emery in the Fast-Growing Air-Express Market," *The Wall Street Journal Stories,* Sept. 11, 1979; Milton Moskowitz, "The Overnight Delivery Revolution," *The San Francisco Chronicle,* Jan. 4, 1985, p. 35.

12. Tim Berners-Lee and Mark Fischetti, *Weaving the Web: The Original Design and Ultimate Destiny of the World Wide Web by Its Inventor,* HarperCollins, New York, 1999, p. 21.

13. Ibid., p. 37.

14. Ibid., p. 36.

15. *Other sources:* David Bank, "Changing the Course of the Information Highway Executive, Students Team Up on Plan to Expand Internet," *Los Angeles Daily News,* June 6, 1994, p. B5; Tim Berners-Lee, Robert Cailliau, Ari Luotonen, Henrik Frystyk, and Nielsen Arthur Secret, "The World-Wide Web," *Communications of the ACM,* Aug. 1, 1994, p. 76; Jim Clark and Owen Edwards, *Netscape Time: The Making of the Billion-Dollar Start-Up That Took on Microsoft,* St. Martin's Press, New York, 1999; Joe Clark, "Browsers Help You Forge Lynx in Internet Chain," *The Toronto Star,* Final, Oct. 13, 1994, p. J5; Della De LaFuente, "The Champaign Net Work//Whiz Kids from U. of I. Make Millions in Cyberspace," *Chicago Sun-Times,* Sept. 17, 1995, p. 33; Katie Hatner and Mathew Lyon, *Where Wizards Stay Up Late,* Touchstone, New York, 1996; Greg R. Notess, "Comparing Web Browsers: Mosaic, Cello, Netscape, WinWeb and InternetWorks Lite," *Online,* March/April 1995, pp. 36–40; Jian-Zhong Zhou, "The Internet, the World Wide Web, Library Web Browsers and Library Web Servers," *Information Technology and Libraries,* Mar. 1, 2000, p. 50.

chapter 6

1. King C. Gillette, "Origin of the Gillette Razor," *The Gillette Blade,* February 1918, p. 7.

2. Russell B. Adams, Jr., *King C. Gillette: The Man and His Wonderful Shaving Device,* Little, Brown, Boston, 1978, p. 29.

3. Ibid., p. 30.

4. Gillette, op. cit., p. 6.

5. Gillette, op. cit., p. 7.

6. *Other sources:* Adams, op. cit.; George B. Baldwin, "The Invention of the Modern Safety Razor: A Case Study of Industrial Innovation," *Explorations in Entrepreneurial History,* vol. 4(2), December 1951, pp. 75–104; Anne Bezanson, "The Invention of the Safety Razor: Further Comments," *Explorations in Entrepreneurial History,* vol. 4 (4), May 15, 1952, pp. 193–198; Gordon McKibben, *Cutting Edge: Gillette's Journey to Global Leadership,* Harvard Business School Press, Boston, 1998; King C. Gillette, "Origin of the Gillette Razor," *The Gillette Blade,* March 1918, pp. 7–14; William E. Nickerson, "The Development of the Gillette Safety Razor," *The Gillette Blade,* December 1918, pp. 5–13; William E. Nickerson, "The Development of the Gillette Safety Razor," *The Gillette Blade,* January 1919, pp. 6–18; William E. Nickerson, "The Development of the Gillette Safety Razor," *The Gillette Blade,* May 1918, pp. 3–6.

7. Harry Tecklenburg, "A Dogged Dedication to Learning," *Research Technology Management,* July–August 1990, p. 13.

8. "The Great Diaper Rush," *Forbes,* Dec. 15, 1970, pp. 24–30.

9. Tecklenburg, op. cit., p. 12.

10. *Other sources:* "Diapers," *Consumer Reports,* August 1954, pp. 160–164; "Disposable Diapers," *Consumer Reports,* March 1961, pp. 151–152; "For Babies Only—Chux Throw-Away Diapers," *Delineator,* August 1935, p. 6; "The Great Diaper Rash," *Forbes,* Dec. 15, 1970, p. 24; "All Those Leaky Diapers," *Forbes,* Feb. 15, 1975; Lawrence G. Foster and F. Robert Kniffen, Press Release 81B11, Johnson & Johnson, New Brunswick, NJ, 1981; Michael E. Porter, "The Disposable Diaper Industry in 1974," Harvard Business School Case 380-175 (1980); Procter & Gamble, *Annual Report,* 1977; Tecklenburg, op. cit., pp. 12–15; "The Great Diaper Battle," *Time,* Jan. 24, 1969, pp. 69–70.

11. Nick Lyons, *The Sony Vision,* Crown Publishers, New York, 1976, p. 150.

12. "Agencies Eye Sony Home TV Recorder for Storyboard Uses," *Advertising Age,* June 21, 1965, p. 101; "Sony Portable Tape Recorder to Bow in Ads," *Advertising Age,* July 18, 1966, pp. 2, 136; "RCA SelectVision Bows: Home Sports Fans Become TV Producers in Early '70s," *Advertising Age,* Oct. 13, 1969; Ampex, *Annual Reports,* 1969–1976, 1980; "More Gear for Home Movie Fans," *Business Week,* July 16, 1966, p. 94; "Hotter Competition in Video Recorders," *Business Week,* Apr. 25, 1977, p. 36; "A Flickering Picture for Video Recorders," *Business Week,* Aug. 21, 1978, p. 28; "Color TV," *Consumer Reports,* November 1961, pp. 612–613; "Home Video Tape Recorder," *Consumer Reports,* June 1966, p. 280; "The Betamax: How Well Does It Work," *Consumer Reports,* May 1977, p. 291; "The Greatest Thing Since the Nickelodeon?" *Forbes,* July 1, 1970; James P. Forkan, "Video Cassette Man Prognosticate Unit Sales Up to 60,000 in '72," *Advertising*

Age, Oct. 2, 1972; James P. Forkan, "Sony Begins Roll of Video Cassette Unit in N.Y. Market," *Advertising Age,* Nov. 3, 1975; Sumantra Ghoshal and Christopher A. Bartlett, "Matsushita Electric Industrial (MEI) in 1987," Harvard Business School Case 9-388-144 (1988); Lawrence Lessing, "Stand By for the Cartridge TV Explosion," *Fortune,* June 1971, p. 80; Mark R. Levy, "The VCR Age: Home Video and Mass Communication," Sage Publications, Newberry Park, CA, 1989; Ralinda Young Lurie, "The World VCR Industry," Harvard Business School Case 9-387-098 (1987); Lyons, op. cit.; Matsushita, *Annual Reports,* 1971–1973, 1975, 1977, 1979, 1981, 1985; Peter Nulty, "Matsushita Takes the Lead in Video Recorders," *Fortune,* July 16, 1979, pp. 110–116; Richard S. Rosenbloom and Karen Freeze, "Ampex Corporation and Video Innovation," in Richard S. Rosenbloom, ed., *Research on Technological Innovation, Management and Policy,* Vol. 2, JAI Press, Greenwich, CT, 1985; Richard S. Rosenbloom and Michael A. Cusumano, "Technological Pioneering and Competitive Advantage: The Birth of the VCR Industry," *California Management Review,* XXIX:51–76 (Summer 1987); Scott R. Schmedel, "Sony TV Tapes Stir U.S. Firms to Act; Separation Spreads to Canada's West," *The Wall Street Journal,* Mar. 28, 1977, p. 6; Sony, *Annual Reports,* 1973–1974, 1976–1982, 1984; *The Wall Street Journal,* "VCR Owners," May 1, 1986, p. B5; David B. Yoffie, "The World VCR Industry," Harvard Business School, Jan. 23, 1990.

13. John H. Dessauer, *My Years with Xerox: The Billions Nobody Wanted,* Doubleday, Garden City, NY, 1971, p. 42.

14. Joseph C. Wilson, "The Product Nobody Wanted," *Nation's Business,* February 1969, p. 69.

15. John Brooks, "Xerox, Xerox, Xerox, Xerox," *The New Yorker,* April 1, 1967, pp. 73–74.

16. Ibid., p. 74.

17. *Other sources:* Ibid., pp. 46–90; "Out to Crack the Copying Market," *Business Week,* Sept. 19, 1959, p. 86; "Two Men & an Idea," *Forbes,* Sept. 15, 1962, p. 17; Gary Jacobson and John Hillkirk, *Xerox: American Samurai,* Macmillan, New York, 1986; Douglas K. Smith and Robert C. Alexander, *Fumbling the Future,* William Morrow, New York, 1988; Wilson, op. cit., pp. 67–70.

18. Robert Slater, *Portraits in Silicon,* MIT Press, Cambridge, MA, 1987, p. 266.

19. Ibid., pp. 265, 266.

20. David Allison, "Bill Gates Interview," National Museum of American History, Smithsonian Institution, http://www.americanhistory.si.edu/csr/comphist/gates.htm.

21. Doug Bartholomew, "Bill Gates Envisions the Enterprise," *Industry Week,* Dec. 12, 1996, p. 9.

22. Daniel Gross, *Greatest Business Stories of All Time,* Wiley, New York, 1996, p. 340.

23. Paul Carroll, *Big Blues: The Unmaking of IBM,* Crown Publishers, New York, 1993, p. 9.

24. "Dropping Out of Harvard Pays Off for a Computer Whiz Kid Who's Making Hard Cash from Software," *People,* Dec. 26, 1983, p. 37.

25. Bill Gates, "They're Talking, We're Selling," *The Wall Street Journal,* Mar. 16, 1995, p. A22.

26. Allison, op. cit.

27. Gross, op. cit.

28. *Other sources:* Paul Carroll, "The Day Bill Gates Overthrew Big Blue," *The*

Wall Street Journal, Aug. 16, 1993, pp. B1, B3; Paul E. Ceruzzi, *A History of Modern Computing,* MIT Press, Cambridge, MA, 1999; Robert X. Cringley, *Accidental Empires,* Addison-Wesley, Reading, MA, 1993; Paul Freiberger and Michael Swaine, *Fire in the Valley: The Making of the Personal Computer,* Osborne/McGraw-Hill, Berkeley, CA, 1984; Amar Gupta and Hoormin D. Toong, "The First Decade of Personal Computers," in Amar Gupta and Hoormin D. Toong, eds., *Insights into Personal Computers,* IEEE Press, New York, 1985; Janet Lowe, *Bill Gates Speaks: Insight from the World's Greatest Entrepreneur,* Wiley, New York, 1998; Joel N. Shurkin, *Engines of the Mind: A History of the Computer,* Norton, New York, 1984; Don E. Waldman, "The Rise and Fall of IBM," in David I. Rosenbaum, ed., *Market Dominance: How Firms Gain, Hold or Lose It and the Impact on Economic Performance,"* Praeger, Westport, CT, 1998, pp. 131–152.

29. Peter N. Golder and Gerard J. Tellis, "Will It Ever Fly? Modeling the Growth of Really New Consumer Durables," *Marketing Science,* 16(3):256–270 (1997).

30. Rajesh Chandy and Gerard J. Tellis, "The Incumbent's Curse? Incumbency, Size and Radical Product Innovation," *Journal of Marketing,* 64(3):1–17 (July 2000); Rajesh Chandy and Gerard J. Tellis, "Organizing for Radical Product Innovation," *Journal of Marketing Research,* 35:474–487 (November 1998); Clayton M. Christensen, *The Innovator's Dilemma,* Harvard Business School Press, Boston, 1997; R. Foster, *Innovation: The Attacker's Advantage,* Summit Books, New York, 1986; James M. Utterback, *Mastering the Dynamics of Innovation,* Harvard Business School Press, Boston, 1994.

chapter 7

1. Rajesh Chandy and Gerard J. Tellis, "Organizing for Radical Product Innovation," *Journal of Marketing Research,* 35:474–487 (November 1998); Rajesh Chandy and Gerard J. Tellis, "The Incumbent's Curse? Incumbency, Size and Radical Product Innovation," *Journal of Marketing,* 64(3): 1–17 (July 2000).

2. "Hat in Hand," *Fortune,* Oct. 31, 1930, p. 46.

3. *Other sources:* Russell B. Adams, Jr., *King C. Gillette: The Man and His Wonderful Shaving Device,* Little, Brown, Boston, 1978; "Gaisman, Who Will Head Gillette, Is an Incorrigible Inventor," *Business Week,* Nov. 26, 1930, pp. 20–21; "Stirring Battle Rages for Vast Razor Blade Market," *Business Week,* Sept. 3, 1930, pp. 11–12; "Hat in Hand," op. cit., pp. 46–52, 147; Richard Austin Smith, "Gillette Looks Sharp Again," *Fortune,* June 1952, pp. 100–172; King C. Gillette, "Centralized Ideas—The Foundation of Progress," *The Gillette Blade,* February 1920, pp. 9–10; King C. Gillette, "Paper Read by King C. Gillette, President of the Gillette Safety Razor Company, at the Banquet of the Annual Convention, Algonquin Club, Boston, Wednesday Evening, April 13, 1921," *The Gillette Blade,* August 1921, pp. 3–7; Gordon McKibben, *Cutting Edge: Gillette's Journey to Global Leadership,* Harvard Business School Press, Boston, MA, 1998; William E. Nickerson, "Turning the Tables," *The Gillette Blade,* March 1922, pp. 3–4.

4. Lawrence Ingrassia, "Gillette Holds Its Edge by Endlessly Searching for a Better Shave," *The Wall Street Journal,* Dec. 10, 1992, p. 1.

5. Ibid.

6. *Other sources:* Adams, op. cit.; "Gillette to Spend $4,000,000 on Stainless Blade," *Advertising Age,* Sept. 2, 1963, pp. 4,46; Cal Brumley, "Stainless-Steel Razor Blades Could Be Shaver's Boon, Makers' Problem," *The Wall Street Journal,* Dec. 25, 1962, p. 7; "What Words in an Ad Can't Say," *Business Week,* May 14, 1960, pp. 45–48; "Cheek by Trowel," *Business Week,* Dec. 22, 1962, pp. 81–82; William M. Carley, "Battle of the Blades," *The Wall Street Journal,* Sept. 26, 1969, p. 38; Subrata N. Chakravarty, "We Had to Change the Playing Field," *Forbes,* Feb. 4, 1991, pp. 82–86; Edward T. Ewen, "Revolution on the Razor's Edge," *The New York Times Magazine,* Oct. 6, 1963, p. 58; "Boston Blue Bladers," *Forbes,* Nov. 15, 1952; "The Coming Close Shave at Gillette," *Forbes,* Dec. 15, 1976, p. 29; Walter Guzzardi, Jr., "Gillette Faces the Stainless-Steel Dragon," *Fortune,* July 1963, p. 159; "Who Wants a Stainless Reputation?" *Financial Times (London),* Sept. 5, 1963; Ingrassia, op. cit.; McKibben, op. cit.; "Keen Drama: A Razor Is Born," *Newsweek,* Oct. 11, 1971, pp. 78–82; John M. Lee, "Gillette Will Market Its New Product in Two Cities," *The New York Times,* Aug. 27, 1963, p. 41; "Blade-Snatching," *Newsweek,* Nov. 22, 1962, pp. 89–90; "How Gillette Plans to Keep Its No. 1 Spot," *Printers Time,* Dec. 4, 1959, pp. 65–66; Kenneth S. Smith, "Razor Blade War Growing Hotter," *The New York Times,* Dec. 2, 1962; Richard Austin Smith, op. cit., p. 100; "Gillette Plans to Offer Stainless Steel Razor Blade in Few Months," *The Wall Street Journal,* Nov. 19, 1962, p. 7; Neil Ulman, "Gillette Chairman Takes a Long View in Program to Brighten Profit Picture," *The Wall Street Journal,* June 28, 1977, p. 12.

7. Andrew S. Grove, *Only the Paranoid Survive: How to Exploit the Crisis Points That Challenge Every Company and Career,* Currency/Doubleday/Bantam Doubleday Dell Publishing Group, New York, 1996.

8. *Other sources:* Paul E. Ceruzzi, *A History of Modern Computing,* MIT Press, Cambridge, MA, 1999; Paul Freiberger and Michael Swaine, *Fire in the Valley: The Making of the Personal Computer,* Osborne/McGraw-Hill, Berkeley, CA, 1984; Grove, op. cit.; Tim Jackson, *Inside Intel,* Dutton/Penguin Putnam, New York, 1997; Albert Yu, *Creating the Digital Future: The Secrets of Consistent Innovation at Intel,* Free Press/Simon & Schuster, New York, 1998.

9. Thomson is apparently bitter that he first introduced the idea of developing a better browser to NCSA, but Andreessen won the assignment and all the glory. His perspective is described well by Alan Deutschman, "Imposter Boy," *Gentleman's Quarterly,* January 1997. However, the history of innovation and of markets is replete with similar examples, some recounted in this book. Success belongs not to the first but to the one with the vision and persistence to realize that vision.

10. George Gilder, "Telecosm: The Coming Software Shift," *Forbes ASAP,* Aug. 28, 1995, p. 147.

11. Deutschman, op. cit.

12. Tim Berners-Lee, "Spinning the Web: A Place for Everything, and Everything on the Web?" *Data Communications,* Oct. 21, 1997, p. 48.

13. *Other sources:* Allison, op. cit.; Paul Andrews, "Web Browser Finds No Honor at Its Illinois Academic Birthplace," *The Seattle Times,* Oct. 9, 1997; Tim Berners-Lee and Mark Fischetti, *Weaving the Web: The Original Design and Ultimate Destiny of the World Wide Web by Its Inventor,* HarperCollins, New York, 1999; Tim Berners-Lee, Robert Cailliau, Ari Luotonen, Henrik Frystyk, and Nielsen Arthur Secret, "The World-Wide Web," *Communications of the ACM,* Aug. 1,

1994, p. 76; Hal Berghel, "Who Won the Mosaic War?" *ACM,* vol. 41 (10), October 1998, pp. 13–16; Jim Clark and Owen Edwards, *Netscape Time: The Making of the Billion-Dollar Start-Up That Took on Microsoft,* St. Martin's Press, New York, 1999; Della De LaFuente, "The Champaign Net Work//Whiz Kids from U. of I. Make Millions in Cyberspace," *Chicago Sun-Times,* Sept. 17, 1995, p. 33; Peter Elstrom and Kathy Rebello, "A Big Bet on Minibrowsers: Can Spyglass Score in the Net Appliance Market," *Business Week,* Oct. 28, 1996, p. 54; Katie Hafner and Mathew Lyon, "Where Wizards Stay Up Late," Touchstone, New York, 1996; Kim S. Nash, "Browsers Compete for Spotlight," *Computerworld,* November 1995, p. 61; Greg R. Notess, "Comparing Web Browsers: Mosaic, Cello, Netscape, WinWeb and InternetWorks Lite," *Online,* March/April 1995, pp. 36–40; Gary Samuels, "Tale of Two Interneters: Netscape Has Gotten the Headlines, but Spyglass Is Making Money," *Forbes Inc.,* September 1995, p. 48; Jared Sandberg, "Designers of Internet's Mosaic Software Plan New Version in Bid to Set Standard," *The Wall Street Journal,* Oct. 13, 1994, p. B6; Jian-Zhong Zhou, "The Internet, the World Wide Web, Library Web Browsers and Library Web Servers," *Information Technology and Libraries,* Mar. 1, 2000, p. 50.

14. Peter N. Golder and Gerard J. Tellis, "Will It Ever Fly? Modeling the Takeoff of Really New Consumer Durables," *Marketing Science,* 16(3):256–270 (1997).

chapter 8

1. Some of the ideas in this section have been shaped by the following sources: Rajesh Chandy and Gerard J. Tellis, "The Incumbent's Curse? Incumbency, Size and Radical Product Innovation," *Journal of Marketing,* 64(3):1–17 (July 2000); Rajesh Chandy and Gerard J. Tellis, "Organizing for Radical Product Innovation," *Journal of Marketing Research* 35:474–487 (November 1998); Clayton M. Christensen, *The Innovator's Dilemma: When New Technologies Cause Great Firms to Fail,* Harvard Business School Press, Boston, MA, 1997.

2. Gary Jacobson and John Hillkirk, *Xerox: American Samurai,* Macmillan, New York, 1986, p. 214.

3. Michael Hiltzik, *Dealers of Lightning: Xerox PARC and the Dawn of the Computer Age,* HarperBusiness/HarperCollins, New York, 1999, p. 36.

4. George E. Pake, "Research at Xerox PARC: A Founder's Assessment," *IEEE Spectrum,* 22(10):56 (October 1985).

5. *Other sources:* "A Market Mostly for the Giants," *Business Week,* June 30, 1975, pp. 71–80; "Xerox's Bid to Be No. 1 in Offices," *Business Week,* June 22, 1981, pp. 77–78; Robert X. Cringley, *Accidental Empires,* Addison-Wesley, Reading, MA, 1993; "Xerox: The McColough Era," *Forbes,* July 1, 1969, pp. 24–32; "An Apple for Xerox?" *Forbes,* July 1, 1971, pp. 32–34; "Does Collision," *Forbes,* Aug. 15, 1972, pp. 40–42; Jacob E. Goldman, in Richard S. Rosenbloom, ed., "Innovation in Large Firms," *Research in Technological Innovation, Management and Policy,* vol. 2, JAI Press, Greenwich, CT, 1985, pp. 1–10; Hiltzik, op. cit.; Jeff Johnson and Teresa L. Roberts, "The Xerox 'Star': A Retrospective," *IEEE Computer,* September 1989; Peter Kilborn, "Can Xerox Copy Itself?" *The New York*

Times, Dec. 1, 1974, section 3, p. 1; Pake, op. cit.; George E. Pake, "From Research to Innovation at Xerox: A Manager's Principles and Some Examples," in R. S. Rosenbloom, ed., *Research on Technological Innovation, Management and Policy,* vol. 3, JAI Press, Greenwich, CT, 1986, pp. 1–32; Tekla S. Perry and Paul Wallich, "Inside the PARC: The 'Information Architects,'" *IEEE Spectrum,* 22(10):54–76 (October 1985); Douglas K. Smith and Robert C. Alexander, *Fumbling the Future,* William Morrow, New York, 1988; Gene Smith, "A Series of Promotions to the Top Post," *The New York Times,* May 26, 1968; Chuck Thacker, "Personal Distributed Computing: The Alto and Ethernet Hardware," in Edele Goldberg, ed., *A History of Personal Workstations,* ACM Press, New York, 1988, pp. 267–335.

6. "A Market Mostly for the Giants," op. cit.; "Xerox's Bid to Be No. 1 in Offices," op. cit.; Cringley, op. cit.; "Xerox: The McColough Era," op. cit.; "An Apple for Xerox?" op. cit.; "Does Collision," op. cit.; Goldman, op. cit.; Hiltzik, op. cit.; Johnson and Roberts, op. cit.; Kilborn, op. cit.; Pake, "Research at Xerox PARC," op. cit.; Pake, "From Research," op. cit.; Perry and Wallich, op. cit.; Smith and Alexander, op. cit.; Smith, Gene, op. cit.; Thacker, op. cit.

7. Hiltzik, op. cit., p. 131.

8. Ibid.

9. Ibid., p. 132.

10. Ibid., p. 133.

11. Ibid.

12. Ibid., p. 144.

13. Della De Lafuente, "The Champaign Net Work//Whiz Kids from U. of I. Make Millions in Cyberspace," *Chicago Sun-Times,* Sept. 17, 1995, p. 33.

14. John Markoff, "A Free and Simple Computer Link," *The New York Times,* Dec. 8, 1995, p. D1.

15. Della De Lafuente, op. cit., 1995.

16. Ibid.

17. *Other sources:* Paul Andrews, "Web Browser Finds No Honor at Its Illinois Academic Birthplace," *The Seattle Times,* Oct. 9, 1997; Jim Clark and Owen Edwards, *Netscape Time: The Making of the Billion-Dollar Start-Up That Took on Microsoft,* St. Martin's Press, New York, 1999; Alan Deutschman, "Imposter Boy," *Gentleman's Quarterly,* January 1997; Stan J. Liebowitz and Stephen E. Margolis, *Winners, Losers and Microsoft: Competition and Antitrust in High Technology,* The Independent Institute, Oakland, CA, 1999; "A Short Sleep before Exploring Version 5.0," ABIX (Australia news abstracts), Aug. 20, 1996; Hal Berghel, "Who Won the Mosaic War?" *ACM,* vol. 41 (10), October 1998, pp. 13–16; Michael A. Cusumano and David B. Yoffie, *Competing on Internet Time: Lessons from Netscape and Its Battle with Microsoft,* Free Press/Simon & Schuster, New York, 1998; Gilder George, "Telecosm: The Coming Software Shift," *Forbes ASAP,* Aug. 28, 1995, pp. 147 ff.; Katie Hafner and Mathew Lyon, "Where Wizards Stay Up Late," Touchstone, New York, 1996; Robert D. Hof, "From the Man Who Brought You Silicon Graphics. . . . Can Jim Clark Score Again with User-Friendly Internet Software?" *Business Week,* Oct. 24, 1994, p. 90; Scott McMurray, "Diplomas and Dollars: The University of Illinois Churns Out Big-Time Software Entrepreneurs, Champaign, Ill." *U.S. News & World Report,* 1996, pp. 48–49; Paul Merrion, "A Tangle in School's Netscape Win," *Crain Communications Inc.,* 09, Oct. 19, 1995; Julie Pitta,

"Investors Get Caught Up in the Netscape," *Los Angeles Times,* 1995, pp. D3, D5; Vivian Pospisil and John Teresko, "50 R&D Stars to Watch," *Industry Week,* Dec. 19, 1994, p. 60; "University of Illinois and Netscape Communications Reach Agreement," *PR Newswire,* Dec. 21, 1994; Gary Samuels, "Tale of Two Interneters: Netscape Has Gotten the Headlines, but Spyglass Is Making Money," *Forbes Inc.,* Sept. 1995, p. 48; Jared Sandberg, "Netscape Has Technical Whiz in Andreessen," *The Wall Street Journal,* Aug. 11, 1995, p. B1.

18. "Looking Ahead," *Fortune,* Dec. 28, 1992, p. 32.

19. "ASAP Interview Bill Gates," *Forbes ASAP,* Dec. 7, 1992, pp. 63, 74.

20. David Allison, "Bill Gates Interview," National Museum of American History, Smithsonian Institution, http://www.americanhistory.si.edu/csr/comphist/gates.htm.

21. Jeffrey Young, *Greatest Technology Stories,* Wiley, New York, 1998, p. 258.

22. "ASAP Interview Bill Gates," op. cit., p. 71.

23. Daniel Ichbiah and Susan Knepper, *The Making of Microsoft,* Prima Publishing, Rocklin, CA, 1991, p. 40.

24. *Other sources:* Paul E. Ceruzzi, *A History of Modern Computing,* MIT Press, Cambridge, MA, 1999; Cringley op. cit.; Paul Freiberger and Michael Swaine, *Fire in the Valley: The Making of the Personal Computer,* Osborne/McGraw-Hill, Berkeley, CA, 1984; Janet Lowe, *Bill Gates Speaks: Insight from the World's Greatest Entrepreneur,* Wiley, New York, 1998; Joel N. Shurkin, *Engines of the Mind: A History of the Computer,* Norton, New York, 1984; Randall E. Stross, *The Microsoft Way,* Addison-Wesley, Reading, MA, 1996.

chapter 9

1. Robert A. Sigafoos, *Absolutely, Positively Overnight!* St. Luke's Press, Memphis, TN, 1983, p. 34.

2. Ibid., p. 36.

3. Ibid., pp. 49–50.

4. Ibid., p. 62.

5. Ibid., p. 23.

6. *Other sources:* "A New Kind of Flight Plan for Small Freight," *Business Week,* Nov. 3, 1973, p. 3; "Why Airlines Fear the 'Federal Express Bill,'" *Business Week,* Sept. 13, 1976, p. 116; Christopher H. Lovelock, "Federal Express (A)," Harvard Business School Publishing, 9-577-042, Boston, 1976; Christopher H. Lovelock, "Federal Express (B)," Harvard Business School Publishing, 9-579-040, Boston, 1978; Sigafoos op. cit.; Winston Williams, *The New York Times,* Jan. 1, 1979, p. 1; John D. Williams and Steve Frazier, "Federal Hustles to Keep Ahead of Emery in the Fast-Growing Air-Express Market," *The Wall Street Journal Stories,* Sept. 11, 1979; Milton Moskowitz, "The Overnight Delivery Revolution," *The San Francisco Chronicle,* Jan. 4, 1985, p. 35.

7. Robert D. Hof, "From the Man Who Brought You Silicon Graphics. . . . Can Jim Clark Score Again with User-Friendly Internet Software?" *Business Week,* Oct. 24, 1994, p. 90.

8. Jim Clark and Owen Edwards, *Netscape Time: The Making of the Billion-Dollar Start-Up That Took on Microsoft*, St. Martin's Press, New York, 1999, pp. 120–121.

9. Rick Tetzeli and Shaifali Puri, "What It's Really Like to Be Marc Andreessen . . . ," *Fortune*, Dec. 9, 1996, p. 136 ff.

10. Jim Clark and Owen Edwards, op. cit., p. 191.

11. *Other sources:* Paul Andrews, "Web Browser Finds No Honor at Its Illinois Academic Birthplace," *The Seattle Times*, Oct. 9, 1997; Jim Clark and Owen Edwards, *Netscape Time: The Making of the Billion-Dollar Start-Up That Took on Microsoft*, St. Martin's Press, New York, 1999, pp. 120–121; Stan J. Liebowitz and Stephen E. Margolis, *Winners, Losers and Microsoft: Competition and Antitrust in High Technology*, The Independent Institute, Oakland, CA, 1999; "A Short Sleep before Exploring Version 5.0," ABIX (Australia news abstracts), Aug. 20, 1996; Hal Berghel, "Who Won the Mosaic War?" *ACM*, vol. 41(10), October 1998, pp. 13–16; "Mosaic Quest Closes in Redmond Original," *Computer Business Review*, Feb. 1997, p. 1; Michael A. Cusamano and David B. Yoffie, *Competing on Internet Time: Lessons from Netscape and Its Battle with Microsoft*, Free Press/Simon & Schuster, New York, 1998; Katie Hafner and Mathew Lyon, *Where Wizards Stay Up Late*, Touchstone, New York, 1996; Hof, op. cit.; Scott McMurray, "Diplomas and Dollars: The University of Illinois Churns Out Big-Time Software Entrepreneurs; Champaign, Ill." *U.S. News & World Report*, 1996, pp. 48–49; Julie Pitta, "Investors Get Caught Up in the Netscape," *Los Angeles Times*, 1995, pp. D3, D5; Vivian Pospisil and John Teresko, "50 R&D Stars to Watch," *Industry Week*, Dec. 19, 1994, p. 60; "University of Illinois and Netscape Communications Reach Agreement," PR Newswire, Dec. 21, 1994; Gary Samuels, "Tale of Two Interneters: Netscape Has Gotten the Headlines, but Spyglass Is Making Money," *Forbes Inc.*, September 1995, p. 48; Jared Sandberg, "Netscape Has Technical Whiz in Andreessen," *The Wall Street Journal*, Aug. 11, 1995, p. B1; Jared Sandberg, "Designers of Internet's Mosaic Software Plan New Version in Bid to Set Standard," *The Wall Street Journal*, Oct. 13, 1994, p. B6; Gordon McKibben, *Cutting Edge: Gillette's Journey to Global Leadership*, Harvard Business School Press, Boston, 1998.

12. King C. Gillette, "Origin of the Gillette Razor," *The Gillette Blade*, February 1918, p. 7.

13. King C. Gillette, "Origin of the Gillette Razor," *The Gillette Blade*, March 1918, p. 7.

14. *Other sources:* Russell B. Adams, Jr., *King C. Gillette: The Man and His Wonderful Shaving Device*, Little, Brown, Boston, 1978; George B. Baldwin, "The Invention of the Modern Safety Razor: A Case Study of Industrial Innovation," *Explorations in Entrepreneurial History*, 1951, pp. 71–104; King C. Gillette, "Intensive Cooperation," *The Gillette Blade*, August 1918, p. 5; King C. Gillette, "How the 'Gillette' Looks to Mr. Gillette after Twenty-Five Years," *The Gillette Blade*, September 1920, pp. 3–6; William E. Nickerson, "The Development of the Gillette Safety Razor," *The Gillette Blade*, December 1918, pp. 5–13; William E. Nickerson, "The Development of the Gillette Safety Razor," *The Gillette Blade*, January 1919, pp. 6–18.

15. Michael Krantz, "Cruising inside Amazon," *Time* Dec. 27, 1999, pp. 68–71.

16. Debra Aho Williamson, "Marketer of the Year: Amazon.com," *Advertising Age*, Dec. 13, 1999, pp. 1, 36.

17. Seth Schiesel, "Payoff Still Elusive in Internet Gold Rush," *The New York Times,* Jan. 2, 1997, p. C17.

18. Jeff Bezos, Amazon.com, *Annual Report,* 1997.

19. Jeff Bezos, Amazon.com, *Annual Report,* 1998.

20. Doreen Carvajal, "The Other Battle over Browsers: Barnes & Noble and Other On-Line Booksellers Are Poised to Challenge Amazon.com," *The New York Times,* Mar. 9, 1998, pp. D1, D4.

21. "A Fable Concerning Ambition," *The Economist,* June 21, 1997, p. 69.

22. *Other sources:* Amazon.com, *Annual Report,* 1999; Amazon.com Web site, www.amazon.com; Amazon.com, Inc., *10-K Report,* 1998; Amazon.com, Inc., *10-K Report,* 1999; Amazon.com, Inc., *10-K Report,* 2000; Lynda M. Applegate and Meredith Collura, "Amazon.com: Exploiting the Value of Digital Business Infrastructure," Harvard Business School Case 9-800-330 (2000); Barnes and Noble Web site, www.bn.com; Borders Web site, www.borders.com; Allison Fass "Amazon Leads in Holiday Advertising," *The New York Times,* Dec. 13, 2000, p. 7; Pankaj Ghemawat and Bret Baird, "Leadership Online: Barnes & Noble vs. Amazon.com," Harvard Business School Case 9-798-063 (1998); John Heilemann "The Networker," *The New Yorker,* Aug. 11, 1997, pp. 28–36; Nick Higham, "Amazon Success Story Built on Traditional Marketing Expertise," *Marketing Week,* Oct. 14, 1999, p. 17; Robert D. Hof, "The Most Influential People in Electronic Business," *Business Week,* Sept. 27, 1999, p. 25; Carol Hymowitz "How Amazon.com Staffs a Juggernaut: It's Not about Resumes," *The Wall Street Journal,* May 4, 1999, p. B1; Paul C. Judge and Heather Green, "The Name's the Thing: Dot.com's Are Spending like Mad to Establish an Identity," *Business Week,* Nov. 15, 1999, pp. 36–39; G. Bruce Knecht, "How Wall Street Whiz Found a Niche Selling Books on the Internet," *The Wall Street Journal,* May 16, 1996, pp. A1, A8; Carin-Isabel Knoop and Cate Reavis, "Selling Books Online in Mid-1998," Harvard Business School Case 9-899-038 (1998); "Delphi Service Features Books & Software from HarperCollins," *Link-Up,* April 1995, p. 44; "Amazon.com Posts Loss, but Less Than Expected," *Los Angeles Times,* Apr. 29, 1994, p. 4; Rebecca Quick, "Barnes & Noble.com to Replace Amazon.com as Top Bookseller Advertising on Yahoo!" *The Wall Street Journal,* Sept. 19, 2000, p. B23; Rebecca Quick, "E-Retailers Say, 'Bah Humbug!' to Lavish Ads," *The Wall Street Journal,* Sept. 22, 2000, p. B1; Joshua Quittner, "An Eye on the Future," *Time,* Dec. 27, 1999; Jeffrey F. Rayport and Dickson L. Louie, "Amazon.com (A)," Harvard Business School Case 9-897-128 (1997); Calvin Reid, "Amazon.com's Jeff Bezos," *Publisher's Weekly,* Jan. 5, 1998, p. 12; William A. Sahlman and Laurence E. Katz, "Amazon.com—Going Public," Harvard Business School Case 9-899-003 (1998); Robert Spector, *Get Big Fast: Amazon.com,* HarperBusiness, 2000; Randall E. Stross, "Why Barnes & Noble May Crush Amazon," *Fortune,* Sept. 29, 1997, pp. 248–250; John R. Wilke "Visiting a Bookstore by Switching on a PC," *The Wall Street Journal,* Jan. 11, 1993, p. B1; Wordworth Web site, www.wordsworth.com.

chapter 10

1. In some cases, strengths in production facilities, sales force, and distribution systems can also be transferred easily. For example, Coca-Cola and Anheuser-

Busch leveraged their strengths in these areas, as well as their strong brands, in their very successful late entries, Diet Coke and Bud Light, respectively. However, as we discuss subsequently, in many other cases these same types of assets cannot be transferred easily to a new category and need to be viewed as specialized assets.

2. Rajesh Chandy and Gerard J. Tellis, "Organizing for Radical Product Innovation," *Journal of Marketing Research*, 35:474–487 (November 1998).

3. Leah Nathans Spiro and Linda Himelstein, "With the World Wide Web, Who Needs Wall Street," *Business Week*, Apr. 29, 1996, p. 120.

4. Beth Healy, "Battle of the Brokers Heats Up," *The Boston Globe*, Apr. 2, 2000, p. K7.

5. Spiro and Himelstein, op. cit.

6. Rebecca McReynolds, "Doing It the Schwab Way," *US Banker*, July 1998, p. 47.

7. Erick Schonfeld, "Schwab Puts It All Online," *Fortune*, Dec. 7, 1998, pp. 94–96.

8. Ibid.

9. *Other sources:* Ameritrade Web site, www.ameritrade.com; Stephen P. Bradley and Takia Mahmood, "Retail Financial Services in 1998: Charles Schwab," Harvard Business School Case 9-799-052 (1998); Robert A. Burgelman and Jeff Maggioncalda, "The Charles Schwab Corporation in 1996," Stanford University Graduate School of Business Case SM-35 (1996); Gaston F. Ceron, "Online Brokers Are Expected to Post Weakened Results," *The Wall Street Journal*, Jan. 16, 2001; Charles Schwab Web site, www.schwab.com; E*trade Web site, www.etrade.com; Saroja Girishankar, "Schwab Makes the Trade—Migrating Millions of Customers and Huge Legacy Systems to the Web Was an Eye-Opener for Precocious Charles Schwab," *Internetweek*, May 25, 1998, p. 30; John Gorham, "Charles Schwab Version 4.0," *Forbes*, Jan. 8, 2001, p. 88; Linda Himelstein, "Schwab Is Fighting on Three Fronts," *Business Week*, Mar. 10, 1997, p. 94.

10. Douglas K. Smith, and Robert C. Alexander, *Fumbling the Future*, William Morrow, New York, 1988, p. 183.

11. Tekla S. Perry and Paul Wallich, "Inside the PARC: The 'Information Architects,'" *IEEE Spectrum*, 22(10): 54–76 (October 1985).

12. Ibid.

13. Smith and Alexander, op. cit.

14. In 1981, Xerox did finally introduce an integrated office computer system called the Star. It was based on the Alto and came with a network, a graphical user interface, a mouse, word processing, and a laser printer. However, it was too late with too high a price of $16,595 for its time. By that time, dedicated word processors were available for half that price, while inexpensive personal computers were available for under $3000. Once again Xerox's products were overpriced.

15. Michael Hiltzik, *Dealers of Lightning: Xerox PARC and the Dawn of the Computer Age*, HarperBusiness/HarperCollins, New York, 1999, p. 359.

16. *Other sources:* "A Market Mostly for the Giants," *Business Week*, June 30, 1975, pp. 71–80; "Why Xerox's Money Machine Slows Down," *Business Week*, Apr. 5, 1976, p. 60; "The New Lean, Mean Xerox," *Business Week*, Oct. 12, 1981, pp. 126–132; "Xerox's Bid to Be No. 1 in Offices," *Business Week*, June 22, 1981, pp. 77–78; Susan Chace, "Xerox Introduces an Office System for Nontypists," *The*

Wall Street Journal, Apr. 28, 1981, p. 4; Robert X. Cringley, *Accidental Empires,* Addison-Wesley, Reading, MA, 1993; "Two Men & an Idea," *Forbes,* Sept. 15, 1962, p. 17; "Xerox: The McColough Era," *Forbes,* July 1, 1969, pp. 24–32 (innovation and asset leverage); Jacob E. Goldman, "Innovation in Large Firms," in Richard S. Rosenbloom, ed., *Research in Technological Innovation, Management and Policy,* vol. 2, JAI Press, Greenwich, CT, 1985, pp 1–10; Hiltzik, op. cit.; Michael A. Hiltzik, "Fans Celebrate Fallen Xerox Star," *The Los Angeles Times,* June 22, 1998; Gary Jacobson and John Hillkirk, *Xerox: American Samurai,* Macmillan, New York, 1986; Jeff Johnson and Teresa L. Roberts, "The Xerox 'Star': A Retrospective," *IEEE Computer,* September 1989; David T. Kearns and David A. Nadler, *Prophets in the Dark,* Harper Business, New York, 1992; Peter Kilborn, "Can Xerox Copy Itself?" *The New York Times,* Dec. 1, 1974; Roger Lowenstein, "History of Xerox Is a Cautionary Tale for Netscape," *The Salt Lake Tribune,* Aug. 18, 1995, p. B10; George E. Pake, "Research at Xerox PARC: A Founder's Assessment," *IEEE Spectrum,* 22, (10) 54–61 (1985); George E. Pake, "From Research to Innovation at Xerox: A Manager's Principles and Some Examples," in R. S. Rosenbloom, ed., *Research on Technological Innovation, Management and Policy,* vol. 3, JAI Press, Greenwich, CT, 1986, pp. 1–32; Perry and Wallich, op. cit.; Andrew Pollack, "Xerox Stalks the Automated Office," *The New York Times,* May 3, 1981, section 3, p. 4; Joel Shurkin, *Engines of the Mind: The Evolution of the Computer from Mainframes to Microprocessors,* Norton, New York, 1996; Smith and Alexander, op. cit.; Gene Smith, "A Series of Promotions to the Top Post," *The New York Times,* May 26, 1968; Chuck Thacker, "Personal Distributed Computing: The Alto and Ethernet Hardware," in Edele Goldberg, ed., *A History of Personal Workstations,* ACM Press, New York, 1988, pp. 267–335; Bro Utall "Xerox Is Trying Too Hard," *Fortune,* Mar. 13, 1978, pp. 84–94; An Wang and Eugene Linden, *Lessons: An Autobiography,* Addison-Wesley, Reading, MA, 1986. Joseph C. Wilson, "The Product Nobody Wanted," *Nation's Business,* February 1969, pp. 67–70.

17. William Gates, "The Internet Tidal Wave," http://www.microsoft.com/presspass/trial/mswitness/maritz/maritz_full.asp (1995).

18. Jim Clark and Owen Edwards, *Netscape Time: The Making of the Billion-Dollar Start-Up That Took on Microsoft,* St. Martin's Press, New York, 1999, p. 59.

19. Mark Evans, "Fight to Finish: Microsoft, Netscape Step Up Race for Control of Internet Software Market," *The Financial Post,* Mar. 14, 1996, p. 8.

20. Charles Williford and Dan Moore, "Will Microsoft Catch Netscape?" *Computerworld* vol. 29, April 1996, p. 81.

21. Gates, op. cit.

22. William Gates, http://www.microsoft.com/BillGates/speeches/12-7-95 (1995).

23. David B. Yoffie, "Microsoft Goes Online: MSN 1996," Harvard Business School Publishing case, 9-798-019, Boston, Nov. 24, 1997.

24. Robert X. Cringley, "Triumph of the Nerds," http://www.pbs.org/nerds/transcript.html (1996).

25. Ibid.

26. Paul Carroll, *Big Blues: The Unmaking of IBM,* Crown Publishers, New York, 1993, p. 1.

27. "Personal Computers: And the Winner Is IBM," *Business Week*, Oct. 3, 1983, p. 86.

28. James Chposky and Ted Leonsis, *Blue Logic: The People, Power and Politics behind the IBM Personal Computer*, Facts on File, New York, 1988, pp. 62–63.

29. "Personal Computers: And the Winner Is IBM," op. cit.

30. Michael W. Miller, "IBM's Watson Offers Personal View of the Company's Recent Difficulties," *The Wall Street Journal*, Dec. 21, 1992, p. A3. *Other sources:* "Microcomputers Catch on Fast," *Business Week* July 12, 1976, p. 50; "Computer Stores," *Business Week*, Sept. 28, 1981, pp. 76–80; "Personal Computers: And the Winner Is IBM," op. cit., pp. 76–95; Jim Carlton, "They Could Have Been a Contender," *Wired*, November 1997, pp. 122–149; Jim Carlton, "Popularity of Some Computers Means Buyers Must Wait," *The Wall Street Journal*, Oct. 21, 1993, p. B1; Carroll, op. cit.; Paul Carroll, "The Day Bill Gates Overthrew Big Blue," *The Wall Street Journal*, Aug. 16, 1993, pp. 16, B1, B3; Paul E. Ceruzzi, *A History of Modern Computing*, MIT Press, Cambridge, MA, 1999; Cringley, op. cit.; Robert X. Cringley, *Accidental Empires*, Addison-Wesley, Reading, MA, 1993. David S. Evans, Albert Nichols, and Bernard Reddy, "The Rise and Fall of Leaders in Personal Computer Software," National Economic Research Associates, Cambridge, MA, Jan. 7, 1999; Paul Freiberger and Michael Swaine, *Fire in the Valley: The Making of the Personal Computer*, Osborne/McGraw-Hill, Berkeley, CA, 1984; Amar Gupta and Hoormin D. Toong, in Amar Gupta and Hoormin D. Toong, eds., "The First Decade of Personal Computers," *Insights into Personal Computers*, IEEE Press, New York, 1985; John B. Judis, "Innovation, a Casualty at IBM," *The Wall Street Journal*, Oct. 17, 1991, p. A23; Dennis Kneale, "IBM Earnings Increased 23% in 1st Quarter," *The Wall Street Journal*, Apr. 13, 1984, p. 1; Mitchell Lynch, "Investors Buying Nautilus for Shares in Apple Are Told to Watch for a Worm," *The Wall Street Journal*, Oct. 8, 1980, p. 10; Michael J. Miller and Laurence Hooper, "Signing Off," *The Wall Street Journal*, Jan. 27, 1993; Michael W. Miller, "IBM's Watson Offers Personal View of the Company's Recent Difficulties," *The Wall Street Journal*, Dec. 21, 1992, p. A3; Gerald E. Nelson and William R. Hewlett, "The Design and Development of a Family of Personal Computers for Engineers and Scientists," in Gupta and Toong, eds., op. cit.; Joel N. Shurkin, *Engines of the Mind: A History of the Computer*, Norton, New York, 1984; "The Third Age (A Survey of the Computer Industry)," *The Economist*, Sept. 17, 1994, p. C3; Don E. Waldman, "The Rise and Fall of IBM," in David I. Rosenbaum, ed., *Market Dominance: How Firms Gain, Hold or Lose It and the Impact on Economic Performance*, Praeger, Westport, CT, 1998, pp. 131–152; Kathleen K. Wiegner, "Tomorrow Has Arrived," *Forbes*, Feb. 15, 1982, pp. 111–119; Grant F. Winthrop, "Whom the Apples Fell On," *Fortune*, Jan. 12, 1981, p. 68.

chapter 11

1. Scott Ward, Larry Light, and Jonathan Goldstine, "What High-Tech Managers Need to Know about Brands," *Harvard Business Review*, July–August 1999, pp. 85–95.

2. For example, Gregory S. Carpenter and Kent Nakamoto, "Consumer Prefer-

ence Formation and Pioneering Advantage," *Journal of Marketing Research,* 26: 285–298 (August 1989); Philip Kotler, *Marketing Management,* Prentice-Hall, Upper Saddle River, NJ, 2000.

3. George Burton Hotchkiss and Richard B. Franken, *The Leadership of Advertised Brands,* Doubleday, Page & Company, Garden City, NY, 1923.

4. For details of this research, see Peter N. Golder, "Historical Method in Marketing Research with New Evidence on Long-Term Market Share Stability," *Journal of Marketing Research,* 37:156–172 (May 2000).

5. At the time we collected data for this particular study, market shares leaders were based on 1997 sales data.

6. Ellen Graham, "McDonald's Pickle: He Began Fast Food but Gets No Credit," *The Wall Street Journal,* Aug. 15, 1991, p. A5.

appendix 1

1. Barbara Tuchman, *Practicing History,* Knopf, New York, 1981, p. 9.

2. The general discussion of the historical method is based on Peter N. Golder, "Historical Method in Marketing Research with New Evidence on Long-Term Market Share Stability," *Journal of Marketing Research,* 37:156–172 (May 2000).

This paper relies on multiple sources:

Baron, Salo W.: *The Contemporary Relevance of History,* Columbia University Press, New York, 1986.

Brooks, Philip C.: *Research in Archives,* University of Chicago Press, Chicago, 1969.

Eisenhardt, Kathleen M.: "Building Theories from Case Study Research," *Academy of Management Review,* 14(4):532–550 (1989).

Elton, G. R.: *The Practice of History,* Thomas Y. Crowell, New York, 1967.

Fogel, Robert William, and G. R. Elton: *Which Road to the Past? Two Views of History,* Yale University Press, New Haven, CT, 1983.

Goodman, Robert S., and Evonne Jonas Kruger: "Data Dredging or Legitimate Research Method? Historiography and Its Potential for Management Research," *Academy of Management Review,* 13 (2):315–325 (1988).

Gottschalk, Louis: *Understanding History: A Primer of Historical Method,* Knopf, New York, 1969.

Hughes, H. Stuart: *History as Art and Science,* Harper & Row, New York, 1964.

Johnson, Allen: *The Historian and Historical Evidence,* Charles Scribner's Sons, New York, 1934.

Langlois, C. V., and C. Seignobos: *Introduction to the Study of History,* Henry Holt, New York, 1898.

Marwick, Arthur: *The Nature of History,* MacMillan, London, 1970.

Salvemini, Gaetano: *Historian and Scientist,* Harvard University Press, Cambridge, MA, 1939.

Shafer, Robert Jones: *A Guide to Historical Method,* Dorsey Press, Homewood, IL, 1974.

Todd, William: *History as Applied Science,* Wayne State University Press, Detroit, 1972.

Tuchman, Barbara: *Practicing History,* Knopf, New York, 1981.

bibliography

Aaker, David A., and George S. Day: "The Perils of High-Growth Markets," *Strategic Management Journal,* 7:409–421 (September–October 1986).

Abell, Derek F.: "Strategic Windows," *Journal of Marketing,* 42:21–28 (July 1978).

———— and John S. Hammond: *Strategic Market Planning: Problems and Analytical Approaches,* Prentice-Hall, Englewood Cliffs, NJ, 1979.

Adams, Russel B., Jr.: *King C. Gillette: The Man and His Wonderful Shaving Device,* Little, Brown, Boston, 1978.

"Agencies Eye Sony Home TV Recorder for Storyboard Uses," *Advertising Age,* June 21, 1965, p. 101.

"All Those Leaky Diapers," *Forbes,* Feb. 15, 1975, pp. 49, 50.

Allison, David: "Oral History Interview with Marc Andreessen," Computer History Collection, Smithsonian National Museum of American History, http://www.americanhistory.si.edu/csr/comphist/ma1.html (1995).

————: "Bill Gates Interview," National Museum of American History, Smithsonian Institution, 1995, http://www.americanhistory.si.edu/csr/comphist/gates.htm.

Alpert, Frank H., Michael A. Kamins, and John L. Graham: "An Examination of Reseller Buyer Attitudes toward Order of Brand Entry," *Journal of Marketing,* 56:25–37 (July 1992).

Amazon.com: *Annual Report,* 1999.

"Amazon.com Posts Loss, but Less Than Expected," *The Los Angeles Times,* Apr. 29, 1994, p. 4.

Amazon.com Web site, www.amazon.com.

Amazon.com, Inc.: *10-K Report,* 1998.

————: *10-K Report,* 1999.

————: *10-K Report,* 2000.

Ameritrade Web site, www.ameritrade.com.

Ampex: *Annual Reports,* 1969–1976, 1980.

Ameritrade Web site, www.ameritrade.com.

Ampex: *Annual Reports,* 1969–1976, 1980.

Anderson, Paul F: "Marketing, Strategic Planning and the Theory of the Firm," *Journal of Marketing,* 46:15–26 (Spring 1982).

Andrews, Paul: "Web Browser Finds No Honor at Its Illinois Academic Birthplace," *The Seattle Times,* Oct. 9, 1997.

Andrews, Paul, and Michele Matassa Flores: "Internet Wars—Microsoft vs. Netscape: Goliath Takes on David. Navigator Still Ahead but Losing Ground," *The Seattle Times,* Final, Mar. 11, 1997, p. A1.

"An Apple for Xerox?" *Forbes,* July 1, 1971, pp. 32–34.

Applegate, Lynda M., and Meredith Collura: "Amazon.com: Exploiting the Value of Digital Business Infrastructure," Harvard Business School Case 9-800-330 (2000).

"*ASAP* Interview: Bill Gates," *Forbes ASAP,* Dec. 7, 1992, pp. 63–74.

Aspray, William: "The Intel 4004 Microprocessor: What Constituted Invention," *IEEE Annals of the History of Computing,* 19(3):1–15 (1997).

Bain, Joe S.: *Barriers to New Competition,* Harvard University Press, Cambridge, MA, 1956.

Baldwin, George B.: "The Invention of the Modern Safety Razor: A Case Study of Industrial Innovation," *Explorations in Entrepreneurial History,* vol. 4(2), December 1951, pp. 73–104.

Bank, David: "Changing the Course of the Information Highway: Executive, Student Team Up on Plan to Expand Internet," *Los Angeles Daily News,* June 6, 1994, p. B5.

Barnes and Noble Web site, www.bn.com.

Baron, Salo W.: *The Contemporary Relevance of History,* Columbia University Press, New York, 1986.

Bartholomew, Doug: "Bill Gates Envisions the Enterprise," *Industry Week,* Dec. 12, 1996, p. 9.

Bass, Frank M. and T. L. Pilon: "A Stochastic Brand Choice Framework for Econometric Modeling of Time Series Market Share Behavior," *Journal of Marketing Research,* 17: 486–497 (1980).

Berghel, Hal: "Who Won the Mosaic War?" *ACM,* 41(10):13–16 (October 1998).

Berners-Lee, Tim: "Spinning the Web: A Place for Everything, and Everything on the Web?" *Data Communications,* Oct. 21, 1997, p. 48.

―――― and Mark Fischetti: *Weaving the Web: The Original Design and Ultimate Destiny of the World Wide Web by Its Inventor,* HarperCollins, New York, 1999.

――――, Robert Cailliau, Ari Luotonen, Henrik Frystyk, and Nielsen Arthur Secret: "The World-Wide Web," *Communications of the ACM,* Aug. 1, 1994, p. 76.

"The Betamax: How Well Does It Work," *Consumer Reports,* May 1977, p. 291.

Bezanson, Anne: "The Invention of the Safety Razor: Further Comments," *Explorations in Entrepreneurial History,* vol. 4, May 15, 1952, pp. 193–198.

Bezos, Jeff: *Amazon.com Annual Report* (1997).

――――: *Amazon.com Annual Report* (1998).

"Blade-Snatching," *Newsweek,* Nov. 22, 1962, pp. 89–90.

Bond, R. S., and D. F. Lean: "Sales, Promotion, and Product Differentiation in Two Prescription Drug Markets," U.S. Federal Trade Commission, 1977.

Borders Web site, www.borders.com.

"Boston Blue Bladers," *Forbes,* Nov. 15, 1952. (Innovation)

Bradley, Stephen P., and Takia Mahmood: "Retail Financial Services in 1998: Charles Schwab," Harvard Business School Case 9-799-052 (1998).

Brooks, John: "Xerox, Xerox, Xerox, Xerox," *The New Yorker,* Apr. 1, 1967, pp. 46–90.

Brooks, Philip C.: *Research in Archives,* University of Chicago Press, Chicago, 1969.

Brumley, Cal: "Stainless-Steel Razor Blades Could Be Shavers' Boon, Makers' Problem," *The Wall Street Journal,* Dec. 25, 1962, p. 7.

Burgelman, Robert A.: "Fading Memories: A Process Theory of Strategic Business Exit in Dynamic Environments," *Administrative Science Quarterly,* 39:24–56 (1994).

Burgelman, Robert A., and Jeff Maggioncalda: "The Charles Schwab Corporation in 1996," Stanford University Graduate School of Business Case SM-35 (1996).

Buzzell, Robert D., and Bradley T. Gale: *The PIMS Principles: Linking Strategy to Performance,* Free Press, New York, 1987.

Bylinsky, Gene: "How Intel Won Its Bet on Memory Chips," *Fortune,* November 1973, pp. 142–147, 186.

Carley, William M.: "Battle of the Blades," *The Wall Street Journal,* Sept. 26, 1969, p. 38.

Carlton, Jim: "They Could Have Been a Contender," *Wired,* November 1997, pp. 122–149.

———: "Popularity of Some Computers Means Buyers Must Wait," *The Wall Street Journal,* Oct. 21, 1993, p. B1.

Carpenter, Gregory S., and Kent Nakamoto: "Consumer Preference Formation and Pioneering Advantage," *Journal of Marketing Research,* 26:285–298 (August 1989).

Carroll, Paul: *Big Blues: The Unmaking of IBM,* Crown Publishers, New York, 1993.

———: "The Day Bill Gates Overthrew Big Blue," *The Wall Street Journal,* Aug. 16, 1993, pp. B1, B3.

Carter, Dennis and Robert Burgelman: "Intel Corporation: The Evolution of an Adaptive Organization," Academy of Management Conference, Chicago, August 6–11, 1999, http://www.aom.pace.edu/meetings/1999/INTEL1.htm.

Carvajal, Doreen: "The Other Battle over Browsers: Barnes & Noble and Other On-Line Booksellers Are Poised to Challenge Amazon.com," *The New York Times,* Mar. 9, 1998, pp. D1, D4.

Ceron, Gaston F.: "Online Brokers to Post Weakened Results," *The Wall Street Journal,* Jan. 16, 2001, p. 1.

Ceruzzi, Paul E.: *A History of Modern Computing,* MIT Press, Cambridge, MA, 1999.

Chace, Susan: "Xerox Introduces an Office System for Nontypists," *The Wall Street Journal,* Apr. 28, 1981, p. 4.

Chakravarty, Subrata N.: "We Had to Change the Playing Field," *Forbes,* Feb. 4, 1991, pp. 82–86.

Chandler, Alfred D.: "The Enduring Logic of Industrial Success," *Harvard Business Review,* vol. 68, March–April 1990, pp. 131–139.

Chandy, Rajesh, and Gerard J. Tellis: "Organizing for Radical Product Innovation," *Journal of Marketing Research,* 35:474–487 (November 1998).

———, and ———: "The Incumbent's Curse? Incumbency, Size and Radical Product Innovation," *Journal of Marketing,* 64(3):1–17 (July 2000).

Charles Schwab Web site, www.schwab.com.

"Cheek by Trowel," *Business Week,* Dec. 22, 1962, pp. 81–82.

Chposky, James, and Ted Leonsis: *Blue Logic: The People, Power and Politics behind the IBM Personal Computer,* Facts on File, New York, 1988.

Christensen, Clayton M.: *The Innovator's Dilemma: When New Technologies Cause Great Firms to Fail,* Harvard Business School Press, Boston, 1997.

Clark, Jim, and Owen Edwards: *Netscape Time: The Making of the Billion-Dollar Start-Up That Took on Microsoft,* St. Martin's Press, New York, 1999.

Clark, Joe: "Browsers Help You Forge Lynx in Internet Chain," *The Toronto Star,* Final, Oct. 13, 1994, p. J5.

Coe, Brian: *Cameras: From Daguerreotypes to Instant Pictures,* Crown Publishers, New York, 1978.

Cogan, George W.: "Intel Corporation (A): The DRAM Decision," Graduate School of Business, Stanford University, Palo Alto, CA, 1989.

"Color TV," *Consumer Reports,* November 1961, pp. 612–613.

"The Coming Close Shave at Gillette," *Forbes,* Dec. 15, 1976, p. 29.

"Computer Stores," *Business Week,* Sept. 28, 1981, pp. 76–80.

Cooper, Robert G.: "The Dimensions of Industrial New Product Success and Failure," *Journal of Marketing,* 43:93–103 (Summer 1979).

Cortese, Amy, et al.: "America Online's Global Push," *Business Week,* April 22, 1996, p. 78.

Cringley, Robert X.: *Accidental Empires,* Addison-Wesley, Reading, MA, 1993.

———: "Triumph of the Nerds," http://www.pbs.org/nerds/transcript.html (1996).

Cusumano, Michael A., and David B. Yoffie: *Competing on Internet Time: Lessons from Netscape and Its Battle with Microsoft,* Free Press/Simon & Schuster, New York, 1998.

Day, George S., and Jonathan S. Freeman: "Burnout or Fadeout: The Risks of Early Entry into High Technology Markets," in Michael W. Lawless and Luis R. Gomez-Mejia, eds., *Strategic Management in High Technology Firms,* JAI Press, Greenwich, CT, 1990, pp. 43–65.

———, Allan D. Shocker, and Rajendra K. Srivastava: "Customer-Oriented Approaches to Identifying Product-Markets," *Journal of Marketing,* 43:8–19 (Fall 1979).

DeKimpe, Marnik G. and Dominique M. Hanssens: "Empirical Generalizations About Market Evolution and Stationarity," *Marketing Science,* 14 (Number 3, Part 2 of 2), G109–G121 (1995).

De LaFuente, Della: "The Champaign Net Work/Whiz Kids from U. of I. Make Millions in Cyberspace," *Chicago Sun-Times,* Sept. 17, 1995, p. 33.

"Delphi Service Features Books & Software from HarperCollins," *Link-up,* April 1995, p. 44.

Dessauer, John H.: *My Years with Xerox: The Billions Nobody Wanted,* Doubleday, Garden City, NY, 1971.

Deutschman, Alan: "Imposter Boy," *Gentleman's Quarterly,* January 1997.

"Diapers," *Consumer Reports,* August 1954, pp. 160–164.

"Disposable Diapers," *Consumer Reports,* March 1961, pp. 151–152.

"Disposable Diapers," Internal Report and Planning Document, Johnson & Johnson Archives, New Brunswick, NJ, 1969.

"Does Collision," *Forbes,* Aug. 15, 1972, pp. 40–42.

Deutschman, Alan: "Imposter Boy," *Gentleman's Quarterly,* January 1997.

"Dropping Out of Harvard Pays Off for a Computer Whiz Kid Who's Making Hard Cash from Software," *People,* Dec. 26, 1983, p. 37.

E*trade Web site, www.etrade.com.

Ehrenberg, Andrew S.C.: *Repeat Buying: Facts, Theory and Data,* Second edition, Oxford University Press, New York, 1988.

———: "New Brands and the Existing Market," *Journal of the Market Research Society,* 33: 285–299 (1991).

Eisenhardt, Kathleen M.: "Building Theories from Case Study Research," *Academy of Management Review,* 14(4):532–550 (1989).

Elstrom, Peter, and Kathy Rebello: "A Big Bet on Minibrowsers: Can Spyglass Score in the Net Appliance Market," *Business Week,* Oct. 28, 1996, p. 54.

Elton, G. R.: *The Practice of History,* Thomas Y. Crowell, New York, 1967.

Erickson, Jim: "Internet Time: It Flies at Warp Speed Microsoft Programmer Scurried for Explorer 3.0," *Seattle Post-Intelligencer,* Final, Aug. 12, 1996, p. B3.

Evans, David S., Albert Nichols, and Bernard Reddy: "The Rise and Fall of Leaders in Personal Computer Software," National Economic Research Associates, Cambridge, MA, Jan. 7, 1999.

Evans, Mark: "Fight to Finish: Microsoft, Netscape Step Up Race for Control of Internet Software Market," *The Financial Post.* Mar. 14, 1996, p. 8.

Ewen, Edward T.: "Revolution on the Razor's Edge," *The New York Times Magazine,* Oct. 6, 1963, p. 58.

"A Fable Concerning Ambition," *Economist,* June 21, 1997, p. 69.

Faggin, Elvia: "Faggin Contributed to First Microprocessor," *San Jose Mercury News,* Oct. 3, 1986, p. 6B

Fass, Allison: "Amazon Leads in Holiday Advertising," *The New York Times,* Dec. 13, 2000, p. 7.

"Federal Express Battles Emery for Growing Air-Express Market," *Dow Jones News Service-Edited Wall Street Journal Stories,* Sept. 11, 1979.

"A Flickering Picture for Video Recorders," *Business Week,* Aug. 21, 1978, p. 28.

Fogel, Robert William, and G. R. Elton: *Which Road to the Past? Two Views of History,* Yale University Press, New Haven, CT, 1983.

"For Babies Only—Chux Throw-Away Diapers," *Delineator,* Aug. 1935, p. 6.

Forkan, James P.: "Video Cassette Man Prognosticate Unit Sales Up to 60,000 in '72," *Advertising Age,* Oct. 2, 1972.

———: "Sony Begins Roll of Video Cassette Unit in N.Y. Market," *Advertising Age,* Nov. 3, 1975.

Foster, R.: *Innovation: The Attacker's Advantage,* Summit Books, New York, 1986.

Freiberger, Paul, and Michael Swaine: *Fire in the Valley: The Making of the Personal Computer,* Osborne/McGraw-Hill, Berkeley, CA, 1984.

"Gablinger's Goes to Gumbinner; Grey Gets Knickerbocker as 2 Shops Resign," *Advertising Age,* Nov. 27, 1967, p. 2.

"Gaisman, Who Will Head Gillette, Is an Incorrigible Inventor," *Business Week,* Nov. 26, 1930, pp. 20–21.

Gates, Bill: "They're Talking, We're Selling," *The Wall Street Journal,* Mar. 16, 1995, p. A22.

Gates, William: "The Internet Tidal Wave," http://www.microsoft.com/presspass/trial/mswitness/maritz/maritz_full.asp (1995).

———: http://www.microsoft.com/BillGates/speeches/12-7-95 (1995).

Ghemawat, Pankaj, and Bret Baird: "Leadership Online: Barnes & Noble vs. Amazon.com," Harvard Business School Case 9-798-063 (1998).

Ghemawat, Pankaj, and Benjamin Esty: "Gillette's Launch of Sensor," Case No. 9-792-028, Harvard Business School Publishing Division, Boston, MA, 1992.

Ghoshal, Sumantra, and Christopher A. Bartlett: "Matsushita Electric Industrial (MEI) in 1987," Harvard Business School Case 9-388-144 (1988).

Gilbert, R. J., and D. M. G. Newberry: "Preemptive Patenting and the Persistence of Monopoly," *American Economic Review,* 72:514–526 (June 1982).

Gilder, George: "The Coming Software Shift," *Forbes ASAP,* Aug. 28, 1995, pp. 146–157.

Gillette, King C.: "Origin of the Gillette Razor," *The Gillette Blade,* February 1918, pp. 3–12.

———: "Origin of the Gillette Razor," *The Gillette Blade,* March 1918, pp. 7–14.

———: "Intensive Cooperation," *The Gillette Blade,* August 1918, p. 5.

———: "Centralized Ideas—The Foundation of Progress," *The Gillette Blade,* February 1920, pp. 9–10.

———: "How the 'Gillette' Looks to Mr. Gillette after Twenty-Five Years," *The Gillette Blade,* September 1920, pp. 3–6.

———: "Paper Read by King C. Gillette, President of the Gillette Safety Razor Company, at the Banquet of the Annual Convention, Algonquin Club, Boston, Wednesday Evening, April 13, 1921," *The Gillette Blade,* August 1921, pp. 3–7.

"Gillette Looks Sharp Again," *Fortune,* June 1952, pp. 100–172.

"Gillette to Spend $4,000,000 on Stainless Blade," *Advertising Age,* Sept. 2, 1963, pp. 4, 46.

"Gillette Plans to Offer Stainless Steel Razor Blade in Few Months," *The Wall Street Journal,* Nov. 19, 1962, p. 7.

Girishankar, Saroja: "Schwab Makes the Trade—Migrating Millions of Customers and Huge Legacy Systems to the Web Was an Eye-Opener for Precocious Charles Schwab," *Internetweek,* May 25, 1998, p. 30.

Glazer, A.: "The Advantages of Being First," *American Economic Review,* 75:473–480 (June 1985).

Golder, Peter N.: "Historical Method in Marketing Research with New Evidence on Long-Term Market Share Stability," *Journal of Marketing Research,* 37:156–172 (May 2000).

——— and Gerard J. Tellis: "Pioneer Advantage: Marketing Logic or Marketing Legend?" *Journal of Marketing Research,* 30:158–170 (May 1993).

——— and ———: "Will It Ever Fly? Modeling the Takeoff of Really New Consumer Durables," *Marketing Science,* 16(3):256–270 (1997).

Goldman, Jacob E.: "Innovation in Large Firms," *Research in Technological Innovation, Management and Policy,* vol. 2, 1985, pp. 1–10.

Goodman, Robert S., and Evonne Jonas Kruger: "Data Dredging or Legitimate Research Method? Historiography and Its Potential for Management Research," *Academy of Management Review,* 13(2):315–325 (1988).

Gorham, John: "Charles Schwab Version 4.0," *Forbes,* Jan. 8, 2001, p. 88.

Gottschalk, Louis R.: *Understanding History: A Primer of Historical Method,* Knopf, New York, 1969.

Graham, Ellen: "McDonald's Pickle: He Began Fast Food but Gets No Credit," *The Wall Street Journal,* Aug. 15, 1991, p. A1.

"The Great Diaper Rash," *Forbes,* Dec. 15, 1970, p. 24.

"The Greatest Thing Since the Nickelodeon?" *Forbes,* July 1, 1970.

Gross, Daniel: *Greatest Business Stories of All Time,* Wiley, New York, 1996.

Grove, Andrew S.: *Only the Paranoid Survive: How to Exploit the Crisis Points That Challenge Every Company and Career,* Currency/Doubleday/Bantam Doubleday Dell Publishing Group, New York, 1996.

Guasch, J. L., and A. Weiss: "Adverse Selection of Markets and the Advantages of Being Late," *Quarterly Journal of Economics,* vol. 94, pp. 453–466 (May 1980).

Gupta, Amar, and Hoormin D. Toong: "The First Decade of Personal Computers," in Amar Gupta and Hoormin D. Toong, eds., *Insights into Personal Computers,* IEEE Press, New York, 1985.

Guzzardi, Walter, Jr.: "Gillette Faces the Stainless-Steel Dragon," *Fortune,* July 1963, p. 159.

Hafner, Katie, and Matthew Lyon: *Where Wizards Stay Up Late: The Origins of the Internet,* Touchstone/Simon & Schuster, New York, 1969.

"Hat in Hand," *Fortune,* Oct. 31, 1930, pp. 46–52, 147.

Healy, Beth: "Battle of the Brokers Heats Up," *The Boston Globe,* Apr. 2, 2000, p. K7.

Heilemann, John: "The Networker," *The New Yorker,* Aug. 11, 1997, pp. 28–36.

Higham, Nick: "Amazon Success Story Built on Traditional Marketing Expertise," *Marketing Week,* Oct. 14, 1999, p. 17.

Hill, Christian G.: "Clark Is Starting Firm to Provide Internet System," *The Wall Street Journal,* May 9, 1994, p. B2.

Hiltzik, Michael A.: "Fans Celebrate Fallen Xerox Star," *The Los Angeles Times,* June 22, 1998, p. D4.

———: *Dealers of Lightning: Xerox PARC and the Dawn of the Computer Age,* HarperBusiness/HarperCollins, New York, 1999.

Himelstein, Linda: "Schwab Is Fighting on Three Fronts," *Business Week,* Mar. 10, 1997, p. 94.

Hof, Robert D.: "From the Man Who Brought You Silicon Graphics. . . . Can Jim Clark Score Again with User-Friendly Internet Software?" *Business Week,* Oct. 24, 1994, p. 90.

———: "The Most Influential People in Electronic Business," *Business Week,* Sept. 27, 1999, p. EB25.

Hoff, Marcian E., Jr.: "Patents Don't Tell Whole Microprocessor Tale," *San Jose Mercury News,* Oct. 12, 1986, p. 10B.

"Home Video Tape Recorder," *Consumer Reports,* June 1966, p. 280.

Hotchkiss, George Burton and Richard B. Franklin: *The Leadership of Advertised Brands,* Doubleday, Page & Company, Garden City, NY, 1923.

"Hotter Competition in Video Recorders," *Business Week,* Apr. 25, 1977, p. 36.

"How Gillette Plans to Keep Its No. 1 Spot," *Printers Time*, Dec. 4, 1959, pp. 65–66.

"How Miller Won a Market Slot for Lite Beer," *Business Week*, Oct. 13, 1975, p. 116.

Hughes, H. Stuart: *History as Art and Science*, Harper & Row, New York, 1964.

Hymowitz, Carol: "How Amazon.com Staffs a Juggernaut: It's Not about Resumes," *The Wall Street Journal*, May 4, 1999, p. B1.

Ibuka, Masaru: "How SONY Developed Electronics for the World Market," *IEEE Transactions on Engineering Management*, 22(1):15–19 (February 1975).

Ichbiah, Daniel and Susan Knepper: *The Making of Microsoft*, Prima Publishing, Rocklin, CA, 1991.

Ingrassia, Lawrence: "Gillette Holds Its Edge by Endlessly Searching for a Better Shave," *The Wall Street Journal*, Dec. 10, 1992, p. 1.

"Intro of Gablinger's Leads to Top-Level Shift at Rheingold," *Advertising Age*, Apr. 1, 1968, p. 6.

"IRS Approval of Low-Calorie Claim Clears Way for Gablinger's Expansion," *Advertising Age*, Feb. 17, 1969, p. 37.

Jackson, Tim: *Inside Intel*, Dutton/Penguin Putnam, New York, 1997.

Jacobson, Gary, and John Hillkirk: *Xerox: American Samurai*, Macmillan, New York, 1986.

Jesdanun, Anick: "AOL Succeeds by Keeping It Simple; Critics Call It 'Internet on Training Wheels.' " *Chicago Sun-Times*, Dec. 3, 2000, p. 57.

Johnson, Allen: *The Historian and Historical Evidence*, Scribner's New York, 1934.

Johnson, Jeff, and Teresa L. Roberts: "The Xerox 'Star': A Retrospective," *IEEE Computer*, September 1989.

Jones, Sandra: "Net Browser Spyglass Plans 2-for-1 Stock Split," *Chicago Sun-Times*, Nov. 29, 1995, p. 69.

Judge, Paul C., and Heather Green: "The Name's the Thing: Dot.com's Are Spending Like Mad to Establish an Identity," *Business Week*, Nov. 15, 1999, pp. 36–39.

Judis, John B: "Innovation, a Casualty at IBM," *The Wall Street Journal*, Oct. 17, 1991, p. A23.

Kadiyali, Vrinda: "Eastman Kodak in the Photographic Film Industry: Picture Imperfect?" in David I. Rosenbaum, ed., *Market Dominance: How Firms Gain, Hold, or Lose It and the Impact on Economic Performance*, Praeger, Westport, CT, 1998.

Kalyanaram, Gurumurthy, and Glen L. Urban: "Dynamic Effects of the Order of Entry on Market Share, Trial, Penetration, and Repeat Purchases for Frequently Purchased Consumer Goods," *Marketing Science*, 11(3):235–251 (1992).

Karakaya, Fahri, and Michael J. Stahl: "Barriers to Entry and Market Entry Decisions in Consumer and Industrial Goods Markets," *Journal of Marketing*, 53: 80–91 (April 1989).

Kearns, David T., and David A. Nadler: *Prophets in the Dark*, Harper Business, New York, 1992.

"Keen Drama: A Razor Is Born," *Newsweek*, Oct. 11, 1971, pp. 78–82.

Kilborn, Peter: "Can Xerox Copy Itself?" *The New York Times*, Dec. 1, 1974, section 3, p. 1.

Kneale, Dennis: "IBM Earnings Increased 23% in 1st Quarter," *The Wall Street Journal*, Apr. 13, 1984.

Knecht, G. Bruce: "How Wall Street Whiz Found a Niche Selling Books on the Internet," *The Wall Street Journal*, May 16, 1996, pp. A1, A8.

Knoop, Carin-Isabel, and Cate Reavis: "Selling Books Online in Mid-1998," Harvard Business School Case 9-899-038 (1998).

Kotler, Philip: *Marketing Management: Analysis, Planning, Implementation, and Control*, Ninth edition, Prentice-Hall, Upper Saddle River, NJ, 1997.

Krantz, Michael: "Cruising inside Amazon," *Time*, Dec. 27, 1999, pp. 68–71.

Kroc, Ray, and Robert Anderson: *Grinding It Out: The Making of McDonald's*, Regnery, Chicago, 1977.

Kummel, Charles M., and Jay E. Klompmaker: "The Gillette Company," Case No. 9-581-619, Harvard Business School International Case Clearing House, Boston, MA, 1982.

Laderman, Jeffrey M.: "Remaking Schwab," *Business Week*, May 25, 1998, p. 122.

Lal, Rajiv and V. Padmanabhan: "Competitive Response and Equilibria," *Marketing Science*, 14 (Number 3, Part 2 of 2), G101–G108 (1995).

Lambkin, Mary: "Order of Entry and Performance in New Markets," *Strategic Management Journal*, 9:127–140 (Summer 1988).

——— and George S. Day: "Evolutionary Processes in Competitive Markets: Beyond the Product Life Cycle," *Journal of Marketing*, 53:4–20 (July 1989).

Lampson, Butler W.: "Personal Distributed Computing: The Alto and Ethernet Software," ACM Conference on the History of Personal Workstations, Palo Alto, CA, 1986.

Lane, W. J.: "Product Differentiation in a Market with Endogenous Sequential Entry," *Bell Journal of Economics*, 11:237–260 (Spring 1980).

Langlois, C. V., and C. Seignobos: *Introduction to the Study of History*, Henry Holt, New York, 1898.

Lee, John M.: "Gillette Will Market Its New Product in Two Cities," *The New York Times*, Aug. 27, 1963, p. 41.

Lessing, Lawrence: "Stand By for the Cartridge TV Explosion," *Fortune*, June 1971, p. 80.

Levitt, Theodore: "Marketing Myopia," *Harvard Business Review*, September–October, 1975, pp. 1–3.

Levy, Mark R.: "The VCR Age: Home Video and Mass Communication," Sage Publications, Newberry Park, CA, 1989.

Lieberman, Marvin B., and David B. Montgomery: "First-Mover Advantages," *Strategic Management Journal*, 9:41–58 (1988).

Liebowitz, Stan J., and Stephen E. Margolis: *Winners, Losers and Microsoft: Competition and Antitrust in High Technology*, The Independent Institute, Oakland, CA, 1999.

Lilien, Gary L., and Eunsang Yoon: "The Timing of Competitive Market Entry: An Exploratory Study of New Industrial Products," *Management Science*, 36:568–585 (May 1990).

Loken, Barbara, and James Ward: "Alternative Approaches to Understanding the Determinants of Typicality," *Journal of Consumer Research*, 17:111–126 (September 1990).

"Looking Ahead," *Fortune*, Dec. 28, 1992, p. 32.

Lothrop, Eaton S., Jr.: *A Century of Cameras*, Morgan & Morgan, Dobbs Ferry, NY, 1973.

Louis, J. C., and Harvey Yazijian: *The Cola Wars*, Everest House, New York, 1980.

Lovelock, Christopher H.: "Federal Express (A)," Harvard Business School Publishing, 9-577-042, Boston, 1976.

————: "Federal Express (B)," Harvard Business School Publishing, 9-579-040, Boston, 1978.

Lowe, Janet: *Bill Gates Speaks: Insight from the World's Greatest Entrepreneur*, Wiley, New York, 1998.

Lowenstein, Roger: "History of Xerox Is a Cautionary Tale for Netscape," *The Salt Lake Tribune*, Aug. 18, 1995, p. B10.

Lurie, Ralinda Young: "The World VCR Industry," Harvard Business School Case 9-387-098 (1987).

Lynch, Mitchell: "Investors Buying Nautilus for Shares in Apple Are Told to Watch for a Worm," *The Wall Street Journal*, Oct. 8, 1980, p. 10.

Lyons, Nick: *The Sony Vision*, Crown Publishers, New York, 1976.

"A Market Mostly for the Giants," *Business Week*, June 30, 1975, pp. 71–80.

Markoff, John: "A Free and Simple Computer Link," *The New York Times*, Dec. 8, 1995, p. D1.

Marwick, Arthur: *The Nature of History*, MacMillan, London, 1970.

Matsushita: *Annual Reports*, 1971–1973, 1975, 1977, 1979, 1981, 1985.

McKibben, Gordon: *Cutting Edge: Gillette's Journey to Global Leadership*, Harvard Business School Press, Boston, 1998.

McMurray, Scott: "Diplomas and Dollars: The University of Illinois Churns Out Big-Time Software Entrepreneurs; Champaign, Ill." *U.S. News & World Report*, 1996, pp. 48–49.

McReynolds, Rebecca: "Doing It the Schwab Way," *US Banker*, July 1998, pp. 46–56.

"Meister Brau Wins Amylase Patent Suit," *Advertising Age*, Mar. 30, 1970, p. 62.

Merrion, Paul: "A Tangle in School's Netscape Win," *Crain Communications*, Oct. 9, 1995, p. 19.

"Microcomputers Catch on Fast," *Business Week*, July 12, 1976, p. 50.

Miller, Michael W.: "IBM's Watson Offers Personal View of the Company's Recent Difficulties," *The Wall Street Journal*, Dec. 21, 1992, p. A3.

Moore, Michael J., William Boulding, and Ronald C. Goodstein: "Pioneering and Market Share: Is Entry Time Endogenous and Does It Matter?" *Journal of Marketing Research*, 28:97–104 (February 1991).

"More Gear for Home Movie Fans," *Business Week*, July 16, 1966, p. 94.

"Mosaic Quest Closes in Redmond Original," *Computer Business Review*, Feb. 1, 1997.

Moskowitz, Milton: "The Overnight Delivery Revolution," *The San Francisco Chronicle*, Jan. 4, 1985, p. 35.

Nash, Kim S.: "Browsers Compete for Spotlight," *Computerworld*, November 1995, p. 61.

Nelson, Gerald E., and William R. Hewlett: "The Design and Development of a Family of Personal Computers for Engineers and Scientists," in Amar Gupta and Hoormin D. Toong, eds., *Insights into Personal Computers*, IEEE Press, New York, 1985.

Nevett, Terence: "Historical Investigation and the Practice of Marketing," *Journal of Marketing,* 55:13–23 (July 1991).

"A New Kind of Flight Plan for Small Freight," *Business Week,* Nov. 3, 1973. p. 3.

"The New Lean, Mean Xerox," *Business Week,* Oct. 12, 1981, pp. 126–132.

Newhall, Beaumont: *The History of Photography,* Little, Brown, Boston, 1982.

Nickerson, William E.: "The Development of the Gillette Safety Razor," *The Gillette Blade,* December 1918, pp. 5–13.

———: "The Development of the Gillette Safety Razor," *The Gillette Blade.* May 1918, pp. 3–6.

———: "The Develpment of the Gillette Safety Razor," *The Gillette Blade,* January 1919, pp. 6–18.

———: "Turning the Tables," *The Gillette Blade,* March 1922, pp. 3–4.

Nilles, Jack M.: *Technology Assessment of Personal Computers: Volume 2, Personal Computer Technology, Users, and Uses,* University of Southern California team sponsored by National Science Foundation, document available from National Technical Information Service, U.S. Department of Commerce, 1980, pp. 2–5.

Notess, Greg R: "Comparing Web Browsers: Mosaic, Cello, Netscape, WinWeb and InternetWorks Life," *Online,* March/April 1995, pp. 36–40.

Noyce, Robert N. and Marcian E. Hoff, Jr.: "A History of Microprocessor Development at Intel," *IEEE Micro,* February 1981, pp. 8–20.

Nulty, Peter: "Matsushita Takes the Lead in Video Recorders," *Fortune,* July 16, 1979, pp. 110–116.

"The Online World of Steve Case," *Business Week,* Apr. 15, 1996, pp. 78–87.

"Out to Crack the Copying Market," *Business Week,* Sept. 19, 1959, p. 86.

Pake, George E.: "Research at Xerox PARC: A Founder's Assessment," *IEEE Spectrum,* 22(10):54–61 (1985).

———: "From Research to Innovation at Xerox: A Manager's Principles and Some Examples," in R. S. Rosenbloom, ed., *Research on Technological Innovation, Management and Policy,* vol. 3, JAI Press, Greenwich, CT, 1986, pp. 1–32.

Parry, Mark, and Frank M. Bass: "When to Lead or Follow? It Depends," *Marketing Letters,* vol. 1, November 1990, pp. 187–198.

Perry, Tekla S., and Paul Wallich: "Inside the PARC: The 'Information Architects,'" *IEEE Spectrum,* 22(10):54–76 (1985).

"Personal Business," *Business Week,* June 4, 1960, p. 129.

"Personal Computers: And the Winner Is IBM," *Business Week,* Oct. 3, 1983, pp. 76–95.

Peterson, Pete W. E.: *Almost Perfect: How a Bunch of Regular Guys Built WordPerfect Corporation,* Prima Publishing, Rocklin, CA, 1994.

Pitta, Julie: "Investors Get Caught Up in the Netscape," *The Los Angeles Times,* 1995, pp. D3, D5.

Pollack, Andrew: "Xerox Stalks the Automated Office," *The New York Times,* May 3, 1981, section 3, p. 4.

Porter, Michael E.: "The Disposable Diaper Industry in 1974," Harvard Business School Case 380-175 (1980).

Pospisil, Vivian, and John Teresko: "50 R&D Stars to Watch," *Industry Week,* Dec. 19, 1994, p. 60.

Prescott, E., and M. Visscher: "Sequential Location among Firms with Foresight," *Bell Journal of Economics,* 8:378–393 (1977).

Procter & Gamble: *Annual Report,* 1977.

Quick, Rebecca: "Barnes & Noble.com to Replace Amazon.com as Top Bookseller Advertising on Yahoo!" *The Wall Street Journal,* Sept. 19, 2000, p. B23.

———: "E-Retailers Say, 'Bah Humbug!' to Lavish Ads," *The Wall Street Journal,* Sept. 22, 2000, p. B1.

Quittner, Joshua: "An Eye on the Future," *Time,* Dec. 27, 1999, pp. 56–64.

Ratneshwar, S., and Allan D. Shocker: "Substitution in Use and the Role of Usage Context in Product Category Structures," *Journal of Marketing Research,* 28: 281–295 (August 1991).

Rayport, Jeffrey F., and Dickson L. Louie: "Amazon.com(A)," Harvard Business School Case 9-897-128 (1997).

The Razor Anthology, Knife World Publications, Knoxville, TN, 1995.

"RCA SelectVision Bows; Home Sports Fans Become TV Producers in Early '70s," *Advertising Age,* Oct. 13, 1969, p. 57.

Rebello, Kathy, May Cortese, and Rob Hof: "Inside Microsoft: The Untold Story of How the Internet Forced Bill Gates to Reverse Course," *Business Week,* July 15, 1996, p. 56.

Reid, Calvin: "Amazon.com's Jeff Bezos," *Publisher's Weekly,* Jan. 5, 1998, p. 12.

Ries, Al, and Jack Trout: *The 22 Immutable Laws of Marketing,* HarperCollins, New York, 1993.

Roberts, Stephen: "Early Laser Printer Development," http://www.printer works.com/Catalogs/CX-Catalog/CX-HP LaserJet-History.html (1994).

Robinson, Phillip: "Dot-Matrix History, 300 dpi Becoming Passé for Printers," *The Orange County Register,* Oct. 5, 1992, p. C24.

———: "HP LaserJet 4 Introduces a New World of Printing," *Austin American-Statesman,* Dec. 28, 1992, p. E2.

Robinson, William T.: "Sources of Market Pioneer Advantages: The Case of Industrial Goods Industries," *Journal of Marketing Research,* 25:87–94 (February 1988).

——— and Claes Fornell: "Sources of Market Pioneer Advantage in Consumer Goods Industries," *Journal of Marketing Research,* 22:305–317 (August 1985).

Rosenbloom, Richard S., and Karen Freeze: "Ampex Corporation and Video Innovation," in Richard S. Rosenbloom, ed., *Research on Technological Innovation, Management and Policy,* vol. 2, JAI Press, Greenwich, CT, 1985.

——— and Michael A. Cusumano: "Technological Pioneering and Competitive Advantage: The Birth of the VCR Industry," *California Management Review,* XXIX: 51–76 (Summer 1987).

Sahlman, William A., and Laurence E. Katz: "Amazon.com—Going Public," Harvard Business School Case 9-899-003 (1998).

"Sales Bubble for Diet Drinks," *Business Week,* June 27, 1964, pp. 88–92.

Salvemini, Gaetano: *Historian and Scientist,* Harvard University Press, Cambridge, MA, 1939.

Samuels, Gary: "Tale of Two Interneters: Netscape Has Gotten the Headlines, but Spyglass Is Making Money," *Forbes Inc.,* September 1995, p. 48.

Sandberg, Jared: "Designers of Internet's Mosaic Software Plan New Version in Bid to Set Standard," *The Wall Street Journal,* Oct. 13, 1994, p. B6.

———: "Netscape Has Technical Whiz in Andreessen," *The Wall Street Journal,* Aug. 11, 1995, p. B1.

Savitt, Ronald: "Historical Research in Marketing," *Journal of Marketing,* 44:52–58 (Fall 1980).

Scherer, F. M.: "Editorial: Post-Patent Barriers to Entry in the Pharmaceutical Industry," *Journal of Health Economics,* 4:83–87 (March 1985).

Schiesel, Seth: "Payoff Still Elusive in Internet Gold Rush," *The New York Times,* Jan. 2, 1997, p. C17.

Schmalensee, Richard: "Entry Deterrence in the Ready to Eat Breakfast Cereal Industry," *Bell Journal of Economics,* 9:305–327 (Autumn 1978).

———: "Product Differentiation Advantages of Pioneering Brands," *American Economic Review,* 72:349–365 (June 1982).

Schmedel, Scott R.: "Sony TV Tapes Stir U.S. Firms to Act; Separation Spreads to Canada's West," *The Wall Street Journal,* Mar. 28, 1977, p. 6.

Schnaars, Steven P.: "When Entering Growth Markets, Are Pioneers Better Than Poachers?" *Business Horizons,* vol. 29, March–April 1986, pp. 27–36.

Schonfeld, Erick: "Schwab Puts It All Online," *Fortune,* Dec. 7, 1998, pp. 94–100.

Shafer, Robert Jones: *A Guide to Historical Method,* Dorsey Press, Homewood, IL, 1974.

"A Short Sleep before Exploring Version 5.0," ABIX (Australia news abstracts), Aug. 20, 1996.

Shurkin, Joel: *Engines of the Mind: A History of the Computer,* Norton, New York, 1984.

———: *Engines of the Mind: The Evolution of the Computer from Mainframes to Microprocessors,* Norton, New York, 1996.

Sigafoos, Robert A.: *Absolutely, Positively Overnight!,* St. Luke's Press, Memphis, TN, 1983.

Sinclair, Frank: "Diet-Rite Budget Boosted; It's 'Not Fad, but Forever,'" *Advertising Age,* Oct. 28, 1963, pp. 1–2.

Slater, Robert: *Portraits in Silicon,* MIT Press, Cambridge, MA, 1987.

Smith, Douglas, K., and Robert C. Alexander: *Fumbling the Future,* William Morrow, New York, 1988.

Smith, Gene: "A Series of Promotions to the Top Post," *The New York Times,* May 26, 1968, section 3, p. 3.

Smith, Kenneth S.: "Razor Blade War Growing Hotter," *The New York Times,* Dec. 2, 1962, pp. 1, 18.

Smith, Richard Austin: "Gillette Looks Sharp Again," *Fortune,* June 1952, p. 100.

Sony: *Annual Reports,* 1976–1982, 1984.

"Sony Portable Tape Recorder to Bow in Ads," *Advertising Age,* July 18, 1966, pp. 2, 136.

Spector, Robert: *Get Big Fast: Amazon.com,* HarperBusiness, New York, 2000.

Spence, M.: "Entry, Capacity, Investment, and Oligopolistic Pricing," *Bell Journal of Economics,* 8:534–544 (1977).

———: "The Learning Curve and Competition," *Bell Journal of Economics,* 12:49–70 (1981).

Spiro, Leah Nathans, and Linda Himelstein: "With the World Wide Web, Who Needs Wall Street," *Business Week,* Apr. 29, 1996, p. 120.

Stevens, Tim: "Bellcore: Its Flexible Rechargeable Plastic Battery Could Revolutionize Design of Portable Consumer Electronics, Telecommunications Backup Power, Electric Vehicles and More," *Industry Week,* Dec. 23, 1994, p. 56.

"Stirring Battle Rages for Vast Razor Blade Market," *Business Week,* Sept. 3, 1930, pp. 11–12.

Stross, Randall E: *The Microsoft Way,* Addison-Wesley, Reading, MA, 1996.

———: "Why Barnes & Noble May Crush Amazon," *Fortune,* Sept. 29, 1997, pp. 248–250.

"Study: Majority of 25 Leaders in 1923 Still on Top," *Advertising Age,* Sept. 19, 1983, p. 32.

Sujan, Mita, and James R. Bettman: "The Effects of Brand Positioning Strategies on Consumers' Brand and Category Perceptions: Some Insights from Schema Research," *Journal of Marketing Research,* 26:454–467 (November 1989).

Sullivan, Mary: "Brand Extension and Order of Entry," Marketing Science Institute Working Paper, Report No. 91–105, Marketing Science Institute, Boston, 1991.

Swisher, Kara: *AOL.com: How Steve Case Beat Bill Gates, Nailed the Netheads and Made Millions in the War for the Web,* Random House, Time Business, New York, 1998.

Tecklenburg, Harry: "A Dogged Dedication to Learning," *Research Technology Management,* July–August 1990, pp. 12–15.

Tellis, Gerard J., and Golder, Peter N.: "First to Market, First to Fail? The Real Causes of Enduring Market Leadership," *Sloan Management Review,* 37(2):65–75 (1996).

Tetzeli, Rick and Shaifali Puri: "What It's Really Like to Be Marc Andreessen . . . ," *Fortune,* Dec. 9, 1996, p. 136 ff.

Thacker, Chuck: "Personal Distributed Computing: The Alto and Ethernet Hardware," in Adele Goldberg, ed., *A History of Personal Workstations,* ACM Press, New York, 1988, pp. 267–335.

"The Great Diaper Battle," *Time,* Jan. 24, 1969, pp. 69–70.

Theodore, Levitt: "Marketing Myopia," *Harvard Business Review,* July–August 1960, pp. 45–56.

"The Third Age (A Survey of the Computer Industry)," *The Economist* Sept. 17, 1994, p. C3.

Todd, William: *History as Applied Science,* Wayne State University Press, Detroit, MI, 1972.

Tuchman, Barbara: *Practicing History,* Knopf, New York, 1981.

"Turmoil among the Brewers: Miller's Fast Growth," *Business Week,* Nov. 8, 1976, pp. 58–67.

"Two *Men* & an Idea," *Forbes,* Sept. 15, 1962, p. 17.

Ulman, Neil: "Gillette Chairman Takes a Long View in Program to Brighten Profit Picture," *The Wall Street Journal,* June 28, 1977, p. 12.

"University of Illinois and Netscape Communications Reach Agreement," *PR Newswire,* Dec. 21, 1994.

Urban, Glen L., Theresa Carter, Steven Gaskin, and Zofia Mucha: "Market Share Rewards to Pioneering Brands: An Empirical Analysis and Strategic Implications," *Management Science,* 32:645–659 (June 1986).

Utall, Bro: "Xerox Is Trying Too Hard," *Fortune,* Mar. 13, 1978, pp. 84–94.

Utterback, J.: *Mastering the Dynamics of Innovation,* Harvard Business School Press, Boston, 1994.

―――― and W. J. Abernathy: "A Dynamic Model of Process and Product Innovation," *Omega,* 3:639–656 (1975).

"VCR Owners," *The Wall Street Journal,* May 1, 1986, p. B5.

Waits, Robert K.: "Safety Razor Reference Guide" (Privately published) by Robert K. Waits, 1990.

Waldman, Don E.: "The Rise and Fall of IBM," in David I. Rosenbaum, ed., *Market Dominance: How Firms Gain, Hold or Lose It and the Impact on Economic Performance,"* Praeger, Westport, CT, 1998, pp. 131–152.

Walker, Rob: Interview with Marcian (Ted) Hoff, Oral Histories of Semiconductor Industry Pioneers, Program in History and Philosophy of Science, Department of History, Stanford University, March 3, 1995.

Wang, An, and Eugene Linden: *Lessons: An Autobiography,* Addison-Wesley, Reading, MA, 1986.

Ward, Scott, Larry Light and Jonathan Goldstine: "What High-Tech Managers Need to Know About Brands," *Harvard Business Review,* July–August 1999, pp. 85–95.

"What Words in an Ad Can't Say," *Business Week,* May 14, 1960, pp. 45–48.

Whitten, Ira T.: "Brand Performance in the Cigarette Industry and the Advantages of Early Entry," U.S. Federal Trade Commission, 1979.

"Who Wants a Stainless Reputation?" *Financial Times (London),* Sept. 5, 1963.

"Why Airlines Fear the 'Federal Express Bill,'" *Business Week,* Sept. 13, 1976, p. 116.

"Why Xerox's Money Machine Slows Down," *Business Week,* Apr. 5, 1976, p. 60.

Wiegner, Kathleen K.: "Tomorrow Has Arrived," *Forbes,* Feb. 15, 1982, pp. 111–119.

Wilke, John R.: "Visiting a Bookstore by Switching on a PC," *The Wall Street Journal,* Jan. 11, 1993, p. B1.

"Will Microsoft Catch Netscape?" *Computerworld,* Apr. 29, 1996, pp. 80–81.

Williams, Winston: "Overnight Delivery: The Battle Begins," *The New York Times,* Jan. 1, 1979, Sec. 3, pp. 1, 9.

Williamson, Debra Aho: "Marketer of the Year: Amazon.com," *Advertising Age,* Dec. 13, 1999, pp. 1, 36.

Williford, Charles, and Dan Moore: "Will Microsoft Catch Netscape?" *Computerworld,* Apr. 29, 1996, pp. 80–81.

Wilson, Joseph C.: "The Product Nobody Wanted," *Nation's Business,* February 1969, pp. 67–70.

Winthrop, Grant F.: "Whom the Apples Fell On," *Fortune,* Jan. 12, 1981, p. 68.

Wordworth Web site, www.wordsworth.com.

"Xerox Corp.," *Forbes,* Oct. 15, 1965, pp. 32–37.

"Xerox: The McColough Era," *Forbes,* July 1, 1969, pp. 24–32.

"Xerox's Bid to Be No. 1 in Offices," *Business Week,* June 22, 1981, pp. 77–78.

Yip, George S.: *Barriers to Entry,* Lexington Books, D. C. Heath, Lexington, MA, 1982.

Yoffie, David B.: "The World VCR Industry," Harvard Business School, Case 9-387-098, Jan. 23, 1990.

————: "Microsoft Goes Online: MSN 1996," Harvard Business School Publishing, 9-798-019, Boston, 1997.

Young, Jeffrey: *Greatest Technology Stories,* Wiley, New York, 1998.

Yu, Albert: *Creating the Digital Future: The Secrets of Consistent Innovation at Intel,* Free Press/Simon & Schuster, New York, 1998.

Zhou, Jian-Zhong: "The Internet, the World Wide Web, Library Web Browsers and Library Web Servers," *Information Technology and Libraries,* Mar. 1, 2000, p. 50.

index

about the authors

Gerard Tellis holds the Jerry and Nancy Neely Endowed Chair in American Enterprise at the Marshall School of Business, the University of Southern California, Los Angeles. He has a Ph.D. in business administration from the University of Michigan, Ann Arbor. Previously he worked as a sales development manager for Johnson & Johnson, where he was responsible for brand management, new product introduction, and sales promotion.

Dr. Tellis specializes in market entry, technological innovation, new product growth, and advertising. He has published over 40 articles and books. His articles have appeared in leading scholarly journals, including the *Journal of Marketing Research*, *Journal of Marketing*, *Marketing Science*, *Strategic Management Journal*, *Sloan Management Review*, and *Journal of Advertising Research*. Many of his articles have won honors, including the Maynard Award for the best article in the *Journal of Marketing*, the Odell Award for the best article in the *Journal of Marketing Research*, and the Bass Award for the best article in *Marketing Science*. He has been on the editorial review boards of the *Journal of Marketing Research*, *Journal of Marketing*, and *Marketing Science* for several years.

Peter Golder is Associate Professor of Marketing at New York University's Stern School of Business. He holds a Ph.D. in Business Administration from the University of Southern California and a B.S. from the University of Pennsylvania. Prior to earning his Ph.D., he worked for Conoco and Northrop.

Professor Golder's research focuses on market pioneering, new products, long-term leadership, and branding. His papers have been published in the top scholarly journals, including *Sloan Management Review*, *Journal of Marketing Research*, and *Marketing Science*. His research has been featured in *The Wall Street Journal* several times, as well as in *The Economist* and *Advertising Age*. Also, it has been recognized with three of the marketing discipline's most prestigious best-paper awards. He has appeared on CNN and advised large and small companies on issues related to his research specialties.